ECONOMICS
An Integrated Approach

Benjamin G. Davis

PRENTICE HALL
Upper Saddle River, N.J. 07458

Library of Congress Cataloging-in-Publication Data
Davis, Benjamin (Benjamin G.)
    Economics : an integrated approach / Benjamin Davis. — 1st ed.
      p.   cm.
    Includes index.
    ISBN 0-13-082810-6
    1. Economics.   I. Title.
HB171.5.D266   1997
330—dc21   96-47277
                                                                        CIP

Acquisitions Editor: Elizabeth Sugg
Production Editor: Andrea Bednar (Carlisle Publishers Services)
Production Liaison: Eileen M. O'Sullivan
Production Manager: Mary Carnis
Director of Manufacturing & Production: Bruce Johnson
Manufacturing Manager: Ed O'Dougherty
Marketing Manager: Danny Hoyt
Cover Design: Rosemarie Votta
Creative Director: Marianne Frasco
Editorial Assistant: Emily Jones
Interior Design: Rosemarie Votta
Development Editor: Roberta Moore
Photo Coordinator: Debra Hewitson
Photo Researcher: Teri Stratford
Formatting/Page Make-up: Carlisle Communications, Ltd.
Printer/Binder: Banta-Harrisonburg

©1997 by Prentice-Hall, Inc.
A Simon & Schuster Company
Upper Saddle River, N.J. 07458

All rights reserved. No part of this book may be
reproduced, in any form or by any means,
without permission in writing from the publisher.

Printed in the United States of America

10 9 8 7 6 5 4 3 2 1

ISBN 0-13-082810-6

Prentice-Hall International (UK) Limited, *London*
Prentice-Hall of Australia Pty. Limited, *Sydney*
Prentice-Hall Canada Inc., *Toronto*
Prentice-Hall Hispanoamericana, S.A., *Mexico*
Prentice-Hall of India Private Limited, *New Delhi*
Prentice-Hall of Japan, Inc., *Tokyo*
Simon & Schuster Asia Pte. Ltd., *Singapore*
Editora Prentice-Hall do Brasil, Ltda., *Rio de Janeiro*

Dedicated to J.M.G.D.

Contents

Forward xvii
Preface xix
Introduction xxi

PART I: UNDERSTANDING THE WORLD AROUND US 1

Chapter 1: Introduction to Economics 2

An Introduction to the Dismal Science 4
Defining Economics 4
Economics as a Science 4
Economic Models 6
The Four Economic Questions 6
- *What? 5*
- *How? 5*
- *For Whom? 5*
- *When? 6*

Resources in Economics 7
- *Land 7*
- *Labor 7*
- *Capital 8*
- *Entrepreneurship 8*

Costs and Scarcity 9
Rational Self-Interest 9
Money and Markets 9
Macroeconomics and Microeconomics 11
Problems in Doing Good Economics 11
- *Detachment Is Required 12*
- *Fallacy of Composition 12*
- *False-Cause (post hoc) Fallacy 13*
- *Equity vs. Efficiency 13*
- *A Conclusion—and a Beginning 14*

Summary 14
Key Terms 14
Review Questions 15
Problem Solving Practice 15

Chapter 2: Understanding—and Lying with—Graphs 16

- The Importance of Data 18
- Reading Charts and Data Tables 19
- Reading Pictorial Graphs 21
  - *Bar Charts 21*
  - *Circle or Pie Charts 21*
- Reading Relational Graphs 22
- Lying with Charts and Graphs 24
- Back on Track with Charts and Graphs 29
- Summary 30
- Key Terms 30
- Review Questions 30
- Problem Solving Practice 30

Chapter 3: Trends in the World and Our Economy 32

- The Importance of Trends 34
  - *We Learn about Our Society Today 34*
  - *We Gain an Understanding of Our Past 34*
  - *We Can Anticipate the Future 35*
- Overall Social Trends 35
- Economic Trends in the United States 36
  - *Employment: Who's Working? 36*
  - *Unemployment: Who's Not Working? 38*
  - *Income: How Much Do We Earn? 41*
  - *The Government: What Do We Get and How Much Do We Pay? 42*
  - *International Issues: How Do We Relate? 45*
- Identifying Tomorrow's Trends:
  - *Anticipating the Future 45*
- So What? 47
- Summary 47
- Key Terms 47
- Review Questions 48
- Problem Solving Practice 48

PART 2: ECONOMIC PRINCIPLES 49

Chapter 4: Basic Ideas and Concepts in Economics 50

- The Idea of Value 52
- The Creation of Value 52
- The Production Possibilities Curve 53
- Exchange and International Trade 56
  - *The Reasons for Trade 56*
  - *Benefits from Trade 58*
  - *Barriers to Trade 59*

Producing Wealth—a Summary 63
Summary 63
Key Terms 63
Review Questions 63
Problem Solving Practice 64

Chapter 5: Supply and Demand 66

It's All We Know 68
Demand 68
Definition of the Term Demand 68
The Law of Demand 69
Factors Affecting Demand 71
Market Demand 72
Supply 73
Definition of the Term Supply 73
The Law of Supply 74
Factors Affecting Supply 75
Market Supply 77
Markets and Equilibrium 77
Markets 77
How Equilibrium Works 77
The Cost of Messing Around with Equilibrium 79
Setting Prices Too High: A Price Floor 80
Setting Prices Too Low: A Price Ceiling 82
Summing Up Supply and Demand 83
Summary 84
Key Terms 84
Review Questions 84
Problem Solving Practice 84

Chapter 6: Elasticity 86

A Big Idea in a Small Package 88
The Concept of Elasticity 88
Elasticity Is the Key 88
Price Elasticity of Demand 88
Elasticity 88
Factors Affecting Elasticity 91
Elasticity and Revenue 92
Other Elasticities 93
Elasticity of Supply 93
Income Elasticity of Demand 94
Cross Elasticity of Demand 94

viii CONTENTS

    Elasticity and Public Policy 94
        U.S. Drug Policy 95
        Health Care Policy 96
    Using This Tool 97
    Summary 97
    Key Terms 98
    Review Questions 98
    Problem Solving Practice 98

Chapter 7: Understanding Costs 100

    Scarcity and Costs 102
    The Idea of Cost 102
    Explicit Costs 103
    Implicit Costs 103
    Total Cost 103
    Measuring Profit 105
        Accounting Profit 105
        Economic Profit 105
    Sunk Cost 107
    Marginal Cost 108
    Costs—a Not-So-Final Look 108
    Summary 109
    Key Terms 109
    Review Questions 109
    Problem Solving Practice 109

PART 3: ECONOMIC STRUCTURES 111

Chapter 8: The Consumer 112

    The Role of the Consumer 114
    Assumptions about Consumer Behavior 114
        Consumers Are Rational 115
        Consumers Desire Many Goods 116
        Consumers Have to Pay for Goods 116
        Consumers Have Limited Income 116
    Utility: How Consumers Decide 117
        Utility Defined 117
        Total vs. Marginal Utility 117
        Diminishing Marginal Utility 117
    Costs and Utility: Getting the Most for Your Money 118
    Once the Consumer Has Voted 121
    Summary 122

Key Terms 122
Review Questions 122
Problem Solving Practice 122

Chapter 9: Labor, Unions, and the Distribution of Income 125

Workers of the World, Untie! 126
Labor 126
The Demand for Labor 126
The Supply of Labor 128
Human Capital 131
Labor Unions 132
Definition and History 132
Types of Labor Unions 132
Labor Union Terms 133
The Effect of Unions on Wages 134
How Unions Can Affect Wages 136
Labor Unions: A Final Assessment 138
Income Distribution 139
Definition and Factors Affecting the Distribution of Income 139
The Components of Income 140
The Actual Distribution of Income 141
Discrimination 143
Definition 143
The Effects of Discrimination 144
Solutions to the Discrimination Problem 144
Labor Retied 145
Summary 146
Key Terms 146
Review Questions 146
Problem Solving Practice 147

Chapter 10: The Firm 148

The How of Economics: The Firm 150
Definition of a Firm 150
Controlling the Firm 150
Internal Control of the Firm 151
Things That Are Said About Managers 151
Major Firm Managers 152
The Major Types of Firms 153
Sole Proprietorships 153
Other Ways of Organizing Firms 155
Labor-Managed Firms 155
Not-for-Profit Firms 155
Publicly Owned Firms 157

Firms and Markets 157
    Definition of a Market 157
    Types of Markets and Competition 158
Summary 158
Key Terms 158
Review Questions 158
Problem Solving Practice 158

Chapter 11: Competition and Monopoly 160

Perfect Competition and Monopoly as Models 162
Perfect Competition: The Dream 163
    The Conditions Required 163
    The Frequency of Perfect Competition 165
Monopoly: The Nightmare 166
    The Conditions Required 166
    The Frequency of Monopoly 169
The Benefits and Costs of Perfect Competition and Monopoly 169
Supply and Demand in Perfect Competition and Monopoly 170
Summary of Competition and Monopoly 172
Economic Concentration and Its Measures 173
    Aggregate Concentration 173
    Industry Concentration 173
Mergers 174
    The Structure of the Productive Process 174
    Definition of Merger 174
    Types of Mergers 175
    Concerns about Mergers 175
Solutions to the Monopoly Problem 176
    Prohibition 176
    Price Regulation 176
    Government Ownership 176
    Laissez Faire 177
From Fiction to Reality 177
Summary 177
Key Terms 178
Review Questions 178
Problem Solving Practice 178

Chapter 12: Imperfect Competition 180

And Now for Something Completely Different 182
Two Models of Imperfect Competition 182
    Monopolistic Competition 183
    Oligopoly 183
Understanding Oligopoly 184
How Oligopolists Compete 188

How Oligopolists Raise Prices 189
Price Leader 189
Mark-up Pricing 189
Collusion 189
The Role of Advertising 190
Cartels 191
Definition 191
Organizing and Maintaining a Cartel 192
A Final Look at Real Markets 192
Summary 193
Key Terms 193
Review Questions 193
Problem Solving Practice 193

Chapter 13: Rent, Interest, and Profit 194

Factors of Production and Their Returns 196
Rent 196
Defining the Term 196
Inframarginal Rent 197
Pure Economic Rent 198
Quasi Rent 199
Monopoly Rent 200
Rents—A Summary 200
Interest 200
Capital: The Goods 201
Capital: The Funds 201
Overall Interest Rates 202
The Nominal vs. the Real Rate of Interest 203
Profits 205
Entrepreneurship 205
Profit as a Residual 205
Accounting vs. Economic Profit 205
Profit Rates Since 1945 206
By Way of a Summary 206
Summary 207
Key Terms 207
Review Questions 207
Problem Solving Practice 207

PART 4: ECONOMIC ORGANIZATION 209

Chapter 14: Economic Systems 210

Scarcity Yet Again 212
Definition of Economic Systems 212
Economic Systems *vs.* Political Systems 212

Characteristics and Types of Modern Economic Systems 213
   Characteristics 213
   Types 213
Capitalism 213
   Definition of Capitalism 214
   Conditions Required for Capitalism 214
   Effects of Capitalism 215
Socialism 216
   Definition of Socialism 216
   Conditions Required for Socialism 217
   Effects of Socialism 218
Mixed Economies 219
Concluding Thoughts 220
Summary 220
Key Terms 220
Review Questions 220
Problem Solving Practice 221

Chapter 15: Government and Taxes 222

Why Government 224
The Role of Government 224
   Government in Socialism 224
   Government in Capitalism 224
Market Failure 225
Causes for Government Intervention in Capitalism 226
   Antitrust and Monopoly Regulation 226
   Externalities 226
   Public Goods 228
   Common Ownership 229
   Income Redistribution 230
   Economic Stabilization 231
A Final Look at Government 232
Paying for Government: Taxes 232
   Defining Taxes 232
   Issues about Taxes: Efficiency and Equity 233
   Types of Taxes 233
      The Effect of Taxes 234
      Tax Shifting and Tax Incidence 235
      Tax Progressivity 237
      A Final Look at Taxes 239
Budget Deficits and Debt 240
   Budget Deficits 240
   Budget Philosophies 241
   Causes of Debt 242
   The Size of the Debt 242
   Effects of Budget Deficits and Debt 242

Now What? 244
Summary 244
Key Terms 245
Review Questions 245
Problem Solving Practice 245

Chapter 16: The National Economy 246

The Big Picture 284
National Accounting 249
 Expenditures vs. Income Approaches 249
 Uses for National Accounts 250
Gross Nations Product *vs.* Gross 251
Domestic Product 251
Difficulties in Using National Accounts 251
Aggregate Demand and Aggregate Supply 253
 Aggregate Demand 253
 Aggregate Supply 255
Macroeconomic Policy 256
 A History of Macroeconomic Policy 256
 The Purpose of Policy Adjustments 257
Current Debates in Macroeconomic Policy 259
Summary 260
Key Terms 260
Review Questions 260
Problem Solving Practice 261

Chapter 17: Money, Banks, and the Interest Rate 262

Money Matters 262
Money 264
 The Definition of Money 264
 The Functions of Money 264
 The Supply of Money 265
 The Demand for Money 266
 The Market for Money 267
The U.S. Financial System 267
 A Brief History of Banking in the United States 267
 The Federal Reserve System 268
 Banks 273
Interest Rates 274
 The Definition of Interest 274
 Factors That Affect Interest Rates 274
 The Effects of High and Low Interest Rates 275
The Banking Industry Today—and Tomorrow 275
Summary 275
Key Terms 276

Review Questions 276
Problem Solving Practice 276

Chapter 18: Economic Growth, Development, and Inflation 278

Economic Growth 280
The Definition of Growth 280
Business Cycles 280
Sources of Growth 281
Measuring Growth 281
The Effects of Growth 281

Economic Development 281
Definition 282
Characteristics of Underdevelopment 282
The Desirability of Development 283
Measuring Development 284
The Keys to Economic Development 284
Sources of Economic Development 284
The Special Role of Government 285
The Effects of Economic Development 286

Inflation 286
Definition 286
Types of Inflation 286
The Effects of Inflation 288

A Final Look at Growth and Development 289
Summary 289
Key Terms 290
Review Questions 290
Problem Solving Practice 290

Chapter 19: The Global Economy 292

Gaining a Perspective 294
International Trade 294
Politics vs. Economics 297

The Good Old Days 299
In the Beginning 299
Tribalism 299
Mercantilism 299
Colonialism 299
Capitalism and Socialism 300

The Present 300
The Fork in the Road 300
Tariffs and Trade 300
Common Markets 300
Multinational Firms 302
The Language of Trade 302
"Resistance Is Useless" 303

Tomorrow 303
   Revolution, Not Evolution 303
   The Communications Revolution and the Service Sector 304
   The Increased Mobility of Human and Financial Capital 304
   The Triumph of Economics over Politics (or "Economics: The Integrating Approach") 304
Summary 305
Key Terms 306
Review Questions 306
Problem Solving Practice 306

PART 5: A SUMMARY 307

Chapter 20: Economics: a Final Look 309

We Made It! 310
Key Ideas in Economics 310
   There Is No Free Lunch 310
   Costs Are More Than Dollars 310
   Trade Benefits All 310
   The Market Works (Mostly) 311
Is Economics All? 312
   People May Not Live by Bread Alone, but Everything Has Its Price 312
   Two Economists Yield Three Theories 312
Efficiency and Equity One More Time 312
Edmund Burke Revisited 312
Key Terms 313
Review Questions 313
Problem Solving Practice 313

Glossary 315
Index 323

PHOTO CREDITS

Chapter 1, Wall Street, NY, Photo by Thierry Cariou, Courtesy of the Stock Market

Chapter 2, Female Executives in Busy Office at Computer, Photo by Jose Palaez, Courtesy of the Stock Market

Chapter 3, Commuters at Train Station, Photo by Michael Dwyer, Courtesy of Stock Boston

Chapter 4, Currency Sign, Photo by Reginald Wickham, Courtesy of Simon & Schuster/PH College

Chapter 5, Warehouse, Photo by Reginald Wickham, Courtesy of Simon & Schuster/PH College

Chapter 6, Grocery Store Shelves, Photo by Reginald Wickham, Courtesy of Simon & Schuster/PH College

Chapter 7, Businessmen and Women Working in Busy Office, Photo by Terry Vine, Courtesy of Tony Stone Images

Chapter 8, Shopping Mall—Chicago, Photo by Alan Carey, Courtesy of The Image Works

Chapter 9, Ford/Mazda Manufacturing Plant, Courtesy of AutoAlliance

Chapter 10, Business People Having a Meeting—Skyline in Background, Photo by Kaluzny/Thatcher, Courtesy of Tony Stone Images

Chapter 11, Young Professional Person, Photo by Michael A. Keller Studio Ltd., Courtesy of the Stock Market

Chapter 12, Sunoco Gas Pump, Photo by Reginald Wickham, Courtesy of Simon & Schuster/PH College

Chapter 13, Current Money Rates Sign, Photo by Reginald Wickham, Courtesy of Simon & Schuster/PH College

Chapter 14, The Main Equities Trading Floor at the NY Stock Exchange, Courtesy of New York Stock Exchange

Chapter 15, Albert Gallatin Statue in Front of U.S. Treasury, Washington, D.C. Head 1801–1814, by T. Jefferson, Photo by Mark C. Burnett, Courtesy of Stock Boston

Chapter 16, Cars on Car Dealership Lot, Photo by Reginald Wickham, Courtesy of Simon & Schuster/PH College

Chapter 17, Mint Dollar Bill Production, Printing & Engraving Bureau, Photo by George Chan Photography, Courtesy of Photo Researchers, Inc.

Chapter 18, Grand Opening of Ice Cream Store, Photo by The Photo Works, Courtesy of Monkmeyer Press

Chapter 19, International Currencies Sign, Photo by Reginald Wickham, Courtesy of Simon & Schuster/PH College

Chapter 20, Buying Sneakers, Photo by Jeffry W. Myers, Courtesy of Stock Boston

Foreword

Like an alien entity, capitalism harbors the seeds of its own destruction. At least, that's what Karl Marx claimed. Adam Smith theorized that an "invisible hand" guides the workings of the marketplace. (Had they lived in the modern era, the two could have collaborated on a blockbuster economic version of the movie *Independence Day*.) Fortunately, students have Benjamin Davis' clever tome to whet their appetites about the dismal science.

In spirit and in fact, *Economics: An Integrated Approach* leads the readers without preaching. This is the classic definition of education: to lead or bring forth. Professor Davis lets the word go forth unerringly. He guides students through economic paradoxes by integrating outside events that impinge on economic remedies. Unlike most textbook authors, he allows the real world to enter into the equation. This causes a gleam of recognition among students, accelerating comprehension.

The author argues the merits of capitalism and socialism—the two primary economic systems in the world today—from the perspective of a true believer. That one is ascendant and the other appears consigned to the ash heap of history does not deter Davis from making a cogent case for each. He provides existing exemplars of both systems. And he offers a rational and dispassionate conclusion that debunks the myths surrounding capitalism's compassion gap and socialism's egalitarian edge. Few economics texts can make this claim. Davis does it by using the indisputable logic of incentives, productivity, and income redistribution.

The latter chapters of the book are also notable for the context they afford the reader. An economic system is differentiated from a political system, something only alluded to in most other introductory economics books. Davis makes the old guns versus butter dichotomy less of a shopworn phrase and more of a living definition. In addition to recycling the four basic questions that every economic system must answer—What, How, For Whom, and When—Davis gives his readers terms they will never forget. It is worth highlighting: "Economic systems have to do with how people use resources. Political systems have to do with how people use power. Economic systems have to do with who's got the goods. Political systems have to do with who's got the guns."

Lest anyone think otherwise, Professor Davis' discussions of microeconomic concepts are just as enthralling. Okay, perhaps informative is a more appropriate superlative. My enthusiasm for the good professor's work is sincere. Take his passages on rents, for example. Any instructor worth his chalk finds classroom excursions into this area to be as arid as sojourns in the Sahara. Davis, instead, makes the most of this mundane yet essential term. Simply expressed, rent is the remuneration for land. But it is far more. The author traces the origin of rent and expands it to encompass inframarginal, quasi, monopoly and pure economic rent. Davis' explanation is a step-by-step building-block approach that few economic writers bother to explain. He does so with precision and clarity.

Rosario Iaconis
Briarcliffe College

Preface

WELCOME TO ECONOMICS

"The age of chivalry is gone. That of sophisters, economists, and calculators has succeeded, and the glory of Europe is extinguished forever."

Well! Was Edmund Burke having a bad day when he wrote that passage, or was he right? Does economics (and those other dismal sciences) push aside all chivalry and extinguish the glory of Europe and, presumably, the United States? Do I hear the occasional "You bet!"? Are economists the bane of our existence and should we attempt to ignore them all or is economics of some real value for life today? Can we find some real usefulness in economics and, perhaps, even in those dreaded people, economists?

I want to let you in on a little surprise: you are already an economist! You already make decisions about what to buy, whether or not to go to college, and whether you should work another day or take some vacation. You probably have voted on spending proposals by your city or county regarding more roads or streetlights, and you have an opinion about whether tax money should be spent on aid to the needy, military hardware, or college tuition assistance. Whatever else they may be, those are *all* economic questions, and those who answer them are economists.

Those decisions, and many others like them, are important, and you want to make them well. I hope by the time you finish this book and course that you will be better equipped to make the myriad economic decisions that face you daily, and that you will make them with an eye to both efficiency (getting the most output for what you spend) and equity (doing what is fair, right, and just).

Whereas it is true that all of us are economists—we all make decisions about how resources should be used—some of us are more intentional when we make these decisions. Some of us tend to think in terms of the *real* costs of doing our tasks and the *total* benefit that can be obtained, and that is where we are headed with this book.

The basic goal of this book is to help you develop a new—or at least more intentional—way of thinking about economic issues. As we do this, we are going to try to keep the text and the materials that are presented very relevant and practical. Far too many economics textbooks go to great pains using graphs and mathematical equations to get across an idea when a few carefully chosen words could accomplish the same thing with much greater clarity. In this text we will use graphs and equations when they are essential to the discussion. Otherwise we will rely on the English language to carry us. And the language we will use will take us into discussions of issues that are of current interest and importance. We will examine how people decide what to buy, why our national drug policy is not working, the overall impact of labor unions, how we can deal with income inequalities, and how the real business world operates.

I ask two things during our exploration: first, we have to be concerned about *both* efficiency *and* equity. We will need to look at *both* what works best *and* at what is the just or right thing to do. Efficiency or low-cost production at the expense of justice or fairness doesn't help our nation or its residents and citizens in the long run. A concern for fairness that ignores the efficient use of resources can only hurt those toward whom we are trying to be fair in the long run. Concern for both equity and efficiency must, and will, be a part of all of our discussions.

The second thing I ask is that we adopt a sense of humility as we propose answers to economic questions. Honest people, looking at the same situation, will often arrive at very different conclusions and recommendations for policy changes. Should we raise the minimum wage, or keep it the same, or eliminate it? In the long run which of these approaches would most help the low-wage worker? All three proposals have been suggested by people who are genuinely concerned with the welfare of low-wage workers. We need to respect the proposals and suggestions made by each other, aware that we can learn something from them at a minimum and that, for Heaven's sake, we *may* be wrong! So we will try to keep the rhetoric and polemics to a minimum in this book. As you will quickly see, for instance, there is a free-market bias to the presentation, but hopefully the inadequacies of the totally free market will be displayed just as obviously as the bias toward it. And so you are invited and urged to remain open to a free exploration of economics and to its possibilities for making life better—and not just in a financial sense.

Benjamin Davis

ACKNOWLEDGMENTS

A few years ago I complained to Alice Barr, Prentice Hall's regional representative, that the book by another publisher that I was using wasn't quite right for my economics course. Alice shared a few of her own texts with me and, after we agreed that none was exactly what was needed, she invited me to propose a text that would work. This book is the result of that invitation. Alice's help in initiating the process and her friendship in guiding it along its initial steps is very much appreciated.

To make certain that the book remained on track and would be easy for students to use, a number of reviewers and contributors have provided their own insights and suggestions. Thanks are extended to

Mostafa Aleseyed, Salem-Teikyo University, Salem West Virginia
Robert P. Cunningham, Binghamton University, New York
William Ganley, Buffalo State University, New York
Emily Hoffman, Western Michigan University, Michigan
Rosario Iaconis, Briarcliffe College, New York
Leonard Lardaro, University of Rhode Island, Rhode Island
Nola Reinhardt, Smith College, Massachusetts
Marianne C. Zipf, Plaza Business Institute, New York
Chris Grevesen, DeVry Technical Institute, New Jersey
Sam Ruggeri, Rochester Business Institute, New York
Barbara Podkowka, Commonwealth College, Virginia

Finally, I want to thank my fellow students. I truly mean fellow students, for in a good class the professor will learn as much as those who pay tuition. Together we were able to develop and live out the "so what?" attitude that is central to this book and which always seeks to immerse the hot steel of theory in the cold water of reality. That practical focus has helped me to hone my understanding of economics and to become a better teacher in the process.

Introduction

This book has been designed to help you gain an overall view of economics and to be able to place it in the context of today. We will begin by looking at the world around us. We need to know what economics is—and isn't—and what the world we live in looks like. We need to know what it is like today, where it has come from, and how it is changing so we can apply economics to help make it better. Once we gain this basic understanding, we will discuss fundamental economic ideas and principles such as costs and benefits, supply and demand, specialization and trade, and elasticity. These concepts and theories will allow us an in-depth look at the economic structures of the world. We will examine individuals and how they decide what to buy, how much to work, and the extent to which they benefit from the economy; we will look at firms and how they function; we will examine competition—and the lack of it—in the market place; and we will see how governments and overall economic systems (capitalism, socialism, and mixed economies) really work. Following the text itself, you will find a *Glossary* of useful terms and an *Index* of words and ideas that you can use as you explore economics during the semester.

The chapters have been structured to help you to acquire a comprehensive knowledge of the topics at hand. Each chapter is introduced with a short paragraph that explains why the information being presented is important. This is followed by a list of the key objectives for learning the material in the chapter. Many of the chapters have been purposefully kept short, to assist you in focusing on one basic idea at a time. All of the chapters have interesting examples that help you relate the information to economics in everyday life. Additional elements within the chapters include:

Key terms are highlighted and defined when they are first used in the text. Terms and definitions are also called out in the margins of the page for easy reference.

Graphs, charts, and illustrations throughout the text provide concrete examples and help clarify the concepts to help you remember them in a practical way.

Core-Info boxes provide brief summaries of important information at strategic points in the chapter. These are useful for testing your understanding of the material and for review.

"Issues" boxes highlight current issues that apply economics to the real-life problems and situations encountered in life as a student, citizen, worker, family member, and potential business owner or manager.

A **Summary** at the end of each chapter reviews the key points covered in the chapter.

Review Questions test your recall and understanding of the chapter content.

Problem-Solving Practice provides an opportunity to apply the principles learned in the chapter to solving interesting problems.

TO THE INSTRUCTOR

The text is structured as the most straight-forward guide to economics in the classroom today. The chapter lengths, for the most part, have been kept relatively short to encourage thorough reading. Graphs and mathematical equations have been kept to an absolute minimum in order to avoid confusing the students. It has not been assumed that students have freely elected to take this course. A practical, applied approach has been taken, therefore, to encourage students to find economics extremely relevant and related to their everyday lives.

Supplements Package

Ancillary materials to accompany the text provide support for the text and offer additional course guidelines.

Instructor's Manual with Transparency Masters provides lecture notes, recommended course syllabi, guides for using the Study Guide with the text, and masters for preparing acetate transparencies.

Test Item File and Electronic Test Item File provide a complete bank of test questions both in print and in electronic format that can be reorganized and reworked for many uses.

Study Guide provides students with additional instruction and practice applications that reflect economic issues in everyday life.

TO THE STUDENTS

You are about to begin a semester-long voyage into economics. I am aware that this is *not* likely to be the reason you chose to go to college. For most of you, this course will be a requirement and one you would not have selected voluntarily. That's O.K. I am going to try to make this as painless as possible. I will be showing real-world applications for all of the theories that are presented, and I will try to help you see how useful these concepts are for your everyday personal and professional lives. As a suggestion, read the assigned chapter *before* the class session in which it will be discussed. Think for a minute about how much you have invested in just being in class for the day—tuition costs, the hour lost, etc. (If any instructors are reading this, I know I have joined sunk costs to opportunity costs here; don't worry: we will separate them later.) When students sit in my classroom, they are aware that they have already spent $50 just to have the session on their schedules. To maximize the benefit from the lectures, prereading the text is most useful. In addition to reading the chapter, kept relatively short for your convenience, take a few minutes to *think* about what you have read and the pictures and charts you have seen. What do they mean? How might they apply to your own lives? Where have you experienced these ideas and theories before? Try to develop a "so what?" attitude toward the theories so you will begin to search for immediate applications. Then, before class, try to answer the questions at the end of the chapter. Answer them as if you were talking with a friend. Use plain, simple English, not *economeze* to explain the topic. When you can do this, you will be in great shape to understand the supplementary information that your instructor will be providing during the class sessions.

When you finish this book and semester, you will understand economics. You will know the basic ideas of economics, you will understand how our economy works—and doesn't work—and you will have a knowledge of the major issues and terms that are used everyday. In short, you will be able to discuss real world issues with any business person or trained economist on an equal basis. Oh, they may have studied economic theory more deeply in certain areas than you have, but you will have the breadth of knowledge needed to hold your own in any discussion. Guaranteed!

PART 1
UNDERSTANDING THE WORLD AROUND US

Chapter 1: Introduction to Economics

Chapter 2: Understanding—and Lying with—Graphs

Chapter 3: Trends in the World and Our Economy

CHAPTER 1

Introduction to Economics

CHAPTER OUTLINE

A. An Introduction to the Dismal Science
B. Defining Economics
C. Economics as a Science
D. Economic Models
E. The Four Economic Questions
   1. What?
   2. How?
   3. For Whom?
   4. When?
F. Resources in Economics
   1. Land
   2. Labor
   3. Capital
   4. Entrepreneurship
G. Costs and Scarcity
H. Rational Self-Interest
I. Money and Markets
J. Macroeconomics and Microeconomics
K. Problems in Doing Good Economics
   1. Detachment Is Required
   2. Fallacy of Composition
   3. False–Cause (*post hoc*) Fallacy
   4. Equity *vs.* Efficiency?
L. A Conclusion—and a Beginning

The purpose of this chapter is to introduce the basic issues in economics and to set the study of economics in its broader social science context.

AFTER COMPLETING THIS CHAPTER, YOU WILL BE ABLE TO:

1. Describe the central concern of economics.
2. Differentiate microeconomics and macroeconomics in the real world.
3. Identify the four economic questions and corresponding answers in a capitalistic economy.
4. Define the term *resources* and identify the four economic resources.
5. Compare rational self-interest and selfishness.
6. Identify the three basic problems and one key concern in doing economic studies.
7. Define *equity* and *efficiency* as they relate to and support each other.

An Introduction to the Dismal Science

Welcome to economics, the "Dismal Science!"[1]

Why would anyone want to be introduced to anything called dismal? Anyone who has read the Preface knows it is too late: you are already an economist. You make decisions about how to use resources every day. You have decided to go to college and add to your abilities rather than go into the labor force with less training. You decided whether to go out or stay at home last weekend—at least partly an economic decision—and how much to spend. You have decided whether to buy a new or used copy of this textbook, whether or not you like the president's latest health care proposal, and how much time you will spend reading this chapter today. Your personal preferences are displayed in each case, of course, but that is what economics is all about. Through the use of our resources, we show our preferences and set in motion a vast economic system. To the extent that we understand how this economic system works, we are more likely to make good decisions, decisions that will produce more long-term satisfaction.

If you give economics half a chance, you will find that far from being dismal it is quite enlightening. You will discover a new way of looking at the world around you and will develop a new set of tools that will serve you well in all aspects of life. That's no small claim, but the science of economics can deliver.

DEFINING ECONOMICS

Definitions are important. How we define something sets the tone and provides direction for our study. Thus, this definition is well worth noting. Don't just memorize the definition: think and *learn* it. **Economics** is the science that studies how scarce resources are allocated to meet competing and unlimited wants. Economics is the science that studies how human beings satisfy their material wants and needs.

Those 32 words say a lot. Terms such as *science, resources, allocated,* and *wants and needs* all require careful examination. This chapter will explore these concepts and fill in a few details along the way.

> **Economics**
> The science that studies how scarce resources are allocated to meet competing and unlimited wants and how human beings satisfy their material wants and needs.

ECONOMICS AS A SCIENCE

Ever since the period known as the Enlightenment, we have attempted to apply science to almost all of what we do as human beings. Science is an attempt to organize information in a logical way so people can discover, understand, explain, and predict. While the scientific method does not give answers, and science never *proves* anything, this approach does help make some sense out of the multitude of information that surrounds us.

There are two major branches of science. In the **physical sciences** we examine the natural phenomena that we encounter. Physics, chemistry, and geology are physical sciences because they each focus on the physical world. The second branch of science is the **social sciences.** In this branch, we examine the relational aspects of life and try to understand how people relate to one another. Psychology, sociology, anthropology, and economics are all social sciences because they examine how people behave both individually and in groups. While economics does look at the use of physical goods and land, its main goal is to examine how these physical assets work to meet human needs.

> **Physical Sciences**
> The systematic study of the physical world around us.
>
> **Social Sciences**
> The systematic study of all aspects of human relationships.

---

[1] Thomas Carlyle gave economics this name. He thought that economics was "a dreary, desolate, and indeed quite abject and distressing" science because it seemed aloof and impersonal to him. We will discover plenty of evidence to refute Carlyle's opinion.

CHAPTER 1 • INTRODUCTION TO ECONOMICS

ECONOMIC MODELS

Model
A simplified view of the world that helps to illustrate one aspect of reality.

All sciences use **models.** Models are simplified views of reality that help us to understand what is happening. No one has seen the inner workings of an atom, but physicists have created a model, or point of view, that represents the protons, neutrons, electrons, and dozens of subatomic particles all present in the atom. This model best explains what physicists observe when they study the atom. So, too, with economics. Economists use models to try to simplify complex situations so we can understand them. One example may help to explain why models are important in economics. Everybody knows that if a beachfront stand lowers the price of t-shirts, people will buy more of them. This is a simple economic model known as the law of demand (see Chapter 5). Economists say this is always true *ceteris paribus,* if everything else is held constant. If the weather is bad or if a competitor lowers his price even more, sales may fall even with the drop in prices. An economic model helps to examine how and why things such as t-shirt sales vary so you can predict what would happen if . . ..

Ceteris Paribus
A Latin term that means all else being equal.

THE FOUR ECONOMIC QUESTIONS

We use economic science to help understand and answer the four great **economic questions.** Every economic system has to answer these questions:

Economic Questions
The four basic questions that every economic system must answer.

1. What will be produced?
2. How will the goods and services be provided?
3. Who will get the goods and services that are produced?
4. When will we get the output?

Let's look at each of these four questions to examine what they mean and how they are answered in a capitalist economy such as that of the United States.

What?

The first—and as we shall see most fundamental—question in economics is what shall we produce? Will we have more hospitals or cancer research or will we have transportation services? Will we have mass transit or will we produce cars? Will we have Fords or Chevrolets or Hondas? Will we have coupes or four doors? Red cars or blue cars? Milano Red or Redondo Red? A million decisions must be made in any economy every day. In a capitalist economy, consumers make the **what** decision. Consumers vote with their dollars, francs, or pounds. By their willingness to spend money, consumers determine not only what final goods and services will be produced, but what machinery will have to be made to produce all of these final goods. Figure 1.1 shows you how consumers have voted with their dollars in the United States over a period of 14 years.

What?
The economic question that deals with the decisions about which goods and services will be produced in an economy.

How?

Once consumers have decided what they want, the goods and services must be produced. If consumers decide they want food, it could be produced by using a lot of machinery and a few workers as we do in the United States or by using lots of workers and very little machinery as they do in India. Either way can be appropriate depending upon what it costs to hire workers and rent or buy machinery. Producers look at the situation and make this decision in a capitalist economy. Thus, firms make the **how** decision.

How?
The economic question that deals with the decisions about the means by which goods and services will be produced in an economy.

For Whom?

Who?
The economic question that deals with the decisions about the individuals or groups that will receive the goods and services produced in an economy.

Next we must decide how to allocate these goods and services to the various people in the economy. Do we give all or some of the goods away? Do we give a lot to a few people and very little to many people? Somehow we have to decide **who** gets the goods. In capitalism we let prices make this decision. People take their preferences, consider their incomes and the prices of the various goods, and make the decision as to which and how much of the goods they will buy. Personally I

FIGURE 1.1
The economy is changing and more and more of our output is in the form of services rather than goods or buildings. *Source:* U.S. Bureau of Economic Analysis.

Percentage Distribution of Gross Domestic Product			
	Goods	Services	Structures
1980	43.4	44.9	11.7
1985	40.9	48.0	11.8
1987	39.5	49.9	10.5
1988	39.6	50.2	10.2
1989	39.9	50.3	9.7
1990	39.4	51.4	9.2
1991	38.8	52.9	8.2
1992	38.1	53.6	8.3
1993	37.9	53.7	8.4
1994	38.4	53.1	8.6

would very much like to own a new Porsche 911. I suppose theoretically I could afford it if I sold my house, but the price in both dollar and nondollar terms is too high for me, so I don't own a Porsche. Capitalism is based on the belief that, as people look at their resources and the prices of goods, they will make better decisions than someone else would in deciding for them.

When?

When?
The economic question that deals with the decisions about whether the goods and services produced in an economy will be received in the present or the future.

Finally we must decide **when** we will get the goods. Will we get all the goods and services that we could produce today, or will we forgo some consumption today so we can have more to spend tomorrow? One way or another we have to decide this critical question. College students should appreciate the importance of this decision: you have decided to give up some earning and spending today so you can invest in yourself and be more productive tomorrow. That is how the basic **when** decision is made in a capitalist economy (see Figure 1.2). Consumers (and, to a lesser extent, businesses through retained earnings) decide when goods and services will be produced.

The following table summarizes the four economic questions and how they are answered in a capitalist economy. As we shall see, these four questions are answered in a very different way in socialism. In that type of economic system, the government makes all of the key economic decisions and, thus, answers the four economic questions.

How the Four Economic Questions Are Answered in Capitalism

1. What?	Consumers
2. How?	Firms
3. For whom?	Prices
4. When?	Consumers and Firms

The four key economic questions are:
1. What will be produced?
2. How will it be produced?
3. Who will get the goods and services produced?
4. When will the goods be received?

[2.] The term *core-info* refers to the essential concepts you need to remember from each section. Obviously you need to read the chapter to understand what they mean, but you can easily use the Core-Info as your test review triggers. Look at the terms. If you know what they mean, go on to the next section. If you don't remember, stop and review the section.

FIGURE 1.2
As people change their "when" decision, the savings rate rises and falls significantly. *Source:* Bureau of Economic Analysis, U.S. Department of Commerce.

Personal Savings Rate	
Personal Savings	
Year	Percent of Disposable Income
1960	5.6%
1965	7.1
1970	8.0
1975	8.6
1980	6.0
1981	6.7
1982	6.2
1983	5.4
1984	6.1
1985	4.4
1986	4.1
1987	3.2
1988	4.2
1989	4.6
1990	5.1
1991	4.7
1992	4.8
1993	4.1
1994	4.1

RESOURCES IN ECONOMICS

Once the four economic questions have been answered, the next step is to produce goods and services and get them to the right people at the right time. The things used to produce and distribute goods and services are called **resources** in economics. (You may also hear them called *inputs* or *factors of production,* and these terms can be used interchangeably.) Everything that is made comes from some combination of these four resources.

Land

Land in economics refers to natural resources. These resources are only available through nature. They are limited and, at least relatively, irreplaceable. The surface of the earth itself (the noneconomist's "land") is limited in size; people must choose how to use it. Oil and coal are finite and can't be replaced for millions of years. Even timber is pretty much irreplaceable. While the new, fast-growing tree varieties can be replaced in a decade or so, for now they are considered to be land. (You may want to speculate, after you finish reading the definitions of all four economic resources, as to what type of resource a *really* fast-growing strain of timber would be.)

Labor

Labor is the work put forward by human beings. Labor is what people add to the productive process. Labor is *both* manual labor and intellectual labor. Whether you are digging a ditch or repairing a computer or conducting a symphony orchestra, you are doing labor. You are also doing labor when you sit at home with your feet propped up and plan the next week's work schedule for your office. There is no distinction between labor and management in economics: both do labor.

Labor has one unique characteristic: it exists only in the present tense. By this economists mean that you can't "save" labor in the same way that you can save money. There is no way to put labor aside today so it can be used tomorrow. If labor is not used today, it is lost forever. The output that could have been produced is gone. Yes, you *could* work extra hours the next day, but you could have done that

Resources
The things that are used to produce and distribute goods and services in an economy. These include land, labor, capital, and entrepreneurship. They are also known as factors of production.

Land
The term applied to the category of resources that is given by nature; natural resources.

Labor
The term applied to the category of resources that includes the mental and physical work done by human beings.

anyway. The labor hours that were lost because they weren't used are gone forever and with them goes what they could have produced. That permanent loss is one of two reasons why economists so strongly dislike unemployment. While a full discussion of the issue of unemployment will be reserved for a later chapter, unemployment not only means that people are not working (with all the economic and psychological problems attached to that) but unemployment falls more heavily on some groups than on other groups. Blacks, Hispanics, older people, and women are much more likely to be unemployed than whites, middle-agers, and males. Unemployment is not an equal opportunity oppressor.

Capital

Capital
The term applied to those resources, made by people, that include machines and equipment that can be used to produce other goods and services; capital goods do not directly satisfy human wants.

The term **capital** must be defined very carefully; this is one of those words we think we understand except that economists twist the meaning just a little. Capital does NOT mean money. Read that again: capital does NOT mean money. As an economic resource, money is useless. Oh, we economists find our salaries useful, but money *per se* is of no use until it is converted into something that brings satisfaction. For most people, little green pieces of paper with faces from history books on them don't bring much satisfaction. However, people can use those greenbacks to buy goods and services that bring a great deal of satisfaction, or to purchase the capital needed to produce those goods and services.

Capital goods or resources are productive goods. They are things we can touch and feel that are used to produce other goods and services. Capital goods are not produced or purchased so we can have capital goods themselves, but so we can produce other things. Garages, stoves, stamping plants, and trucks are all capital goods. Each of these goods is used to produce something else.

Consumer Goods
Goods and services that directly satisfy human wants.

The ultimate goal of economics is to produce goods and services for people. To that end, we must first produce capital goods. In contrast with labor, capital is future oriented. Capital is produced or purchased to generate a stream of **consumer goods** for some extended period into the future. To produce capital goods requires foregoing the production of consumer goods for a time. We always face a trade-off, therefore between capital goods and consumer goods: producing more of one by definition means producing less of the other *today*. Of course, producing more capital goods today means that we will be able to produce more consumer goods tomorrow.

Entrepreneurship

Entrepreneurship
The creative resource in economics that combines other resources in new and unique ways to produce goods and services.

Entrepreneurship is the last of our four resources or factors of production. Entrepreneurship is the intuitive, creative side of economics. Entrepreneurs are not people with lots of money to invest. Entrepreneurs are people with vision who can see an opportunity, accept the risk, and try something different. Entrepreneurs, in economics, develop new products or find new ways to do old things. There is no guaranteed return to entrepreneurship. If you add one more acre of land or one more ton of coal, if you add one more labor hour, if you add one more piece of capital equipment, you can pretty much predict what the result will be. The outcome of using additional units of those three types of resources or factors of production can be anticipated in advance. This is not the case with entrepreneurship, and many a would-be entrepreneur has found that the hoped-for outcome from the pursuit of a new path did not materialize. Risk is a part of entrepreneurship, and it is this willingness to accept risk, combined with creativity, that makes a true entrepreneur.

Core-Info

The four economic resources are:
1. Land
2. Labor
3. Capital
4. Entrepreneurship

CHAPTER 1 • INTRODUCTION TO ECONOMICS

COSTS AND SCARCITY

Scarcity
The idea that all resources are limited and inadequate to meet all human wants.

Free Goods
Those goods that are available to meet all human demand at a zero price. There are none.

Cost
Anything that is given up in order to obtain something else; a result of scarcity.

Scarcity is a way of life—maybe we should say *the* way of life. Goods, in economics, are either scarce or free. **Free goods** are available in an unlimited supply at a price of zero. Free goods cost nothing; you don't have to give up anything to get them. Scarce goods, on the other hand, do cost something: you have to give up something to get them, and that is what **cost** is.

Cost is anything you have to give up to get something else. We will spend a good deal of time discussing costs in Chapter 7, but for now it is important to remember that *everything* has a cost: you must give up something to get anything else. Even if you are just giving up some of your free time to do something, that means that you can't be doing something else at the same time. Until we reach Chapter 7, remember that some costs can be measured in terms of the dollars you must spend (these are called **explicit costs**) and some costs are measured in terms of opportunities lost (these are called **implicit costs**). Both the dollars used and the opportunities lost are important to economists, because something is given up. Resources are used.

Core-Info

The two basic types of costs are:
1. Explicit costs
2. Implicit costs

Explicit Costs
The actual dollar or accounting cost associated with obtaining something.

Implicit Costs
The opportunity cost of resources that are used in obtaining something and for which there is no explicit payment.

Rational Self-Interest
The view of human behavior that states that all human decisions involve a weighing of the costs and benefits perceived to be associated with them in order to maximize the outcome. Economists use this approach in explaining all human actions.

RATIONAL SELF-INTEREST

Economics is based on the assumption that people act out of **rational self-interest.** Rational self-interest means that individuals weigh the costs and benefits *as they perceive them* and make decisions that will increase their welfare. This includes decisions to buy and sell, to invest or save, to take a job or retire, to spend on one's self or give to charity. In short, economists think that all of our decisions are based on rational self-interest. While some economists have begun to question this model, it appears to explain personal economic (and other human) behaviors better than any other approach.

It is important to remember two things about rational self-interest. First, what may appear to be crazy to one person is quite logical to another. One car buyer may choose Honda while another favors a Pontiac. One couple may dine at restaurants three times a week, while another couple eats out once a month. The key is that all people maximize their welfare as they perceive it. To change that behavior—to convince Honda drivers to buy Pontiacs, for instance—requires showing people how the change would benefit their self-interest. They must see how the benefits of the proposed change outweigh the costs. *Then* they will be willing to change. People will always act in their own self-interest. Period.

The second thing to remember is that there is a world of difference between "self-interest" and "selfish," and people give to charity out of their self-interest (see Figure 1.3). When people act selfishly, they want what they want even if—and sometimes especially if—they have to take it from someone else. When you are selfish, if another person has to lose so you can win, so be it. With self-interest, however, your only concern is improving your own situation in life. If another person can improve his or her own lot, too, that's fine; it doesn't diminish your improvement. In fact, if one person improves his or her situation, it probably helps other people as well. Selfish people want their income to rise, not the pay of other people. Self-interested people don't mind if the pay of others increases—as long as theirs does too.

MONEY AND MARKETS

As we study economics and see how individuals, pursuing their own self-interest, benefit the overall economy, we will come to understand that exchange is the basis

FIGURE 1.3
Source: American Association of Fund-Raising Council, Inc., AAFRC Trust for Philanthropy.

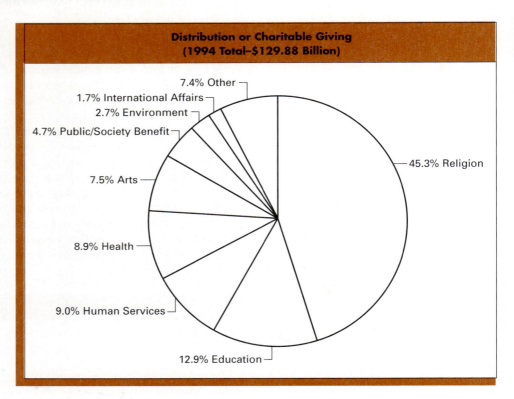

Core-Info

Rational self-interest means doing the best you can for yourself as you understand it.

of all economics. One person exchanges what he or she has too much of with someone else who has too much of something else. I trade my labor services to you for a pair of shoes. You trade an hour of legal assistance for a bushel of apples. One way or another, we trade things we don't want for things we do. The place where and the means by which we make these exchanges is known as a **market.**

People can do this trading directly, and that is how all economies begin. I trade you some of the fish I have caught for a coat you have made. We **barter** with each other. In barter, people directly trade goods for goods. To do this they must negotiate over the price of each trade. Thirty fish equal one coat; two fish equal three loaves of bread, and so forth. To barter, people must meet, set the price, and exchange the goods. This can be quite cumbersome if many exchanges must take place, and almost impossible if people want some goods from very far away. Trading the fish I caught in Maine for some California wines would be difficult even today. The way people get around the limitations of barter is money.

Money is anything people agree is money. That may seem like a silly definition, but it is true. As long as people agree that something is money, it is, regardless of what the government says. Cigarettes and chocolate served as money in Europe after World War II. If people don't think that something is money, then it will not serve as money even if it has been printed by the government. Some European currencies were all but useless following World War II: people were afraid that these monies would be worthless, so they refused to accept them for purchases. We will look in depth at money in Chapter 17, but for now, think of money as anything that people can use to facilitate exchange and that they can use to accumulate wealth to later spend. Figure 1.4 shows the dramatic increase in the amount of money in circulation.

Market
The place where buyers and sellers exchange goods and services produced and desired in an economy and which, if allowed to function freely, results in equilibrium.

Barter
The exchange of one good for another without the use of money as a medium of exchange.

Money
Anything two parties agree is money. Money serves as a medium of exchange, a measure of value, and a store of value.

FIGURE 1.4
Source: Board of Governors, Federal Reserve System.

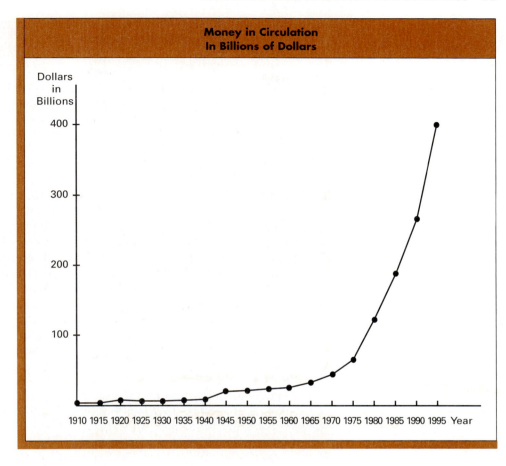

MACROECONOMICS AND MICROECONOMICS

As you can probably tell from our discussion so far, there are two basic approaches in economics. We will be pursuing both in this book. The first approach is called **macroeconomics.** Macroeconomics is economics of the entire economy taken together. Included in this aspect are questions such as the balance of trade with Japan, the overall level of Gross Domestic Product, the rate of inflation, and the level of unemployment. Any question that affects the entire economy is a macroeconomic question.

The other economic approach is known as **microeconomics.** Microeconomics deals with the activities and decisions of an individual decision maker such as a consumer, household, or business firm. The decisions to buy a new shirt or attend college or open a new shoe store are all microeconomic decisions. Even General Motors' billion dollar decision to start a new Saturn division was a microeconomic, not macroeconomic decision. As a rule of thumb, if it affects the entire economy, it is macroeconomics; if a part, it is microeconomics, regardless of the size of the decision.

Macroeconomics
The study of the economy as a whole.

Microeconomics
The study of individual decision makers, both people and businesses, within an economy.

Macroeconomics has to do with the study of the whole economy.
Microeconomics has to do with the study of any part of the economy.

PROBLEMS IN DOING GOOD ECONOMICS

Becoming a good economist is not easy. The "stuff" of economics is occasionally difficult, and the path is not always clear. What we want to do is to make certain that we do not compound our difficulties by falling victim to any of the three common problems that are frequently encountered.

Detachment Is Required

Economics touches us all on real gut-level issues. We are dealing with whether to pursue a cure for AIDS or spend more money on cancer research. We are dealing with whether it is better—for individuals and for the economy—to have a higher minimum wage or lower welfare costs or a flat tax. We are dealing with the issue of inequalities in income and opportunity in our society. It is hard to be neutral with issues such as these, and we shouldn't be. Anyone who argues that values have no place in good economic analysis is just flat wrong. Personal values *should* be a part of the analysis. How and when you apply your values is the issue.

There are two ways of looking at issues, two ways of doing science. There is the **positive** approach and the **normative** approach. The positive approach, or positive economics, is also called descriptive economics because it attempts to describe as accurately as possible what is there. "There are approximately 250 million people living in the United States" is a positive statement. "It is 279 miles from Detroit to Chicago" is a positive statement. "Women earn 70 percent of what men earn for equal work" is also a positive statement. You don't have to agree with the statement or want it to be true to call it a positive statement. If the statement describes reality, it is a positive statement whether you like what it says or not.

Normative statements are quite different. Normative statements are value statements. In normative statements we voice our opinions, so words such as "should" or "ought" are generally a part of such statements. "We should spend more money on finding a cure for Parkinson's Disease" states a value. It is a normative statement.

"Women earn less than men" is positive; "women should earn the same as/more than/less than men" is normative.

Throughout this book we will attempt to be aware of our biases so we can guard against them. We will start with positive statements and descriptions so we know what the facts are and then move to applying our values to each situation. With any luck, we will agree on the descriptive or positive issues. If we disagree as to the facts, we can go and look them up and find the correct answer. *Then* we will apply our values and, perhaps, have some disagreements. If we all try to operate this way, and if you carry this approach into all of your economic analysis, our time together will be enlightening, and you will do a much better job with economics.

Fallacy of Composition

The **fallacy of composition** is the place where macroeconomics and microeconomics can appear to collide. The fallacy of composition states that what is true of an isolated case is not necessarily true of everything; what is good for one person is not necessarily good for all. A couple of examples will help here. Let's say you're at a college football game and are having trouble seeing. You can see better if you stand up, right? Now the people behind you have to stand up, too? In fact, why doesn't *everybody* in the stadium stand up? The problem now is that when everyone stands up, you are right back where you started: you can't see. Another example: you drive to college and always get into a traffic jam trying to get to your 8:00 A.M. class. One morning you notice that if you leave 10 minutes earlier, you avoid all of the traffic *and* get a good spot in the parking lot. However, if everyone tries your solution, the result is simply moving the traffic jam 10 minutes earlier.

In economics, the same fallacy of composition is often the case. If I can convince the president of my college to double my salary, I will certainly benefit. Since it is good for me, why not double everyone's salaries? If everyone brings home twice as much money, all costs and prices will double and we will be right back where we started. In a final example, if you decide to save money this year rather than spend so you can buy a house next year, you are quite likely to be better off.

Positive
The approach to science—and economics—that describes or deals with data, facts, and reality.

Normative
The approach to science—and economics—that deals with values, judgments, and opinions, not facts.

Fallacy of Composition
The faulty reasoning that assumes that what is true for a part is necessarily true for the whole.

Converging Approach, Diverging Views

News Flash!! Limbaugh and Kennedy Agree!
A late-breaking news story from Washington, D.C., today reports that conservative commentator Rush Limbaugh may have been inspired by the late Robert F. Kennedy. This story has taken political pundits by surprise as most felt that Limbaugh and a Kennedy would never agree on *anything*. A quotation made by Kennedy very closely parallels the name of Limbaugh's daily political commentary program. Kennedy's quote is: "Some men see things as they are and say why. I dream things that never were and say, why not." Limbaugh similarly has titled his program "America: The Way It Ought to Be." Commentator's hasten to point out that this is not the first time political opposites have agreed on the means, if not the ends.

What is going on? How is it that Limbaugh agrees with Kennedy? Their viewpoints converge on an approach to politics, not on positions. Both men have approached political issues from a *normative,* not a positive position. Their statements are opinions on how America should be shaped. Once they slip into the world of opinion, we have to sharpen our listening skills, for we are out of the realm of fact. Facts may be very much a part of the arguments of a Limbaugh or a Kennedy, but when they begin to tell us how things should work, we need to listen more critically.

What is true for Limbaugh and Kennedy is also true of every other politician. Remember to listen carefully to politicians and apply your analytical skills to their statements. When we begin to separate fact from a politician's opinions, we can reclaim our role as leaders, not just followers.

What would happen if everybody decided to save and not spend anything this year? The economy would take a nose dive (economists' talk for a depression).

These examples should demonstrate the need to be careful when extrapolating any economic prescription from the particular (the individual) to the general (all of us). All too often, this sort of logic backfires. Look very carefully, therefore, at any proposal that says that it was good for one family or one company or one city or one anything else and *therefore* it will be good for all of us. That just may not be the case.

False–Cause Fallacy

False–Cause (*Post Hoc*) Fallacy
The mistaken linking of cause and effect; mistaking correlation for causation.

The **false–cause (or *post hoc*)** fallacy is the last of our three potential problems in doing good economics. In the case of a false-cause fallacy, we confuse correlation with causation. Correlation means that two things happen at the same time. Causation means that one thing makes another thing happen. There is a big difference between the two of these, but it is easy to confuse them in economics. Why did the economy have its latest upturn/downturn? Was it because of the president's recently passed economic program? Was it because consumer spending increased/decreased? Was it because businesses increased/decreased their investment in new capital because of what they thought might happen? In economics it is often *very* hard to tell for certain.

Core-Info

The three problems we face in doing good economics are:
1. We get too personally involved; detachment is required.
2. We assume that what is true for one person is true for all people; avoid the fallacy of composition.
3. We mistake correlation for causation; watch out for false-cause fallacy.

Equity vs. Efficiency?

Efficiency
Doing things right; getting the maximum output for the minimum input.

A final concern as we begin our economic journey has to do with the oft-supposed trade-off between **efficiency** and **equity.** Efficiency has to do with getting the most for the least, with using your resources as frugally as possible, with doing things right.

Equity
Doing the right thing; including a sense of justice and fairness in decision making.

Equity, on the other hand, has to do with justice and fairness, with doing the right things. Some economics textbooks contend that there is a trade-off between the two. There isn't. Early industrialists might have argued that paying children pennies a day to work in sweatshops made their goods more affordable for the masses, but not even economists call this examplary behavior. Henry Ford discovered after he raised his workers' wages to $5.00 per day, that they were more productive and he sold more cars and made more money. In our study of economics, we shall see that business does not have to choose between equity and efficiency and that, in fact, the two go hand in hand.

Core-Info

The balance that is required throughout economics is that of equity and efficiency. Both *can* be achieved together, hence the subtitle of this book.

A CONCLUSION—AND A BEGINNING

As we continue our foray into economics, we will examine how the economy can work and how we can make good decisions and effective use of resources. Along the way, we will discover that we may have to give up some of our previous assumptions about how the world works, assumptions that seem so obviously true. We will discover that rent controls put in place to help renters actually hurt them. We will find that import controls put into place to aid our economy actually damage it. And, we will learn that the U.S. policy of attempting to reduce the supply of drugs coming into the country is one of the best things that could have happened to drug dealers, sort of an American Drug Dealer Welfare Program.

How can anything that can give us insight into issues such as these be called "dismal"?

SUMMARY

- Economics is the study of how we use our scarce resources. Macroeconomics considers the whole economic system while microeconomics is the study of individual decision makers within the overall economy.
- The four economic questions are what will be produced, how will it be produced, who will get the goods and services, and when will they be received.
- The four resources are land, labor, capital, and entrepreneurship. These are the elements used to produce goods and services.
- Rational self-interest means that people are always trying to do the best for themselves, not that they are trying to take something away from anyone else.
- The three basic problems we face in doing economics are the need for detachment, the idea of the fallacy of composition, and the issue of false-cause fallacy.
- Equity means doing the right thing. Efficiency means doing things the right way. They go hand in hand in economics.

KEY TERMS

Barter	False-cause (*post hoc*) fallacy	Normative
Capital		Physical sciences
Ceteris paribus	Free goods	Positive
Consumer goods	How	Rational self-interest
Cost	Implicit costs	Resources
Economic questions	Labor	Scarcity (scarce goods)
Economics	Land	Social sciences
Efficiency	Macroeconomics	What
Entrepreneurship	Market	When
Equity	Microeconomics	Who (for whom)
Explicit costs	Model	
Fallacy of composition	Money	

REVIEW QUESTIONS

1. Define economics and explain why it is considered to be a social science.
2. Explain why economics uses models in explaining how people act.
3. State the four economic questions and briefly explain who makes the decision for each one in a capitalist economy.
4. Identify the four resources of economics and give two examples of each.
5. What is the difference between explicit and implicit cost? Give two examples of each type of cost.
6. Macroeconomics or microeconomics can be discussed using positive and/or normative statements. Explain the significance of each approach.
7. Explain how individuals can pursue their own self-interest without being selfish in the process.
8. Define equity and efficiency. Give one economic example that you have observed for things that are equitable, inequitable, efficient, and inefficient.

PROBLEM-SOLVING PRACTICE

Provide a short analytical answer to each of the following.

1. How does a modern market economy answer the four economic questions? In what ways would a subsistence economic economy answer these questions differently?
2. Identify which of the following goods are free goods and which are economic goods and explain your selection.

a freeway	a toll road
free food from a food bank	food from a grocery store
sea water	fresh water

3. Determine whether each of the following is a positive or normative economic statement:
   (a) Most prices are determined by the supply and demand of a product.
   (b) The next president of the United States should reduce the unemployment rate to zero.
   (c) The price of gasoline in the United States should never exceed $1.40 per gallon.
   (d) The average price for a new computer is $2,000.
   (e) The chief executive officers of the largest U.S. corporations earn about 200 times more than the average worker.
   (f) Housing should be affordable for all American families.
   (g) An increase in the minimum wage will increase unemployment in the United States.
   (h) The minimum wage in the United States should be increased to help the poor.

CHAPTER 2

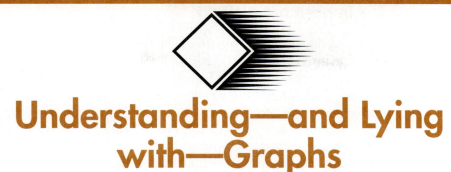

Understanding—and Lying with—Graphs

CHAPTER OUTLINE

A. The Importance of Data
B. Reading Charts and Data Tables
C. Reading Pictorial Graphs
   1. Bar Charts
   2. Circle or Pie Charts
D. Reading Relational Graphs
E. Lying with Charts and Graphs
F. Back on Track with Charts and Graphs

The purpose of this chapter is to introduce the ways of using and misusing quantitative data displays in presenting information in economics.

AFTER COMPLETING THIS CHAPTER, YOU WILL BE ABLE TO:

1. Use charts and graphs to explain economics.
2. Read and draw pictorial and functional graphs.
3. Identify misleading information in graphs.

The Importance of Data

Chapter 1 provided a basic view of economics and its central concepts. Readers whose curiosity has been piqued probably have snuck a look at the chapters to come. Even if you haven't, you have no doubt seen what this chapter is about in local newspapers and magazines. We are going to deal now with charts and graphs.

There are two ways to present information in economics. We can use words to describe something (for instance, "I studied a lot for that stupid econ quiz") or we can use numbers ("I studied for three hours for that fine quiz that I just took"). Using descriptive words helps to convey feelings, but makes it impossible to make comparisons. How long did the first student in our example here study? More or less than the second student? What he or she calls "a lot" may be one hour or ten hours. If both students say it in numbers, it is possible to make comparisons, to add their study time for this quiz to the time they studied for the last one to calculate a total, or to determine the average amount of time everybody studied. Numbers can be very helpful in economics.

Numbers aren't everything, of course. As the last chapter noted, some of the science of economics is to talk normatively, to bring into play values, and here it is very difficult to speak numerically. Just how important is it that women be paid the same as men for the same work? What does "very" important mean? It's pretty hard to measure "very." Where we can, however, we are going to try to use data. We need data in order for our normative statements to be worth anything.

When people use numerical information, they need some way to present it. They could write a paragraph with all of the data included in it. For instance, a student describing the composition of this economics class could write a paragraph that included the total number of students, the number of each gender, the number from each state, and so forth. The information would all be there, but it would be hard for people to dig it out without a great deal of effort. With charts and graphs, data can be presented in a way that people can readily see what the composition of the class is.

Those of you who have already studied how to read charts and graphs in mathematics or some other class may figure you don't need to read this chapter. However, the focus here is not only conveying and interpreting data in graphs, but how that data can lead people astray. About 40 years ago, Darrell Huff and Irving Geis wrote a book called How to Lie with Statistics. Just as they showed how statistics can be used to mislead others, this chapter will demonstrate how graphs can do precisely the same thing. Properly drawn and correctly interpreted, graphs can provide a wealth of good, solid information for decision making. On the other hand, data graphed improperly can not only mislead but can lead someone to believe just the opposite of what is true.

Is the purpose of this chapter to encourage lying with graphs? Of course not. The goal here is to encourage you to become careful graph drawers and expert graph readers so you won't be misled by others. The first step is to look at charts to see how they are composed and how to read them. We will then discuss how graphs are drawn and interpreted. Finally, we will see just how easy it is to mislead with—or be misled by—graphs.

Core-Info

Using data in economics provides an understandable measure of the subject under discussion.

READING CHARTS AND DATA TABLES

In the first place, charts are just lists. A chart's author takes raw data and organizes it into a list that readers can easily understand. For instance, information about the number of people who live in the five most populous states can be organized as shown in Figure 2.1.

Figure 2.1 is straight forward, yet it contains everything that a good chart should have. Each chart should be able to stand by itself. Anyone who found a chart on a page ripped from a book should be able to understand it without having to locate the book it came from. The chart has a number so readers can find it in the text and a title that describes what it is about. The information has been organized in a logical way that makes sense to readers. Finally, the source of the information contained in the table has been listed. This last item is *very* important; submitting charts or graphs in an economics report without citing sources is likely to net a significant loss of points on the assignment.

A second example of a type of chart is shown in Figure 2.2. This chart presents the average earnings of women in the United States by occupational category and states how earnings compare with men in the same occupational group. The chart illustrates that women don't fare particularly well in our economy. Chapter 9 will examine this phenomenon and explore why this might be the case. For now, the chart that presents the information shows how to compare data with information that does not appear in the chart itself.

FIGURE 2.1
Source: Department of Commerce, Bureau of the Census.

Population of the Largest States—1990	
State	Population
California	29,760,021
New York	17,990,455
Texas	16,986,510
Florida	12,937,926
Pennsylvania	11,881,643

FIGURE 2.2
Source: U.S. Department of Labor, Bureau of Labor Statistics.

Weekly Earnings of Full-time Women Workers—1991		
Occupational Group	Median Weekly Earnings (1)	Percent of Men's Weekly Earnings
Managerial and professional	$527	70.0
Technical, sales, and administrative support	$350	68.8
Service occupations	$244	73.9
Skilled workers	$341	69.0
Unskilled workers	$271	70.5
Framing, forestry, and fishing	$224	83.3
ALL OCCUPATIONS	$368	74.0

(1) Median means that half of the people in this group earn more than the number shown, and half earn less.

Finally, take a look at Figure 2.3. If you can make sense of *this* chart, you can understand *any* chart you will ever see.

This chart contains whole numbers, decimals, fractions, some kind of code with letters and numbers together, and dashed numbers. There is a footnote to the graph. The decimals aren't even expressed correctly! And yet, most economics students can quickly read this chart and either understand it or figure it out very quickly. It is a highly complex table that requires a fairly sophisticated level of analysis, but you can understand it. Take a minute to look at the chart. If you haven't paid much attention to a chart like this before, get together with a fellow student and talk about it. Once you master it, you should feel justifiably proud of yourself and confident of handling *any* chart you will see in this course or in any document you will ever read.

How do you read a complex chart like the baseball standings in Figure 2.3? Start by making sure you know precisely what the chart is about. This chart provides the records of the American League teams. (While it doesn't say it in the chart, *this* American League is in baseball: readers must bring that piece of knowledge with them when they read this chart.) Look first at the chart headings and footnotes, if there are any, to help decipher the data. In this case, there are two divisions in the American League, the data are as of a given date, and there was one night game from the previous day (Detroit *vs.* Texas, designated by the letter "x" before the names of both teams) that hasn't been reported in the table.

Once you understand which subject the chart addresses, you can move on to the information contained in it. Charts are read in two directions, horizontally and vertically. Reading horizontally, across the rows, you can learn a number of details about a single team. Detroit, for instance, has won 48 games and lost 41 for a winning percentage of 53.9 percent. Standard baseball usage, you will notice, incorrectly reports this percentage as .539, just over one half of one percent, but people reading the graph know what .539 means, so the number continues to be reported this way. By reading further across the row, you can learn how many games behind the division leader Detroit is, what its record in the last ten games is, and so forth. You can repeat the process for other teams and evaluate how they are doing.

FIGURE 2.3

American League Standings								
EAST	W	L	Pct	GB	L10	Strk	Home	Away
Toronto	50	41	.549	—	2-8	L1	29-20	21-21
Baltimore	49	41	.544	½	6-4	W2	26-17	23-24
xDetroit	48	41	.539	1	4-6	L2	27-17	21-24
New York	49	42	.538	1	2-8	W1	26-15	23-27
Boston	46	43	.517	3	6-4	W1	26-15	20-28
Cleveland	41	49	.456	8½	4-6	L1	27-16	14-33
Milwaukee	37	51	.420	11½	5-5	L2	21-24	16-27
WEST	W	L	Pct	GB	L10	Strk	Home	Away
Chicago	47	41	.534	—	6-4	W3	23-17	24-24
xTexas	45	42	.517	1½	9-1	W5	23-16	22-26
Kansas City	45	43	.511	2	5-5	W1	25-21	20-22
Seattle	45	45	.500	3	6-4	L1	28-20	17-25
California	44	44	.500	3	6-4	W1	28-20	16-24
Oakland	39	47	.453	7	5-5	L1	26-23	13-24
Minnesota	36	51	.414	10½	3-7	L4	22-23	14-28

x-Late game.

The other direction to read a chart is vertically, up and down the columns. By reading this chart vertically, you can learn how all teams have done on a single statistic and can therefore compare one team to another. Reading the "Home" column for the American League West, for instance, you can see that with the exception of Minnesota, which has won 22 games and lost 23, all teams have won more games than they have lost when playing on their home fields. You can then select another statistic of interest and look at that column.

If you use the pattern established in the preceding two paragraphs, you can interpret any chart. First, decide what you want to learn. Next, find that item in either the top row or the first column. Finally, run your finger across the row or down the column until you learn what you want to know.

Core-Info

Charts and data tables are organized displays of numerical information.

READING PICTORIAL GRAPHS

Fortunately, graphs are about as easy to understand as charts are. Graphs are data put into picture form. Why use pictures to display numerical information? The advantage is the ability to *see* the data or view the relationships or comparisons between different statistics. These graphs can be of two basic types: pictorial and relational. Pictorial graphs use pictures or visual aids of some sort to show comparative information. Relational graphs use lines to show changes.

When reading a graph of any kind, it is important to begin by looking at the title, the source, any footnotes, and the axes before considering the graph itself. Reading the title should elicit what is being presented in the graph. Knowing the source of the information in the graph may indicate a potential for bias in the data. For instance, graphs drawn by the United Auto Workers labor union are likely to look very different from those drawn by General Motors Corporation during contract negotiations. The footnotes should provide any explanations needed for interpreting the information contained in the graph. Finally, the axes lay out how the data are being presented and whether readers need to be extra careful when interpreting the graph (more about this in the upcoming discussion on lying with graphs).

Bar Charts

The most common types of pictorial graphs are bar graphs and circle or pie graphs. Bar graphs are used to show comparative data and use bars of different lengths to show the amount of each item presented. Figure 2.4 is a good example of a bar graph. This graph compares the unemployment rates in several countries in 1990. The vertical axis shows the possible unemployment rates, increasing from zero at the origin (where the two axes intersect) to 12 percent or more. Along the horizontal axis are displayed the countries in question in order of increasing unemployment rate. An analysis of the graph indicates that in 1990 the United States had a better unemployment rate than any other country in the survey.

Circle or Pie Charts

Circle graphs are the other major type of pictorial graph. Circle graphs are shaped like a pie (hence their alternate name) cut into pieces representing how the whole is divided into its various parts. A circle graph could be used to show the sources of revenues that the United States government collects. Figure 2.5 presents these data for 1993. Because the federal government won't know exactly how much it collected in the 1994 **fiscal year** until some years later, an estimate is reported in the graph. As you can see from the graph, 43 percent of the federal government's revenue comes from individual income taxes and an additional 37 percent comes

Fiscal Year
The twelve-month accounting period over which data are collected.

FIGURE 2.4
Source: United Nations, Monthly Bulletin of Statistics

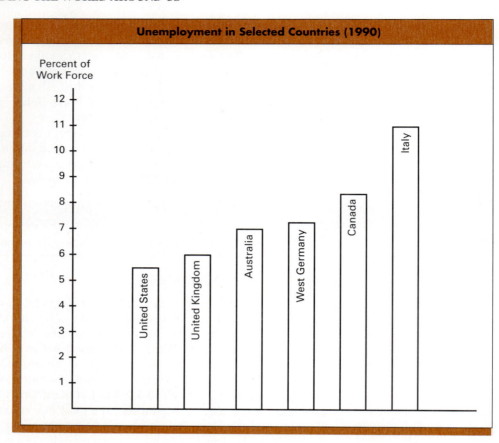

from social insurance taxes (the Social Security and Medicare taxes that you pay either directly or indirectly). About 9 percent of the federal revenue comes from corporate income taxes which, in turn, come from higher prices on the products that firms sell (as we shall see in Chapter 15, only people actually pay taxes); 4 percent comes from excise taxes; and 5 percent comes from all other sources. Do you like the way the federal government collects revenue? Whether you answer yes or no, you now have literally *seen* the data and can make an informed decision.

READING RELATIONAL GRAPHS

Relational graphs show the relationship between two **variables.** Variables are figures that change, such as the birth rate in a given year. **Independent variables** cause change to occur (in this example, year) whereas **dependent variables** are the resulting changes (the birth rate). Figure 2.6 presents these data for the past 80 years in the United States. As you can see, the independent variable (year) is along the **x-axis** (the horizontal axis) and the dependent variable (the birth rate) is on the **y-axis** (the vertical axis). Tracing your finger along the vertical axis will show a break or change in the scale. The scale begins at zero and proceeds 1, 2, 3, 4, and 5 before skipping to 15. The "lightning bolt" on the axis is the warning that the scale has changed at that point. Entering the statistical data yields the graph as shown. Standing back and looking at the graph provides the general and correct impression that the birth rate has been declining this century. A closer look indicates that, while there has been a general decline, the birth rate rose following World War II and again in 1990. Both the general view and the detailed view of data are important to gain an understanding of what is really happening. Figure 2.6 and the other graphs used in this book will allow you to develop both understandings of economic data.

Variable
Something that changes or is changed.

Independent Variable
A variable that is believed to influence the value of a second variable; a causal variable.

Dependent Variable
A variable that is affected by another variable.

X-Axis
The horizontal axis of a graph.

Y-Axis
The vertical axis of a graph.

CHAPTER 2 • UNDERSTANDING—AND LYING WITH—GRAPHS   23

FIGURE 2.5
Source: Executive Office of the President, Office of Management and Budget.

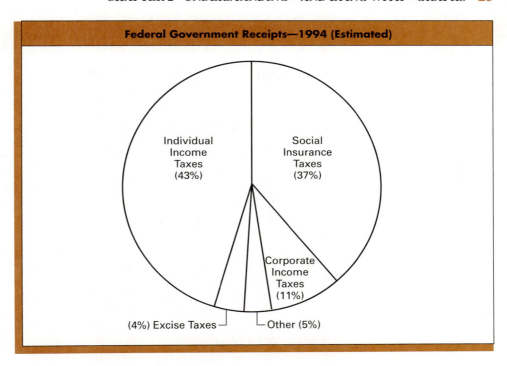

FIGURE 2.6
Source: Department of Health and Human Services, National Committee for Health Statistics.

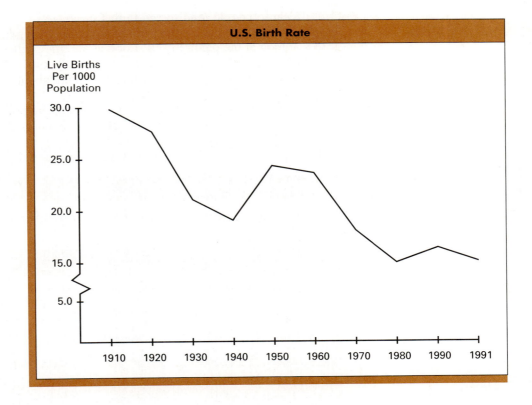

Core-Info

Relational graphs show how two variables are related to each other and in particular how one variable affects the other.

LYING WITH CHARTS AND GRAPHS

This section was not written as a guide to learning to lie with data. Anybody can lie. Lying is easy to do, and you don't need any help. However, it is morally wrong. Thus the focus here is how people can be misled by charts and graphs. Remember, charts and graphs are ways in which information is organized and presented so people can learn what is going on and make effective decisions.

The ways in which people can be misled with charts has to do with what information is included and what is left out. By carefully selecting what information is included, the chart maker can get the reader to see what he or she wants the reader to see. One example is a chart conveying information about the economies of three countries around the world. The information could be presented either as Figure 2.7 or Figure 2.8. The charts are quite different, aren't they? Based on the two tables, which country would you say had the biggest or best economy? A trade specialist concerned with potential world markets might choose Figure 2.7 to show that China's economy is more than 60 percent greater than that of Australia. A rabid anticommunist might select Figure 2.8 to show how little the socialist economy of China provides to its citizens. The selection of which table to present combined with the words used to describe the data have a major impact on what readers believe after they read the charts.

Lying—or misleading—with graphs is just as subtle and just as effective. What people try to do when they set out to mislead others with graphs is to take advantage of the expectations or preconceptions that people have. People typically think in standard ways. If the graph drawer is aware of these standards, he or she can take advantage of them.

Because people tend to see things in set ways, you must start to look at a graph, which is just data in the form of a picture, by reading around the picture before you look at the picture itself. Look at the title of the graph. What is the graph supposed to be describing? What do you already know about that subject that you can use to compare with the information you are about to see? What is the source of the data contained in the graph?

Are you aware of any inherent biases that the author might have that could affect what he or she *wants* you to see? If the graph has axes, what units of measure are used on them and do they make sense? The chief requirement to correctly read and interpret a graph is that you *think* and think carefully.

Core-Info: Pictorial graphs present information through the use of graphics and visual displays.

FIGURE 2.7
Source: Information Please Almanac.

National Gross Domestic Product (1992)

Country	Gross Domestic Product (in billions)
China	$413.0
Brazil	$297.0
Australia	$254.4

FIGURE 2.8
Source: Information Please Almanac.

National Gross Domestic Product per Person (1992)

Country	Gross Domestic Product Per Capita
Australia	$14,980
Brazil	$ 2,020
China	$ 370

The ways in which graphs are drawn can mislead. Take the standard circle graph as an example. Let's say that you are reporting the labor costs for a manufacturing firm and that these costs are one fifth of the company's total expenditures. The standard way to report this on a circle graph can be seen in Figure 2.9. In this graph, a standard coin is divided so that one fifth goes for labor costs and four fifths goes for everything else. That is pretty easy to see from the graph. This graph is unambiguous. What if you want to overemphasize or underemphasize labor costs? If this report is going to the labor union, the company might want to show that it really spent a lot on its valued workers. In that case, it could use the approach shown in Figure 2.10A. If, on the other hand, the company is reporting to its stockholders and wants to show them how well it is controlling labor costs, it could use the format shown in Figure 2.10B. The graphs certainly look different, don't they? Placing labor costs in the front of the now-leaning coin overemphasizes them. With these costs on the back side of the coin, they are downplayed. Be certain to check any circle graph that you read for tilting or false perspective as it will affect what you see.

Perspective is one way to control what people see. Adjusting the axes is another. Figures 2.11A and 2.11B provide another example of how what people see can be easily influenced by the way in which a graph is drawn. These two graphs allegedly say the same thing. They are adapted from graphs, which appeared on the same day in two different newspapers. Do they *look* the same? Figure 2.11A portrays a postal service that has gotten out of control in the last 30 years. Figure 2.11B appears to show a post office that has had slowly and steadily rising prices over the past century. Study the two graphs carefully to see why they look so different. (Hint: look at the axes.) As you can see, the vertical axes are different. The graph in Figure 2.11A has a vertical axis that is stretched out in comparison with the axis in Figure 2.11B. This stretching will exaggerate any increase or decrease that takes place in a vertical direction. By way of contrast, Figure 2.11B under-

FIGURE 2.9

FIGURE 2.10A & B

FIGURE 2.11A

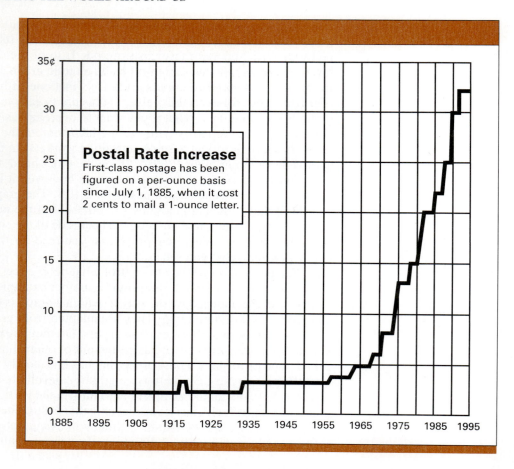

Postal Rate Increase
First-class postage has been figured on a per-ounce basis since July 1, 1885, when it cost 2 cents to mail a 1-ounce letter.

FIGURE 2.11B

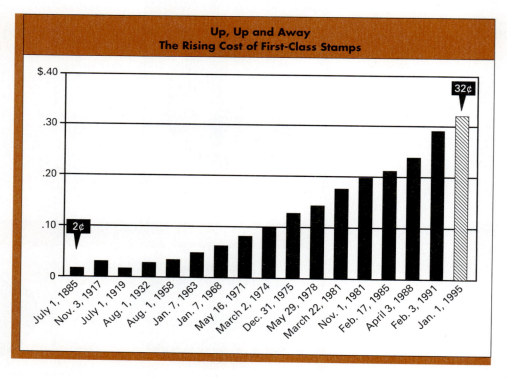

Up, Up and Away
The Rising Cost of First-Class Stamps

emphasizes the changes that have taken place. The horizontal axes are different as well. The horizontal axis in Figure 2.11A is evenly divided into decades. The period from 1885 to 1895 covers precisely the same distance as the decade from 1975 to 1985. This certainly is not the case in Figure 2.11B. This graph has a varying scale along the horizontal axis and shows the dates on which the new postal rates went into effect. Thus, the distances between the first two bars designates 32 years. The distance between the last two bars, by way of contrast, covers just three years. Varying the scale along the horizontal axis as has been done in Figure 2.11B will smooth out the variations and make them appear much more regular. If you read the axes carefully before you look at the graph itself, you will have a better chance of understanding how the author may be trying to influence what you think.

A third way in which graphs can be presented to create an impression in people's minds is to change the way in which years are presented. The previous example is typical in that data are presented with lower years on the left and higher years on the right. This is rather standard practice, and people are used to reading graphs from left to right. There is nothing sacred about this, however, and the years *can* be reversed. The effect of this can be seen in Figures 2.12A and 2.12B. These figures show the total exports of automobiles that were made in factories in the United States. In Figure 2.12A, the data have been presented in the standard way, and they show that exports have been decreasing over the four-year period of the report. To create a different impression, the chart maker could reverse the years as shown in Figure 2.12B. Now, instead of illustrating the decrease in automobile exports, the graph depicts how auto exports are developing (note that the "development" is negative!). If you read around the graph before you look at the graph itself, you would notice the title and the fact that the years were backwards compared to what is typical. Knowing that, you can correctly read and interpret the graph and not be misled by its author.

The final example of how people can be misled by graphs—and why it is critical to read graphs *very* carefully—can be seen in Figure 2.13A and Figure 2.13B.

FIGURE 2.12A
Source: Motor Vehicles Manufacturers Association of the U.S.

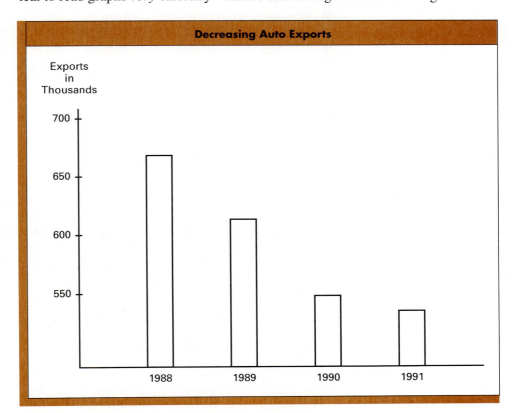

FIGURE 2.12B
Source: Motor Vehicle Manufacturers Association of the U.S.

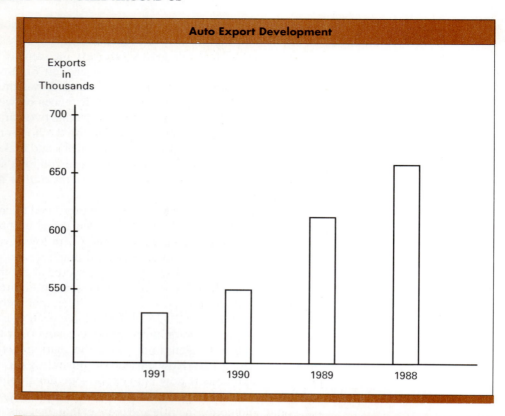

FIGURE 2.13A
Source: Food and Agriculture Organization of the United Nations.

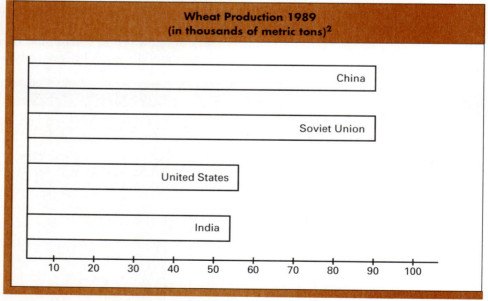

This example compares the output of wheat by the top four producers in the world in 1989. As you can easily see in the correctly drawn bar graph in Figure 2.13A, the United States ranks a distant third in production after China and the former Soviet Union. During the Cold War, this would have been an embarrass-

---

[2.] As you are reading this graph, think for a moment about the numbers that are contained in it. China produced more than 91 million metric *tons* of wheat in 1989. That is more than 200 *billion* pounds of wheat. In total, the world produced over one trillion pounds of wheat that year and almost as much rice and corn. With 5 billion people in the world, that means that every man, woman, and child alive could have had more than 1.5 pounds of those three products every day all year long. It makes you wonder, doesn't it?

FIGURE 2.13B
Source: Food and Agriculture Organization of the United Nations.

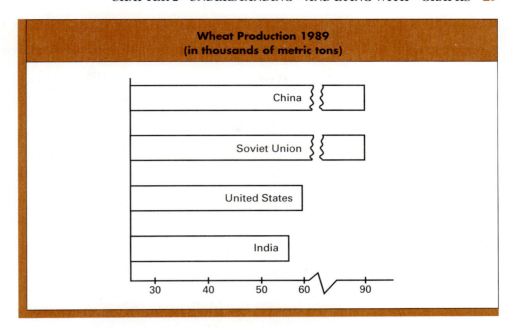

ment to the United States. To save face, a graph could be produced like that shown in Figure 2.13B which literally cuts China and the Soviet Union down to size. Looking at the axes first provides the clue as to what is going on. This is confirmed by looking at the graph itself. On the horizontal axis, the scale is not consistent. The scale reads 30, 40, 50, 60, 90. Most numbering systems include 70, and 80, but not this one. A segment of the bars for China and the Soviet Union has been cut out. This is shown by the jagged-edged parts that are missing. It is also shown in that little lightning bolt that appears on the horizontal axis. This indicates that something has been cut out and serves as a warning to read the graph carefully.

Graphs can mislead just as easily as they can present factual information. Great care must be taken when reading graphs.

BACK ON TRACK WITH CHARTS AND GRAPHS

As you have learned from the past few pages, the data in charts and graphs can be manipulated. They can be used to provide clear, concise information so everybody can understand what is going on or they can be used to mislead and manipulate people into seeing what the author wants.

When you read charts and graphs, be careful. Think *before* you begin. Why are you reading the item? What are you trying to learn? What do you expect to find? Think *when* you are looking at the chart or graph. Start by looking around the figure at the title, axes, source, and so forth. Only then look at the graph or chart itself. Read the figure carefully, comparing the numbers or drawings with what you already know about the subject and then decide what you have learned.

When you draw a graph or make a chart, be careful. Think about what you are trying to say and what your readers' expectations are likely to be. Then design your chart or graph carefully. It is unethical to mislead your readers, but you can help guide them to a "correct" understanding if you do your work right. Good luck!

SUMMARY

- Graphs and charts are used in economics to present information in ways that are easy to see.
- Pictorial graphs are frequently used to display data through the use of pictures, bar graphs, or other simple visual techniques.
- Relational or functional graphs present a visual picture of how one variable directly affects another variable.
- Graphs can mislead as well as present accurate information. Great care must be exercised when reading graphs to be certain that the data are accurately displayed.

KEY TERMS

Dependent variables Independent variables X-axis
Fiscal year Variables Y-axis

REVIEW QUESTIONS

1. Why are charts and graphs used in economics?
2. What is a "fiscal year" and why might it be different from a calendar year?
3. What is a bar graph and what type of information does it display?
4. What is a pie graph and what type of information does it display?
5. What is the difference between a dependent variable and an independent variable?
6. When would it be appropriate to use relational graphs in economics?
7. Identify three ways in which graphs may present information that is likely to be misinterpreted by the reader.

PROBLEM-SOLVING PRACTICE

1. The following figures represent the U.S. federal budget expenditures for 1995.
   (a) Construct a bar graph with this.
   (b) Construct a pie chart.

   Where the federal budget goes

Individual benefit	48%
Defense	16%
Interest on debt	16%
State/local grants	15%
Federal programs	5%

   Source: Office of Management and Budget

2. A survey in an economics class indicated these hourly pay rates for students in the class working at part-time jobs.

$4.00–4.99	3
$5.00–5.99	6
$6.00–6.99	12
$7.00–7.99	10
$8.00–8.99	7
$9.00–9.99	2

   Construct a bar graph with the data.
   Construct a pie chart with this data by converting the table into percentages.

3. The following represents information about the market for a new t-shirt, with estimated sales at varying prices per shirt. Plot a graph with price on the vertical axis and estimated sales on the horizontal axis and interpret its meaning.

Price per T-shirt	Estimated Sales
$2.99	1,500
3.99	1,000
4.99	800
5.99	500
6.99	400
7.99	200

CHAPTER 3

Trends in the World and Our Economy

CHAPTER OUTLINE

A. The Importance of Trends
   1. We Learn about Our Society Today
   2. We Gain an Understanding of Our Past
   3. We Can Anticipate the Future
B. Overall Social Trends
C. Economic Trends in the United States
   1. Employment: Who's Working?
   2. Unemployment: Who's Not Working?
   3. Income: How Much Do We Earn?
   4. The Government: What Do We Get and How Much Do We Pay?
   5. International Issues: How Do We Relate?
D. Identifying Tomorrow's Trends: Anticipating the Future
E. So What?

The purpose of this chapter is to introduce the concept of trends in society with a goal of learning to take advantage of existing trends.

AFTER COMPLETING THIS CHAPTER, YOU WILL BE ABLE TO:

1. Explain the advantages of having an awareness of trends in society.
2. Identify the Megatrends that shape the world in which you live.
3. Analyze the impact of general trends in society, the business world, and government on your personal career goals.
4. Utilize a methodology to predict the future trends that will affect your career.

The Importance of Trends

To make much sense out of this economic muddle we've gotten ourselves into requires an understanding of the world around us. Just knowing a lot of great economic theory from a textbook, even this one, is not enough. We have to know what the economic world really looks like before we can decide what to do about it.

Remember from earlier chapters how easy it is to be sidetracked by biases and prejudices. One problem in economics is differentiating between positive statements and normative statements. Wise choices require decision makers to know the facts, to think positively, before allowing preferences and values to enter—thinking normatively. Considering factual data will go a long way toward accomplishing these tasks.

In order to make sense of our world we need to gather three types of information: information about today, information about yesterday, and information about tomorrow. Once this information has been collected, the next step is to see how it has changed—and is expected to change—over time. In short, we must understand not only today but the trends that are taking place in the world around us. These data provide the foundations for making good decisions.

The analysis of trends helps in three ways:

1. We learn about our society today.
2. We gain an understanding of our past.
3. We can anticipate the future.

We Learn about Our Society Today

To begin to understand how the economic system functions and how to use it to accomplish objectives, you must first know what society is today. Only by knowing the world *as it is* can you begin to put anything into context. To understand economic reality, we must gather data or information about the people of our country and the world. This data must be gathered dispassionately. The key is to approach the task positively (as opposed to normatively) and learn as much as possible. The information gathered must describe the good and the bad to avoid screening out a crucial item of importance. For instance, it is important to know that women tend to be paid significantly less than men who do the same work. Learning and reporting this does not signify an endorsement of the differential, but unless we understand just how different wages are today we cannot be in a position to discuss today or predict tomorrow.

We Gain an Understanding of Our Past

Looking at trends can provide more than just an understanding of the world today. By looking backward, we can begin to understand where society has come from and, occasionally, why it is where it is today. This backward look is critical to offer clues about what to do if today is not what people want it to be. In the case of women's wages, knowing that they are below men's wages is a start, but looking back provides a wider perspective. Were women's wages always below men's? By the same amount as today? More? Less? Knowing what the differential was and how this has changed over time certainly could go a long way toward helping to prescribe a solution for the economy. For instance, if the gap between men's and women's wages was much greater in the past than it is today—if the gap is closing—the right action may be to get out of the way and let the economy continue to do its job. On the other hand, if the wage differential was the same as or less than it is today, direct action may be needed to accomplish the goal of equal pay for equal work. Looking at the past and comparing it with today uncovers the information needed to make this decision.

Extrapolation
To project or make guesses about the future based on what is known or has already happened.

We Can Anticipate the Future

Once we understand where society is today and where it has come from, we can look forward to the future. This looking forward is known as **extrapolation.** Extrapolation means to project based on what is known. If you like what you see, great! You can relax and look forward to a bright future. If you don't like what you see, you take this projection or extrapolation as a challenge and try to do something to change the future.

Two examples of extrapolation offer an understanding of what is meant by accepting or working to change the future. A review of the incomes earned by different groups of individuals in the United States demonstrates that the gap between men's and women's incomes is closing while the income gap between blacks and whites has remained about the same for the past 40 years. The first case produces some measure of happiness. Without accepting the existing difference between men's and women's incomes as justified, people can be pleased that the gap is closing and continue to work for its disappearance. In the second case, the continuing gap between blacks and whites should sound alarms. Much effort has allegedly been put forward in both the personal and political arenas to close the gap. That it has remained constant throughout this period should both inspire us to action and encourage the search for new approaches to the problem. The old ones are *not* working. Perhaps the differential would have widened in the absence of efforts to date. Perhaps it would have closed *without* interference with the market. Whatever we might think normatively, the positive data offers something to really think about. Applying this kind of thinking to all trends creates the opportunity to help create a better future.

OVERALL SOCIAL TRENDS

The first pieces of information to consider are the overall trends taking place in society. Society tends to go through stages or phases during which some issues are hot and some are not. Looking at the last four decades, for instance, economists might categorize them by focus:

1950s—Homogeneity; the corporation man

1960s—Group rights (for women and minorities); pacifism

1970s—Individual rights at the expense of group rights

1980s—Acquisitiveness and material gain

The complete accuracy of these examples might be open to argument, but they should have a ring of truth to them and portray the tenor of the times to further understanding why people and economic systems may have acted the ways they did during those periods.

Core-Info

Understanding trends is important because they:
1. Help people to learn about today.
2. Provide an understanding of the past.
3. Form the foundations to predict the future.

Major, underlying trends in the world today affect everything. An awareness of these trends allows people to take advantage of them.

Another way to look at general trends is to examine the "Megatrends" that are occurring. John Naisbitt developed the technique and popularized this approach with his 1982 book of the same title. Through his research, Naisbitt attempts to identify the key trends that are taking place in the world today. He has identified ten key trends for U.S. society and the world at large, as shown in Figure 3.1.

FIGURE 3.1

Megatrends[1]

1. From an industrial society to an information society
2. From forced technology to high tech/high touch
3. From national economies to a world economy
4. From short term to long term
5. From centralization to decentralization
6. From institutional help to self-help
7. From representative democracy to participatory democracy
8. From hierarchies to networking
9. From north to south
10. From either/or to multiple options

FIGURE 3.2

Megatrends 2000[2]

1. A global economy
2. A renaissance in the arts
3. The emergence of free market socialism
4. Global lifestyles and cultural nationalism
5. Privatization of the welfare state
6. The rise of the Pacific rim
7. Women in leadership
8. The age of biology
9. Religious revival of the new millennium
10. The triumph of the individual

If you consider each of these trends for a few minutes, you can begin to see why they are so important and how they affect all aspects of life today. For instance, the trend about the world's movement from a series of national economies to an integrated world economy has major ramifications for all businesses and individuals, even those who do not think that they are involved in some form of international trade. Look at the other trends and think about how they affect you personally as well as the overall economy.

In more recent years, Naisbitt, along with Patricia Aburdene, has published a new list of Megatrends, this time titled *Megatrends 2000*. This later list of what Naisbitt and Aburdene believe to be the ten overall trends is shown in Figure 3.2. These trends may well supplant Naisbitt's original list; only time will tell. Until then, the first list of Megatrends is most useful for understanding how our world is changing.

ECONOMIC TRENDS IN THE UNITED STATES

The next step is to focus on the trends that are more specific and localized to the United States. Remember that the goals are to gain an understanding about where society was, where it is now, and where it is headed to support decisions about what to do in the future.

Employment: Who's Working?

The first area to examine is employment. Knowing who is working and what types of jobs are held contributes a great deal to an understanding of the economy.

---

[1] Naisbitt, John. *Megatrends.* New York: Warner Books, Inc., 1982.
[2] Naisbitt, John, and Aburdene, Patricia. *Megatrends 2000: Ten New Directions for the 1990s.* New York: William Morrow and Co., Inc., 1990.

FIGURE 3.3
Source: U.S. Department of Labor, Bureau of Labor Statistics

Composition of U.S. Labor Force (in thousands of workers and percent)					
Year	Women		Men		Total
	Number	Percent	Number	Percent	
1950	18,408	29.0	41,646	71.0	60,054
1960	23,268	32.5	46,609	67.5	69,877
1970	31,580	37.2	50,469	62.8	82,049
1980	45,611	42.0	60,474	58.0	106,085
1990	56,719	44.9	68,463	55.1	125,182

FIGURE 3.4
Source: U.S. Department of Labor, Bureau of Labor Statistics

Industrial Composition of U.S. Employment				
Sector	1950	1970	1980	1990
Agricultural	13.7%	4.7%	3.6%	2.8%
Manufacturing	35.3%	31.7%	27.4%	22.1%
Service	51.0%	63.6%	69.0%	75.0%

Figure 3.3 provides a wealth of information—and much grist for our thinking mills. On the surface, all the data show is the total U.S. employment over the past 40 years and the portion of the total composed of females and males. So far, so good. But look at the data more closely. The number of males has increased, though not dramatically, while the number of females has skyrocketed. Whereas women made up 29 percent of the 60-million person labor force in 1950, by 1990 they composed 45 percent of this group of now more than 125 million people. The major portion of growth has been the result of the increase in women's participation.

Two questions result: why and what does it mean?

Why? A new set of choices and options for women. Changing societal expectations for women. An increase in the divorce rate, forcing women to work outside the home. A shift in the occupational composition from manufacturing to jobs relying more on brains than on brawn.

What does it mean? Two-income families. The need for day care for children. No one home all day to manage the cooking and cleaning (thus, more demand for cleaning services, dining out, fast foods, frozen gourmet foods, microwaves). As you can see, this one trend has many implications.

The Megatrends indicate that the United States is rapidly moving away from being a manufacturing nation to one that has services as its major occupational focus. Figure 3.4 brings that idea home graphically. Both agricultural employment and manufacturing employment have been declining as a percentage of the labor force throughout the past 40 years. Even in individual terms, the number of farm workers has decreased continuously, and the number of manufacturing workers has also declined in the past decade.

While the farm population has been declining, farm production has been increasing. How has this been accomplished? The trick has been to use much more expensive capital equipment on farms (the average farm worker has more equipment at his or her disposal than the average factory worker) and to use much greater amounts of petrochemicals. In fact, the current use of chemicals is more than six times that of 40 years ago. That trend leads to speculation about the long-range implications of the continued use of great quantities of chemical pesticides and fertilizers.

As manufacturing employment has fallen, so, too, has labor union membership. In general, how people feel about unions is largely determined by whether or

FIGURE 3.5
Source: U.S. Department of Labor, Bureau of Labor Statistics

Union Membership as a Percent of the Labor Force	
Year	Percent
1950	31.5%
1955	33.2%
1960	31.4%
1965	28.4%
1970	27.3%
1975	25.3%
1980	21.9%
1985	18.0%
1990	16.1%
1994	15.5%

not their parents or grandparents were union members. To some, unions are the only thing between the struggling working person and the whims of an oppressive, greedy capitalist. To others, unions are the one group that has forced wages up and made American products uncompetitive on world markets. As we shall see when we discuss unions in some depth, both of these positions are erroneous. For the present, however, it is sufficient to look at union membership as reported in Figure 3.5. As you can see, the proportion of workers who are members of labor unions has declined steadily since the mid 1950s.

There are some reasons to be concerned about this decline, but one of them is *not* that wages will now begin to slip backward. As we shall see, the key factor that determines wage rates is the supply of and demand for labor. Labor unions can take advantage of these trends (and can also work to eliminate pockets of oppressive wage practices), but they cannot set wages. The market does that. In fact, wages in nonunionized sectors are growing more rapidly than is the case for union members. Between June 1981 and December 1988, union wages increased an average of 38.6 percent. During that same period, the wages of nonunion workers rose 43.9 percent. The image of unions as the great raiser of wages is about to pass into oblivion.

Unemployment: Who's Not Working?

Equally critical is the other side of working—not working. In the United States, the line between working and not working is a fuzzy one, to say the least. It should seem clear—either you are working or you are unemployed—but it is not that simple. In the United States, people may be employed, unemployed, or not in the labor force; to qualify as "unemployed," people must have actively looked for work and been unable to find any during the past week. Those who have lost their jobs, have unsuccessfully looked for work for months, and have finally given up in desperation are no longer considered unemployed. By not looking for work, they have removed themselves from the labor force, are no longer unemployed, and have improved the nation's unemployment statistics. That may seem illogical, but how else are we to know who *really* wants to work?

The other part of the problem with the term *unemployment* has to do with full-time versus part-time workers. Workers who are working part-time but would accept a full-time job if they could find one are considered to be fully employed.

Because of these two factors, the unemployment figures for the United States always underreport the extent of unemployment in the country. This underreporting is likely to be exaggerated for some groups of workers, such as minorities, who are less likely to have had jobs that would place them in the pool of those who would be counted for unemployment purposes.

Given those cautions, let's look at unemployment in the United States for the past 45 years. Figure 3.6 presents this information. What do you see when you look at the table? An obvious observation is the wide variation in the unemployment

FIGURE 3.6
Source: U.S. Department of Labor, Bureau of Labor Statistics

Unemployment Rate in the United States	
Year	Percent
1950	5.3%
1955	4.8%
1960	5.5%
1965	4.5%
1970	4.9%
1975	8.5%
1980	7.1%
1985	7.2%
1990	5.5%
1995	5.6%

FIGURE 3.7
Source: U.S. Department of Labor, Bureau of Labor Statistics

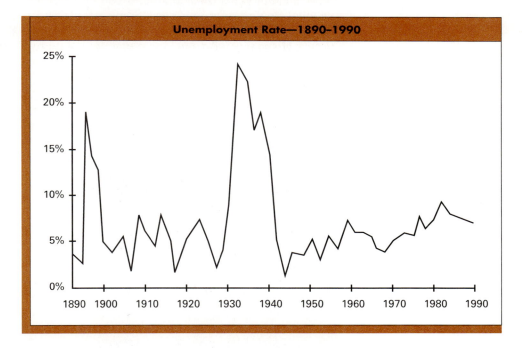

rate. If it is high this year it is likely to be lower next year and vice versa. Through the use of its macroeconomic tools, the federal government generally acts to control the amount of unemployment, keeping it from going too high or too low; the former is an obvious problem, the latter would cause inflation.

What do you see? Next, look at the section of Figure 3.7 that covers the same time period. Stand back figuratively and you can see a general upward trend in the unemployment rate. Whereas the average unemployment rate was a little less than 5 percent during the 1950s and 1960s, in the '70s and '80s the rate has risen rather steadily. Speculate for a moment on why this might be. Think about the need to make consumer goods in the 1950s after the end of World War II. Think about the Vietnam War and the War on Poverty in the 1960s. Think about the shift from manufacturing to services that escalated in the 1970s and 1980s. Any other ideas coming to mind? Give it some thought, for it is a real economic and political problem for the nation.

Finally, let's put unemployment into perspective. Look again at Figure 3.7. Examining unemployment over the past century presents a very different picture—one that gives us pause. During the Depression, the national unemployment rate hit 25 percent. In many localities such as Detroit, the rate was much higher. The economic cost to the nation and to families was incredible, even worse than it appears at first glance. Today most families have two wage earners. It is not likely that both workers are unemployed at the same time. If one person loses a job, the other person can still provide income for the family. In the 1930s, however, most families had only one wage earner. When that person lost his or her job, the family was without income. Those differences sharpen the views of not only unemployment but also the people who went through the Depression.

On the surface, the problem with unemployment is twofold: people are out of work and goods don't get made. When the production of goods falls, fewer things are available for people's daily lives. While some goods may be considered frivolous, many others, such as food, shelter, and medical care, are considered to be essential. In periods of unemployment, these essentials don't get produced. Because unemployed people don't have the money to buy goods anyway, joblessness can begin to have a cumulative effect.

As with most other issues, unemployment requires an examination beyond the surface. If everyone had an equal chance of being unemployed at any point in time, unemployment would at least be fair. But unemployment is not fair: it is an unequal opportunity oppressor. Some people and some groups are much more likely to become unemployed than others. Figure 3.8 shows this quite clearly. Black, Hispanic, and young people are much more likely to be unemployed than white or older people. *Why* unemployment rates vary is the key question, and one with which we must all concern ourselves.

Unemployment rates between races and age groups may be different, but at least there are programs to help end this inequity, right? After all, the Equal Employment Opportunity Commission has been in place since 1965 to implement and monitor programs for just this purpose. However, Figure 3.9 indicates that the gap is far from closed.

FIGURE 3.8
Source: U.S. Bureau of Labor Statistics

Unemployment Rates by Race and Age			
Age	Rate	Race	Rate
16–19	18.3%	Black	14.5%
20–24	10.7%	Hispanic	10.6%
25–54	5.7%	White	6.0%
55+	3.9%		

FIGURE 3.9
Source: U.S. Bureau of Labor Statistics

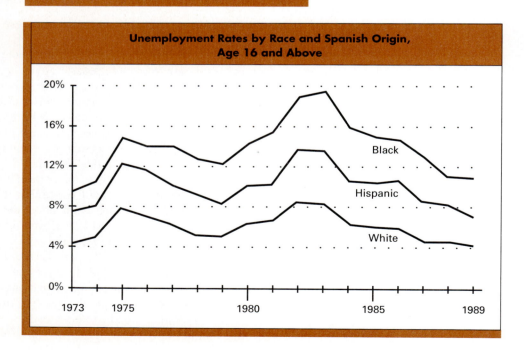

Unemployment Rates by Race and Spanish Origin, Age 16 and Above

Income: How Much Do We Earn?

People work so they can contribute to society and to help fellow human beings, but the bottom line is that they work so they can earn money. Having a job is nice, but if people don't earn enough to pay the bills, they are likely to be unhappy no matter how much they are contributing to others. The distribution of income is critical to people individually and to society as a whole.

Figure 3.10 offers a first look at the income distribution in the United States. This graph presents the median weekly earnings (half of the population earns more, half earns less) of full-time workers by race and sex. The data are displayed in what is known as constant dollars, from which the effect of inflation has been removed (if salaries increase 5 percent this year but there has been a 5 percent inflation rate, people stand still in terms of buying power). This graph indicates that white male earnings have consistently been above those of other groups. Women and males of color earn significantly less, and as with unemployment, the gap has been a steady one for the past 20 years.

Figure 3.11 confirms these findings. Family incomes have been significantly different over the same time period. While these data look serious on the surface, reality is even bleaker. Average family sizes differ by race—white families average four, blacks six, and Hispanics eight—so that the amount of income per capita is even lower and the differential is even wider.

As you have seen, the income of women is significantly less than that of men. In the United States, women earn approximately 70 percent of what men earn. Figure 3.12 shows this information. While the gap remains, the decade of the 1980s seems to have worked toward greater equity in wages. The gap is slowly closing.

One reason for this declining differential is the fact that the occupational distinctions that once existed seem to be breaking down, and women are entering jobs that were once considered to be "man's work." So-called "men's jobs" typically paid a higher wage than "women's jobs," so as women enter these fields in greater numbers, a higher degree of equality should result. Figure 3.13 presents this information for the past 30 years.

FIGURE 3.10
Source: U.S. Bureau of Labor Statistics

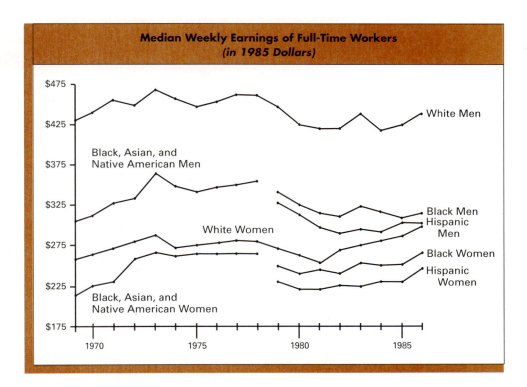

FIGURE 3.11
Source: U.S. Bureau of Labor Statistics

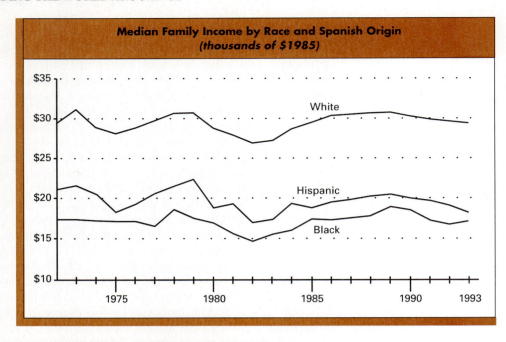

Median Family Income by Race and Spanish Origin
(thousands of $1985)

FIGURE 3.12
Source: U.S. Bureau of Labor Statistics

Women's Earnings as a Percent of Men's	
Year	Percent
1960	60.7
1970	59.4
1980	60.2
1982	61.7
1984	63.7
1986	64.3
1988	66.0
1990	71.6

FIGURE 3.13
Source: U.S. Bureau of Labor Statistics

Percent of Positions in Fields Held by Women				
Occupation	1960	1970	1980	1986
Engineers	1%	2%	5%	7%
Lawyers and Judges	3%	5%	14%	17%
Doctors	6%	8%	12%	16%
Managers	15%	18%	30%	38%

The Government: What Do We Get and How Much Do We Pay?

Consider this fact: the U. S. federal government's budget is about $1.6 trillion. That means the government spends $48,000 every second of every minute of every day all year long.

The federal government takes in money (revenues) each year from a variety of sources and spends it (expenditures) on many programs and services. Figure 3.14 presents an overview of the sources of federal revenues in 1960 and 1993. Figure 3.15 shows amounts of taxes collected between 1936 and 1994. It appears as though there has been a major shift in the way taxes are collected, doesn't it? Maybe the critics are right: business is getting a free ride while the average citizen is paying more and more taxes. But consider for a moment who really pays taxes. Do corporations pay

FIGURE 3.14
Source: U.S. Office of Management and Budget.

Sources of Revenue for Federal Government		
Source	1960	1993
Taxes on personal income	53%	82%
Taxes on corporate income	28%	9%
Sales and other taxes	19%	9%

FIGURE 3.15
Source: U.S. Office of Management and Budget.

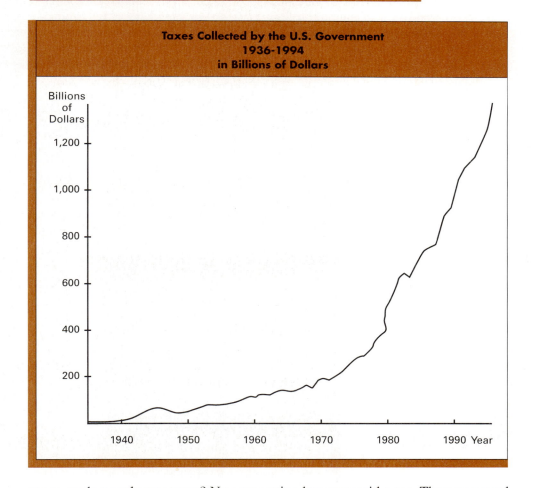

taxes, or do people pay taxes? No corporation has ever paid a tax. They may send checks to the government, but where does that money come from? Of course, it comes from the prices of the goods they sell. Any tax placed on a corporation is passed on to consumers in the form of higher prices. Thus, when the government requires corporations to pay taxes, we are only fooling ourselves if we believe that this means that our personal tax burden has been lightened.

Figure 3.16 illustrates that the federal government also has changed its spending patterns. As you will quickly note, there has been a major shift in national priorities as demonstrated by federal spending. Whereas the defense budget was the major consumer of resources in the 1960s, social programs (social security, Medicare, food and housing assistance, disability insurance, etc.) now absorb the lion's share of our funds.

Finally, to one extent, the federal budget is like a personal budget: if people spend more than they earn, they owe money at the end of the year. In other words, they run a deficit. In every year since 1969, the federal government has spent more money than it has received in taxes. Figure 3.17 presents a summary of the annual budget deficits of the federal government since 1965.

The Rapid Growth of the Federal Government

Lots of people complain about how big the federal government has become. To an extent, they are right. The federal government now spends $1,600,000,000,000 per year. Where they err is in their perception of the relative size of the government. The table below illustrates the shift toward an increasingly numerically dominant state and local influence.

This trend fits nicely with another observed by John Naisbitt. The move toward an increasing influence of state and local government employees is a part of his Megatrend shift "from centralization to decentralization." This trend is expected to continue. Both political parties have pledged themselves to a decreased federal role. People may have to find something else to complain about.

Government Employment
(in thousands and percent)

Year	Federal		State & Local	
1950	2,117	(33%)	4,285	(67%)
1960	2,421	(27%)	6,387	(73%)
1970	2,881	(22%)	10,147	(78%)
1980	2,898	(18%)	13,315	(82%)
1990	3,105	(17%)	15,263	(83%)

FIGURE 3.16
Source: U.S. Office of Management and Budget.

Federal Government Spending		
Program Area	1960	1993
Military spending	58%	19%
Social spending	34%	55%
Net interest	8%	14%
Other	8%	12%

FIGURE 3.17
Source: U.S. Office of Management and Budget.

Annual Budget Deficits	
Year	Amount in Dollars
1965	$ 1,596,000,000
1970	2,845,000,000
1975	45,108,000,000
1980	58,961,000,000
1985	202,813,000,000
1990	220,388,000,000

In all, the total federal deficit is more than $3.5 trillion. Before you pack up and move to the Antarctic, remember two things. First, those dollar figures do not take inflation into account. When the more recent deficits are adjusted to constant dollars (as in a previous graph of personal incomes), they are significantly smaller than they appear in comparison with those of decades ago. Second, throughout this period, the economy has been growing rapidly. As a result, the annual budget deficit has been shrinking as a portion of the nation's gross national product. Figure 3.18 presents a summary of this relationship for the past decade.

Thus, while federal budget deficits are high and are consuming a significant portion of revenues, they are proportionally less important in the same way that people can personally handle more debt when their income rises.

FIGURE 3.18
Source: U.S. Office of Management and Budgets.

Federal Deficits as a Portion of GNP	
Year	Portion of GNP
1983	6.26%
1985	5.37%
1987	3.38%
1989	2.90%
1991	1.10%

FIGURE 3.19
Source: U.S. Bureau of Economic Analysis

U.S. Exports and Imports (in billions)			
	1980	1985	1990
Exports—all goods and services	$343.2	$366.0	$652.9
Exports—services alone	36.5	45.0	123.3
Imports—all goods and services	333.9	461.2	722.7

International Issues: How Do We Relate?

Just as John Donne wrote that "no man is an island," no one nation's economy stands alone. We are increasingly interrelated with other nations of the world. We visit and are visited; we buy their goods and they buy ours; we invest in and are invested in. We couldn't live in anything like the manner to which we have become accustomed without an extensive network of international trade and relations. Yet many Americans worry that international trade will be their nation's downfall. Figure 3.19 provides an overview of U.S. exports and imports during the last decade. Both exports and imports doubled during the 1980s. What is more interesting, however, is what happened to the export of services. As was indicated in our earlier review of the overall trends in society, we have become a service-producing economy. As a result, the export of services has grown at a rate nearly double that of all exports combined.

If people are concerned about the level of imports into the United States from other countries, imagine how worried other nations must be given the size and strength of the U.S. economy. Figures 3.20 and 3.21 should help to provide a basis for understanding this perspective. Figure 3.20 shows total U.S. gross domestic product. Figure 3.21 contrasts the sales of three American corporations with the total gross domestic product of three nations. It's a staggering comparison. Several U.S. corporations have annual sales well in excess of major nations of the world. It is easy to understand why other countries could be concerned when, for instance, Exxon is considering building a new refinery in their nation. Even assuming the best of intent and actions, the arrival of an economic power the size of Exxon will have a major and permanent impact on the country. As Woody Allen once noted, "The lion and the calf shall lie down together, but the calf won't get much sleep."

Core-Info

The U.S. economy has been undergoing radical changes in recent years. The changes involve people who are working and those who are not, where work takes place, how much people earn, and how the government spends money.

IDENTIFYING TOMORROW'S TRENDS: ANTICIPATING THE FUTURE

Once you have a sense of a trend that is taking place today, you will probably want to look into the future to see if the trend will continue. Many books available in the library can suggest a number of great techniques to use in making these projections. Here are two easy-to-use approaches that you can put to work right away.

FIGURE 3.20
Source: U.S. Office of Management and Budget.

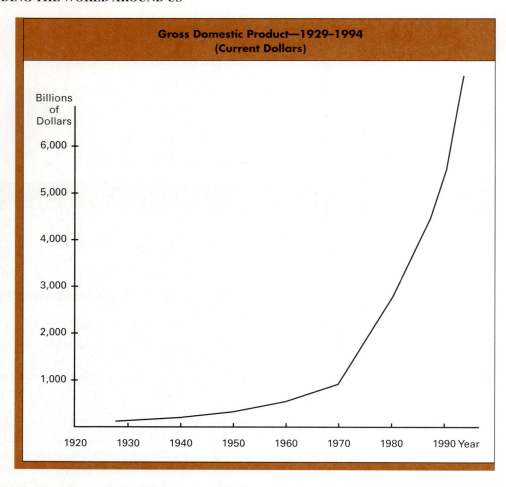

FIGURE 3.21

Sales of Three Corporations and the GDP of Three Nations			
Nation	GDP	Corporation	Sales
Singapore	$34.6 B	General Motors	$123.8 B
Kenya	$ 8.5 B	Exxon	$103.2 B
El Salvador	$ 5.1 B	Ford Motors	$ 89.0 B

The first of these approaches is that of straight-line projections. With this technique, you look at how something is changing and project that change into the future. If a person's income has been increasing at a rate of 5 percent per year, you can assume that rate will continue unless there are indications to the contrary. If the sales of wheat to foreign customers have grown by 50 million bushels per year, it is logical to assume that this rate of increase will continue. If, on the other hand, sales were 50 million bushels in 1980, 45 million bushels in 1985, and 40 million bushels in 1990, the logical projection for 1995 sales is 35 million bushels. While this technique is not very sophisticated and does not consider other factors that could influence the variable, the approach generally provides an answer that proves to be relatively close to reality.

The other approach that can be easily used is known as the Delphi technique. In this approach, you assemble a group of individuals (your classmates, for instance), provide them with some background information about the projection that you are trying to make, and ask them to individually arrive at their best guess as to what the projected figure will be. Once everybody has done this, you collect their estimates, calculate an average, and return the group's average to all members. The group members are then given the opportunity to revise and resubmit their own estimates, and a new average is calculated. Once again this average is returned to group members to think about and make another revision. Once this process is repeated three or four times, you have a group estimate that should prove very accurate for your projection. The advantage of the Delphi technique is that it draws upon the collective strengths of a number of people and thus provides a better estimate than individuals could on their own.

Core-Info

Two approaches that can be used to project the future are:
1. Straight-line projections
2. The Delphi technique

SO WHAT?

Trends may be interesting to consider and project, but of what use are they to you? The answer to that question varies from person to person. Which trends are useful and which may be beneficial will be determined by your own personal interests and professional aspirations. Those planning careers in politics will find some trends useful while those planning to enter the world of business will find others more applicable. Your job is to find trends of interest or applicability to *your* life and consider them. Prop this book open to a trend of interest and just think about it for one minute. What does it mean? Where have you seen examples of this trend? Where has the trend *not* been true? Where is it going? How will you be affected? When you begin to ask—and answer—these questions, you will have gone a long way toward bringing economic issues and concern onto the center stage of your life.

Finally, mark some of the key trends for later review. When you have finished studying this course and reading the book, go back and rethink these key trends with your newly developed knowledge. What do these trends mean to you now? You should be able to make even more insightful analysis on your second reading and appreciate what you have learned between the two readings.

SUMMARY

- We need to be aware of trends in society because they are the long-term changes in the economy that affect everything people do.
- There are ten key Megatrends as identified by John Naisbitt. Among these ten trends are the shift from national economies to a world economy, the change from institutional help to self-help, and the move from either/or to multiple options.
- Women's roles in the work force have increased in terms of both participation and relative income.
- The United States is now and always will be a service-based economy.
- Unemployment is a critical issue as its burden of lost wages and self-esteem are not equally borne by all segments of society.
- Incomes have been rising, but the racial disparity remains as large as ever.
- Federal government spending has shifted from military to social programs over the past 30 years.

KEY TERMS

Extrapolation

REVIEW QUESTIONS

1. State the three ways in which the analysis of trends helps us in our evaluation in the study of economics.
2. Define the term "extrapolation." Give at least one example of extrapolation.
3. Identify your first job after college. Select four *Megatrends* and apply them to your forthcoming occupation.
4. What are some implications of the increase of the number of women in the labor force?
5. Explain the term "unemployed."
6. Define and describe the two easy-to-use approaches used to project the future.

PROBLEM-SOLVING PRACTICE

1. According to statistics, fewer workers are employed in agriculture today than 40 years ago.
   (a) What are the primary reasons for this trend?
   (b) What are the implications for this trend for society?
2. The decline in manufacturing employment has specific implications for labor union membership.
   (a) What has been the trend in union membership since World War II?
   (b) What is the relationship between the trend in the labor market and union membership?
   (c) What underlying conditions could have led to the early rise and recent decline in labor union membership?
3. To identify and analyze employment trends in the economy, a student needs to understand the measurement of employment and unemployment. With that in mind, answer the following questions.
   (a) For people to be counted as "unemployed," what conditions must they meet?
   (b) In terms of measurement of unemployment, what happens to those people who are unemployed, but do not meet the conditions of part (a)?
   (c) Over the past 60 years, is there any reason why the number of people who were unemployed, yet not officially counted as unemployed, would have gone up or down?
   (d) Analyze the relationship between white, black, and Hispanic unemployment rates over the past two decades.

PART 2
ECONOMIC PRINCIPLES

Chapter 4: Basic Ideas and Concepts in Economics

Chapter 5: Supply and Demand

Chapter 6: Elasticity

Chapter 7: Understanding Costs

CHAPTER 4

Basic Ideas and Concepts in Economics

CHAPTER OUTLINE

A. The Idea of Value
B. The Creation of Value
C. The Production Possibilities Curve
D. Exchange and International Trade
   1. Reasons for Trade
   2. Benefits from Trade
3. Barriers to Trade
   a. Natural Trade Barriers (Costs)
   b. Diffused Benefits and Concentrated Cost
   c. Artificial Trade Barriers (Controls)
E. Producing Wealth—a Summary

The purpose of this chapter is to provide a basic understanding of concepts that are central to the science of economics.

AFTER COMPLETING THIS CHAPTER, YOU WILL BE ABLE TO:

1. Describe the two ways of creating value in an economy.
2. Relate the production possibilities curve to individual decisions and economic production.
3. Explain the two reasons why international trade occurs.
4. Analyze the impact of international trade on individuals, businesses, and the overall economy.
5. List the barriers to international trade and describe the effect of each barrier on individuals, businesses, and the overall economy.

The Idea of Value

We're ready now to move another step deeper into the basic issues of economics. Remember that the definition of economics encompasses the disparity of scarce resources and unlimited wants. The definition emphasizes the reason why we study economics. If it weren't for the fact that resources are scarce, we wouldn't have to worry about these issues. But resources are scarce: the materials needed to produce the goods that people want are limited. That means that the amount of goods that can be produced is also limited. As a human race we will never have everything we want. Needs and wants will always exist, and people will always try to do better in life. Thus economics will be with us as long as people want to add to their wealth, to increase their welfare (well-being).

As you consider the concept of unlimited wants, it is important to remember that just getting more and more goods may not be the solution. The story of King Midas is helpful in understanding this caveat. Midas *loved* gold. He wanted more and more and more gold. As a "favor," his wish was granted by Dionysus. What Dionysus gave Midas was the "Midas Touch"—*everything* he touched would turn to gold. What a perfect gift for someone who loved gold! Midas touched the table; it turned to gold. Midas touched his chair; it turned to gold. Then his daughter came into the room, and Midas was so overjoyed at his great gift that he kissed her ... and she turned to gold. Midas now had 117 pounds of extra gold, but he was crushed. He had more gold, but he lost what he valued. That is where economics reenters the picture. Getting more "stuff" is *not* what economics is about. Getting more of the things people value is the focus.

The two great underlying issues of economics are efficiency and equity. In its basic conception, efficiency is an engineering idea. It means doing things right, getting more output from your input. That is a good start, but it is not enough. The pursuit of efficiency alone may yield lots of output, but the issue of equity remains. Equity means doing the right thing. Equity means being fair, being just. Some old economics books suggest that there is a tradeoff between equity and efficiency, that society must give up some of one to get the other. That is not the case. Just getting more stuff is not the answer. What people want is to get more of the stuff they value, and that is what this chapter—and economics—is all about.

THE CREATION OF VALUE

There are two ways in which people can get more of what they value. First, they can produce things they want. They can grow their food or make their clothing. They can make their own music or repair their car. In all of these ways, people add to their welfare because they have more things they want. The second way to increase wealth is to exchange something that you have for something that someone else has that you want more. We will consider both of these wealth-creating mechanisms in turn and learn how value is created in both cases.

Core-Info

Increasing our welfare means more than just getting more "stuff." It means getting more of the things people value. Value is created in two ways:
1. Production
2. Exchange

CHAPTER 4 • BASIC IDEAS AND CONCEPTS IN ECONOMICS

THE PRODUCTION POSSIBILITIES CURVE

The first way to create wealth is the one people tend to think of first: make something. By combining resources, people can produce something they want. They look for ways to combine resources to produce all of the many things people want, and therein lies the rub. People want not just one thing but many things. They want shirts and shoes and Chevrolets. Very quickly people learn that they cannot produce all of the shirts and shoes and cars they want at the same time. If people want more shirts, that might mean producing fewer cars. If they want more Chevrolets, that might require taking some workers and machines away from shoe factories and converting them to auto production. In short, when people try to produce a lot of different goods, they quickly discover that there are tradeoffs. Getting more of one thing almost always means getting less of something else. Within this phenomenon lies a lot of basic economics.

A central concept in this phenomenon is the **production possibilities curve.** To explore this concept, we will use a very much simplified version of how things get produced. Our model will compare how much of two different goods can be produced with a given set of resources.

Consider this scenario. It is 7:30 Sunday evening, and for the past week you have been planning to use the time between 8 P.M. and midnight to complete a set of 40 short-answer economics questions that your professor assigned. When the questions were distributed in class, you looked at them briefly and realized that some would be quite easy to answer, some were a bit harder, and some would be real puzzles, but with four hours to work on them, you felt confident that you could answer all 40 correctly. As you sit down to begin the assignment, the telephone rings and you learn that your boss needs you to come into work for the evening because of an emergency. If you go to work, you will be paid your usual $6 per hour wage rate. You are now faced with a dilemma. If you go to work, you can earn some much-needed cash, but you will lose the time that you had planned to spend on your economics assignment. If you don't go to work, you can do your assignment and work toward the grade you want, but you will lose the opportunity to earn some money.

It's a real tradeoff, isn't it? If you use your time to work on the economics assignment, you will produce some points but give up some money. If you use your labor resources to go to work, you will produce an income but give up some points in the class. You can't produce all the possible points and all the possible income at the same time. You have to give up some of one to produce the other.

Figure 4.1A lays out the options that you face. You can decide to go in to work all night, in which case you will have no time to write your answers. That is Option A: zero hours writing your assignment and four hours working. You could turn down your boss's request and stay home and work on your assignment. That is Option E: four hours spent writing and zero hours producing an income. Alternatively, you might talk your boss into allowing you to work for a part of the evening so that you would have some time available to work on your assignment. That possibility can be seen in Options B, C, and D where you produce both work and some answered economics questions.

What should you do? It depends on what you can get by selecting each of the options and on what is important to you. Consider the possible outcomes of the evening. Let's examine what you could produce if you spent your evening only working or only writing or doing some of each.

Figure 4.1B outlines the five possible outcomes that you face. If you go with Option A and work for four hours while doing no economics, you will earn $24 but will answer no questions. If you can talk your boss into Option B, you will lose $6 of income but answer all 20 of the easy questions. The **marginal cost** of spending that first hour on your economics assignment is $6. The **marginal benefit** of spending that hour on economics is 20 correctly answered questions. That is the tradeoff

---

Production Possibilities Curve
A curve that shows all possible combinations of two goods that can be produced with a given set of resources, fixed technology, and full employment.

Marginal Cost
The extra cost involved in producing one more unit of output.

Marginal Benefit
The additional benefit received by obtaining one more unit of a good.

FIGURE 4.1A & B

A — Options

	Write	Work
A	0 hours	4 hours
B	1 hour	3 hours
C	2 hours	2 hours
D	3 hours	1 hour
E	4 hours	0 hours

B — Outcomes

	Write	Work
A	0 questions	$24
B	20 questions	$18
C	30 questions	$12
D	36 questions	$ 6
E	40 questions	$ 0

you face in the first hour. If you choose Option C and spend two hours on economics (one additional hour), you lose another $6, but you can answer more questions correctly. The marginal cost of spending that second hour on economics is $6, and the marginal benefit is 10 additional questions answered. Why isn't your second hour spent on economics as productive as the first? In the first hour you answer the easy questions, the ones that you are best suited to answer. You are now moving on to the more difficult questions, the ones that you aren't as well prepared to deal with. You can anticipate what would happen if you chose Option D or Option E, and these options are described in Figure 4.1B.

What is the cost of working? A lower grade. What is the cost of studying? Lost income. These are opportunity costs. You have to give up one thing to get another.

As you know by now, anything that has numbers in it can be turned into a graph, and that's what we are going to do. The goal is to plot the possible outcomes on a graph. The graph will illustrate the possible production combinations in this four-hour period if you get right to it and do the best you can. We are going to draw a production possibilities curve.

The first set of outcomes (Option A) results from spending no time writing the answers to the economics questions and putting in four hours at work. The outcome of this decision is $24 and a grade of zero. This is plotted as Point A on the graph in Figure 4.2. In Option B, one hour of work on the economics questions and three hours of earning money produces less income but answers to 20 of the 40 questions. This option is shown as Point B on the graph. The other three possible outcomes likewise are plotted on the graph.

This graph is your production possibilities curve for the evening, and this curve demonstrates a number of important things about economics. First, it shows the maximum that you could produce if you used all your time on either working or studying. Second, it is a model. It helps us to understand the world around us and to make predictions about what would happen "if." Third, it lays out the cost of choices. You can see that there are tradeoffs in life and that these tradeoffs constitute opportunity costs.

Is it possible to get outside the production possibilities curve? Could you answer 30 questions *and* earn $18? That's not possible with the situation as described. With a change in technology, however, you could get outside the *current* production possibilities curve. If you could use a friend's word processor, you might be able to answer the questions more quickly. If you could talk your boss into paying you time-and-a-half for working (if you could get more output from your input), you could shift the production possibilities curve. (Sketch out these two possibilities and see how the shape of the production possibilities curve changes.) Point F on Figure 4.3 is an example of an impossible position to achieve given current resources and technology.

If you can't get outside your production possibilities curve, is it possible to be inside the curve? Could you answer 20 questions and earn $12? That could happen if you didn't use all of the time either for economics or for working. If you were to study for one hour, work for two hours, and watch television for an hour, you could

FIGURE 4.2

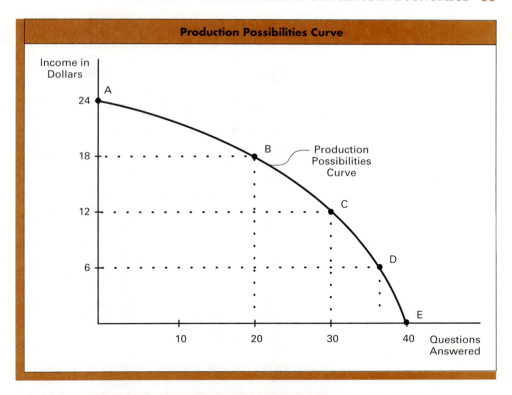

FIGURE 4.3

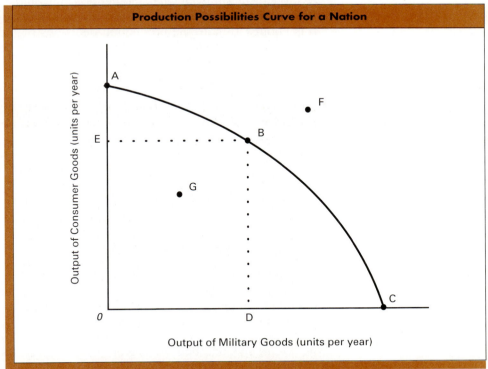

be inside your production possibilities curve. If you were to do this, you would not have used all of your time, all of your resources, in producing output. In economics terminology, you would have had *unemployed resources*. When the United States has people who are out of work or pieces of capital equipment that are sitting idle, it has unemployed resources; it is operating inside its production possibilities curve.

Just as you could have more of either grade or income or both by using all of your resources, so does this concept apply to the economy. Point G on Figure 4.3 is an example of being inside the production possibilities curve with utilized resources and unrealized output.

Thus, the production possibilities curve is not just for individuals and their personal microeconomic choices; it is for the entire economy at the macroeconomic level. Figures 4.3, 4.4A and 4.4B show a national perspective. Whether the tradeoff is between food and clothing, or CD players and sofas, or guns and butter, people must give up some of one thing to produce more of another. Everything has an opportunity cost, and choices must be made at all levels. Figure 4.4A shows an economy that is expanding and increasing its production possibilities. Figure 4.4B shows an economy that is contracting due to war, national disaster, or a decline in technology, with a decrease in production possibilities.

Let's return to the study-work example. Which choice *should* you make? Which of the five possible options should you choose? That depends on a number of variables. What are your preferences today? What do you want? If your grade is really solid in economics, perhaps the points you could earn from the assignment wouldn't be worth the time (even though you would learn an exceptional amount!) and you would choose to work. If your grade was hovering at 78 percent and the extra points could push you over the line to a B, maybe you should do the assignment. If your child is ill and you need the $18 to pay for a prescription, you would probably choose to work three hours whatever that might mean for your grade. This decision is in the arena of normative economics now, so each person's values come into play. What you might choose could be quite different from what another person would choose in the same situation. We will consider later how consumers make their buying decisions, but for now it is enough to note the production decisions of individuals and countries are based on the expected outcomes of what could be produced and the value people place on those outcomes.

Core-Info

Production possibilities curves show the maximum amount of production of two goods:
1. Given current technology
2. Given existing resources
3. With all resources fully employed

EXCHANGE AND INTERNATIONAL TRADE

Producing goods is one way to increase wealth. When people have more goods that they value, they are better off. A second and more subtle way to increase wealth or welfare is exchange. When I was in high school, I had a bow and arrow set that was collecting dust in my basement. A friend had a guitar that was accomplishing the same thing in his basement. He liked to hunt and I liked music. We traded, and both of us were happier. We experienced an increase in our welfare as a result of the trade. No new goods were produced, but the act of exchange made us both better off.

The Reasons for Trade

What was true for my friend and me is true of all free exchanges. Both sides are better off as a result of the exchange. Trades take place for two reasons: **differing resources** and **comparative advantage.** Differing resources refers to the fact that

Differing Resources
The fact that some resources are either completely absent or in extremely limited supply in some economies.

Comparative Advantage
The idea that each economy has a relative advantage in producing some goods in terms of the amounts of other goods that will be given up in their production.

FIGURE 4.4A
An increase in the resource base or an improvement in technology can move the production possibilities curve outward.

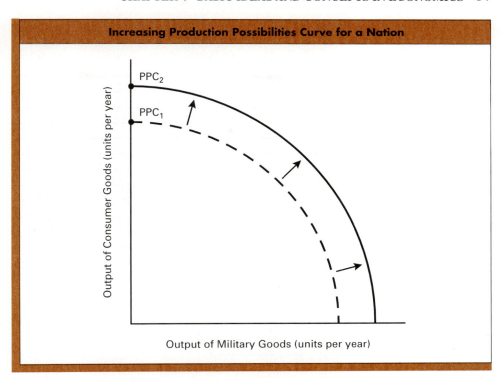

FIGURE 4.4B
Wartime bombing or natural disasters can move the production possibilities curve inward.

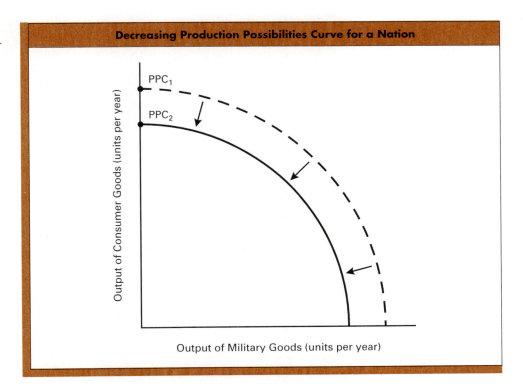

FIGURE 4.5

While labor costs are important, they are only one factor in the balance of trade. We import more from Germany than we export to it, and export more to Mexico than we import. *Source:* U.S. Bureau of Labor Statistics.

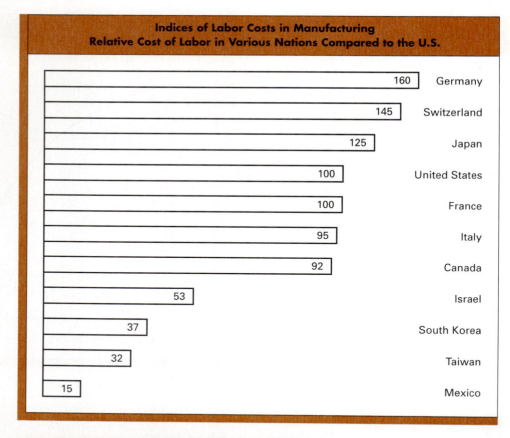

Indices of Labor Costs in Manufacturing
Relative Cost of Labor in Various Nations Compared to the U.S.

Country	Index
Germany	160
Switzerland	145
Japan	125
United States	100
France	100
Italy	95
Canada	92
Israel	53
South Korea	37
Taiwan	32
Mexico	15

FIGURE 4.6

Source: U.S. Bureau of the Census

U.S. Exports by States of Origin—1994 in Millions of Dollars

	State	Amount
1.	California	$66,292
2.	Texas	51,818
3.	New York	25,912
4.	Michigan	25,830
5.	Washington	23,629
6.	Illinois	19,097
7.	Ohio	19,007
8.	Florida	16,287
9.	Louisiana	14,549
10.	North Carolina	11,863

each participant in a trade has something that the other wants. That was the case with the long-ago trade between my friend and me. The same situation can exist at the international level. The United States produces wheat and beef in abundance. Saudi Arabia doesn't, but it does produce a lot of oil and sand. The United States may not have much demand for sand, but it does trade for oil. When countries have differing resources, trade is all but inevitable.

The other reason why people or countries trade is a bit more complex. That reason is comparative advantage, when one person or country has a relative advantage in producing a good over another person or country.

Benefits from Trade

As you can tell by this time, everybody benefits from trade. As long as people think they are better off by trading, they will do it. The minute they believe they would

Fish Gotta Swim and Birds Gotta Fly: Why We Specialize

If the United States doesn't have some natural resources, the country trades for them. But if the country can do everything else, why should we trade? After all, doesn't it take away from us to buy things from foreign countries? In a word, no. Let's take a look at a two-person universe as an example and see why this is the case.

Jack is a painter and Jill is an accountant. It is April and both of them have to do their taxes and both want to get their houses painted. Jill earns $50 per hour at her work and Jack earns $15 per hour at his. Both could paint their own homes and both could do their own taxes. The question is: should they?

The chart shows how long it would take for Jack and Jill to do both jobs.

	Jill the Accountant (Earns $50/hour)	Jack the Painter (Earns $15/hour)
PAINT THE HOUSE	30 hours	40 hours
DO THE TAXES	2 hours	10 hours

Oh, yes, the missing detail is that Jill worked her way through college painting houses. She was *very* good at it. In fact, Jill is better at both tasks than Jack. Jill has what is known as an absolute advantage in both areas. However, Jill has a comparative advantage in accounting and Jack has a comparative advantage in painting. At these costs, Jill should hire the painter and Jack should hire the accountant. If Jill paints her own house, it will take her 30 hours during which she could have earned $50 per hour for $1,500. If Jack paints the house, he will do it in 40 hours at $15 per hour for a total of $600. Jill saves $900 if Jack paints her house.

If Jack does his taxes, it will take him 10 hours during which he could have earned $15 per hour for $150. If Jill does the taxes, she will do it in 2 hours at $50 per hour for a total of $100. Jack saves $50 if Jill does his taxes.

The recommended action? Specialize and trade. Jill should specialize in accounting and Jack should specialize in painting. They have a comparative advantage in these areas, and specializing and trading will benefit both of them.

be better off without trading, they stop. Therefore, by definition, everybody (both sides in a trade) benefits through personal trade and through international trade. Does that mean that all traders do equally well? Not necessarily. If you are a more skillful negotiator than I or if you are more powerful and can intimidate the person you are trading with, you may be able to gain more benefit from the trade. In any case, however, as long as both sides are willing to trade, both benefit. Has the United States "taken advantage" of its trading partners in the Third World? Yes. Did those countries benefit from the trade? Yes. Does that excuse bad behavior or ill manners on our part? Certainly not, so let's criticize ourselves for that sin and not for impoverishing underdeveloped countries.

Barriers to Trade

If trade is so wonderful, why don't we do more of it? Given that the benefits of trade are so great and that everybody benefits, there must be some reason or reasons why people don't trade all the time and why the newspapers are full of stories about one group or another opposing it. In fact, three reasons or barriers rein in increasing exchange or trade: first, there are **natural trade barriers** or hindrances; second, the benefits are diffused while the costs are concentrated; and, third, **artificial trade barriers** can be imposed.

Natural Trade Barriers (Costs). Trade is not free. If we are to exchange goods with someone else, something has to happen. Some costs to trade cannot be avoided. These costs are known as natural barriers to trade.

Two types of costs are considered to be natural barriers: **transactional costs** and **transportation costs.** Transactional costs are the costs of making the deal. When the United States trades with businesses in another country, it must first learn about what they have to offer, compare their goods with those available elsewhere,

---

Natural Trade Barriers
The exchange costs involved in doing trade.

Artificial Trade Barriers
The restrictions imposed by government to restrict trade.

Transactional Costs
The costs involved in "making the deal" so trade can happen.

Transportation Costs
The costs involved in shipping the goods involved in trade.

FIGURE 4.7
Source: Bureau of Economic Analysis, U.S. Department of Commerce.

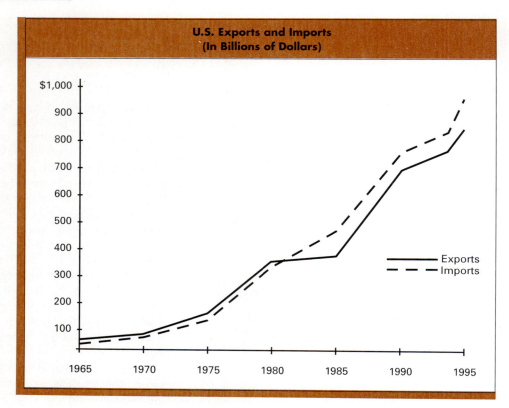

negotiate with their business people regarding prices and delivery schedules, and monitor the whole process. All of this takes time, and time costs something; there is an opportunity cost. In the time a company spends negotiating with a foreign supplier, it could be doing something else. Making the deal means that the company gives up the chance to pursue other business opportunities. When their transactional costs are low, people are more likely to trade with others. If transactional costs are high, trade is restricted. This is one reason why senators, representatives, and governors visit other countries, attempting to make it easier for American business leaders to work with business people in other countries.

Diffused Benefits and Concentrated Costs. Consider for a minute what would happen if the United States dropped its trade barriers with Japan. Those barriers include restrictions on the number of cars that Japan can export to this country and restrictions on how much rice the United States can ship to Japan. If those barriers were removed today, what would happen? The United States would import more Japanese automobiles, and the Japanese would import more rice from the United States. Both countries would benefit from this exchange. The free movement of goods would make more rice available in Japan, helping to bring down prices for the Japanese consumer, and more Hondas and Nissans would be available in the United States, lowering prices in this country as well. With the restrictions gone and prices lower, the Japanese would buy more U.S. rice—and less of their own—while Americans bought more Japanese cars—and fewer made in the United States. If Americans are buying more Japanese cars and fewer domestic models, some autoworkers would lose their jobs. Some Japanese rice farmers would face the same problem. While all consumers would benefit a little by the increased trade, some workers in both countries would pay a very high cost—their jobs. The benefits of trade are diffused, but the costs are highly concentrated. Because many people benefit a little while some are hurt a lot, those who do pay the high price tend to be "noisier" than those who benefit a little, and democratic governments tend to respond to noise.

Artificial Trade Barriers (Controls). The second reason for limited international trade often results in our third factor: artificial barriers. Artificial barriers are restrictions or controls that are intentionally put into place to reduce the amount of trade that can take place. The first of these artificial barriers is **prohibition.** Occasionally, some governments will prohibit trade between their country and another. These prohibitions are generally put into place for political reasons. There are prohibitions against trading with Cuba and Iraq, and many have called for a prohibition of trade with South Africa. For decades there were prohibitions against trading some goods (such as super computers or nuclear technology) with the Soviet Union. In each case, political considerations were the factors that led to the prohibitions. Even if there are valid political (or survival) reasons for prohibiting trade with another country, both nations suffer because of it.

> **Prohibitions**
> Government-established restrictions in all trade in a good.

The second artificial barrier is the **quota.** Quotas are limitations in the amount of a good that can be imported into another country. Sometimes quotas are set by the importing country, and sometimes they are "voluntarily" set by the exporting country. The latter is the case with Japanese automobiles. The Japanese agreed to limit their automobile exports to the United States to no more than 1.8 million cars per year. The reason for this "voluntary" restriction was that Japanese automobile manufacturers were afraid that if they didn't do it themselves, the United States might set an even lower quota. This limiting of imports to the United States reduces the supply of Japanese cars and pushes prices up for *all* automobiles.

> **Quotas**
> Government-established restrictions as to the amount of a good that may be traded.

The third artificial barrier to trade is the **tariff.** Tariffs are taxes placed on the price of a good when it enters the country. This tax raises the price of the foreign good to the consumer in the importing country, so demand for the product will fall. When the demand for the foreign good falls, the demand for the domestic good rises. When the demand for a good increases, its price also rises. The net result of a tariff, therefore, is that the price of both foreign and domestic goods rise, and the consumer's cost of living goes up as a result. The tariff has protected some jobs in the importing country, but the prices paid by all consumers of the good have risen.

> **Tariffs**
> Government-established taxes on imported goods.

Tariffs have one further, even more insidious, result. This cost is the waste that results as foreign firms look for ways to get around the tax. A prime example of this waste occurred in 1984 when Harley Davidson requested and was granted a tariff against Japanese motorcycles with engines of more than 700 cc. Harley Davidson's goal was to limit competition against its then hopelessly outdated 883 cc motorcycles. The tariff granted was a decreasing tariff that began at 44 percent of the import price. What was the response of Japanese motorcycle manufacturers? They all developed new motorcycles with engines of 699 cc, thus avoiding the tariff. So the effect of the tariff was to cause Honda and Yamaha to spend resources redesigning their motorcycles to avoid the tariff. This is a wasteful expenditure, but it is a natural response to *any* tax and one to expect any time a new or higher tariff is put into place.

The final type of artificial barrier to trade is known as **non-tariff barriers (NTBs).** Non-tariff barriers are rules that countries use to restrict the amount of trade that can occur. Automobile safety regulations that vary from country to country reduce the amount of trade that can take place by raising the costs that manufacturers face in selling in different markets. Licensing requirements that take months or years to complete also limit trade. Packaging or product testing requirements are another example. For instance, the U.S. Food and Drug Administration will not accept testing data from other countries but requires that all imported drugs be tested in approved American laboratories. This is a safety precaution, certainly, but it also functions as a barrier that can keep some foreign drugs off American shelves for years. These non-tariff barriers may be subtle and much less obvious than prohibitions or quotas, but they are just as effective in their result.

> **Non-tariff Barriers**
> Government-established rules and requirements that effectively limit foreign trade.

None of the artificial barriers need to exist. These barriers to international trade exist solely because countries choose to have them. Whereas trade will always face some level of natural barriers (it will always cost something to negotiate with others, and it will always cost something to ship goods), governments could eliminate all artificial barriers in an instant. Artificial barriers exist for political reasons. People who propose and support these barriers should understand the cost to both countries if trade is limited. As long as those costs are considered, choosing to put an artificial barrier in place can be legitimate.

Core-Info

Both trading partners benefit from free trade.
  Natural barriers to trade include:
1. Transactional costs
2. Transportation costs
  Artificial barriers to trade include:
1. Prohibitions
2. Quotas
3. Tariffs
4. Non-tariff barriers

National Defense Argument
The argument that trade in some goods should be restricted because the industry or good is vital to the survival of the nation.

Infant Industry Argument
The argument that trade in some goods should be restricted because the industry is young and unable to compete effectively on the world market.

Is it *ever* permissible to restrict international trade? Is *all* foreign trade marvelous and wonderful? There are two—and only two—acceptable arguments for limiting international trade. All other possible reasons are unacceptable. Any restriction of international trade entails an economic cost, so the reasons for limiting it have to be pretty good. They are. The first argument is known as the **national defense argument** against foreign trade. This argument contends that if the defense of the country is at stake, it has the right and obligation to limit foreign trade. The United States shouldn't export nuclear weapons or poison gas technology to a country that may use them against us. That makes sense even to an economist. Similarly, the country may not want to become dependent on a particular import if its survival could be at stake if the supplier suddenly decides to curtail shipments. The problem with these two national defense arguments is that it is almost impossible to know where to draw the line. Hydrogen bombs and super computers *may* be obvious (although the United States exports both—to its "friends"), but what about shoes? The national defense argument has been used to try to keep foreign-made shoes out of the country (the military would need shoes to go to war, so we had better make them here). Properly applied, the national defense argument makes sense, but the term *properly* means different things to different people.

The other argument that carries some legitimacy in terms of limiting foreign trade is known as the **infant industry argument.** To understand this argument, remember the first few days you spent at your most recent job. You probably weren't very productive. It takes a while to learn how to do the job and be as efficient as someone who has been doing it longer. If you had been expected to perform as well as an experienced worker, you probably would have been fired. While you were an "infant" at your job, the boss probably gave you some leeway and "protected" you against being measured by the same standard as other workers. Now that you have been on the job for a while, you are most likely expected to perform by the same standards as other workers. That is the crux of the infant industry argument. When a country is developing a new industry that must compete in the world market against older, more established firms, the new industry may need some short-term protection until it learns how to be as efficient as its older competitors. This argument is most frequently used by economists or political leaders who want to protect infant industries in underdeveloped countries. The problem with this argument is that what may be an "infant" to some may be an old-timer to others. Case in point: the U.S. steel industry (a century old) has requested infant industry protection against imports by the Japanese steel industry (30 years old) on the grounds that it is trying to modernize and compete against the more efficient Japanese. That is a poor application of the argument. Used appropriately in a limited way for a very short period of time, the infant industry argument can, however, be quite beneficial to a developing economy.

Core-Info

The only possible arguments against free trade are:
1. National defense argument
2. Infant industry argument

PRODUCING WEALTH—A SUMMARY

The nation's economy is based on the idea of generating wealth for its citizens. All people's economic—and other—activities are aimed at increasing their welfare. They can do this through production, by making more goods, but there are some tradeoffs in doing this. People can also increase their wealth through trade and exchange, although many would try to prevent this approach from working. As we move further into our examination of economics, keep in mind that *both* production and exchange produce wealth, and limiting either will reduce the welfare of the world.

SUMMARY

- The two ways in which value is created in an economy are production and exchange.
- The production possibilities curve shows the tradeoffs that must occur between the production of any two items.
- International trade occurs because of differing resources and because of comparative advantage.
- The benefits of international trade are a greater variety of goods at a lower cost for both trading partners.
- Natural and artificial barriers get in the way of free international trade and reduce the welfare of society.

KEY TERMS

Artificial barriers
Comparative advantage
Differing resources
Infant industry argument
Marginal benefit
Marginal cost

National defense argument
Natural barriers
Nontariff barriers
Production possibilities curve
Prohibitions

Quotas
Tariffs
Transactional costs
Transportation costs

REVIEW QUESTIONS

1. What are the two ways that value can be increased in an economy?
2. What is the central issue behind the production possibilities curve?
3. What are the two reasons why nations engage in foreign trade?
4. What are the two types of barriers that limit the amount of trade that can take place?

64 PART 2 • ECONOMIC PRINCIPLES

5. Identify the ways that government limits international trade.
6. If trade is truly unrestricted and open, who will benefit from the exchange?
7. How do the infant industry and national defense arguments apply to international trade?

PROBLEM-SOLVING PRACTICE

1. When fully employed, the island of Tuesday has the resources to produce a variety of combinations of two types of products: cookies and cars.

Point	Cookies (in tons)	Cars (units of 1,000)
A	15	0
B	12	2
C	9	4
D	6	6
E	3	8
F	0	10

    (a) From the data, draw a production possibilities curve for Tuesday.
    (b) If Tuesday is at Point B, what is the marginal cost of increasing car production to 4,000?
    (c) If Tuesday is at Point C, what is the marginal cost of increasing cookie production to 12,000?
    (d) Plot a new combination 8 tons of cookies and 3,000 cars as Point G. Where is Point G relative to the production possibilities curve? What does this mean?
    (e) Plot a new combination 8 tons of cookies and 8,000 cars as Point H. Where is Point H relative to the production possibilities curve? What does this mean?

2. Two countries, Richland and Poorland, can produce millions of bottles of wine and beer. The following table describes how much output two countries can produce of two products when both countries have a full employment of all resources. (Each measure is millions of bottles.)

	Beer	Wine
Richland	12	4
Poorland	8	2

    (a) Calculate the opportunity cost of producing beer in both countries.
    (b) Calculate the opportunity cost of producing wine in both countries.
    (c) If the two countries decide to engage in trade between each other, which should specialize in wine production? Which should specialize in beer production?
    (d) Explain your answers to Part C.

3. The country of Apples can produce more guns and more food than its neighbor, Oranges. The respective production of guns and food at full employment of all resources are represented in the following table (all figures in billions of units).

	Guns	Food
Apples	10	10
Oranges	4	8

    (a) Although Apples is more productive in both guns and food, which of the two should it specialize in if it decided to trade with Oranges? Explain the answer in terms of comparative advantage.
    (b) Although Oranges is lower in production capabilities than Apples, it still has a comparative advantage in one type of production. What should Oranges export? Provide an economic explanation for your answer.

4. If no money changes hands, how can you say that someone's wealth has increased as a result of merely trading goods?
5. Don't barriers that restrict trade protect American jobs by keeping foreign goods out? How can reducing barriers benefit the country?
6. For a number of years, the United States has enforced restrictions on the import of foreign-made clothing. What would happen if these barriers were eliminated? Should the United States do something if it eliminated the barriers? What? Why?

CHAPTER 5

Supply and Demand

CHAPTER OUTLINE

A. It's All We Know
B. Demand
   1. Definition of the Term *Demand*
   2. The Law of Demand
   3. Factors Affecting Demand
   4. Market Demand
C. Supply
   1. Definition of the Term *Supply*
   2. The Law of Supply
   3. Factors Affecting Supply
   4. Market Supply
D. Markets and Equilibrium
   1. Markets
   2. How Equilibrium Works
E. The Cost of Messing Around with Equilibrium
   1. Setting Prices Too High: a Price Floor
   2. Setting Prices Too Low: a Price Ceiling
F. Summing Up Supply and Demand

The purpose of this chapter is to introduce the central economic concepts of supply and demand and to begin the process of understanding markets.

AFTER COMPLETING THIS CHAPTER, YOU WILL BE ABLE TO:

1. Apply the law of demand to how purchasing decisions are made.
2. Describe the factors, other than price, that affect demand.
3. Draw a demand curve and apply it to the way people buy.
4. Apply the law of supply to production decisions by the firm.
5. Describe the factors, other than price, that affect supply.
6. Draw a supply curve and apply it to the way firms produce goods.
7. Apply the concept of equilibrium to markets and explain the effects of interfering with equilibrium.

It's All We Know

If you were to back an economist into a corner and demand to be told everything he or she knows, you would likely hear, "Benefits and costs, supply and demand." While that is not really all we know, everything else is essentially elaboration on these two themes. The elaborations can be extremely complex and the theorems and analyses quite elegant, but they are all some form of variation on one of those two basic themes. Given that, it would probably be to your advantage to know supply and demand fairly well (especially if passing an introductory course in economics is of interest).

The central tenets of economics are that goods and services are provided to people and that people act in their own self-interest. Supply and demand theory brings those tenets together. On the supply side are suppliers who might be willing to make goods and services available to others (if the price is right). On the demand side are demanders who want to acquire goods and services (again, if the price is right). Supply and demand theory is about how suppliers and demanders, producers and consumers, express their own self-interest—how they try to do the best they can for themselves.

To learn about supply and demand, we will examine them separately even though they ultimately must be brought together. We will discuss them separately for two reasons: to understand how each one works by itself and to develop the habit of analyzing their individual effects in real-life economic problems. We will begin with demand because it is easier to understand and because consumer demand is at the heart of our capitalistic system.

DEMAND

As we begin our discussion of demand, the first step is to understand just what that term means, for there is a lot of confusion about it in the world. To an economist, the term *demand* is very different from the terms *need* and *want*. Most people think they need more and better roads between the suburbs where they live and the cities where they work. After all, the roads are jammed every morning with traffic; obviously more roads are needed. Perhaps given the current set of costs and set of substitutes available, more roads might be needed. However commuters would have a different set of "needs" if mass transit were available at no direct cost or if parking cost $100 per day in the city. If free mass transit were available, people probably would say that they "need" more buses or light rail systems. If parking cost $100 per day, commuters would probably "need" fewer parking lots and highways and more mass transit and carpooling. The term "need" seems to be awfully fuzzy, doesn't it?

Similarly, many people say that they want free medical care available to people who need it. Again, "want" and "need" must be clarified. People who join a health maintenance organization (HMO) pay a fixed monthly charge and then pay low or no cost for medical care. Anyone who has access to a so-called free clinic probably goes to their doctor more often than they would if they had to pay the full cost for each visit. When people have to pay $50 for each trip to the doctor's office, they are likely to take aspirin, eat chicken soup, or get a day's rest; they don't go to the doctor unless they are really sick. Because HMOs don't charge by the visit, members are more likely to go to the doctor's office when they feel out-of-sorts (even though the doctor will probably prescribe aspirin or chicken soup or a day's rest anyway). Again, "need" for something depends a great deal on the cost. That is why economists don't talk about needs or wants.

Definition of the Term *Demand*

Needs and desires are subjective and very difficult to measure. Demand, however, can be quantified. **Demand** is desire backed by a willingness and ability to pay for

Demand
The desire for a good or service that is backed by the consumer's willingness and ability to purchase.

The Law of Demand

Our study of supply and demand begins with demand, the realm of consumers or buyers. People are all buyers or demanders. They demand goods and services from shirts to shoes to Chevrolets. Even producers are demanders. Producers buy raw materials and parts and labor. When producers buy, they behave the same way as consumers do. That leads us to the law of demand.

The **law of demand** states that there is a relationship between the price of a good and the amount of it that people are willing and able to buy. In fact, the law of demand stipulates an inverse, or negative, relationship between the price of any good and the quantity that people will buy. When the price of a product rises, people will buy less of it. When the price of a good falls, people will buy more of it. That's the law, and it is observed with such regularity that economists are hard pressed to find goods or services that don't obey it.

In the law of demand (as in the law of supply as you will learn in a minute), price is the cause and quantity is the effect. When the price changes, the quantity demanded changes in response. When the price goes up, the quantity demanded goes down. When the price falls, the quantity demanded goes up. Price causes the change. That is a constant in the law of demand. In mathematical terms, price is the independent variable and quantity is the dependent variable.

Of course, this discussion assumes *ceteris paribus,* that everything else stays the same and that price is the only thing changing. People's tastes don't change, the amount of advertising of the product doesn't change, the prices of other goods don't change, nothing changes except the price of the one good in question. In those conditions, the law of demand explains people's behavior.

The law of demand shows how buyers express their self-interest, how they try to maximize their welfare. When the price of a good rises, it is in the buyer's best interest to cut back on the purchases of that good and look for substitutes. On the other hand, when the price of a good falls, it is in the buyer's best interest to try to substitute that good for other things she or he consumes. Thus, when the price of Big Macs rises, people switch to other fast foods and vice versa. We can write it as follows:

> **Law of Demand**
> The concept that the price of a good or service and the quantity purchased are inversely related. If the price rises, the quantity demanded falls.

Core-Info

The law of demand states that there is an inverse relationship between the price of a good and its sales. The higher the price, the fewer will be sold. The lower the price, the more will be sold.

The relationship between price and sales may seem logical and not particularly earth-shattering, but it is absolutely true and central to economics. It is called a "law" to emphasize that point.

This effect can be illustrated in a table known as a **demand schedule.** A schedule is a list, something like a bus schedule of the times that a bus is supposed to arrive at various places. A demand schedule shows the possible prices of a good or service and the quantities of that good that people are willing and able to buy at each price. A demand schedule shows the desires of buyers.

An example should help to explain the law of demand. Think about your classmates and their desire to buy college sweatshirts. In any month, there is a certain level of demand for sweatshirts, and price plays a key role. If the bookstore puts sweatshirts on sale, students may buy one, but if the price goes up, they are more likely not to buy one. Figure 5.1 shows a demand schedule for college sweatshirts in the bookstore. As you can see, when the price is higher, students buy fewer

> **Demand Schedule**
> A tabular listing of possible prices of a good and the quantities that people are willing and able to purchase at each price.

FIGURE 5.1

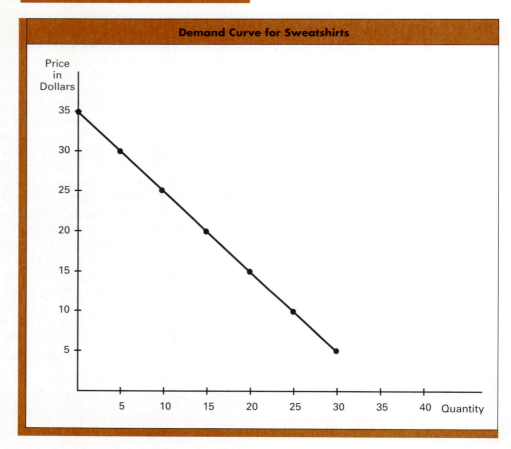

FIGURE 5.2

Demand Curve
The graphic representation of the relationship between possible prices of a good and the quantities that people are willing and able to purchase at each price.

sweatshirts. If the price falls, sweatshirt sales pick up. At a price of $15, students buy 20 sweatshirts. If the price is $20, students are willing to buy only 15 sweatshirts. If sweatshirts are expensive, students may buy t-shirts or jackets or nothing at all. If the bookstore puts sweatshirts on sale, they sell better. A demand schedule helps pinpoint the relationship between price and quantity demand. The listing of prices and quantities organizes the data for further analysis and helps show the strength of the relationship between the two variables.

By now, you should realize that an economist can make a graph of *anything*. Figure 5.2 is a **demand curve** that graphically presents the information contained in the demand schedule. This demand curve shows the relationship between the price of sweatshirts and the quantity that people are willing to buy at each price. A demand curve shows people's intentions or desires; it shows how many of an item they want to buy at each price.

When you draw a demand curve (and you draw a lot of them in economics), price is *always* on the vertical (or "Y") axis and quantity on the horizontal (or "X") axis. Label the axes to show the units you are using (e.g., dollars, cents, thousands of units), and measure the axis based on the range of price and quantity that you

FIGURE 5.3

	Demand Schedule for Sweatshirts	
Price	Quantity Demanded Before Advertising	Quantity Demanded After Advertising
$35	0	5
30	5	10
25	10	15
20	15	20
15	20	25
10	25	30
5	30	35

need to show. Then transfer the information about price and quantity from your demand schedule to the graph to show the relationship. What was a relationship that you could see numerically becomes one that you can see as a picture. Demand curves always look like Figure 5.2. The angle or slope of the line may vary, but they always slope downward from the upper left to the lower right. Why? Because as the price decreases, the quantity demanded increases and vice versa.

Factors Affecting Demand

Some of you may be saying to yourselves, "Law of demand? Ha! That's just not true. Why, I worked at a resort last summer, and in June we raised our prices *and* sold more than we did during April and May combined." That doesn't disprove the law of demand, because *ceteris* wasn't *paribus*. All other factors were not constant. For instance, the number of potential customers was much greater in June than in the previous months. Imagine how much you could have sold if you hadn't raised your prices.

Price is the only factor that affects the *quantity demanded,* but other factors may affect *demand.* That may seem to be just a subtle wording difference, but it makes a big economic difference. A change in the quantity demanded—when people decide to buy more or less as the price changes—represents a move along the demand curve. When economists talk about a change in demand, they are talking about a shift in the entire curve. It moves outward, or to the right, if there is an increase in demand. It moves inward, or to the left, with a decrease in demand. The following list outlines the various factors that affect demand. Consider each of the factors for a moment and decide how the demand curve would shift as they change.

- The number of consumers—more customers, more demand
- The income of customers—as income rises, people generally buy more of a good
- Expected income changes—if people expect their incomes to rise tomorrow, they tend to buy more today
- The prices of related goods
  - Substitute goods—if the price of a substitute drops, people buy less of the original good
  - Complementary goods (goods that go together: coffee and cream, vases and fresh flowers)—as the price of a complement rises, the demand for the original good falls
- People's tastes
- Time—with time, people acquire new information and change their behavior.

Figure 5.3 presents the demand schedule for sweatshirts first listed in Figure 5.1, but adds a column for what the quantity demanded might be if the bookstore began an advertising campaign for sweatshirts in the college newspaper. More students would probably decide to buy sweatshirts because of the advertising. That being the case, the quantity demanded would be higher than in the past at each of the prices. The new demand curve for this increased demand can be seen in Figure 5.4. At each possible price, the quantity demanded is greater after the advertising campaign than it was before. Anything that increases demand shifts the demand curve as shown. Anything that decreases demand has the opposite effect and shifts the demand curve to the left.

FIGURE 5.4

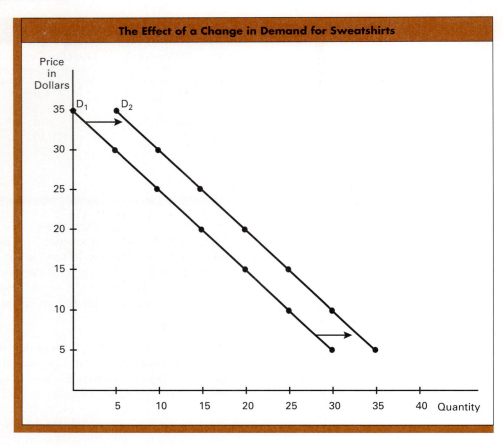

Market Demand

Thus far, the focus has been on demand on the individual level. We have looked at how much of a good *you* would buy at various prices or how much demand a bookstore can expect. It is time to expand that outlook to see what market demand would be. "Market" means the total quantity demanded for the product. This is relatively easy to figure out. Think about the total quantity demand for sweatshirts at the college bookstore. The total quantity demand that the bookstore faces is the sum of the individual quantities demanded by each student. If you would buy one sweatshirt at a price of $10 and your wealthy roommate would buy two at that price, the quantity demanded at $10 would be three. The same approach is used in calculating the market demand for sweatshirts or anything else. Figure 5.5 gives the market demand schedule for sweatshirts, assuming that only three stores carried the item.

This market demand schedule can be made into a market demand curve as shown in Figure 5.6. To draw the total, or market, demand curve, you must add horizontally the quantities demanded at each store. This market demand curve is used to determine the overall price of the good and the actual amount sold.

Demand is only the first half of the equation. It takes into account only what buyers want to do. It is now time to turn to the other half, supply, and consider what sellers want to do.

Core-Info

1. To determine the market or total demand for something, add all the individual demands for the item.
2. To determine the market or total supply of a good, add all the individual producers' supplies of the item.

FIGURE 5.5

Market Demand Schedule for Sweatshirts				
Price	Quantity Demanded			
	Store 1	Store 2	Store 3	Total Market
$35	0	6	1	7
30	5	8	2	15
25	10	11	4	25
20	15	14	7	36
15	20	18	9	47
10	25	21	11	57
5	30	23	14	67

FIGURE 5.6

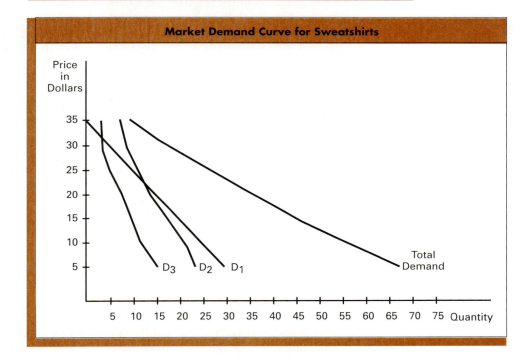

SUPPLY

Supply
The willingness and ability of a producer to make a good or service available for sales to consumers at a variety of prices.

As an introduction to **supply,** start with the basic fact that sellers are in business to make money. Whether a business sells sweatshirts or cars or its expertise, it wants to get as much as it can for what it produces or makes available. In supplying goods to someone else, a business incurs costs, and it wants to get as much as it can from the sale to cover its costs and have something left over at the end of the day.

Definition of the Term *Supply*

Supply is the willingness and ability of a producer to make goods and services available at a variety of costs.

The costs a producer faces are opportunity costs. Producers have a range of options before them. They could produce a number of things. They could produce sweatshirts or t-shirts or slacks or something else. They could produce four-door cars or two-door cars or coupes or station wagons in a variety of models. People could work for (sell their labor to) McDonald's or Wendy's or Burger King or someplace else. Producing more of one thing means giving up the opportunity to produce something else and using resources (inputs) as well. Because producers face costs, both explicit and implicit, the price they receive for their product is critically important. The combination of price and costs leads to the law of supply.

The Law of Supply

Law of Supply
The concept that the price of a good or service and the quantity produced for sale are directly related. If the price rises, the quantity supplied increases.

The **law of supply** states that there is a relationship between the price of a good and the amount that people are willing and able to produce of it. The relationship in this case is a direct or positive one. When the price that suppliers can receive for a product increases, they are willing to produce more of that product. That makes sense: when someone is willing to pay you more, you are likely willing to work a greater number of hours, aren't you? Just the opposite is true as well. When the price that suppliers can receive for a product decreases, they are less interested in producing that good. The same is true for you: when someone is willing to pay you less, you want to work fewer hours for that employer and more for someone else. That is the case with all suppliers. This is how suppliers express their own self-interest, and it is known as the law of supply.

As with the law of demand, price is the independent or causal variable, and the quantity supplied is the dependent or affected variable. When the price they can receive for a good increases, suppliers are willing to supply more of the good. When the price they can receive for a good falls, suppliers are less willing to supply that good. We can show this positive relationship as follows:

Core-Info

The law of supply states that there is a direct relationship between the price of a good and the quantity producers are willing to make available. The higher the price, the more will be offered for sale. The lower the price, the fewer will be produced.

Again, this is a logical relationship; producers do more of what is rewarding and less of what is not. That is how producers express their self-interest, how they act to maximize their welfare.

The positive or direct relationship between price and quantity supplied is shown in a table called a **supply schedule.** A supply schedule is a table that shows the possible prices that producers could receive for something they sell and the quantities that they are willing and able to make available at each price. The supply schedule shows the desires of suppliers.

Supply Schedule
A tabular listing of possible prices of a good and the quantities that producers are willing and able to produce at each price.

Let's return to the sweatshirt example to see how the law of supply works. The college bookstore has a number of items for sale: t-shirts, jackets, book bags, sweatshirts, and many other things. The store is willing to order and carry in inventory any item that is likely to sell well. If sales are good and the price the store receives is high, it is willing to carry (supply) more of the item. If the price it receives for sweatshirts is high, the bookstore will order more, pay for overnight delivery, stay open longer hours and pay overtime wages, and do anything else needed to sell the item. On the other hand, if the price the bookstore can receive for sweatshirts is low, it won't be willing to pay the extra costs necessary to supply a lot of extra sweatshirts and will reduce the quantity it is willing to supply.

Figure 5.7 presents a supply schedule for sweatshirts at the college bookstore. As you can see, at high prices, the quantity supplied is high and vice versa. If the bookstore can get $20 for each sweatshirt, it is willing to supply 15. If it can receive $30 for each one, it is willing to supply 25.

The data from this supply schedule can be converted into graphical form and made into a **supply curve.** Figure 5.8 is the supply curve for sweatshirts at the bookstore. This curve presents what the bookstore is willing to do and shows the positive or direct relationship between price and the quantity supplied. The supply curve angles upward and to the right. The slope of the curve may vary from quite flat to nearly vertical, but it always moves upward and away from the lower left of the graph.

Supply Curve
The graphic representation of the relationship between possible prices of a good and the quantities that a supplier is willing and able to produce at each price.

Again, as with the demand curve, you always put price on the vertical (or "Y") axis and quantity on the horizontal (or "X") axis. Label the axes carefully and enter your data, and you will have a picture of the relationship between price and quantity.

FIGURE 5.7

FIGURE 5.8

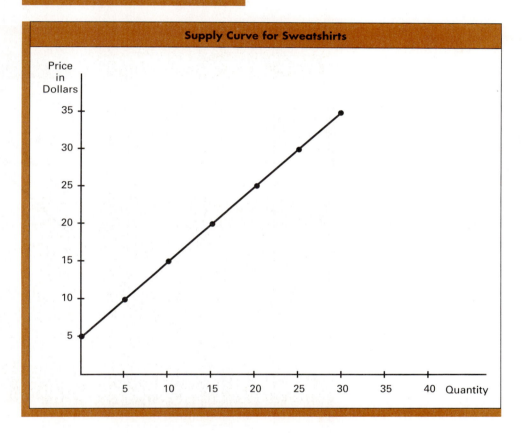

Supply Schedule for Sweatshirts	
Price	Quantity Supplied
$35	30
30	25
25	20
20	15
15	10
10	5
5	0

Factors Affecting Supply

You may be thinking that there must be more to figuring out how much a seller is willing to supply, and you're right. There are a number of factors that affect the supply of a good. The list below outlines these factors.

- Technology—if technology improves, supply will increase
- Input costs—if input costs fall, supply will increase
- Price expectations—if producers expect prices they will receive to rise, they will increase supply
- Time

When a factor is said to cause an increase in supply, it means that the seller is willing to make more available at the same price. When a factor causes a decrease in supply, less is available at each price. A change in supply (just as with a change in demand) means that the entire supply curve moves. An increase in supply moves the curve outward to the right while a decrease in supply moves the curve inward to the left. Take another minute and think about why the supply curve would shift as it does when supply changes.

FIGURE 5.9

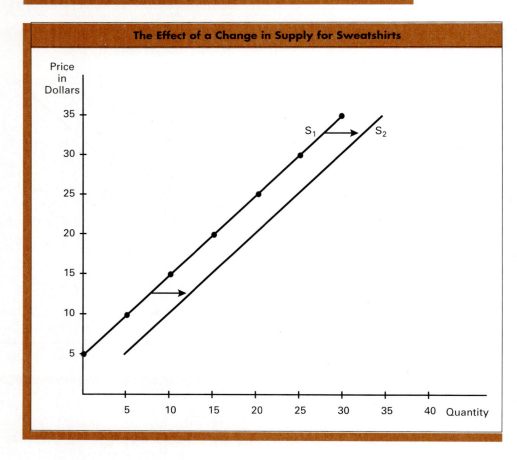

	Supply Schedule of Sweatshirts	
Price	Quantity Supplied Before New Technology	Quantity Supplied After New Technology
$35	30	35
30	25	30
25	20	25
20	15	20
15	10	15
10	5	10
5	0	5

FIGURE 5.10

The Effect of a Change in Supply for Sweatshirts

With the sweatshirt example, assume there has been a breakthrough in the technology of transportation, and the cost of shipping shirts from the manufacturer to the bookstore has been reduced. Because costs have fallen for the bookstore, it is willing to carry and sell more of the sweatshirts at each price. Figure 5.9 shows the supply schedule for sweatshirts at the bookstore. Column 1 is the price, column 2 is the old supply schedule (as shown in Figure 5.7), and column 3 presents the new quantities that the bookstore is willing to sell now that its costs have fallen. Remember: this example demonstrates a *change in supply*. It differs from a *change in the quantity supplied*, which translates as a move along the same supply curve in response to a change in prices. (Note: Be sure to read the questions on your next quiz very carefully. Economics professors just love to ask questions about the effect of an increase in supply or an increase in the quantity supplied.

The effect of a change in supply can be presented graphically, as shown in Figure 5.10. Because there has been an increase in supply due to the new technol-

FIGURE 5.11

Market Supply Schedule of Sweatshirts				
Price	Store 1	Store 2	Store 3	Total
$35	30	20	35	85
30	25	16	28	69
25	20	14	25	59
20	15	10	21	46
15	10	7	17	34
10	5	2	15	22
5	0	1	13	14

ogy, the new supply curve is out and to the right of the old supply curve. A decrease in technology or an increase in the cost of inputs for the manufacturer or the bookstore would result in a decrease in supply, and the curve would move to the left.

Market Supply

Not surprisingly, economists arrive at the total or market supply of a good in much the same way they calculate the market demand for a good: they add the amounts that each seller would be willing to supply at each price. That makes sense. The total number of sweatshirts available for $20 is the sum of the amounts that each store is willing to provide for sale at that price.

Figure 5.11 shows the market supply of sweatshirts for a three bookstore market. Column 1 shows the various possible prices for the sweatshirts. Columns 2 through 4 show what each store is willing to supply at the various prices (their supply schedules). Column 5 shows the total or market supply of sweatshirts. Why do the amounts that the stores would be willing to sell at a given price differ? Each store has its own costs and opportunities for sales. Because the relevant costs and other sales opportunities differ at the various bookstores, the amount that each is willing to supply likewise varies, and thus the individual supply schedules and supply curves vary as well.

Combining the individual supply schedules produces the market supply schedule. Supply curves can also be combined. To draw the market supply curve, add horizontally the individual supply schedules to derive the key curve, the total supply curve as shown in Figure 5.12.

MARKETS AND EQUILIBRIUM

At this point you have studied supply and demand individually and have a pretty good idea of how and why they work. It is now time to bring these two together and see how they interact. This combination of supply and demand takes place in the market.

Markets

A **market** is a place where sellers and buyers, suppliers and demanders, interact. Suppliers offer their products for sale at various prices according to the law of supply, and buyers look at the range of choices available and, given their tastes, select a package of goods to purchase according to the law of demand. This interaction of suppliers and demanders results in some amount of goods exchanging hands at a given price, and an equilibrium is the result.

How Equilibrium Works

Equilibrium is an economic term for a place of rest for the market, a place from which there is no pressure on the part of buyers or sellers to move. To examine equilibrium, you must look at what buyers and sellers are willing to do individually. The desires of buyers are shown in their demand schedule, and the desires of suppliers are shown in their supply schedule. Once these two sets of desires are combined, it is possible find equilibrium.

Market
A place in which buyers and sellers exchange the goods and services produced and desired in an economy and which, if allowed to function freely, will result in equilibrium.

Equilibrium
A situation in which the quantity supplied is equal to the quantity demanded for a good or service. The price at which this occurs is known as the equilibrium price, and the quantity is called the equilibrium quantity. This can occur only when prices can move freely.

FIGURE 5.12

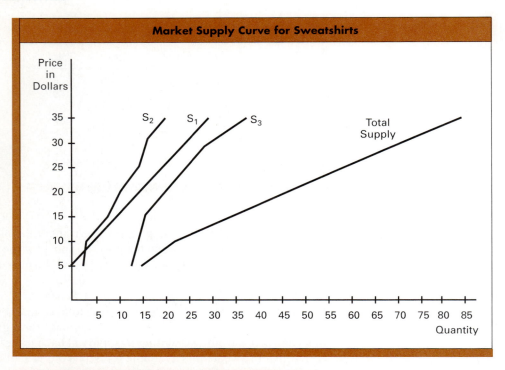

FIGURE 5.13

Supply and Demand Schedules for Sweatshirts		
Price	Quantity Demanded	Quantity Supplied
$35	0	30
30	5	25
25	10	20
20	15	15
15	20	10
10	25	5
5	30	0

To look at equilibrium, consider the college bookstore and its sweatshirts. Figure 5.13 brings together the supply and demand schedules for the store. Column 1 presents the prices, column 2 shows how many sweatshirts buyers are willing to purchase at these prices, and column 3 shows how many the bookstore is willing to sell at each price. As the price decreases, the quantity of sweatshirts demanded increases but the quantity of sweatshirts supplied decreases. At only one place does the quantity of sweatshirts demanded equal the quantity of sweatshirts supplied, and that point is known as equilibrium. At equilibrium, we find the equilibrium price and the equilibrium quantity. At any price above equilibrium, the quantity that sellers supply is greater than the quantity that buyers demand. At any price below equilibrium, the quantity that buyers want is greater than the quantity that sellers are willing to supply. At any price other than equilibrium, the schedule is out of balance.

Figure 5.14 presents the combined supply and demand curves for sweatshirts at the college bookstore and shows the equilibrium price and quantity for the product.

If the price of the sweatshirts was above equilibrium, say at $25, then the quantity demanded is less than the amount that suppliers are willing to sell. Suppliers would provide 20 sweatshirts, but buyers would only be willing to purchase 10 at that price. The result would be too many sweatshirts available; a **surplus** of 10 sweatshirts would exist. What would happen then? Faced with an excessive quantity of sweatshirts, suppliers would lower the price to consumers (who would then

Surplus
The amount by which the quantity demanded is less than the quantity supplied at a price that is above the equilibrium price.

FIGURE 5.14

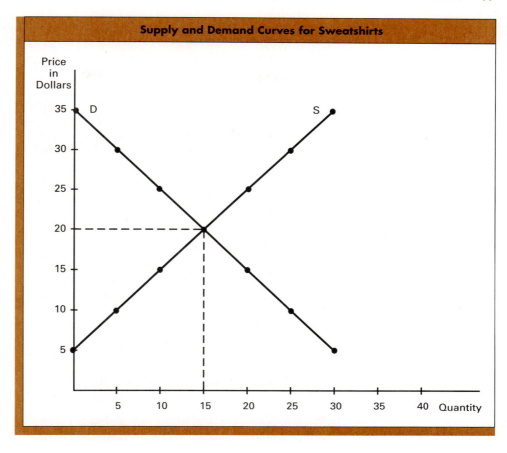

increase the quantity they would purchase), and suppliers would produce fewer sweatshirts in the future now that they know they can't get as much for them.

If the price of sweatshirts were below equilibrium, say $15, then sellers would only be willing to supply 10 sweatshirts. Buyers, on the other hand, would want to purchase 20. The result of this too-low price would be a **shortage.** There would be too few sweatshirts for the number of buyers wanting them. Now what would happen? Some buyers would begin to bid against each other and would be willing to pay a higher price than $15 to get the sweatshirts that were available. This bidding process would raise the market price, driving some consumers out of the market and encouraging suppliers to produce more sweatshirts.

All of the market adjustment that has just been described would happen automatically. No one has to set prices or determine how much should be produced or sold. If prices are not at equilibrium, forces are set into motion to help the market move back to equilibrium automatically. While the real world may never get exactly to equilibrium, the market always moves in that direction if it is allowed to. That is one of the beauties of a capitalistic economy: it is self-regulating in response to the desires of individual buyers and sellers as expressed through their freely determined willingness to act.

THE COST OF MESSING AROUND WITH EQUILIBRIUM

Many years ago, the late Jim Croce had a hit song, "You Don't Mess Around with Jim." The gist of the song was that it is unwise to "tug on Superman's cape" or to "spit into the wind" and that you don't "pull the mask off of no Lone Ranger." If you do tug or spit or pull (*or* mess around with Jim), you face a severe price. Economists would extend the same advice about equilibrium. Messing around with equilibrium exacts a heavy cost, so you had better know what it is and be willing to pay it.

Americans aren't always happy with what the market does. Sometimes they don't like the prices that result from the interaction of supply and demand forces.

Shortage
The amount by which the quantity demanded exceeds the quantity supplied at a price that is below the equilibrium price.

Has Detroit Learned?

Starting about 1975, the U.S. auto industry was written off as a relic of the dinosaur age. Its cars were said to be overpriced, overweight, and overchromed. The answer was seen to be foreign cars, especially Japanese cars. And so, while sales of imports nearly doubled, sales of domestic cars increased by only 0.03 percent. Time to convert Detroit's factories into museums? Maybe not.

As the chart below shows, there has been a remarkable turnaround in world motor vehicle production. U.S. factories are working two shifts while foreign factories are laying off staff. The reasons? American manufacturers responded to demand and reduced the weight, changed the style, and improved the efficiency of their cars. Perhaps even more important is that average American cars now cost *less* than Japanese cars. With product improved and price relatively decreased, is it any wonder that American car sales are soaring?

World Motor Vehicle Production (in thousands)

Year	United States	Europe	Japan
1991	8,811	17,563	13,245
1992	9,729	17,307	12,499
1993	10,898	14,825	11,228
1994	12,263	16,028	10,554

Source: American Automobile Manufacturers Association

Sometimes they don't think that the quantity that is provided by the market is correct. When this is the case, there is a strong temptation to mess around with equilibrium or, as some would put it, to seek an adjustment to the interplay of market forces. Let's look at two common examples.

Core-Info

While equilibrium can be considered the place of rest for the market, nobody is really happy. All goods that are produced are sold, but buyers still would like to get them for less and suppliers would like to sell them for more.

Setting Prices Too High: A Price Floor

Occasionally people believe that the price of a good is too low for the seller to earn a decent living. This is how some people feel about farm prices. While people all want low prices for food, the concern persists that if the prices received by farmers are too low, many family farms will be driven out of business, leaving the market to the corporate giants. Many in the government have felt this way (at least during election years), and the response they have taken is to set minimum prices, a **price floor,** for certain agricultural products such as wheat, rice, and dairy products. The result of this action in the case of wheat can be seen in the supply and demand curves shown in Figure 5.15.

Farmers have a supply curve for wheat. When they are likely to receive low prices for wheat, they plant less wheat, sometimes leaving the fields in clover or other nitrogen-fixing crops. As prices rise, they grow more wheat, shifting away from the production of other crops. At really high prices, farmers plant to the corners of their fields, use petrochemical fertilizers and pesticides, and intensively cultivate the crop. In short, they act like any other rational supplier and have a normal-looking supply curve for wheat.

Consumers have a demand curve for wheat. People want wheat for bread, cakes, rolls, cereal, and a thousand other products. When the price of wheat is high, they reduce their consumption of wheat and substitute other products for wheat products. No Wheaties on the breakfast table; corn flakes will have to do. No wheat bread for dinner; potatoes are passed around instead. Similarly, when the price of wheat and wheat products is low, the quantity of wheat consumers demand rises as they substi-

Price Floor
A government regulation in which a minimum legal price is established for a good or service. Sales below this price are prevented by the government's willingness to purchase all goods or services at this price.

FIGURE 5.15

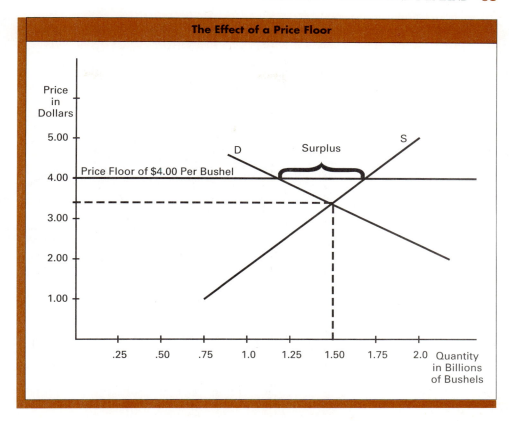

tute the now-cheaper wheat products for other foods. Wheat consumers look like any other demander, and they too have a regular-looking demand curve for wheat.

The interaction of the supply curve for wheat with the demand curve for wheat yields an equilibrium price and quantity for wheat in the United States, as shown in Figure 5.15. In this example, the equilibrium price is $3.25 per bushel, at which some 1.5 billion bushels of wheat would be produced.

If the government feels that $3.25 is too little for farmers to receive, it may—and does—step in and set a price floor, a minimum price that wheat can be sold for. If the market price of wheat is above this minimum price, the government does not interfere. If the market price is below the minimum price, the government guarantees to buy at the minimum price whatever wheat farmers produce. Government sets a fixed price above the equilibrium price, $4 in this example, for wheat. The horizontal line at $4 on Figure 5.15 is this minimum price for wheat.

What happens at this price above equilibrium? Suppliers and demanders both act in their own self-interest. Suppliers increase their production of wheat in response to the higher prices while demanders reduce their consumption of wheat. The result, of course, is a surplus of wheat in the United States, a situation that exists today. Thus, resources are used (farmers' labor, land, capital, fertilizer) to produce a surplus of wheat that consumers don't want to buy. The government, which now owns a great quantity of surplus wheat, must use railroad cars and diesel engines to transport it to the silos that must be built to hold it until it rots so it can be thrown out. Perhaps we may want to think this one through again. One solution that students often suggest for the use of our surplus crops is to send them to India or Bangladesh (give them away if necessary) to help save the lives of people who are starving on the subcontinent. On supply and demand curves, trace through the effects of an increase in the supply of wheat in Bangladesh that would result from the addition of the U.S. surplus. Then think about the number of Bangladeshi farmers who would remain in agriculture and what would probably happen in the year following the U.S. donation of the surplus grain. It should provide some food for thought.

Figure 5.16

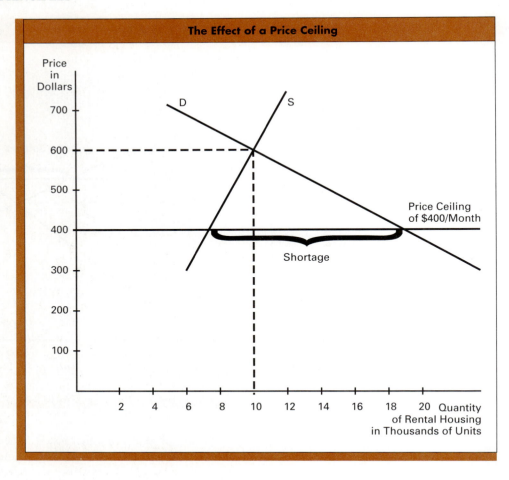

Price Ceiling
A government regulation by which a maximum legal price is established for a good or service. Sales above this price are prohibited.

Rent Controls
A form of price ceiling in which a maximum rental amount is established for an apartment.

Setting Prices Too Low: A Price Ceiling

The reverse of the situation just described is when people think that prices are too high or quantities are too low for some good. These views are all too often accompanied by a call for a **price ceiling.** Some people think this situation applies to rental housing in U.S. cities. It is certainly true that many poor people cannot afford the high rents for apartments and houses that are charged by landlords. If people are unhappy with what the market does, why not intervene? That's just what some city governments have done.

To keep apartment rents from skyrocketing, a number of city councils have set a maximum price that may be charged for an apartment. These government price ceilings are called **rent controls.** By controlling the rent, these governments contend they will make more low-cost apartments available to the poor. Let's see if this is the case.

Figure 5.16 presents the supply and demand curves for rental housing in a city. A normal supply curve exists for rental housing. As rents rise, more apartments become available: the quantity supplied increases. Large houses become subdivided. Basement and attic apartments become available. Rooms open up to renters. The quantity supplied increases. Conversely, when rents fall, people no longer are willing to rent out their spare rooms, apartment buildings are converted to condominiums, and basement apartments are taken off the market. In short, when the price (rent) falls, the quantity supplied (number of apartments) falls.

Renters have a demand curve for housing. As rents decrease, more people want to rent apartments in the city. People who are renting together can afford to have their own place. Those living with their parents or grandparents can move out and be independent. And suburbanites who work in the city are attracted to apartments within the city limits because rents are lower. On the other hand, when rents go up, fewer people want a place of their own, and more are willing to live with someone else or to remain in the suburbs and commute. The interaction of this demand curve with the earlier supply curve results in an equilibrium number of apartments at an equilibrium (or market) price, in this example 10,000 and $600 respectively.

When government enacts rent controls, it sets a price ceiling or maximum rent. The maximum rent that can be charged may be $400 per month, as shown on the graph by the horizontal line at a price of $400. What happens if the price is $400? The quantity demanded would increase significantly, and the quantity supplied would decrease. The result is a shortage of apartments in the city. Rent controls reduce the number of available rental apartments.

Now put yourself in the position of a landlord with a rent-controlled apartment. How much maintenance are you willing to do? To protect your investment, might you not begin to require a key deposit and a cleaning deposit in addition to the first and last month's rent in advance? (Who can afford this? The rich person or the poor?) To whom would you more likely rent: a professional couple with no children who currently live in the suburbs or a welfare mother of four who is just squeaking by economically? Most landlords would choose the tenant best able to pay the rent.

The net effect of rent controls is twofold: the number of available rental apartments drops and those who can rent the now lower priced apartments are not the people the government intended to help in the first place. These are the people who are in fact damaged by rent controls. If landlords appear rapacious and are acting in ways that hurt poor people, the government may decide to do something to encourage them to change their behavior, but rent controls are probably not the way to do it. Controls change landlords' behaviors, but not in the intended direction.

What could governments do to help the poor afford a place to live? Build more rental housing, give landlords tax incentives for making more apartments available (push the supply curve outward), or give the poor a rental assistance check to spend for an apartment (which would also push the demand curve outward). These approaches should help to provide housing for the poor. Rent controls will not. This simple analysis is a good example of how supply and demand theory can help to examine real-life situations and anticipate likely outcomes to determine if the results equal the intent. If they do, that's great. If they do not, the opportunity is there to change the approach before making a big mistake.

Core-Info

Preventing the market from freely adjusting and achieving equilibrium will always cause some problems. What must be decided is whether the problems caused are less serious than the problems that are solved by intervening.

SUMMING UP SUPPLY AND DEMAND

There you have it: supply and demand theory at the core of economics. If you can understand how people make more available as prices rise, how people are willing to buy more as prices fall, what equilibrium means, and how equilibrium can be adjusted, you are already a long way toward achieving success in this course and, quite frankly, in life. Supply and demand analysis can be applied to innumerable situations, including social situations, college tuition, and proposed changes in the medical care program. If you begin to think in terms of supply and demand, you can anticipate the effects of proposed actions or situations and can begin to make better, more informed decisions. Good luck!

SUMMARY

- The law of demand states that there is an inverse relationship between price and the quantity demanded of a good or service.
- The major factors that affect demand are the number and incomes of consumers, the prices of related goods, expectations of tomorrow, people's tastes, and time.
- Demand curves always slope downward from upper left to lower right.
- The law of supply states that there is a direct relationship between price and the quantity supplied of a good or service.
- The major factors that affect supply are technology, input costs, price expectations, and time.
- Supply curves always slope upward from lower left to upper right.
- Equilibrium is the market price and condition in which the quantity demanded equals the quantity supplied.
- Interfering with equilibrium will always yield misadjustment in the market with resulting surpluses or shortages.

KEY TERMS

Demand	Law of supply	Shortage
Demand curve	Market	Supply
Demand schedule	Price ceiling	Supply curve
Equilibrium	Price floor	Supply schedule
Law of demand	Rent controls	Surplus

REVIEW QUESTIONS

1. How does the term "demand" differ from "want" or "need?"
2. What is the relationship between price and quantity when we speak of the quantity demanded? Why?
3. What factors other than price affect demand?
4. Why does a firm decrease production of a good when the price decreases?
5. What factors other than price affect supply?
6. What is the relationship between the quantities demanded by individuals and market demand?
7. What does the term "equilibrium" mean?
8. What is the effect of moving a market away from equilibrium through the use of price floors or ceilings?

PROBLEM-SOLVING PRACTICE

1. The daily demand for fast food hamburgers for students at a university is represented by the following demand schedule:

Quantity Demanded	Price
50	$2.00
100	1.75
300	1.50
600	1.00
750	.75
1200	.50

And the fast food restaurants in the university area have a supply schedule that is represented by the following schedule:

Quantity Supplied	Price
1000	$2.00
800	1.75
700	1.50
600	1.00
400	.75
200	.50

(a) Plot the demand and supply schedules as the demand and supply curves respectively.
(b) At what price do supply and demand curves intersect?
(c) At this *equilibrium* price, what is the equilibrium quantity of hamburgers?
(d) If the price were set at $1.75, what would happen in this market for hamburgers?
(e) If the price were set at $.50, what would happen in this market?

2. In a metropolitan area, car dealers are willing to supply the midsized new model of the Neptune automobile in accord with the following schedule:

Supply Schedules for Neptunes

Quantity Supplied	Price
500	$ 5,000
2,000	10,000
3,000	15,000
4,500	20,000
5,000	25,000

Consumers for midsized new model cars have a demand schedule for Neptunes that is represented by the following:

Quantity Demanded	Price
250	$25,000
1,000	20,000
1,500	15,000
2,000	10,000
3,000	5,000

(a) Construct supply and demand curves for the Neptune in the market.
(b) Determine the market price and quantity exchanged in the market for Neptunes.
(c) If the manufacturer of Neptunes required the selling price of Neptunes to be $20,000 what would happen in this market?
(d) If corporate marketing policy changed and the Neptune were marketed nationally as a $5,000 car, what would happen in this metropolitan market?

3. In the above market for Neptune cars, indicate the changes that would take place in supply and demand by drawing in the necessary changes in the curves for the following changes:

(a) The income of consumers in this metropolitan area goes down.
(b) Improved technology in the production of Neptune reduces the costs of production for Neptunes.
(c) The price of another major midsize automobile increases.
(d) Consumer preferences for midsized cars increases due to increasing gas prices.
(e) The workers producing the Neptune gain significant wage increases through their union's new collective bargaining agreement.

CHAPTER 6

Elasticity

CHAPTER OUTLINE

A. A Big Idea in a Small Package
B. The Concept of Elasticity
   1. Elasticity Is the Key
C. Price Elasticity of Demand
   1. Elasticity
   2. Factors Affecting Elasticity
   3. Elasticity and Revenue
D. Other Elasticities
   1. Elasticity of Supply
   2. Income Elasticity of Demand
   3. Cross Elasticity of Demand
E. Elasticity and Public Policy
   1. U.S. Drug Policy
   2. Health Care Policy
F. Using This Tool

The purpose of this chapter is to introduce the theoretical and practical uses of the concept of elasticity.

AFTER COMPLETING THIS CHAPTER, YOU WILL BE ABLE TO:

1. Explain the concept of elasticity and describe its relationship to the effects of change.
2. Apply the concept of price elasticity of demand to the pricing decisions made by a firm.
3. Apply price elasticity of demand to public policy decisions made by the government.
4. Explain the factors that affect the price elasticity of demand.
5. Apply elasticity of supply and income elasticity to the decisions made by individuals, business, and government.

A Big Idea in a Small Package

The brevity of this chapter is not a message about the importance of its subject. Though this section is short, the theory and application of the idea of elasticity are critically important. The discussion of elasticity is usually grouped with—and lost in—the explanation of supply and demand in economics textbooks, but it certainly rates its own chapter. Pay close attention to the discussion and, if it isn't completely clear, give it a second read-through or talk with your instructor. If you can master the idea of elasticity, this knowledge will help you understand how to change prices in any business you manage and how to make decisions about such issues of national concern as illegal drugs or health care policy.

THE CONCEPT OF ELASTICITY

The last chapter covered supply and demand. These two ideas are central to all of economics, for they explain how buyers and sellers act in their own self-interest and how this brings about market equilibrium. We know, for instance, that whenever the price on a product is increased, the quantity that people are willing and able to purchase decreases. Also, common sense dictates that some goods and services are very responsive to any change in price while other goods and services aren't affected much by a change in their price. Wouldn't it be nice to be able to predict how much the quantity demanded will change when price changes and what this might mean to a business? In fact, such forecasts are possible.

Elasticity Is the Key

The term **elasticity** means responsiveness, and it relates to how much one factor changes as a result of a change in another factor. In particular, elasticity measures how much a dependent variable changes as a result of a change in an independent variable. This chapter will use price elasticity of demand as its primary example because it is so central to how businesses make pricing and output decisions. However, the concept can be applied to any situation where one variable is affected by another. We will look briefly at a few of these situations a bit later.

PRICE ELASTICITY OF DEMAND

Elasticity

The idea of price elasticity intuitively makes sense: the demand for some goods and services respond to a change in their price, and others don't. Economics has a formula for looking at this; the equation compares how much the quantity demanded changes as the price changes.

The Price Elasticity Formula

$$Ed = \frac{\% \Delta Qd}{\% \Delta P}$$

The formula can be translated as follows: the **price elasticity of demand** is equal to the percent change in the quantity demanded divided by the percent change in the price. How much did quantity change as price changed? Because both prices and quantities can be low or high, the calculation is in percentage terms. If the percentage that the quantity demanded changes more than the percentage that price changes, then the elasticity coefficient is greater than one and demand is considered **elastic.** If, on the other hand, the percentage that the quantity demanded changes is less than the percentage that price changes, the elasticity coefficient is less than one and demand is described as **inelastic.**

$$Ed > 1.0 -- \text{ELASTIC}$$
$$Ed < 1.0 -- \text{INELASTIC}$$

Elasticity
The measure of the relative responsiveness of one variable to a change in another variable.

Price Elasticity of Demand
A measurement of how responsive the quantity demanded is when the price of the good or service changes.

Elastic
A situation in which there is a relatively large change in a variable in response to a change in another variable.

Inelastic
A situation in which there is a relatively small change in a variable in response to a change in another variable.

CHAPTER 6 • ELASTICITY   89

Core-Info

1. The term elasticity means responsiveness: how much one variable responds when something else changes.
2. Price elasticity is a measure of how much the quantity demanded responds to a change in its price.

FIGURE 6.1

	Demand Schedule for White Bread	
	Price	Quantity
Point A	$1.00	500 loaves per week
Point B	$1.10	100 loaves per week

FIGURE 6.2

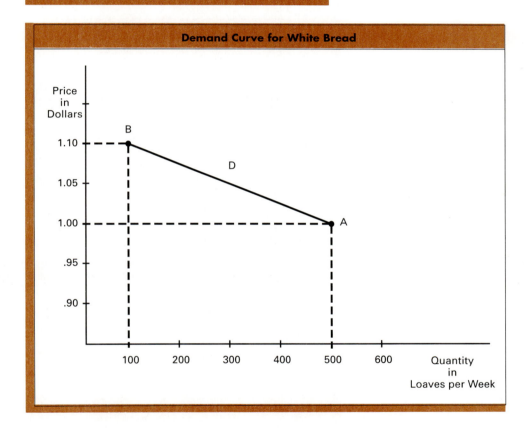

Consider this example of a product that would probably respond greatly to a change in its price: generic white bread. You might expect that sales of ordinary white bread would be greatly affected by the price. After all, there are many readily available, acceptable substitutes for plain white bread: brand name breads, whole wheat, rye, and pumpernickel bread, potatoes, rice, orzo, pancakes, waffles, and muffins. If a store raises the price of white bread, people will quickly switch to something else or nothing at all. Figure 6.1 gives the demand schedule showing the demand for white bread at two different prices in a particular store.

It is pretty obvious that the quantity demanded declined as the price increased. Before you look at the next figure, draw the demand curve for white bread. When you finish, compare and see how you did.

Relatively easy to draw, wasn't it? Check your work against the demand curve in Figure 6.2. Is your drawing pretty close? The curve is very flat, showing that the quantity changed a lot when the price changed. This is always the case for a product that is elastic.

FIGURE 6.3

Demand Schedule for Cigarettes		
	Price	Quantity
Point A	$2.00	7 packs per week
Point B	$2.50	6 packs per week

FIGURE 6.4

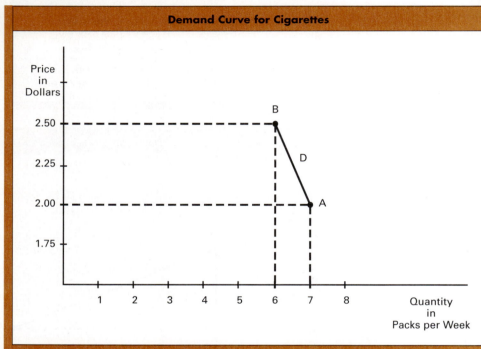

FIGURE 6.5

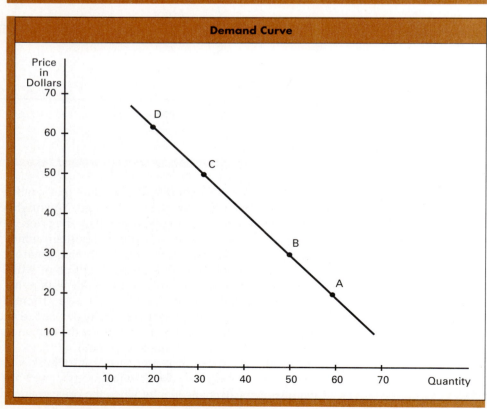

FIGURE 6.6

	Demand Schedule	
	Price	Quantity
Point A	$20	60
Point B	$30	50
Point C	$50	30
Point D	$60	20

Now let's take a product that is not particularly affected by price, say the number of packs of cigarettes an individual smokes each week. For most people who smoke, price is not much of an issue. Smokers may complain about how the price has gone up and threaten to quit if the price ever hits $2 per pack (or $3.50 or $4 or . . .), but they rarely do. This type of response is shown in the demand schedule in Figure 6.3. This time you can see that the quantity fell as the price increased, but not by much. When this demand schedule is converted into a demand curve, Figure 6.4 is the result.

The demand curve in this case is quite steep, showing that the quantity that people buy varies little as the price changes. Other factors influence the decision about whether to buy cigarettes more than price.

The idea of an "elastic" demand curve or an "inelastic" demand curve is misleading. A quick calculation shows that the elasticity coefficient varies along the demand curve. Take a look at Figure 6.5. On this demand curve we have identified four points. Let's calculate the elasticity if we move from Point A to B and from Point C to D.

Our demand schedule for this demand curve is shown in Figure 6.6. As we move from Point A to Point B, price changes from $20 to $30, and quantity demanded changes from 60 to 50. If we plug these data into our elasticity equation, we get the following:

$$E = \frac{\% \Delta Q}{\% \Delta P} \qquad E_{A \text{ to } B} = \frac{17}{50} = 0.34$$

The elasticity of demand as we move from Point A to Point B is 0.34, an inelastic demand curve.

Perform the same calculation for the move from Point C (price equal to $50 and quantity demanded equal to 30) to Point D (with a price of $60 and quantity demanded of 20). This shift produces the following elasticity:

$$E_{C \text{ to } D} = \frac{33}{20} = 1.65$$

Thus, the demand curve between Points C and D has an elasticity coefficient of 1.65; it is elastic. What this means, of course, is that elasticity changes over the range of possible prices, and that if the price is particularly high or low, the elasticity may be different from mid-range values. Technically, therefore, it is incorrect to speak of a product as being "elastic" or "inelastic" or a demand curve as "elastic" or "inelastic." For our purposes, however, we can safely call cigarettes, liquor, and drugs inelastic products with inelastic demand curves. Similarly, we can call bread, automobiles, and furniture elastic products with elastic demand curves.

Factors Affecting Elasticity

What causes people to respond differently to different products? Why do the price elasticities of different products vary? An understanding of what causes this variation can help you to predict how any product will respond as its price changes.

Don't Assume Anything

The headline read: "Cigarette Sales Down in Wake of Tax Increase." Naturally, my interest was piqued. As I read further, I learned how proud the state of Maryland was that the laws of economics had been overthrown. Economists, they claimed, had said that cigarette sales were not affected by the price and that increasing the tax would have no impact. They had shown, they claimed, that economists were wrong.

Here are the facts. The new excise tax had gone into effect and had raised cigarette prices by nearly 20 percent. Cigarette sales had fallen about 5 percent. Frankly, that sounds a lot more like an elasticity issue than an economics error.

Elasticity assumptions have some problems in an open society. The state of Maryland is bordered by the District of Columbia and the Commonwealth of Virginia, and many Maryland residents commute to jobs in those jurisdictions. Rather than buy cigarettes at home, commuters may have stocked up at work and brought them home at the end of the day. (The same phenomenon occurs with alcohol; the District of Columbia tax is lower than the Maryland tax.) In determining elasticity, you must consider not only the product but the context in which it is sold and used. Products which can be shared or purchased in another jurisdiction have apparent elasticities that are very different from those which cannot be shared or purchased elsewhere. Taking these issues into account can help prevent basing programs on erroneous assumptions.

Three basic factors affect price elasticity of demand:

1. The number and availability of substitutes—the more good, readily available substitutes there are, the more responsive a product will be to a change in its price. A small increase will yield a big decrease in the quantity demanded.
2. The proportion of the buyer's budget involved—the larger the price when compared with the buyer's budget (spendable income), the more elastic the product will be. If the price of pencils increases by 50 percent from 10 cents to 15 cents, the number people buy will stay about the same. If the price of Acura four-door sedans increases by the same percentage (from $36,000 to $54,000), their sales would likely plummet.
3. Time—the longer the time period, the more elastic a product is. With time, people can learn about substitutes, change their behavior, or reprogram themselves to take advantage of other opportunities. In the short run, products are often inelastic, only changing the quantity demanded over a longer period of time.

Elasticity and Revenue

Who cares if elasticity coefficients are big or small? They are just numbers, right? They may be just numbers, but they are numbers that convey critical information about profitability. An example should bring this point home.

Let's say that a clothing retailer with two items in its inventory is considering price increases. One product is a man's plain white t-shirt, and the other is a brand name shirt endorsed by Michael Jordan. Which of the two items do you think is likely to have an elastic demand? The plain white t-shirt with lots of good substitutes is likely to be quite elastic, while the Jordan shirt is likely to be inelastic. Let's look at what would happen if the retailer increased the price of both shirts. If the price on both shirts goes up 10 percent, how will the quantity demanded and the revenue to the retailer change?

Figure 6.7 provides the answers. In the case of the (elastic) t-shirt, the quantity demanded falls by 25 percent. In the case of the (inelastic) brand name shirt, the quantity demanded falls by 5 percent. Using our elasticity formula, we find that the elasticity coefficient is 2.5 for the t-shirt and 0.5 for the brand name shirt. Our

FIGURE 6.7

Demand Schedules for Two Products				
	Before Increase		After Increase	
	P1	Qd1	P2	Qd2
T-shirt	$ 5	40/month	$ 5.50	30/month
Brand-name shirt	$50	40/month	$55	38/month

expectations have proven true; the t-shirt is elastic (the quantity changes a lot when the price changes a little) while the brand name shirt is inelastic (the quantity demanded doesn't change much when the price changes).

What would the revenue be for each shirt before and after the price change? The formula for calculating revenue is:

$$\text{Revenue} = \text{Price} \times \text{Quantity} \ (R = P \times Q)$$

The revenue from selling t-shirts at the old price would be $200 ($5 × 40). At the new price, the revenue would be $165 ($5.50 × 30). At the higher price, not only did the quantity demanded fall, but the retailer's *revenue* fell as well. How about the brand name shirt? At the old price, the revenue would have been $2,000 ($50 × 40). At the new price, the revenue would be $2,090. Even though the quantity demanded fell, with the price increase revenues went up. These examples are always true. When a supplier increases the price on an elastic good, revenue will fall. When a supplier increases the price on an inelastic good, revenue will increase. When it is time to raise prices, what should suppliers do? They should estimate the elasticities of demand and strongly consider raising the prices of inelastic goods while *not* raising the prices of elastic goods.

Core-Info

The factors that affect the price elasticity of demand are:
1. The number and availability of substitutes
2. The proportion of consumers' budgets involved
3. Time

If an item is price elastic, raising its price will result in a decrease in revenues. If the item is price inelastic, raising its price will result in an increase in revenues.

OTHER ELASTICITIES

The concept of elasticity is a most useful one. It can be applied in a variety of situations with two related variables by dividing the percentage change in the dependent (affected) variable by the percentage change in the independent (causal) variable. A couple of examples should help to show how very useful the concept can be.

Elasticity of Supply

The law of supply states that the quantity supplied is directly affected by the price of the product: as the price a firm can receive for a product increases, the firm will increase the quantity supplied. The **elasticity of supply** deals with how strong the relationship is. The formula for the elasticity of supply is as follows:

$$E_s = \frac{\% \Delta Q_s}{\% \Delta P}$$

Elasticity of Supply
A measure of a supplier's response to a change in the price he or she can receive by providing the good or service.

The dependent variable is the quantity supplied, and the independent variable is the price the firm can receive. If the elasticity coefficient is large (Es > 1.0), then the product is considered to be elastic, and the firm will vary its quantity supplied quite a bit as the price rises or falls. If, on the other hand, the elasticity coefficient is small (Es < 1.0), then the product is inelastic, and the quantity supplied does not change much as the price changes.

Income Elasticity of Demand

Income elasticity of demand picks up on the idea that people tend to change how much they buy of a good as their income changes, regardless of the price. For goods that are considered "normal," when incomes rise, people buy more of the good. Elasticity measures how responsive they are. The formula for income elasticity of demand is:

$$E_y = \frac{\%\,\Delta\,Q_d}{\%\,\Delta\,Y}$$

The percent change in the quantity demanded is divided by the percent change in income. If $E_y > 1.0$, then the good is elastic, and people consume much more as incomes rise and much less as incomes fall (restaurant meals and fine wines are two examples). If $E_y < 1.0$, the good is inelastic, and people don't change their consumption much as incomes rise or fall (prescription drugs and local newspapers are examples here).

Cross Elasticity of Demand

Demand theory states that many factors affect the level of demand. Prices and incomes are certainly important, but so, too, are the prices of goods that are related to the product in question. For instance, a big increase in the price of compact discs would probably depress the sales of compact disc players, and a change in the price of beef would affect the sales of chicken. Our elasticity formula takes this into account and measures how the quantity demanded of one product is affected by a change in the price of another product. The formula for **cross elasticity of demand** is:

$$E_d = \frac{\%\,\Delta\,Q_{d2}}{\%\,\Delta\,P_1}$$

If the goods are **complements** (they go together like coffee and cream, pretzels and beer, or fish and chips), then an increase in the price of one will cause a decrease in the quantity demanded of the other. If the goods are **substitutes** (like Coke and Pepsi, beef and pork, Manhattan and Van Heusen shirts), then an increase in the price of one will cause an increase in the quantity demanded of the other.

Income Elasticity of Demand
A measure of how responsive consumers of a good are as their income changes.

Cross Elasticity of Demand
A measurement of the amount by which the demand for one good changes in response to a change in the price of another good.

Complements
Pairs of related goods in which an increase in the price of one good results in a decrease in the demand for the other good.

Substitutes
Pairs of related goods in which an increase in the price of one good results in an increase in the demand for the other good.

Core-Info

1. Elasticities can be determined for any two variables in which one is independent and causes an effect on the other variable.
2. Use of elasticity analysis can yield great results for the analysis of public programs as well as in the assessment of proposed business actions.

ELASTICITY AND PUBLIC POLICY

Let's now move out of the personal and product arenas into the sphere of public policy. Here, too, elasticity theory can be very helpful in anticipating the probable outcomes of some government programs. Once we understand how people will be

FIGURE 6.8

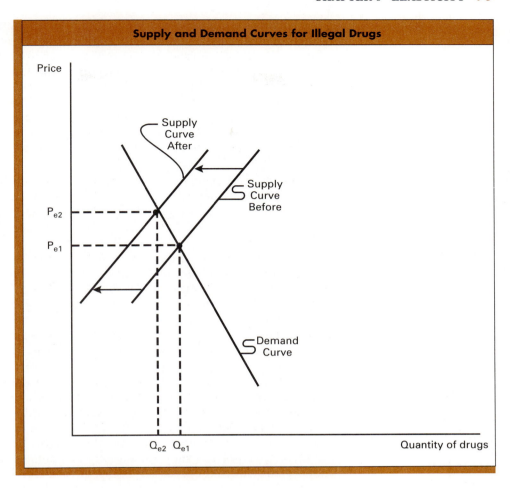

Supply and Demand Curves for Illegal Drugs

affected (how much they will change the amount they will buy or how much they will want of something) as something else changes, we can decide if a program is a good remedy or if a change would be appropriate.

U.S. Drug Policy

With illegal drugs—as with any other good—there are supply and demand curves that show how buyers and sellers express their self-interest. For buyers, an increase in the price of drugs will elicit a decrease in the quantity demanded, but the amount consumed will probably not change by much. Those who use drugs do so for social or other reasons (including dependence) and are not deterred by the price. For sellers, an increase in the street price of drugs will make it worth their while to risk importing more drugs. A decrease in the price of drugs will likely send them into some other shady occupation. The result of these self-interested behaviors, as shown in Figure 6.8, yield an equilibrium (or street) price of P_{e1} and an equilibrium quantity of Q_{e1}.

Now consider the national drug policy. What form has it taken? Other than the occasional "just say no" commercial, the major approach has been to limit the supply of drugs coming into the country. From drug interdiction to paying poppy farmers to grow something else to the occasional military incursion, the goal has been to keep drugs out of the country, to reduce the supply. If the supply of drugs is reduced, the supply curve will be shifted to the left. The shift in the supply curve results in a new equilibrium point with an increased price (much higher at P_{e2}) and a decreased quantity (but only down a little to Q_{e2}).

The amount of drugs consumed has not fallen very much, but the price has risen rather dramatically. With the price higher, drug users (demanders) must generate extra cash from one source or another to pay for their drugs and pass it along to their suppliers. The net beneficiaries of the U.S. drug program, therefore, seem to be the drug dealers.

As an exercise, trace through what the unrestricted importation of drugs would look like. Next, envision what form an effective anti-drug education program could take. Then propose your own policy.

Health Care Policy

Another ongoing public policy debate is over how to best deal with the country's health care crisis. With more people living longer lives and with treatment costs soaring, the cost of medical services has become all but prohibitive for many. Let's apply supply and demand analysis and the idea of the elasticity of supply to this situation.

The demand for medical care has a typical-looking demand curve. At higher prices, the quantity demanded is less than at lower prices. At high prices, people self-medicate (take two aspirin, rest in bed, or eat chicken soup). If the price of doctor visits is low, people go see the doctor whenever they "need" to. Headache? See the doctor. Stomach hurt? See the doctor. Child has a fever? You know what to do. On the other hand, the supply curve for medical care states that as the price people are willing to pay for medical care rises, more medical services will be made available. Doctors can be coaxed off the golf courses on Wednesdays. Hospitals will convert unused rooms to patient care. Retired nurses will return to serve clients. The problem with supply, however, is that there are fairly severe limits on how much and how quickly supply can change in response to major price increases. It takes four years to create a new nurse. It takes ten years to make another doctor. Hospitals require seven years to build. The quantity supplied is really quite inelastic. That being the case, the supply and demand curves are going to look like those shown in Figure 6.9, with an equilibrium price of Pe1 and an equilibrium quantity of medical care used of Qe1.

So far, so good. Now let's introduce a medical care program that permits people who were not previously served (probably lower income families) to have access to medical services. This program increases the demand for medical care. The increase in demand would show up as a new demand curve to the right of the old demand curve. This has been added in Figure 6.9 and appears as the "Demand After Curve," referring to the introduction of the new program. The horizontal movement of the curve (an increase in the quantity demanded at each price) shows how many new people have been added to those who were previously in the health care market. The intersection of new demand curve and the old supply curve indicate a new equilibrium of Pe2 and Qe2. *Both* the number receiving services and the price have risen.

Let's review the effects of the new program. The old demand curve shows those who were in the market before the program. The new demand curve shows the total number in the market after the program (those who would have purchased medical care before and the lower income families who can now receive care). The price that all pay is now higher, but the cost to those who participate in the medical care program is borne by the government (the taxpayers). Facing a higher price, how are the original demanders likely to react? They will reduce the amount of medical care they purchase. As the price increases, the quantity they demand will decrease along their original demand curve. Therefore, the group which used to purchase medical care (middle and upper income families) will buy less medical care at a higher price. Of this

Figure 6.9

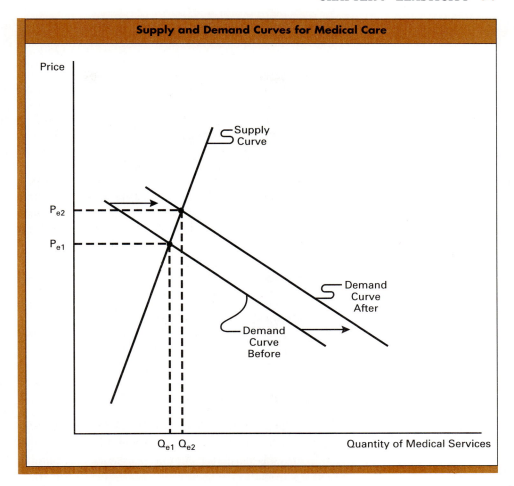

group, upper income families can continue to afford medical care. The lower income groups, with their costs covered by the medical assistance program, will now be served. The middle income group, however, will feel the squeeze. This group will pay higher prices, receive less medical services, and pay the taxes required to support the program.

Is there another way this problem could be addressed? Work on this issue through the supply and demand curve approach. Consider how supply and demand can be increased or decreased, and think about the issue of elasticities. Then propose a method to make your preferred adjustments happen.

USING THIS TOOL

The use of supply and demand analysis in combination with the evaluation of elasticities provides a powerful tool for doing very practical economic analysis. You can predict both individual and group behaviors and can use your new knowledge to anticipate potential difficulties and to propose practical solutions. Use it from time to time. Properly applied, this new knowledge can provide insights and the pleasure of discovery, and I'll bet you never thought that was possible with economics!

SUMMARY

- Elasticity is the measure of the responsiveness of one variable to another variable.

- The formula for price elasticity of demand is

$$Pe = \frac{\% \Delta Qd}{\% \Delta P}$$

- Elastic demand curves tend to be flat while inelastic demand curves tend to be steep.
- The three factors that affect price elasticity of demand are the number and availability of substitutes, the proportion of a buyer's budget involved, and time.
- If a product is price inelastic, raising its price will result in an increase in revenues even though sales will fall.
- Application of price elasticity concepts to proposed government programs can help to anticipate their final impact and effectiveness.
- Elasticity can be applied to other areas such as how supply responds to an increase in price or how people's demands change as their incomes change.

KEY TERMS

Complements
Cross elasticity of demand
Elastic
Elasticity

Elasticity of demand
Elasticity of supply
Income elasticity of demand

Inelastic
Price elasticity of demand
Substitutes

REVIEW QUESTIONS

1. What does the term "elasticity" mean and why is it important?
2. What is the difference between elastic and inelastic?
3. Identify the three factors that determine price elasticity of demand and state how each affects it.
4. Explain how revenues are affected by elastic and inelastic demand.
5. Why do different goods have differing elasticities of supply?
6. How does the concept of income elasticity apply to the demand for a product?
7. Using cross elasticity of demand, explain the terms "complement" and "substitute."

PROBLEM-SOLVING PRACTICE

✷ 1. Mystic Pizza increased the price of its king size pizza from $10 to $11, and the following change in quantity demanded took place: the quantity demanded dropped from 100 pizzas a week to 80 pizzas a week.
    (a) Calculate the elasticity of demand.
    (b) How would the demand elasticity be characterized for Mystic Pizza's king size pizza?
    (c) Suppose the decrease in quantity demanded had only been from 100 to 95. Calculate the elasticity of demand.
    (d) How would you characterize the elasticity of demand in this second situation?

✷ 2. The price of oil decreases from $15 per barrel to $13.50 per barrel. The quantity demanded of oil increases from 100 million barrels to 102 million barrels.
    (a) Calculate the total revenues for it at $15 per barrel.
    (b) Calculate the total revenues at $13.50 per barrel.
    (c) Calculate the elasticity of demand for oil.

(d) Is the demand for oil in the price range elastic or inelastic?

(e) Why do you think the elasticity of demand is what you found it to be in part a?

3. When the average income of customers from the Neptune automobiles went from $30,000 to $33,000 per year, the increase in the quantity demanded in a particular metropolitan market went from 2,000 Neptunes sold to 2,400 Neptunes sold. Calculate the income elasticity of the demand for Neptunes, and characterize it as elastic or inelastic.

CHAPTER 7

Understanding Costs

CHAPTER OUTLINE

A. Scarcity and Costs
B. The Idea of Cost
C. Explicit Costs
D. Implicit Costs
E. Total Cost
F. Measuring Profit
   1. Accounting Profit
   2. Economic Profit
G. Sunk Cost
H. Marginal Cost
I. Costs—a Not-So-Final Look

The purpose of this chapter is to provide a second examination of the nature of costs in economics and, in particular, to help differentiate between costs in a business sense and costs as understood in economics.

AFTER COMPLETING THIS CHAPTER, YOU WILL BE ABLE TO:

1. Apply the concepts of explicit and implicit cost to the decisions made by individuals and businesses.
2. Explain the factors that make accounting profit an ineffective measure of business profitability.
3. Apply the concept of sunk cost to business decisions.
4. Demonstrate the applicability of the concept of marginal cost.

Scarcity and Costs

Scarcity is an economic way of life. That should come as no great surprise to the average college student who is trying to juggle shortages of time, money, and energy. If you want to have more time for studying, you will have less time for socializing. If you want to spend more money on compact discs, you will have less money for going to the movies. Getting more of something means that you must give up something else.

What is true of college life is true of the entire world. If there were no shortages, there would be no need for economics, for economics is the science of how we allocate our scarce resources to competing and unlimited wants. Things are in short supply and many people want them. If they really want something, they must be willing to give something up in order to get it. Everything costs something.

Somehow, people inherently know about costs and the importance of costs. Most people like to consider themselves as being fairly cost conscious, and they think they act pretty rationally where costs are concerned.

If that is so, why, given their cost-conscious nature, don't people car-pool to their jobs or schools? Statistically, very few do even though they know it would save money. It "costs" less to car-pool, but they don't do it. Are people irrational? Do they like to waste money? Of course not.

People who don't car-pool can cite a long list of reasons why not: the difficulty in locating a carpool, the inconvenience, the extra time required, the hassle of riding with a smoker or a driver who likes country music. Any or all of these reasons keeps people from car-pooling and saving money. People obviously feel that they would have to give up something to car-pool, that carpooling would cost them something. While they might save money, they would face other real costs to carpool (the time required to find one, the hassle, the noxious smoke, or the bothersome music). These nondollar costs obviously outweigh the monetary benefit of carpooling for many people. An economist would say that given their assessment of the costs, they are eminently rational in that decision.

THE IDEA OF COST

The problem that most college students have with the economic definition of cost is that they understand the business definition so well. With money tight and expenses high, students tend to have to be very "cost" conscious and to watch every penny carefully. Note that the word "cost" in the last sentence was in quotation marks, for it is that definition of the term that causes problems in the study of economics.

The term *cost* is not limited to the issue of dollars. In fact, to most economists, dollars are not the central issue. Economists like their salaries and aren't going to give them up, but dollars themselves aren't very important. In fact, a $20 bill is all but useless. You can use it as a book marker or fold it into a wedge to keep a dorm window open, but by itself it is not worth much. When that money is converted into something useful, however, like a book, shirt, or 15 gallons of gasoline, then you've got something. Dollars are useful because of the resources they can command. This being the case, *resources* are the issue of concern in economics.

Cost
Anything that is given up to obtain something else; a result of scarcity.

Costs are really a resource concept. Any time you give up or use resources (or the ability to access them), you have a cost. **Costs** are whatever you have to give up to get something else. If you go to a movie and spend $15 and three hours, your costs are $15 and three hours, because that is what you spent. As you can see, costs come in two varieties, and it is to these two basic types of costs that we now turn.

EXPLICIT COSTS

Explicit Costs
The actual dollar or accounting cost associated with obtaining something.

The first kind of costs that exist in economics are known as **explicit costs.** They are called explicit because they are visible. Explicit costs are the dollars that are spent for something. If you go the movie, your explicit cost is $15. Because they are measured in actual, out-of-pocket dollars, explicit costs are also known as **accounting costs.** Explicit costs are fairly easy to determine: all you have to do is add up the dollars spent for something.

Accounting Costs
Costs as determined by an accountant—actual money costs, or explicit costs.

IMPLICIT COSTS

Implicit Costs
The opportunity cost of resources that is used in obtaining something and for which there is no explicit payment.

Implicit costs are something else. **Implicit costs** are the resources that are used to do something but for which explicit payment is not made. Implicit costs are the nondollar costs associated with any activity. Economists are concerned with implicit costs precisely because they have to do with the resources that are used to do something and because economics has to do with how resources are used. Any time resources are used, whether they are paid for or not, a cost is involved.

Explicit costs are easy to measure—dollars are involved. How do you calculate implicit costs where there are no dollars to use as a measure of value? The solution is to estimate. Economists measure implicit costs by estimating their value or worth on the free market. What would they have cost if people had to pay for them? Let's say a bicycle shop owner has a friend who loves bikes and drops in every Saturday to be an unpaid salesperson. The value of that person's time must be estimated. If the shop owner would ordinarily pay a salesperson $7 per hour and the friend works for five hours, the implicit costs for Saturday labor are $35. (The friend, on the other hand, has to measure the cost of giving up a Saturday to work in the bike shop.)

What are some other examples of implicit costs? Free trial samples of products from vendors or suppliers that are given to convince people to use the products. Free legal advice from a sister-in-law who happens to be a tax attorney. A personal car used in a business without taking a mileage allowance. Free advertising in a local newspaper. A rent-free period offered by a landlord in exchange for signing a long-term lease for business space. A mother who tends the cash register or a brother who helps to maintain the business. Finally, the income business owners could have earned as an employee elsewhere is an implicit cost of running their own company; it is an opportunity cost. Any time anything is used in a business but is not paid explicitly for, an implicit cost has been incurred.

The problem with implicit costs is that they are often not visible to an outsider. Whereas any reasonably competent accountant can come into a business and identify its dollar costs (and revenues), it is exceedingly difficult for that accountant to pinpoint nondollar costs. This accountant can ask questions (Did anybody work and not get paid? Did a supplier provide any sample products to try?), but he or she cannot identify implicit costs. Only business owner/managers will know their implicit costs. Only they know what free resources were received by the business. It is their task to estimate the value of these resources so they can be aware of all costs involved in producing the good or service.

TOTAL COST

Total Cost
The sum of all resources used whether or not there is a direct money cost involved. The total of both explicit and implicit costs.

As you would assume by its name, **total cost** includes all costs involved in any action. Total cost is the sum of all explicit and implicit costs. This can be represented in equation form as:

$$TC = EC + IC$$

where: TC is total cost
EC is explicit cost
IC is implicit cost

Air Bags at What Cost?

Air bags in automobiles are touted as a great safety innovation. Air bags, which inflate in a fraction of a second when an accident occurs, are designed to protect the driver and passenger from serious injury in head-on collisions. Federal government regulations have effectively mandated that air bags must be installed in all passenger vehicles. The question of the hour is: are they worth it?

Many people would argue that a life is of infinite value and that we should spend whatever it takes to protect people when a possible solution exists. Mere dollars are not important, it is said, when lives are at stake. Air bags provide an example to consider.

The U.S. Department of Transportation released a study that states that air bags saved 911 lives between 1987 and 1994. Let's apply critical thinking to this situation.

First, treat the number 911 with suspicion. Do you recognize the number? Conveniently, it is the same number to call in emergencies. Suspicious minds might wonder about the coincidence.

Second, even if air bags did save 911 lives, how much did their installation cost? The Department of Transportation estimates that about 21 million cars had air bags. The dollar cost of installing air bags is coming down, but from 1987 to 1994 air bags cost about $500 per vehicle. Multiply $500 by 21 million cars, and you will find that it cost $10.5 billion to save 911 lives. That's $11,525,795 per life saved.

If it were only money and we had tons of it, cost wouldn't matter. But we don't, so it does. The United States lost 950,895 men and women to cardiovascular diseases and 496,152 to cancer in 1989. Nearly 1.5 million lives were lost to these two killers alone in 1989. Here is some food for thought: could that $10.5 billion spent on air bags have saved more lives if it had been spent on medical research and treatment? The cost of anything is what you have to give up to get it. By spending money on air bags, Americans have less to spend on other things. We need to choose carefully to make sure we get the greatest return for our investment.

Here are a few more notes on air bags. Recent reports indicate that when air bags inflate they can actually kill children in front seats or toddlers in rear-facing infant seats. And insurance company research is finding that, while air bags may save lives, they are leaving survivors with costly long-term injuries. Insurance company data also show that it costs $2,000 to $3,000 to replace the air bags after they inflate, so the bags often aren't replaced or the car is junked after a crash. Finally, a recent study has found that drivers in cars with air bags take more risks and drive more dangerously than those without the bags.

Are air bags a good investment? It is certainly a good question to debate, for the total cost is very high.

Total cost is the cost that is important to an economist. Total cost includes the value of all resources used in accomplishing a task; thus, it reflects the true cost of something to society. Total cost is the cost that should be important to business owners and managers because it reflects what it really took to do the job.

Core-Info

1. Costs are the result of scarcity—a fact of economic life.
2. The cost of anything is whatever you have to give up to obtain it.
3. Explicit costs are the actual money costs that are involved in getting the good.
4. Implicit costs are the nonmonetary costs that are involved in getting the good.
5. The total cost of anything is the sum of the monetary and nonmonetary costs that are involved in getting a good or service.

For an example of the importance of total cost (and implicit cost), let's return to the bicycle shop. The shop has been running fairly successfully for some time out of a colleague's spare garage at no dollar cost to the shop owner. In the process the shop owner has accumulated a number of friends who enjoy cycling. These friends like to hang out at the shop and, while there, work alongside the owner for the fun of it. One enthusiast likes to help sell the bikes. Another friend enjoys maintaining and repairing bikes. A third friend handles the bookkeeping tasks. None of these friends is paid for helping out, so the dollar cost (explicit cost) for their work is zero, even though the bike shop wouldn't stay open long without their labor. The same principle applies to the donated garage: no dollar cost, but the bicycle business could not exist without the space. Resources are used but not paid for.

If a business can get some free help or rent-free space, is that bad? Certainly not. As a business person, you want to take advantage of any and all free resources that you can. Just remember that you are not really paying the full cost of doing the job. A look at the issue of profit may help to drive the point home.

MEASURING PROFIT

Let's take the bike shop example one step farther. If it has been successful, the proprietor is likely to have made some profits as well as friends. With a successful operation going and a high level of additional demand for services, what is the shop owner likely to want to do? He may decide to open another shop. After all, if his first shop is so successful, why not open a second?

When the business owner opens another shop, he doesn't have a friend to let him use a spare garage, so he has to pay rent to a landlord. The friend who likes to sell bikes continues to work at no salary at the first shop, but the salesperson at the new shop needs to earn a living and is paid. The bike mechanic also stays at the first shop, and a new mechanic is hired to work at the new location. Are you beginning to see a pattern? At the first shop, the owner depends on a lot of free resources. He pays for some things (explicit costs) but uses quite a number of free resources (implicit costs) in addition. At the new shop, those implicit costs have become explicit costs; he must pay for them. The second shop is less successful, and the owner starts to lose money.

You can probably guess from this example that the now disillusioned businessperson made a mistake somewhere. The shop owner did not consider the total cost of doing business, but focused on dollars only. Big mistake.

Accounting Profit

Because there are two ways of measuring cost, you might guess that there are two ways of measuring profit. You would be right. The first way that profits are determined is the standard, business way. Because they are calculated following traditional business practice, they are called **accounting profits.** To calculate accounting profits, subtract the dollar costs (explicit costs) from the dollar revenue from selling the product to come up with the dollar profit. The equation for accounting profits is:

ACCOUNTING PROFIT = TR − EC

where: TR is total revenue
EC is explicit (or dollar) costs

Because they are based totally on dollars, accounting profits are relatively easy to calculate, and they are exceedingly important. These are the profits on which businesses pay their taxes. These are the profits business owners brag about at board meetings. These are also the profits by which bosses monitor the performance of their employees.

Economic profit

However, accounting profits are nowhere near as important as the other type of profits. These profits are thought by economists to be so critically important, so absolutely essential, so totally bottom-line that we named them after ourselves. These

Accounting Profit
Money profits calculated by subtracting explicit costs from total revenue.

FIGURE 7.1
While we hear about business making gigantic profits, accounting profits really are a small percentage of our Gross Domestic Product.

After Tax Profits As A Percent of G.D.P.—1980–1994	
Year	Profit Percent
1980	5.76
1984	3.87
1985	3.19
1986	2.60
1987	3.55
1988	4.31
1989	3.85
1990	4.09
1991	4.09
1992	4.25
1993	4.56
1994	4.78

Economic Profit
The amount by which total revenues exceed the total cost (explicit plus implicit costs) of producing something.

profits are called **economic profits.** The equation for determining economic profits is slightly different from that for accounting profits:

$$\text{ECONOMIC PROFIT} = TR - TC$$

where: TR is total revenue
TC is total costs

Economic profit is also expressed as:

$$\text{ECONOMIC PROFIT} = TR - (EC + IC)$$

Economic profit can be expressed this way because total cost is the sum of explicit costs plus implicit costs.

The calculation of accounting profit was relatively easy: just subtract dollars out from dollars in. What of economic profit? In this case, you don't have easily identifiable dollar costs to measure against dollar income. Costs now must include nondollar items such as those things received for free that were used in the production process, and so, as with implicit costs, you must develop an estimate of economic profit. Identify the total amount of revenues received, subtract all dollar costs that were incurred (now you've got accounting profit), and subtract from that your estimate of the value of the resources that were used but not paid for (implicit costs). The result is economic profit.

When you compare the two profit equations, you will note that total revenue appears in both the economic profit and the accounting profit equations. From total revenue, you subtract the costs that are associated with each type of profit. In the case of accounting profit, we subtract explicit costs. In the case of economic profit, we subtract the sum of explicit cost and implicit cost, a larger number. Thus, economic profits are always smaller than accounting profits.

The mistake the bicycle shop owner made was to consider only explicit costs and accounting profits. He was making a dollar profit only because he was not paying for all of the resources that he was using. Once he had to pay the total cost of selling and repairing bikes, he started to lose money. He would have known this in advance if he had paid attention to his implicit costs and had estimated his economic profit.

Core-Info

Profit is a residual that is measured by subtracting the cost of production from the revenue received from sales. There are two measures of profit:

1. Accounting profit, which is calculated by subtracting monetary or explicit costs from revenues
2. Economic profit, which is calculated by subtracting total cost from revenues

SUNK COST

Another type of cost is also vitally important to understand. If you can understand the nature of this one, you will be in a much better position for moving forward rather than becoming mired in the past. Once you have a solid understanding of this cost, you will know why to ignore them whenever you find them. The name for this cost is sunk cost.

Have you ever felt guilty? Silly question, right? Everybody feels guilty sometimes. Some people might feel so accomplished at it that they could major in guilt and minor in business administration or medical technology or whatever their college records say. But what are guilt feelings?

Guilt feelings are negative emotions that people experience today because of something they did yesterday. Guilt feelings exist in the present because of the past. The past cannot be changed. People can change their perspective about the past and either rationalize or better understand it, but they can't change the past no matter how strong their guilt feelings are. Therefore guilt is of no use. Worse yet, feeling too guilty can add extra costs to today and make it impossible to move on in life. Therefore, people must learn to not let guilt feelings control them today and ruin the future. People can learn from guilt feelings, however. Who among us has not said, "Boy was *I* stupid; I'll never do *that* again!" If we don't do it again, guilt helps us to improve our lives. What is true of guilt feelings is also true of sunk costs.

Sunk costs are costs that were previously incurred. Sunk costs are money or expenses spent yesterday. Once the money is gone and cannot be recalled, it becomes a sunk cost. To pay too much attention to sunk costs and not enough to the costs over which a business has some control will just exacerbate its problems.

Let's return to the bicycle shop for a look at the problems associated with sunk costs. The bike shop owner decided to expand the operation and purchased a piece of equipment for $10,000 that would bend tubing for bicycle frames. The day after the purchase, a manufacturer announced that it had developed a new and inexpensive method for constructing built-up carbon fiber frames for bicycles. Naturally, the shop owner would be concerned about the purchase and, most likely, would try to resell it to the supplier. Given the fact that the machine was now used and that there was a new process that made the machine obsolete, the supplier who sold it originally would likely offer the bicycle shop owner only a fraction, say $5,000 at most, for the equipment. What decision should the bike shop owner make? If he sells the machine back to the vendor, he "loses" $5,000. A $5,000 loss is not inconsequential, so reluctantly, the owner might well decide to keep the equipment and continue to make steel frames now less in demand. Or, even worse, he might decide that if people don't want the steel frames and since he can't afford to absorb the loss of selling the machine back to the dealer, he had better just hold on to it in his shop.

The latter choice would be a mistake. Once the piece of equipment was purchased and paid for, the cost became a sunk cost. The cash that was spent on the equipment was, in a sense, converted into a piece of equipment. The issue now is what is the best way to use the resource (the piece of capital). If the shop owner can sell it, that's great. If he can use it for something else, fine. Whatever he can do to maximize his return from the machine is what he should do *without regard to the original cost*. Use it, sell it, put it on display as a museum piece and charge admission—whatever yields a return. The shop owner also can learn from this situation. How did he make the decision that turned out to be wrong? What information did he not get or did he ignore that would help him to make a better decision next time? If he can learn from his sunk costs, he can turn the mistake into something positive for the future. If he allows himself to be afraid of the loss and to be forced into inaction, he will only compound his error and increase his overall losses.

Sunk Cost
Any cost that has been previously incurred and which is irretrievable.

Buy More Than You Need and Throw the Extra Away

Sometimes it makes sense from a self-interested point of view to be wasteful, to buy extra of something and throw out what you never wanted or needed in the first place. Marginal analysis helps to explain why this is the case.

One of my volunteer activities is to help work in a food bank. Each year we thank those who have served in the food bank, and one of my tasks was to get some small award that we could give in appreciation. After looking around, I found just the perfect memento: mugs with the food bank's logo on them. The price structure for the mugs was as follows:

Quantity	Price
1 – 24	$2.49 each
24 – 48	1.99 each
49 +	1.79 each

I needed 22 mugs to give to workers. According to the price schedule I would have to pay $54.78. But if I bought 25, my cost would be $49.75. I can get three extra mugs and save nearly $5. The marginal cost of these last few mugs is negative. Sounds like a winner.

Let's look at the marginal cost of the mugs. For each of the first 24 mugs, the cost is $2.49 each. If I buy between 25 and 48, the cost falls to $1.99 each. The cost table that shows this as follows:

Number Purchased	Cost Each	Total Cost	Marginal Cost
1	$2.49	$ 2.49	$2.49
10	2.49	24.90	2.49
20	2.49	49.80	2.49
24	2.49	59.76	2.49
25	1.99	49.75	–10.01

By buying more mugs than I need, I can save some money. It is definitely in my best interest to buy the extra mugs and use them however I can.

Why would the company that sells the mugs price something as weirdly as this? It has to do with the way mugs are packaged. Mugs come packed 24 to the box. By selling mugs in increments of 24, the business can use full boxes and does not have to incur the additional expense of extra handling and storage that would be involved in dealing with odd lots. It is in its self-interest to price the mugs this way just as it is in my self-interest to buy more than I need. Marginal analysis has been used by both the supplier and the demander, and both are better off because of it.

Core-Info

1. A sunk cost is any cost already incurred and irretrievable. Ignore these costs in current decision making.
2. Marginal analysis examines the extra cost or revenue that results from a change.

MARGINAL COST

Marginal Cost
The extra cost involved in producing or acquiring one more unit of output.

Marginal Benefit
The additional benefit received by obtaining one more unit of a good.

Marginal Revenue
The additional revenue that will be received by selling one more unit of a good.

Marginal Analysis
The idea that people compare the added cost incurred in obtaining something with the added benefit to be received from consuming the good.

The final cost we are going to deal with is marginal cost. **Marginal cost** is the added or extra cost that is involved with any action or decision. Economists think that people engage in **marginal analysis,** that they compare the added, or marginal, costs of doing something with the added benefits, or **marginal benefit,** to be received. If the bicycle shop manager is trying to decide whether or not to make another frame, he compares the extra cost of making the additional frame (marginal cost) with the extra revenue (**marginal revenue**) that he will receive when he sells it. Similarly, if someone is trying to decide whether or not to order another pizza, they compare the extra cost of purchasing the additional pizza (not the total cost of all the pizzas) with the extra (marginal) benefit to be received by getting one more pizza. This type of marginal analysis is done all the time by everybody and underlies most contemporary economic theory.

COSTS—A NOT-SO-FINAL LOOK

Costs, which are central to economics, have taken just a few pages to explain, yet they are key to all the chapters to follow. You should now understand explicit costs and implicit costs and see how, together, they make up the total cost of doing something. These two different definitions of cost lead to two very different views of the concept of profit, accounting profit and economic profit. Focusing only on the number of dollars a business earns can lead to some very bad decisions. Sunk costs cannot be recovered, and if business people who pay too much attention to them can be diverted from optimal decisions. Other key concepts are marginal cost and marginal analysis, which are critical to making economic decisions.

Have you noted the word that was repeated in the previous paragraph (in addition to "cost")? Decisions. Economics is all about making good, effective decisions, about considering all the costs, and about correctly determining which costs are relevant (those you can do something about) and which are irrelevant (those over which you have no control).

SUMMARY

- The term *cost* means whatever has to be given up to get something. It is usually much more than the monetary cost.
- Explicit costs are the actual monetary costs involved in obtaining something. Implicit costs are the nonmonetary costs involved, free goods and services and things lost or done without. Implicit costs often have to be estimated because they do not involve money directly.
- The two measures of profit are accounting profit, determined by subtracting monetary costs from revenues, and economic profit, determined by subtracting total costs from revenues.
- Sunk costs are costs which were incurred in the past and cannot be retrieved.
- Marginal cost is the extra cost involved in obtaining one more unit of a good or service.

KEY TERMS

Accounting costs	Explicit cost	Marginal cost
Accounting profit	Implicit costs	Marginal revenue
Cost	Marginal analysis	Sunk cost
Economic profit	Marginal benefit	Total cost

REVIEW QUESTIONS

1. What is the definition of the term "cost"?
2. What are the two basic types of cost and how do they differ?
3. How is total cost calculated?
4. What does the term "accounting profit" mean and how is it calculated?
5. What does the term "economic profit" mean, how is it calculated, and why is it important?
6. Why should sunk costs not affect your decisions today?
7. Why should you consider marginal cost and marginal benefit when making decisions?

PROBLEM-SOLVING PRACTICE

1. Determine the explicit and implicit costs of attending college this year.
2. Identify the explicit and implicit costs of each of the following:
    (a) A Domino's pizza delivered to your home
    (b) A pizza you make for yourself in your own home
    (c) Ordering and watching a video on cable pay per view
    (d) Using a VCR to record your favorite TV show
    (e) Attending the next Super Bowl Game
    (f) Flying round-trip to Paris for your next holiday

*3. You decide to open a hot dog stand across from the college campus, which will be open 50 weeks of the year. The initial cost of the land and the construction of the stand was $10,000. You lease a grill for $1,000 a year, and hire a helper for $100 a week. On the average you buy 20 pounds of hot dogs per week at $2 a pound. The stand sells on the average 100 hot dogs a week at a price of $2 per hot dog.

(a) Calculate your profits for one year of operation.

(b) After two years of operation, the college offers you a rent-free location on campus, but you are reluctant because you spent $10,000 for the existing stand. The university offers to buy it from you for $3,000. What should you do based on the analysis of costs presented in this chapter?

(c) Your helper wants a raise to $120 a week. You would like to give her the raise. Analyze your decision based on the chapter.

PART 3
ECONOMIC STRUCTURES

Chapter 8: The Consumer

Chapter 9: Labor, Unions and the Distribution of Income

Chapter 10: The Firm and Market Structures

Chapter 11: Competition and Monopoly

Chapter 12: Imperfect Competition

Chapter 13: Rent, Interest, and Profit

CHAPTER 8

The Consumer

CHAPTER OUTLINE

A. The Role of the Consumer
B. Assumptions about Consumer Behavior
   1. Consumers Are Rational
   2. Consumers Desire Many Goods
   3. Consumers Have to Pay for Goods
   4. Consumers Have Limited Income
C. Utility: How Consumers Decide
   1. Utility Defined
   2. Total *vs.* Marginal Utility
   3. Diminishing Marginal Utility
D. Costs and Utility: Getting the Most for Your Money
E. Once the Consumer Has Voted

The purpose of this chapter is to introduce the role of consumers in a capitalistic economy and to describe how and why consumers behave the way they do.

AFTER COMPLETING THIS CHAPTER, YOU WILL BE ABLE TO:

1. Describe the dominant role of consumers in a capitalistic economy.
2. Explain the impact of the four assumptions made about the way consumers behave.
3. Apply the concept of diminishing marginal utility to consumer behavior.
4. Demonstrate the relationship between marginal cost and marginal utility in consumer decision making.

The Role of the Consumer

In music it is said that "love makes the world go 'round." Maybe so, but in economics it is consumers who make things happen.

Consumers *are the engine that drives the economy. From the four economic questions discussed in Chapter 1, we learned that the "What?" question of economics is determined by consumers. Consumers, either directly or indirectly, determine everything that the economy will produce. Directly, consumers decide how many of each of the final goods and services will be produced by voting with their dollars. By purchasing one good and not another, consumers send signals to manufacturers and other suppliers about what should—and what need not—be produced. Through these direct statements, consumers indirectly determine the capital goods and intermediate goods (supplies and inputs) that must be produced to meet the demand for final goods and services. Thus, everything that is produced in the economy is produced because consumers want it.*

With consumers of ultimate importance to the economy, it is essential to understand how they operate and what motivates them. Managers need to know consumers so they can anticipate what consumer demands will be and react to these demands in order to make a profit. At the national level, lawmakers and administrators need to understand how consumers are likely to act so they can set appropriate national policies and help the economy to function smoothly. Therefore, we will look at consumers in some depth. We will consider what we believe to be true of all consumers (assumptions about them) and then examine how consumers make specific purchasing decisions.

ASSUMPTIONS ABOUT CONSUMER BEHAVIOR

You have to be careful when you make assumptions. If people assume too much or too early, they blind themselves to the possibilities that the world may be different than they think. If they make too few assumptions, they spend their lives rethinking every aspect of every action that they might take.

In truth, people make assumptions all the time, and these assumptions help them to live more efficiently. People assume that the buildings they work or attend classes in have been constructed according to the relevant safety codes. They assume the television set will not give them an electric shock when they turn it on. They assume that by-and-large traffic will stop at red lights. They assume all of this even though they know that buildings *do* collapse, that people *do* die of accidental electrocution, and that 1,118 people were killed by drivers who ran stop signs in 1994. They make all these assumptions because to do otherwise would present an unacceptable burden (only sit near escape doors, wear insulated gloves at all times, stop at green lights and check). Making assumptions is quite acceptable, but you need to be certain that your assumptions are correct and once in a while recheck them to be certain that they still hold true.

> **Consumer**
> An individual who purchases and uses a final good or service in the economy.

> **Core-Info**
> The consumer is the driving force in a capitalistic economy. The private sector gets its signals from consumer decisions. Consumers make the "What?" decision of economics.

Economists make four basic assumptions about how consumers operate. These assumptions describe what motivates consumers and underlies their

"Buy." Buy what? "Buy anything."

That quotation is attributed to President Dwight David Eisenhower when the United States was in the middle of a recession. President Eisenhower knew that consumer demand was a prime motivating factor in getting the economy going, and it was his job, he felt, to get Americans buying again. That strategy works, but it may have some long-term consequences depending on how Americans go about making their purchases.

As we all know, one way people get what they want when they want it is to use plastic, those wondrous credit cards that let people buy those oh-so-necessary things. How many Americans put their plastic to use can be seen in the table below.

Year	Credit Outstanding (in billions)	Ratio to Income
1970	$133.8	18.5%
1975	$207.5	18.0%
1980	$355.4	18.2%
1985	$601.6	20.4%
1990	$813.0	19.5%

As can be seen, Americans have accumulated quite a load of debt, an amount equal to about one-fifth of their total income. Getting into debt can be a big spur for the economy. As people go into debt to buy more, businesses produce more and generate more wages, which in turn generates more business. As long as people keep on buying, everything is fine. When they get too much debt to feel comfortable and stop buying, the economy can go into a quick tailspin. This is precisely what has happened a number of times in recent years when a consumer-led boom became a consumer-vacated bust. In addition, at least at the first level, when consumers are paying off their credit cards and other debts, they are paying from today's income for yesterday's party—with interest. The amount available to spend today is reduced because of the equivalent of a financial hangover. Heck of a party, but the cost in the morning is a doozy.

---

decision-making process. As we review the assumptions, check them against how you operate and what motivates you. See if they aren't a pretty close fit to the real world.

Consumers Are Rational

> **Rational**
> The concept that individuals always act in ways that maximize the satisfaction they receive from the things they do.

The first assumption is that consumers are **rational.** By rational economists mean that consumers are trying to do the best they can for themselves as they understand it. Consumers always move toward products and services that give them benefit and always move away from things that cost them. They are trying to maximize their welfare.

This assumption doesn't mean that consumers always decide what is "best" for themselves (i.e., what "experts" would choose) or that consumers don't make mistakes. Consumers do make mistakes, and they don't always choose the way others might think they should. Some people take illegal drugs. Some people go home and drink themselves into oblivion every night. Some people buy fad toys and t-shirts.

Observers would probably agree that people who spend their money on illegal drugs or liquor every night are making irrational decisions. Why would anyone take drugs or get drunk every night? Not rational, right? Economists would respond that those people had weighed the costs and the benefits of drug use and excessive drinking and had selected the option that maximized their welfare as they perceived it. If others think that getting drunk every night or taking illegal drugs is a mistake for those people, the first step is to help them to see the true costs and benefits of what they are doing. Once they realize that alcohol or other drug abuse may cost them their jobs, drive off their families, and shorten their

FIGURE 8.1
Consumer spending varies considerably around the U.S. average of just over $30,000.

Selected Average Annual Expenditures: 1993	
City Area	Amount
San Francisco, CA	$40,969
Washington, DC	40,507
Minneapolis, MN	38,775
New York, NY	35,760
Los Angeles, CA	35,319
U.S. Average	30,692
Cleveland, OH	27,677
St. Louis, MO	27,656
Buffalo, NY	24,297

lives, they may reweigh the costs and benefits and opt for sobriety. Until they reassess the costs and benefits of quitting and decide that the latter outweigh the former, they will continue to drink or use drugs.

People who buy fad products weigh the benefits of spending on those items versus buying a book or a shirt and decide that they prefer to buy a toy. Even consumers purchasing "necessities" such as cars must weigh the benefits of each make and model along with their personal preferences and budget.

Consumers Desire Many Goods

Consumers want a lot of stuff. In the words of *The Hobbit's* Gollum, "We wants!" We wants shirts *and* shoes *and* Chevrolets. We wants Porsches *and* pies *and* pullovers. The whole world tempts consumers and from that world they must make choices every day. Consumers are always weighing one good against another. They compare the benefits that can be gained per dollar of cost, and it is this cost/benefit calculation that is at the heart of their decision-making process.

Consumers Have to Pay for Goods

There's no such thing as a free lunch. If goods were free, there would be no need for economics or economizing (except for the task of making the most of closet space). Goods aren't free, however, so consumers must weigh the costs that they have to pay against the benefits they may receive. Here, again, the consumer may not understand the true or full cost of a good. The costs of excessive alcohol consumption, for instance, may be incurred a number of years in the future, and it may be difficult to accurately understand that toll while under the influence. But consumers do know that everything costs, and it is this cost that they consider in their buying decisions.

Consumers Have Limited Income

This one is easy. Everybody knows that consumers have limited income. People feel it every day. That limitation is behind daily decisions: can you afford another sweater or should you be saving to buy books for next semester's classes? Even Donald Trump has limited income: he can only buy one airline at a time. This limited income forces consumers back to their rational starting point. They have to pay for goods and they want lots of things, so they must make very careful choices and weigh the costs and benefits of every decision. Thus, these four assumptions are played out every day by all consumers as they live their economic lives. This doesn't mean that people are always consciously aware of these factors, just that they live this way.

Core-Info

Economists make four assumptions about consumer behavior:
1. Consumers are rational.
2. Consumers desire many goods.
3. Consumers have to pay for goods.
4. Consumers have limited income.

UTILITY: HOW CONSUMERS DECIDE

When you first encounter the term **utility,** you may decide that economists don't have enough real work to do so they just sit around thinking up weird ways to say things. Not so. What economists have done with the idea of utility is to try to provide some comparative, analytical, *quantitative* way of describing how consumers act.

Let's begin by thinking about some foods you may eat. Can you rank burritos, hamburgers, hot dogs, and pizza? Do you have a preference? Most people do and can come up with a list. Pizza first, then burritos, then hamburgers and hot dogs. Now how about people? Can you measure love? No. Can you rank people? Of course you can. You might list spouse or life partner first, then parents and siblings, then close friends, and so forth. Can you say that you like pizza 2.71 times more than a burrito or that you love your mate exactly 1.96 times more than the second person in your life? Not a chance. What economists try to accomplish is to put numbers to the rankings that they give to the pleasure that the goods give people. Economists put a measure to what people can't measure with numbers but can measure with their hearts. Economists call that utility.

Utility Defined

The definition of the term *utility* is deceptively simple. Utility is a measure of the satisfaction people get from consuming a good. Every good people consume gives some satisfaction. An ice cream cone provides a moment's pleasure and is worth at least a dollar. Cars get people to work, school, entertainment, and church for a number of years and yield a great deal of satisfaction. Tailored suits and name-brand athletic shoes offer some people a lot of satisfaction, while the discount store variety yields somewhat less.

Total *vs.* Marginal Utility

Total utility is the total amount of satisfaction that people get from consuming all units of the good they purchase. **Marginal utility** is the satisfaction that people receive from a single unit of the good, in particular the last unit of the good consumed, or the satisfaction received by consuming one more unit of the good or service. To determine total utility, add up all of the individual marginal utilities or the satisfaction received from each of the units consumed.

Diminishing Marginal Utility

This leads to an important point about utility. If you think about it for a minute, you will realize that not every unit of a good consumed gives the same level of satisfaction. Often, the first unit consumed gives more satisfaction than subsequent units. This idea is known as **diminishing marginal utility.** The theory of diminishing marginal utility states that the more units of a good people consume, the less additional satisfaction each extra unit provides. The example in Figure 8.2 and 8.3 may help explain this theory.

Picture this scene: you're helping a friend move on a hot, hot day in the city. You are *very* thirsty. Your friend offers you one of those trendy carbonated water drinks, and the first bottle provides a lot of thirst-quenching satisfaction. The

---

Utility
The satisfaction received by an individual from consuming a good or service.

Total Utility
The total amount of satisfaction that an individual receives from all the units of a good or service consumed in a given period of time.

Marginal Utility
The additional satisfaction that an individual receives by consuming one more (or the last) unit of a good or service.

Diminishing Marginal Utility
The idea that as individuals consume more units of a good or service, they derive less additional satisfaction from each subsequent unit.

FIGURE 8.2

Utility from Drinking Carbonated Bottled Water		
Number of Bottles	Marginal Utility	Total Utility
0	0	0
1	10	10
2	7	17
3	4	21
4	2	23
5	0	23
6	−12	11

FIGURE 8.3

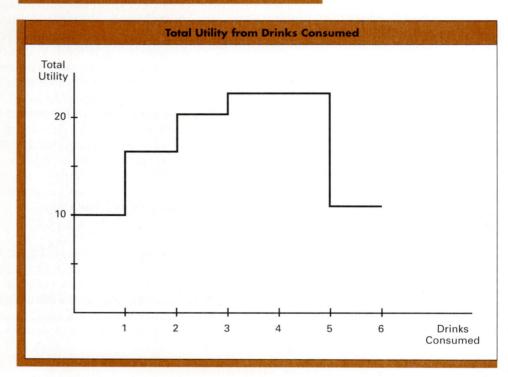

second bottle is still welcome, but it doesn't give quite the same relief as the first bottled water. Same for the third and fourth bottles. Each one gives less additional satisfaction—diminishing marginal utility. When you get to the fifth bottle, the carbonation is starting to build up in your system. The sixth bottle in one afternoon leaves you decidedly uncomfortable and brings negative satisfaction. Figure 8.4 shows this. You can see that as the number of bottled waters increases, the amount of additional satisfaction (the marginal utility) decreases. That is the way you are with bottled water, that is the way some people are with shirts, that is the way customers are when they come into a store. Each visit yields a diminishing level of satisfaction unless the store managers do something to stir their customers' interest and help them to see something new.

COSTS AND UTILITY: GETTING THE MOST FOR YOUR MONEY

Is utility the only factor that is important in the decision to consume a good? Not at all. Utility conveys the benefit that the consumer receives by consuming a good. The other side of this equation is the cost. Consumers weigh the utility they receive against the price they pay. What they try to do is to get as much benefit from a dollar spent on automobiles as they do from a dollar spent on shirts and every other

FIGURE 8.4

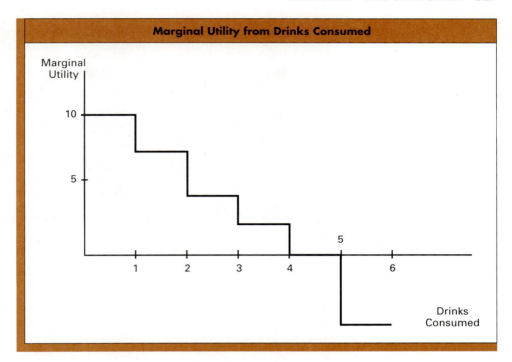

good. In the example in Figure 8.2, if bottled water has no cost, you would consume four or five bottles until you received no additional satisfaction. If the trendy drink costs you something, however, you will weigh the satisfaction that the next bottle will give you against the cost of that drink in deciding whether or not to buy it.

The equation that expresses this attempt of consumers to balance their satisfactions and costs is:

$$\frac{MU(1)}{P(1)} = \frac{MU(2)}{P(2)} = \frac{MU(3)}{P(3)} = \ldots$$

where MU (1) is the marginal utility received from good number one and P (1) is the price of the good, MU (2) is the marginal utility of the second good, and so on. What this equation shows is that consumers attempt to balance the costs and benefits of all their purchases.

How well do consumers make the adjustments? The important issue here is that they try to do it. Consumers make those little adjustments to bring themselves back into line whenever something changes. When the price of good number one goes up, the fraction becomes smaller, and consumers reduce their purchases of this good, driving up the marginal utility received from the last unit consumed, until the balance is restored. If the price of good number two goes down, then consumers will buy more of this good so their marginal utility will decrease. Remember: the equation shows the marginal utility that consumers get from the goods, not the quantity consumed, and with diminishing marginal utility, the more consumed, the lower the marginal utility.

Before we leave diminishing marginal utility, you should know that this concept does not hold true for one group of people. Can you think of who they are? That group encompasses one who is addicted to a substance or a thing. For example, the latest scientific studies show that alcoholism is much more than drinking too much. Alcoholism has been classified as a disease, and some people have a genetic predisposition toward alcoholism. Alcoholics have a trigger in the brain that reacts differently than economics would indicate. Whereas most people quit drinking after a couple of beers because they experience

FIGURE 8.5
Source: U.S. Bureau of Labor Statistics

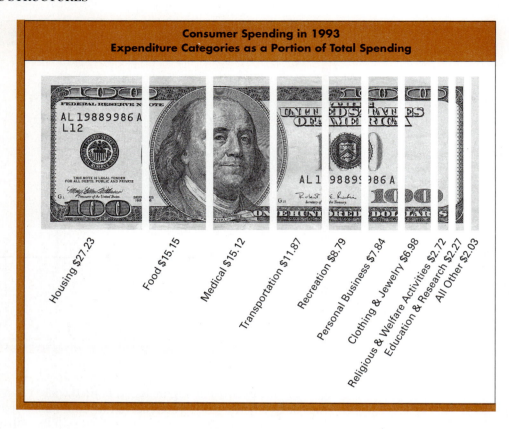

FIGURE 8.6
Source: U.S. Bureau of Economic Analysis

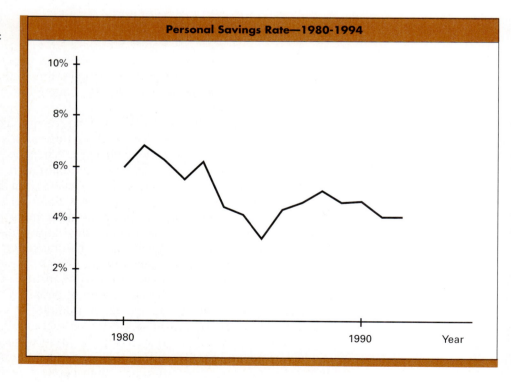

FIGURE 8.7
Consumer spending, the engine of our economy, has done its part over the past 35 years.

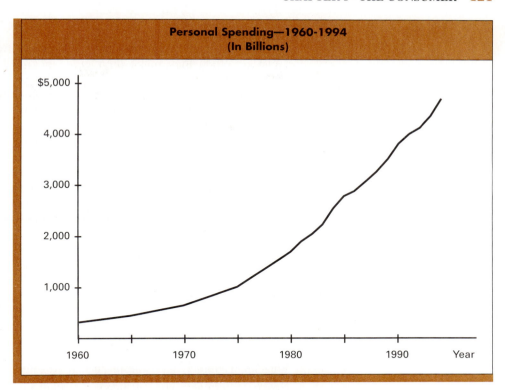

diminishing marginal utility, the alcoholic has a different experience. For the alcoholic, a drink triggers a chemical reaction in the brain that makes the second beer more satisfying than the first, the third beer more satisfying than the second, and so on. Alcoholics experience increasing marginal utility. Given that the price of beer remains constant, it is a rational act for alcoholics to drink more; their benefit-cost ratio improves with each beer. The choice for the alcoholic is an obvious one: do not drink at all.

Core-Info

1. Utility is the key indicator applied to consumers. It is the measure of the amount of satisfaction that consumers get from a specific good or service.
2. In making decisions, consumers compare the satisfaction they receive from a product with its cost and adjust their purchases to maximize their total welfare.

ONCE THE CONSUMER HAS VOTED

Thus, consumers hold great power in a capitalistic economy. Consumers vote with their dollars for the goods they want. If they like something, they buy it. This increases the demand for the good and decreases the demand for some other good. The increased (or decreased) demand for a good sends a ripple effect through the economy. The signals that have been sent affect all aspects of the economy. The goods will be made, machines will be bought to make the goods, workers will be hired to make both the goods and the machines. Businesses respond to the demand to produce what consumers want. Firms pick up when consumers have voted. We will consider firms, but first we will discuss labor. Whereas consumers are the backbone of the demand side, labor is the backbone of the supply side, so it is to labor that we next turn.

SUMMARY

- Consumers are in charge in a capitalistic economy; they make the "What?" decision. When they make their independent decisions, all aspects of the economy move in response.
- The four assumptions we make about consumer behavior are: consumers are rational, they desire many goods, they have to pay for goods, and they have limited income.
- The term *utility* means the satisfaction someone gets from consuming a good or service.
- Diminishing marginal utility means that, as people consume more of any good, they get less and less satisfaction from each additional unit consumed.
- Consumers compare the satisfaction they receive from a good with the cost of that good in an attempt to get the most they can from all the goods they consume.

KEY TERMS

Consumers	Marginal utility	Total utility
Diminishing marginal utility	Rational	Utility

REVIEW QUESTIONS

1. How is it that consumers can be said to have the dominant role in a capitalistic economy?
2. What are the four assumptions that economists make about consumers?
3. How can consumers who buy hula hoops, Barbie dolls, and Mighty Morphin Power Rangers be said to be rational?
4. What is the difference between total and marginal utility?
5. Why is it important for a business to be aware of the principle of diminishing marginal utility?
6. In addition to marginal utility, what two factors does a consumer consider in making purchasing decisions?

PROBLEM-SOLVING PRACTICE

1. One of your friends loves the hot variety of Buffalo chicken wings. Her utility schedule for chicken wings is as follows:

Number of Wings	Total Utility
0	0
1	15
2	25
3	30
4	34
5	37
6	39
7	40
8	39
9	36
10	15

(a) Calculate the marginal utility schedule associated with the total utility schedule presented above.

(b) Construct a graph of the total utility and marginal utility curves for chicken wings for this person.

2. The same friend likes to drink diet cola with her chicken wings. The following total utility schedule presents her preferences for cola.

Glasses of Cola	Total Utility
0	0
1	8
2	15
3	20
4	24
5	21
6	13

   (a) Calculate the marginal utility schedule.
   (b) Plot the total and marginal utility schedules as graphs.
   (c) If the colas are free, how many would she drink? If she has to pay for the drinks, can you tell how many she would drink?

3. On Tuesdays the local pub sells chicken wings for $.10 each and drinks for $.25 each. If your friend is a maximizing consumer, what combination of drinks and wings will she buy?

CHAPTER 9

Labor, Unions, and the Distribution of Income

CHAPTER OUTLINE

A. Workers of the World, Untie!
B. Labor
   1. The Demand for Labor
      a. Labor as a Derived Demand
      b. Determining the Demand for Labor
      c. The Elasticity of Demand for Labor
   2. The Supply of Labor
      a. Factors Affecting the Overall Supply of Labor
      b. Discrimination and the Supply of Labor
      c. The Backward Bending Supply Curve of Labor
   3. Human Capital
      a. Definition
      b. The Creation of Human Capital
      c. The Effect on the Supply and Demand of Labor
C. Labor Unions
   1. Definition and History
   2. Types of Labor Unions
      a. Craft Unions
      b. Industrial Unions
      c. Government Employee Unions
   3. Labor Union Terms
      a. Types of Union/Management Relationships
      b. The Weapons of Labor and Management
   4. The Effect of Unions on Wages
   5. How Unions Can Affect Wages
      a. Through the Supply of Labor
      b. Through the Demand for Labor
      c. Through Nonequilibrium Wages
   6. Labor Unions: a Final Assessment
D. Income Distribution
   1. Definition and Factors Affecting the Distribution of Income
   2. The Components of Income
      a. Income from Labor
      b. Income from Assets
      c. Income Effect of Taxes and Transfers
   3. The Actual Distribution of Income
E. Discrimination
   1. Definition
   2. The Effects of Discrimination
      a. Effects on Those Discriminated Against
      b. Effects on Those Who Discriminate
      c. Effects on the Marketplace
   3. Solutions to the Discrimination Problem
      a. Personal Action
      b. Legislation
      c. *Laissez Faire*
F. Labor Retied

The purpose of this chapter is to introduce the factors which affect the demand for and supply of labor, to describe labor unions and their role and impact in the American economy, to examine the distribution of income in the United States, and to explore the causes of and solutions to discrimination.

AFTER COMPLETING THIS CHAPTER, YOU WILL BE ABLE TO:

1. Describe the factors that affect the supply of and demand for labor in the market.

2. Demonstrate the applicability of the supply of labor curve to the way all workers behave.

3. Describe the three types of labor unions and how they act to affect wages.

4. Describe the actual distribution of income in the United States.

5. Predict the effect of each type of discrimination on individuals and society.

6. Apply the three basic solutions to the problem of discrimination.

Workers of the World, Untie!

Yes, that's right, "untie." You may have thought of a quote from Karl Marx when you read that. The closing statement in Karl Marx's book, The Communist Manifesto, *written in 1848 when capitalism was at its most oppressive, is "Workers of the world, unite!" Marx was trying to call all laborers together in a struggle against capitalism. We have no ideological axe to grind in this chapter. We are going to untie—to pull apart to better understand—labor and all that goes into it. Because labor is the foundation and backbone of every economy in the world, a solid understanding of what labor is and how it functions is essential for anyone who wants to understand the economy.*

The first step is to look at labor itself. We will examine the supply of labor and the demand for labor to understand the unique conditions that apply. We will then look at organized labor—labor unions. Here we will learn what labor unions are, what forms they take, and how they affect the economy. Next we will explore the distribution of income, how the earnings from labor are distributed among all members of society. Finally we will examine discrimination, both economic and social, and the potential solutions to the discrimination problem in the economy.

LABOR

Labor is the key. Nearly 75 percent of the national income of the United States goes to the compensation of employees. The remaining 25 percent is divided among profits, interest, and rents. With three quarters of the nation's income going to workers, labor rates more than a cursory glance.

The Demand for Labor

The demand for and supply of labor are crucial, for it is the interaction of supply and demand that sets wage rates and determines how many workers will have jobs. We will start with demand, for unless somebody wants to hire a worker the number of workers available is of absolutely no consequence—except that it can mean unemployment.

Labor as a Derived Demand. The first point to note about the demand for labor is that nobody wants to hire workers. Managers don't lie awake at night trying to figure new ways to pad the payroll. What they do lie awake and think about is production. Producing goods in response to consumer demand is what business is all about. Once consumers decide (the "What?" question of economics), firms set out to produce the desired goods at the lowest possible cost (the "How?" question). In this effort, firms attempt to combine inputs in the most efficient manner possible. One of the inputs used is labor. Thus, because of the desire to produce goods, firms hire workers and use labor along with the other inputs. Therefore, the demand for

Derived Demand
The idea that the demand for labor is determined by the demand for the products it produces.

workers results from the demand for the product. The term used for this relationship is **derived demand.** The demand for labor is derived from, or determined by the demand for the product.

Determining the Demand for Labor. What affects the demand for labor? What factors cause it to change? Two key factors result in a change in the demand for labor: a change in the demand for the product that the labor helps to produce and a change in labor's productivity. The first factor is pretty straightforward. An increase in demand for the products that workers produce results in an increase in the demand for labor to produce them. If you want to produce more television sets, you need more workers to produce them (assuming that your workers were fully employed at the outset). The demand for labor, therefore, is a derived demand, and there is a direct relationship between the amount of labor used and the amount of products produced. If production goes up, more workers are needed; if production falls, fewer will be employed. That makes sense.

The second factor, on the other hand, isn't quite as straightforward. There is also a direct relationship between the productivity of labor and the demand for that labor. As labor becomes more productive, more workers will be hired. When labor is less productive, fewer workers are hired. On the surface, that may seem contradictory. If a group of workers becomes able to produce more, won't you need fewer of them? Yes, but only for today. Labor is only one of the four inputs or factors of production; remember land, labor, capital, and entrepreneurship? When a firm is deciding how much of each of the four inputs to use, it compares the productivity of each with the cost of employing it. If labor is becoming more productive, a company can increase its output more by adding workers rather than by adding capital. Thus, as labor's productivity increases, more workers are hired.[1] If, on the other hand, labor's productivity is falling when compared with the productivity of the other inputs, fewer workers will be hired and more capital, entrepreneurship, or land will be used.

Core-Info

The two factors that affect the demand for labor are demand for the product and labor's productivity. Both factors are positively correlated with demand.

The Elasticity of Demand for Labor. This issue should be of interest to everyone whether they are employers or employees. The elasticity of demand for labor has to do with what happens to the number of workers who have jobs as the wage rate rises. As with the price of anything, when labor costs go up, fewer workers are hired. If, when wages go up, the number of workers hired decreases only slightly, then workers in general (not those few who have lost their jobs, of course) are better off, and the demand for labor is said to be inelastic. If, on the other hand, when wages go up employers cut their hiring significantly, then workers in an overall sense lose, and the demand for labor is said to be elastic. If the demand for labor is elastic, then wage increases exact a very high cost in terms of the number of workers who will have jobs. The elasticity theory discussed in Chapter 6 can help you determine which sectors are elastic or inelastic and why this is so.

---

[1] The belief that firms are more likely to hire workers if they (the workers) are more productive is seen in the fact that 15 million people are enrolled in colleges and universities in the United States alone. This idea, known as human capital, will be discussed later in the chapter.

Three main factors determine how elastic the demand for labor will be. These factors are:

1. The number and availability of substitutes
2. The proportion of total production costs that labor comprises
3. The elasticity of demand for the product

The first two factors are exactly the same ones that exist in other applications of elasticity. First, if the substitutes for labor (land, capital, and entrepreneurship) are readily available and can be used easily, then an increase in the wage rate will result in a significant decrease in the demand for labor. Rather than use the same amount of labor as the cost of labor rises, employers will make massive switches to, in particular, capital. In this case, the demand for labor is said to be elastic. If, on the other hand, an employer can't easily substitute capital for labor or if capital is very expensive, an increase in the wage rate will have little negative effect on the level of employment; thus, the demand for labor is considered inelastic.

The second factor has to do with how big a portion of total costs labor comprises. If labor is a significant portion of the total cost of a product, any increase in the wage rate will result in a big drop in employment. If labor is only a small part of total costs, wage rate increases will have a minimal effect on total costs. Thus, in the first case labor is said to be relatively elastic whereas in the second it is said to be inelastic.

The third factor has to do with the elasticity of demand for the product itself. If the final product is price elastic, any increase in its price will result in a big drop in its sales. Therefore, an increase in the cost of labor that is passed on in the form of higher product prices (an option, not a requirement!) will result in a significant drop in the sales of the product and an equivalent big drop in the amount of labor employed. Remember that labor is a derived demand.

What does it matter that labor is either elastic or inelastic? In a dynamic environment in which workers hope to have wages rising so they can purchase more goods and services for themselves, they are directly affected by the elasticity of demand for their labor. In an occupational field in which labor is generally elastic and many people will lose their jobs (or work fewer hours) as wages go up, those workers had better strive to make demand for themselves more inelastic by adding to their human capital so they will be among the last to be fired.

The Supply of Labor

As everybody knows, demand is only half of the equation. Demand without supply is like Bonnie without Clyde, hot dogs without mustard, or major league sports without a strike. The supply of labor must be part of the picture that illustrates how wage rates are set. That topic is of interest to all of us.

Factors Affecting the Overall Supply of Labor. Whereas the factors that affect the individual supply of labor tend to be economic, the factors that affect the overall supply of labor tend to be sociological. Attitudes toward work in general and about who should work in which jobs determine the overall supply. Should people be striving to get ahead or be satisfied with their lot in life? Do family duties come before work duties or vice versa? Is the "proper" place for a woman at home or in the work place or both? What about immigrants: are they welcome or should they stay home? How about child labor? Seniors in the work place? Schooling through age 8 or 20? These attitudinal variables are the factors which determine how many people in general will be available for work in any given country.

Discrimination and the Supply of Labor. We will deal with the issue of discrimination in more depth in an upcoming discussion of the distribution of income. Suffice it to say here that racial and gender discrimination both reduce the supply of labor in general and distort relative earnings as women and minorities are either pre-

FIGURE 9.1

Supply Schedule for Labor		
Wage/hr.	Hours Worked	Income/Week
$ .01	0	$ 0.00
.10	0	0.00
1.00	0	0.00
2.50	0	0.00
5.00	10	50.00
7.50	20	150.00
10.00	40	400.00
20.00	50	1,000.00
50.00	60	3,000.00
100.00	70	7,000.00
250.00	60	15,000.00
500.00	40	20,000.00
1,000.00	30	30,000.00
2,000.00	20	40,000.00

vented from working or are relegated to selected occupations. These distortions are extremely costly to both the individual affected and to society as a whole.

The Backward Bending Supply Curve of Labor. Now that we know something about the overall supply of labor, we are going to examine how individuals supply labor to the market. In the process you will learn that people are very much alike whether they are college students, welfare recipients, wealthy professionals, or people in developing countries. The same factors affect all workers, and they all act in similar ways when faced with the same situations. This may seem strange at first, but you should understand the validity of this assertion shortly.

Let's start with an example. Assume that a new business opens and you are an applicant for a job there. The business owner offers you a job at various wage rates. What you must do is tell the owner how many hours per week you would be willing to work for those rates. Take out a piece of paper and write down how many hours per week you would be willing to work if you were paid 1 cent per hour? Ten cents per hour. $1 per hour. $5 per hour. $50 per hour. $5,000 per hour. Remember you have a total of 168 hours available each week (24 hours per day seven days per week) in which to do everything: eat, sleep, play, walk the dog, and work. Working more hours means you have to give up something else. Those tradeoffs are opportunity costs.

Most people would be unwilling to work any hours at 1 cent per hour or 10 cents or $1 or $2.50 per hour. Why? The opportunity cost of working is not offset by what they would earn. In order to work, people must discipline themselves to maintain regular hours, wear whatever type of clothing is considered appropriate, get to and from work, deal with day care if they have children, miss "Guiding Light," and make other adjustments. Working costs. At $5 per hour, the business owner begins to get some attention. You might work 10 hours per week. At $7.50 per hour or $10 per hour, you would be willing to work even more. When the hourly wage is high enough, say $250 per hour, you can work fewer hours and still have all of your income needs met. With the higher income, people can take Wednesdays off and head for the golf course, can go yachting in Bermuda in December, and generally enjoy life. At least you can dream.

Now back to reality. The previous example can be displayed on a chart, as it is in Figure 9.1.

Figure 9.1 looks familiar, doesn't it? It is a standard supply schedule from Chapter 5, with wage rate as the price and the number of hours worked as quantity. As you can see, below a certain wage rate, people aren't willing to go to work. It's

130 PART 3 • ECONOMIC STRUCTURES

FIGURE 9.2

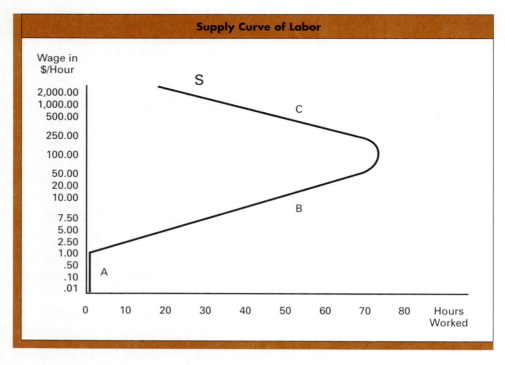

Backward Bending Supply Curve of Labor
The oddly shaped supply curve of labor that reflects the fact that people will work fewer hours when the wage rate rises significantly compared with the wage they are used to.

too much trouble for too little return. Once the wage rate reaches a minimally acceptable level, people begin to work and, for some range of wage rates, they increase their hours as the rate continues to rise. Finally, when the wage rate is really high; people can reduce their hours and still earn a lot of money.

Anything you can put on a supply schedule you can put on a supply curve. Figure 9.2 does just that for this example.

When the data from the supply schedule is plotted on Figure 9.2, you can see that this graph has a unique shape, known as the **backward bending supply curve of labor.** The curve actually has three sections: Section A, the vertical portion; Section B, the normal-looking supply curve; and Section C, which heads back in the opposite direction.

Let's consider this curve in connection with vitriolic statements made about people who collect welfare instead of working. Those people would end up in Section A. Think about most of the jobs available to people who are on welfare. What type of jobs are they? How much do they pay? Low level and low wage, right? What are the costs of taking these jobs? Those costs include transportation, meals, clothes, day care for the children, loss of cash assistance, and the end of free medical care. Just as you wouldn't be willing to work at these low wages, neither would people on welfare. They act precisely the same as people with college educations do. They act just as rationally as anyone else.

If we think that work is better than welfare—and for many people it is—then we need to look at the incentives that people on welfare see. With the likelihood of low wages and high costs, it is irrational to take a job. The solution is to increase the benefits of working, reduce the costs of working, or decrease the benefit of remaining on welfare. If one or more of these changes is not made, then people on welfare will continue to act rationally and not work, just like we would.

Another section of the curve, the portion that bends back, applies to a different group of people—wage earners in underdeveloped countries. When wages go high enough, people begin to substitute leisure for work and put fewer hours in at the office. When wages go up for those in underdeveloped countries, they do the same. We can all be in Section C; the only difference is the wage rate. If the salary of an American business executive were to double, it would increase by tens of thousands of dollars. If the average Bangladeshi's wage were to double, it merely has to move from $200 to $400 per year. (That's right, the per capita income in

Bangladesh is $200 per year. You've probably spent that much on a big dance or date.) To double a person's income in Bangladesh is not difficult. A good development project can quickly result in a significant increase in income for a village. When this happens, many of the people begin to take time off to worship or to relax or to be with their families—just as Americans would. For people in both economies, the choice is a rational one—they are acting just like us.

It turns out that people all over the world act pretty much the same. The same factors that act as incentives for working Americans affect everybody else. Perhaps people who stand ready to label others should withhold judgment until they examine their situations carefully.

Core-Info

The supply curve of labor shows that at low wages, people choose not to work and at high wages they reduce their hours worked. This is true of all people.

Human Capital

As a college student, you probably know more about **human capital** than almost anybody else. It is obvious that you deeply believe in the concept. Why? Because as a college student, you are in the process of investing quite heavily in human capital even, and especially, as you read this paragraph. By going to college, you are participating in a human capital activity.

Definition. The definition of human capital is simple: it is anything that adds to an individual's productive capacity. Education, formal and informal training, and health investments all qualify as they help a person to become more productive.

The Creation of Human Capital. Human capital is created by investing. Rather than work as many hours as you could this year and earn more money, you have chosen to forgo or give up some earnings in order to go to school. An opportunity cost is paid to invest in human capital. This opportunity cost includes both the direct costs of college and the indirect costs such as foregone earnings and time with the family. That is true of all investments in human capital. Whether it is spending on education, training, or health, investing in human capital involves giving something up today in order to have something more tomorrow.

The result of investing in human capital, of forgoing income today, is higher income in the future. This investment is similar to using the thousands of dollars that you are investing in your college education to purchase a business or invest in government bonds. You would receive a stream of increased income for the rest of your life as a result of this investment. The same is true for investments in human capital. Your investment in higher education will pay great financial dividends in the long run.

That leads to a final note about investing in human capital. Not all the money you spend going to college can be considered an investment in human capital. Few economists include Friday night entertainment expenses in this category. To further muddy the waters, building human capital is only one of a number of reasons that people choose to attend college. Some people go to college for the joy of learning with no expectation of a better job. Others attend for the social life; education is not a priority. Only those expenses and activities that add to a person's productive capacity count as investments in human capital.

The Effect on the Supply and Demand of Labor. The effect of investments in human capital on the supply of and demand for labor is pretty straightforward: it increases demand and raises supply. By increasing the demand for labor, the demand curve slides outward to the right. More labor is now desired at every wage rate. Why? Because the workers are more productive and employers substitute labor for capital. By raising the supply of labor, the supply curve now is farther "north" of the graph, and wage rates commanded by the more highly trained workers are higher. The net effect is an increased wage rate for workers and an increased number of workers hired. A rather nice combination, don't you think?

LABOR UNIONS

Labor unions are very much a part of the American economy. While comprising a relatively small percentage of the overall labor force, labor unions have had a significant impact on the economy and are likely to have a lasting effect regardless of their size. Because of this, they are worth examining in some detail.

A major problem in studying labor unions is that of bias. What we think about labor unions is likely to be determined by whether our mother or father belonged to a union or were a part of management. The goal should be to look at unions dispassionately and examine them for what they are. This discussion will try to give them credit for what they have done, point out where they have fallen short, and not blame them for things over which they have no control.

Definition and History

A labor union is a group of workers who have organized collectively to negotiate with management over wages and working conditions and to offer a level of security to its members. Labor unions had their beginnings in the medieval craft guilds, local groups of workers in a specific trade (e.g., gold, silver, hides, barrels) who joined forces to maintain the quality of the product and to train future workers. Although local in geographic area, these guilds were quite powerful, and they served as the training grounds for new apprentices. The earliest American unions followed the same pattern in the 18th century.

Types of Labor Unions

There are three basic types of labor unions today. Each exists for a specific purpose, and each has been established to accomplish unique goals.

Craft Unions. The first of the three types of labor unions is the **craft union.** A craft union is a group of workers who are organized around a specific skill or trade. In this respect, craft unions are similar to the guilds of previous centuries. Craft unions tend to be exclusive in nature. They set rigid standards for apprenticeship and limit the number of members. By keeping down the supply of labor in a particular skill, craft unions can help increase the wage rate for their members. Printers, carpenters, electricians, and doctors all have their own craft unions.

Industrial Unions. While craft unions can work effectively when a single skill is involved, they become quite cumbersome in a large manufacturing plant. Imagine the level of chaos that would exist in an automobile firm if the engine makers had one union, the upholstery workers belonged to a second, and the headlight installers had a third. Obviously, in a large firm, a different type of union is required, and that is the **industrial union.** The industrial union is a group of workers who organize not around the skill of the worker but around the product they produce, and they tend to form where the products are relatively complex. Thus, industrial unions represent the auto workers, the steel workers, and the electrical workers. Industrial unions try to be inclusive rather than exclusive. These unions contend that their greatest strength lies in having as many members as possible. Rather than restrict the supply of labor, industrial unions attempt to assemble the power of numbers for their negotiations with management.

Government Employee Unions. The third type of labor union is the **government employee union.** While craft unions and industrial unions are decreasing in size, government employee unions are growing. These unions consist of people

---

Labor Unions
Groups of workers who join together in an attempt to affect wage rates and working conditions.

Craft Unions
Groups of workers organized around a common skill who attempt to restrict the supply of labor in order to drive up wages.

Industrial Union
A group of workers organized around the product produced. This type of union attempts to drive up wages through market power.

Government Employee Unions
Groups of government workers organized in an attempt to drive up wages and affect working conditions through negotiation.

CHAPTER 9 • LABOR, UNIONS, AND THE DISTRIBUTION OF INCOME

who work for federal, state, or city governments. Teachers, social workers, firefighters, and police often organize in government employee unions. Because these types of jobs are considered essential, there is a restricted ability for government employee unions to strike.

Labor Union Terms

To examine labor unions in more depth, you must understand the language. Once you know the terms and their precise meaning, you will not only understand the rest of this section but can better interpret news stories today.

Types of Union/Management Relationships. A **closed shop** arrangement is one in which people must belong to a union before they can be hired by a firm. The union determines who can—and cannot—be a member, and only those selected by the union can be employed by the firm. Obviously, this position is one that gives unions quite a bit of power in the labor/management relationship, but it does have benefits for the employer. Those persons who are referred to firms for employment have been screened by the union, and this reduces the employer's cost of recruiting and hiring. Overall, however, it works to labor's advantage. Since passage of the Taft-Hartley Act in 1947, the closed shop arrangement has been illegal in the United States.

Another type of labor/management relationship is the **union shop** arrangement. In this situation, the firm may hire anyone it chooses, and new employees must join the union within 30 days of starting to work. The firm has more control over hiring decisions in this arrangement than in closed shops.

Finally, an **open shop** arrangement may exist between labor and management. In open shops, both union members and nonunion employees work side-by-side. Union membership cannot be required of an employee. Obviously, the union is at a real disadvantage in this situation. Both union and nonunion workers are paid the same wage by the employer, but union members pay union dues out of their paychecks to support union activities. Of course union members do receive some benefits from unions as a result of their dues, but often these benefits are less attractive to workers than more money in their paychecks. Some states have institutionalized open shops by passing **right-to-work laws.** Right-to-work laws make it illegal to require a person to join a union as a condition of employment. This approach typically occurs in those states that are rural, conservative, or less industrialized.

Closed Shop
A labor/management arrangement in which workers must be members of a union before they can be hired by an employer.

Union Shop
A labor/management arrangement in which workers must join a particular union after being hired by an employer.

Open Shop
A labor/management arrangement in which workers cannot be forced to join a union as a condition of employment.

Right-to-Work Laws
Laws which prohibit any requirement for a worker to join a union.

Core-Info

The three types of labor unions are:
1. Craft unions
2. Industrial unions
3. Government employee unions

The three types of labor/management relationships are:
1. Closed shop
2. Union shop
3. Open shop

The Weapons of Labor and Management. The goal of labor/management relations is, or at least should be, to work together to settle the wage and working conditions issues in a peaceful way. The process by which they try to do this is called **collective bargaining.** In collective bargaining, both labor and management send an individual or a team of people to represent their constituencies in the best way they can. The labor representative attempts to gain increases in wages and improvements in working conditions. The management representative attempts to get

Collective Bargaining
The process by which labor and management meet to negotiate wages and working conditions.

Strike
A weapon used by labor in which workers collectively withhold labor services.

Work-to-Rule
A weapon used by labor in which workers collectively only do the work that is absolutely required by the terms of their contract.

Lockout
A weapon used by management in which it refuses to permit labor union members to work at their jobs and earn income.

Binding Arbitration
An arrangement in which labor and management agree that a third party will determine the outcome of any disputes.

workers to operate more efficiently. In the best of all worlds, labor and management reach an agreement, and everybody comes away from the collective bargaining sessions at least relatively happy.

However, the world is not always ideal. What happens if both sides can't agree to a settlement? If one or both of the parties can't get what they want through negotiation, both sides may turn to a stronger weapon to accomplish their goals.

A number of strategies are available to both unions and management as the two sides move from negotiation to confrontation. On labor's side are boycotts, picketing, and, finally, the **strike.** In a strike, workers refuse to go to work, preventing production from occurring. In this case, both sides lose. Workers lose the wages they would have earned, and management loses the profits that would have been made. A final, and very effective, weapon for labor is known as **work-to-rule** (sometimes called work-to-the-rule). In a work-to-rule situation, workers do only what is required of them by their contract with the firm. Anything extra that is not specifically called for is not done: no helping others, no working a little late, no cleaning the machinery. In their day-to-day work, most people do many things that are not in their job description. They do them to help out and make the job better for everybody. In a work-to-rule situation, nothing extra is done, and the real loser in this case is management.

Management's options include layoffs and the equivalent action to a strike, a **lockout.** In a lockout, workers are prevented by management from working; they are literally locked out of the office or factory. In this case, both sides lose.

Obviously, neither strikes nor lockouts serve the best interests of labor and management. Strikes and lockouts are to be avoided if possible. If labor and management can't come to an agreement and if it looks like a strike or lockout is the next step, the two sides may call for **binding arbitration.** In binding arbitration, a neutral third party enters the picture. The arbitrator listens to both sides, weighs the arguments and demands of both, and makes a decision. Once the decision has been made, it is binding on both labor and management. Both parties have agreed beforehand that whatever decision the arbitrator makes is acceptable. In this manner, strikes and lockouts are avoided, and neither side loses income to a work stoppage.

The Effect of Unions on Wages

Labor unions cannot force higher wages on an employer. No ifs, no ands, no buts. Unions can negotiate for wage increases, can demand higher wages, can do a lot to try to increase paychecks, but they cannot force employers to pay higher wages without pretty severe consequences on the union and its members. To see what effect an overzealous labor union would have, let's return to the concepts of supply and demand.

Firms have a demand for labor. When wages are low, firms try to hire workers rather than buy machines to do the job. As wages go up, firms want to hire fewer workers and begin to substitute machines where possible. This means that the demand for labor has a demand curve that looks like every other demand curve in the world; it slopes downward from upper left to lower right.

Workers supply their labor. At low wages in any occupation or firm, workers look elsewhere for jobs. As wage rates go up, more workers are willing to work, and they are willing to work more hours. The result is a supply curve for labor that looks like every other supply curve; it slopes upward from lower left to upper right.

When a supply curve and a demand curve are combined, the result is a graph with the usual equilibrium. That's how wages are set. The supply of and demand for labor determine wage rates and the number of workers who will be hired. Unions may push and management may pull, but ultimately supply and demand win. This supply and demand situation is shown in Figure 9.3. On the vertical axis is the wage rate, the price of labor. The horizontal axis shows the number of workers hired (or the number of hours worked), the quantity of labor. The equilibrium wage rate and the number of workers is determined solely by the supply and demand curves.

FIGURE 9.3

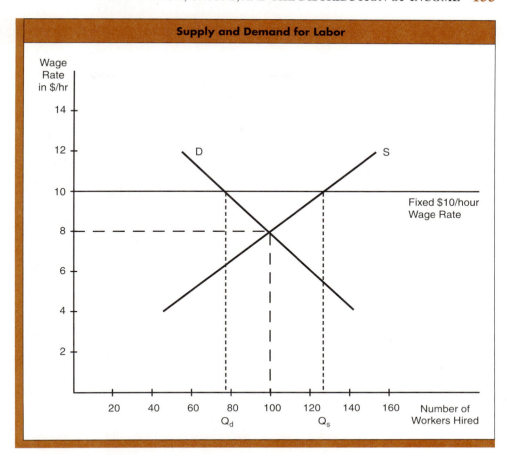

Think of this example as taking place in a local department store. People are willing to take jobs there if the price is right, and management wants to hire people to work if the price is right. In this department store in this city, we have reached an equilibrium. In this example, the equilibrium wage rate is $8 per hour, and the equilibrium number of workers hired is 100. If the wage rate is somehow pushed below equilibrium, what would happen? Management would want to hire a lot of workers, but fewer workers would be willing to take jobs there. At this lower wage rate, some workers would decide to work elsewhere. The result could be a shortage. If, on the other hand, the wage rate is somehow pushed above equilibrium, what would happen? Management would want to hire fewer workers, but many more workers would be willing to take jobs there. At this higher wage rate, we would be in a surplus situation. What is a surplus of labor but too many workers and too few jobs? Unemployment. The result is our equilibrium position as described.

Let's add a labor union to this picture. Assume that the workers in the department store became unionized, and the labor union negotiates new wages of $10 per hour. What would happen? The higher wages would attract a lot of people who want to work at the store while the store's management would hire fewer workers. The number of workers who want to work at the store would rise to Qs in Figure 9.3 while the number of workers who would be hired at that wage would fall to Qd. Qs > Qd. The result of a union forcing the wage rate above the equilibrium is higher wages for those workers with jobs but unemployment for the rest. Forcing wage rates up causes unemployment and results in fewer union members. It is not in the union's best interest to force wages up, and self-interest is the motivating factor in economics. Therefore, it is a very rare situation in which a labor union will attempt to force wages above the level that would result from the natural laws of

FIGURE 9.4

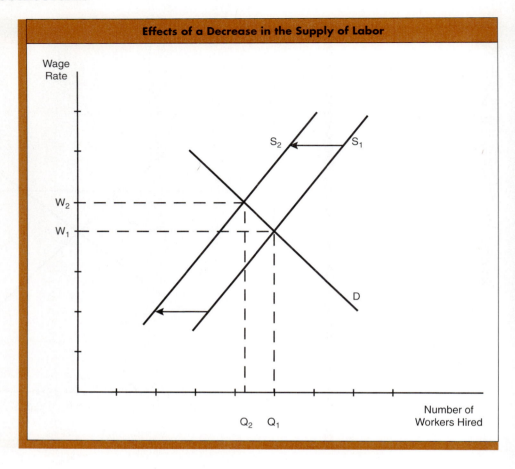

supply and demand.[2] Forcing nonequilibrium wages is a possible way for unions to raise wages, but the cost to everyone but the few who retain their jobs is very high.

How Unions Can Affect Wages

This may be nice theory, but of what use are unions if they cannot increase their members' wages? Can't they have some impact on wages? Yes, labor unions can have an impact on their members' wages, but they have to go about it indirectly. If unions try to force wage rates up, some union members will end up unemployed. What unions must do is change the world around them so wages are driven up through natural causes. They can do this through the natural laws of supply and demand.

Through the Supply of Labor. The first way that unions can approach the issue is through the supply of labor. If unions can reduce the supply of labor and hold down the number of workers looking for jobs, then wage rates will rise naturally. As Figure 9.4 shows, if unions can move the supply curve to the left (from S1 to S2), then wage rates will rise (from W1 to W2) although fewer workers will be hired (from Q1 to Q2).

Labor unions can use numerous methods to help reduce the supply of labor. Think about it for a second. What could be done to reduce the number of available workers? How about these:

1. Required apprenticeship programs for people who want to enter the field. This will screen out some people who can't take the time to go through a formal program.

---

[2] In the 1930s and 1940s, U.S. mineworkers were paid appallingly low wages to work in exceedingly unsafe mines. John L. Lewis, the president of the United Mine Workers, forced wages up through long strikes and other extreme measures. He also wrestled with federal bureaucrats to force greater job safety and to extend some benefits to the mineworkers who lost their jobs.

FIGURE 9.5

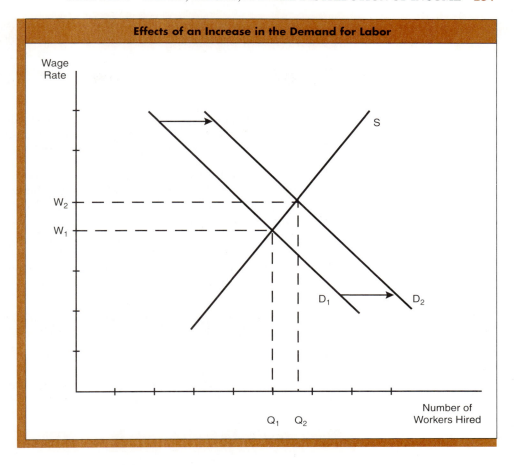

2. Education requirements to work in the field. We seem to want our doctors and barbers to be formally trained. This again thins the field.
3. High initiation fees for membership in a required union. Those who can't afford the membership fees are eliminated from the labor pool.
4. Laws against child labor. If children (through age 14, 16, or 18) can be kept from working, more jobs are available for adult workers.
5. Push for a higher minimum wage. If the minimum wage rises, then all the wages above it are pushed up.
6. Push for earlier retirement. If workers can be forced to retire at a fixed age through mandatory retirement programs or if they can be induced to retire through retirement income programs, the number of available workers drops.

Through the Demand for Labor. The flip side of decreasing the supply of labor is increasing the demand for labor. If unions can somehow increase the demand for labor and make employers want to hire more workers, then wage rates will again rise naturally. As Figure 9.5 shows, if unions can move the demand curve to the right (from D1 to D2), then wage rates will rise (from W1 to W2) and more workers will be hired (from Q1 to Q2).

How can labor unions do something to increase the employer's demand for workers? Again there are a number of strategies, including:

1. Increase the productivity of labor. If workers become more productive, employers have an incentive to hire more workers and use fewer machines. Educating and training workers increases their productivity. This education can be in the form of general education that people may get from the public school systems or specific education through technical or on-the-job programs.

138   PART 3 • ECONOMIC STRUCTURES

2. Increase demand for the product. If people want to buy more of whatever it is that workers produce, more workers are needed to produce it. Unions can help this process by advertising the product either directly (as the United Auto Workers have done with some car companies) or indirectly (through the "Buy American" or "Look for the Union Label" campaigns).

3. Push for higher tariffs. If foreign competition can be reduced or eliminated, demand for the American product increases. By encouraging anti-import legislation in Congress, labor unions can increase the demand for American-made goods, and the demand for workers to produce these goods increases.

Through Nonequilibrium Wages. Unions can force wages up, but only at a very high cost to themselves. As was noted in the footnote about the United Mine Workers, if unions have enough power, they can force firms to pay higher wages. Employers will respond by reducing the number of workers they hire. Those who still have jobs win. Those who end up out of work take it on the chin.

To increase their members' wages, unions can act to reduce the supply of labor or to increase the demand for labor, but they cannot force wages to go up. In the end, it comes down to supply and demand.

Core-Info

Unions cannot force wages to rise without reducing the number of people who can work at that wage.

The ways in which unions can obtain an increase in wage rates are:

1. Increase the demand for labor.
2. Reduce the supply of labor.

Labor Unions: a Final Assessment

If labor unions cannot push up their members' wages, what *can* they do? Actually, labor unions have had a profound effect on the American economy. In addition to

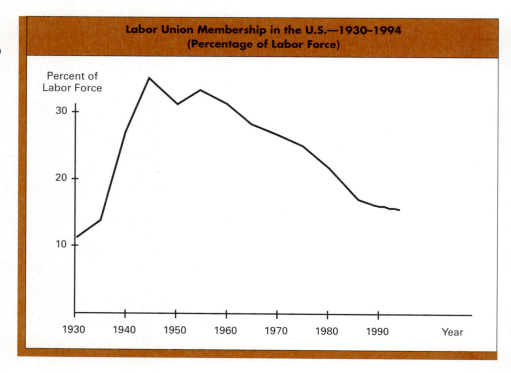

FIGURE 9.6
Labor union membership hit its peak 40 years ago and has been steadily declining since. *Source:* U.S. Bureau of the Labor Statistics.

FIGURE 9.7
The number of strikes has dropped dramatically in the past 30 years due, in part, to the decline in union power. *Source:* U.S. Bureau of Labor Statistics.

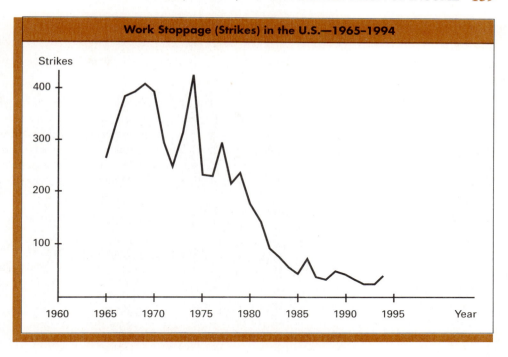

providing a balance to the power of large businesses,[3] labor unions have had a significant impact on social legislation that affects all aspects of society. Labor unions are charged with serving their members. The goals of unions are higher wages and better working conditions. The ways to achieve these goals, especially raising wages, are through affecting the supply of and demand for labor. As you have seen, unions accomplish these goals through such efforts as increasing the productivity of workers, restricting child labor, and improving retirement programs. In their attempt to help their members, labor unions help all of society.

That leads to one final observation about unions. Labor unions are on the decline in terms of the number of members and their impact on the economy and society. Workers' wages are safe; supply and demand will see to that. But what may happen is that those segments of society that have benefitted in the past from the unions' efforts may begin to lose ground. The undereducated, the unprotected, those needing social programs may not have a voice now that unions are declining and having less of an impact. Who will speak for the oppressed?

INCOME DISTRIBUTION

You may not remember the old Goodyear tire slogan, "Where the rubber meets the road" but it certainly applies to this section. Economics is inherently important, but unless there is something in it for us, who cares? If an economic system is incredibly productive but all the money goes to the already wealthy, it doesn't really matter. The distribution of income—who gets it and how much they get—is critical.

Definition and Factors Affecting the Distribution of Income

We will focus our look at individual income. Individual income is the earnings that people receive from all sources. The general factors that affect income include some amount of personal choice (working two jobs or taking a vacation, for instance), luck (being at the right place at the right time—with the right skills), government policies regarding benefits and taxes, and discrimination. This discussion of income should provide a sense of how well the income generated in the economy is distributed to all its participants.

[3.] John Kenneth Galbraith calls this the development of a "countervailing power."

Will Labor Unions Disappear?

The chart below offers a picture of the post-war history of labor unions in the United States. It doesn't look good for the movement, does it? While the labor force has nearly tripled in size, growing from around 40 million to 110 million, labor union membership has risen only 15 percent and numerically has been on the decline since 1980. Is this the death knell for labor unions?

Don't write them off yet. First, labor unions have a long history in the American workforce. The modern union movement dates to 1886 with the formation of the American Federation of Labor out of 25 existing craft unions. Many people today either have belonged to unions or had family members who did. This connection yields a soft spot in the hearts of many Americans. Second, labor unions have accomplished good. Economists contend that unions haven't done much for wages, but they have brought change in other areas, and they have spoken for the poor. This connection with those in need defines a purpose for unions to continue. Finally, there are new areas to organize. Labor union strength has typically been within the manufacturing sector, the area of greatest decline today. Where unions are largely unrepresented is among service workers, the most rapidly growing sector of our economy.

Weep not for unions. They will be with us for a long time to come.

Labor Union Membership

Year	Union Members	Percent of Labor Force
1945	14,322,000	35.5
1955	16,802,000	33.2
1965	17,299,000	28.4
1975	19,611,000	25.5
1985	16,996,000	18.0
1995	16,500,000*	15.0*

*Estimated
Source: Bureau of Labor Statistics, U.S. Department of Labor

The Components of Income

Individual income consists of three basic components: income from labor, income from assets, and the effect on income of taxes and transfer payments.

Income from Labor. The income from labor is by far the largest of the three components. For most people, income from labor is in part a decision about work versus leisure and about the amount of education. If people choose to go to school longer or work more hours, their income will be higher. Some people, however, have fewer options. If you have a physical or mental disability, if you are sick or old or young, if you are a woman or a minority, the choice is not entirely yours. If you face limitations from within or imposed from the outside, your income is more limited than if you don't. The wage rates people earn are a function of their human capital (the amount of education they have invested in themselves), their stage in the life cycle (old workers earn more than young workers), and discrimination.

Income from Assets. Whereas people have a fair amount of say about their labor income, the income from assets is a bit more proscribed. This income is what people receive from savings, capital investments, and land. It is a function of prior earnings, either theirs or someone else's. If your grandparents were hard workers who made it big and passed the money on to you, then you have a pretty good pool of assets to draw on for income. People who have a save-not-spend attitude and who are skillful at investing ultimately have a good deal of asset income. Some churches urge members to work hard but not spend; those church members have quite a bit of asset accumulation in the long run.[4]

Income Effect of Taxes and Transfers. Naturally, the government enters the picture. In considering the impact of government, be aware of two different ways

---

[4] Max Weber and Robert Tawney have written excellent books about the link between religion, in particular Protestantism, and the rise of capitalism.

of looking at how income distribution may be studied. One is called *ex ante* and the other is *ex post*. The *ex ante* income distribution is the income distribution that exists before the impact of any government actions. The *ex post* income distribution takes into account the effect of government actions. What impact does the government have? It imposes taxes and gives transfers, and these can have a major impact on the final distribution of income.

Taxes are monies collected by the government for which people receive no direct and immediate benefit. A fee for entry to a park is not a tax. Neither is a highway toll a tax. Similarly, transfers are monies received from the government that people did not work for and earn today. Government employees receive labor income, not transfers. Examples of transfers are cash assistance or food stamps or a subsidized college loan.

Government transfers may take one of two forms. Transfers may be cash, or they may be "in kind." Cash transfers are easy to understand. If someone receives a check from the government and didn't earn it through work, it is a cash transfer. This distinction should not be interpreted to mean that transfers are unearned or un-

Core-Info

The three components of an individual's income are:
1. Income from labor
2. Income from assets
3. Income from government transfers

deserved. People who receive unemployment compensation earned that transfer by working at least a minimum number of weeks before losing their jobs.

The Actual Distribution of Income

How much income is there? What is the average amount of earnings in the country? That answer is shown in Figure 9.8. The earnings presented in the middle column are shown in "current dollars," and no effect for inflation has been included. We were not 12.4 times as well off in 1990 as we were in 1950. Income improved, but not by that much. Inflation ate up a good portion of the dollar increase in earnings. The third column takes inflation into account and shows the equivalent, effective level of per capita earnings. This column shows that Americans were actually 2.29 times better off in dollar terms in 1990 than they were in 1950 from an income standpoint.[5]

Figure 9.8

Per Capita Income in the United States		
Year	Dollar Income	Effective Income
1950	$ 1,501	$ 6,228
1960	2,219	7,497
1970	3,893	10,034
1980	9,910	12,027
1990	18,635	14,258

[5.] Were people *really* 2.29 times better off in 1990 than they were in 1950? There was AIDS, more crime, and toxic waste dumps in 1990. On the other hand, Americans had eradicated smallpox and ended the Cold War; more than 80 percent had color television sets. It's your call.

Declining American Incomes?

Everybody *knows* that American incomes have not kept pace with inflation. We know it and our politicians reinforce it each time they try to throw out the incumbents. We may *know* it, but is it true? Recent studies indicate that this is not the case. Let's take a look.

There are two ways to look at earnings. First, you can look at paychecks and money received by workers. Second, you can look at the total compensation of workers including benefits. The graph below presents both approaches.

As you can see, if you are looking only at hourly earnings by workers, their real earnings have fallen. While the average wage rate may have been rising, when the effects of inflation are subtracted, real pay has fallen. That would seem to prove our prior belief. When the total compensation package of workers is included, however, a different picture emerges. In this case, real incomes have risen fairly steadily since the mid-1960s.

What, then, is the difference between "earnings" and "compensation"? Earnings includes only direct financial pay. Compensation, on the other hand, includes the benefits that employers provide or are required to pay for. Paid health insurance premiums, pensions, and the employer's share of Social Security and Medicare taxes are examples. These forms of noncash pay have been increasing significantly.

First, business payments for health insurance premiums have risen. In 1970, businesses paid $13.7 billion for health services. By 1991, business' share had risen to $205.4 billion. A second factor is that the Social Security and Medicare tax rates have risen as has the income base on which the tax is applied. In 1970 the maximum payment by employers for Social Security for an employee was $374. By 1993 it had risen to $5,529. Finally, employers and employees have pushed for fringe benefits increases because these benefits are presently exempt from taxation, so the net effect to the employee of a benefit increase is greater than an equal increase in wages.

So there you have it. You are now equipped to argue with those who claim that workers have become worse off because of the lousy Democrats/Republicans/Other who are in office. We are not, and you now have the data to prove it.

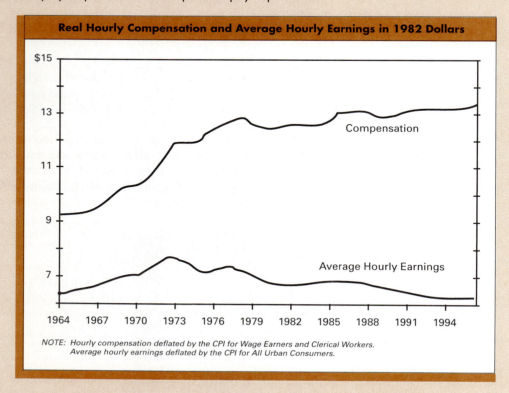

Source: *National Economic Trends.* Federal Reserve Bank of St. Louis. June 1996. p. 1.

FIGURE 9.9

Income Distribution by Quintile			
Quintile	Percentage of Total Income		
	1969	1979	1991
Lowest 20%	4.1%	4.1%	4.5%
Middle 60%	52.9%	51.7%	51.4%
Top 20%	43.0%	44.2%	44.2%

Who gets it? Is income in the United States distributed equally, or is it highly unequal? It should be no surprise that income is unequally distributed. Is it too unequally distributed? That question moves out of the realm of the positive and into the realm of the normative. You can make your own judgment call from Figure 9.9. One source of agreement on this table is that income distribution has been remarkably consistent over the past quarter century. The poorest 20 percent of Americans, the lowest quintile or fifth, consistently received less than 5 percent of the total income while the richest 20 percent, the top quintile, consistently received more than 40 percent. (Note that this is *ex ante* income distribution. Government programs and taxes helped to reduce the inequality.)

Nearly everybody agrees that there should be some income inequality. Why? Incentives, of course. If everyone earned the same income regardless of abilities, education, or efforts, there wouldn't be much incentive to try. The theory is that capitalism allows for greater income inequality than socialism because of capitalism's reliance on monetary incentives. The interesting point is that reality is quite different from theory. The income distribution of families is very, very similar in most developed countries of the world whether capitalist or socialist. There is the same proportion of rich, middle class, and poor in most developed economies. It is not the distribution that differs but the level of efficiency and the size of the economy.

DISCRIMINATION

Some people say, "Discrimination is alive and well in the United States." Frankly, that's wrong. Discrimination is alive and sick. It is to discrimination that we now turn.

Definition

Discrimination means treating people differently based on their race, gender, religion, disability, age, or sexual orientation. People are not treated as equal individuals in a society or work place where discrimination exists; they are classified not on any measure of merit, but based on some external characteristic of a group. These groups are arranged in an artificial hierarchy: males above females, for instance, or blacks above whites, Catholics above Jews, gays above straights.

The resulting discrimination can take one of two forms: economic discrimination and social discrimination. Economic discrimination means hiring, promoting, or paying people differently based on such characteristics as race or sex, not based on the person's ability. Receiving less pay for equal work is economic discrimination. Social discrimination involves unequal treatment in places other than the marketplace. For example, some people might believe it is fine for Jews to become doctors and earn a lot of money, but "they wouldn't feel comfortable in our clubs." That is social discrimination.

We know the results of discrimination. Women earn about 70 percent of what men earn for equal work. Blacks earn approximately 70 percent of what whites earn. Minorities and women are underrepresented in most professional occupations and overrepresented in the lower wage occupations. Even the federal government appears to practice discrimination. A study of government employment shows a steady increase in the percentage of whites in government jobs as the pay and rating scales go up.

The Effects of Discrimination

The effects of discrimination are far reaching. Everybody is affected by discrimination. Discrimination, of course, affects first and foremost those who are discriminated against. However, discrimination also negatively affects those who practice discrimination and the marketplace itself.

Effects on Those Discriminated Against. Obviously, people who are discriminated against suffer. Their pay is lower and opportunities fewer. The effects can begin early in life, with fewer opportunities for education and cultural activities, and can continue through life with lower wages and less desirable jobs. In the end, those discriminated against have poorer nutrition, receive less health care, and die earlier. The cost to people who suffer discrimination is enormous.

Effects on Those Who Discriminate. Discrimination, however, is a double-edged sword. It not only hurts the person at whom it is aimed but also the person who practices it. Think about people who practice discrimination. If they won't hire women or blacks or Jews or Mexicans, they cut themselves off from a large number of people with unique gifts and abilities. They lose these people, and their competitors gain them. People who practice discrimination in hiring significantly reduce their labor supply; their supply of labor curve moves to the left. What happens to the equilibrium price when the supply is reduced? The price goes up. People who practice discrimination must pay more to hire labor, and their profits fall.

Effects on the Marketplace. Not only are individuals affected, but the whole marketplace is affected by discrimination. When discrimination is practiced, limits are placed on people. People are not free to move to occupations or jobs for which they are qualified, and firms do not hire the person best qualified for the job. The net result is that the marketplace cannot adjust efficiently and allow resources to move to those opportunities for which they are best suited. The whole economy suffers when discrimination—either economic or social—is practiced.

Core-Info

The two types of discrimination are:
1. Social discrimination
2. Economic discrimination

Discrimination of any kind hurts:
1. The person discriminated against
2. The person who discriminates
3. The entire market and economy

Solutions to the Discrimination Problem

"I'm mad as hell, and I'm not going to take it any longer!"

Do you remember that line from the movie *Network?* It expressed about the world what many of us feel about discrimination. It is time to end it. Now.

Yes, discrimination exists.

Yes, discrimination hurts everybody.

And no, we don't have to put up with it any longer.

Many strategies can be used effectively to end discrimination. We can take action to change the world and to bring the kind of "level playing field" that politicians like to talk about during an election year.

Personal Action. One obvious step you can take is personal action against discrimination. First, don't practice it. Make sure you are fair and just in all actions from the language you use to the ways you hire to the money you pay to the places you buy. Treat people fairly, and don't patronize places that practice discrimination. The former is just good business sense, as you have seen. The latter is known as "voting with your feet." By not shopping at places that practice discrimination, you help ensure that their sales and profits will fall and their businesses will suffer. And so they should.

Legislation. People can pass and enforce laws that prohibit all forms of discrimination. They can encourage their legislators to pass laws prohibiting discrimination where those laws are lacking. And, even more critical, they can demand that existing laws are actively enforced.[6] Many people—even some economists—believe that there are enough laws to accomplish the goal of a discrimination-free society *if* the laws are enforced. It is certainly worth a try.

Laissez Faire. A final option is *laissez faire,* to leave alone. Why would a rational economist who wants to end discrimination say that the best way to end it is to leave it alone? As stated earlier, if an employer doesn't like women or blacks or Asians or Jews or Hispanics and decides not to hire any, what has he done to his labor supply? He has significantly decreased his available labor supply. If there is a decrease in supply, what happens to the supply curve? It moves to the left. Finally, what happens to the equilibrium price (in this case the wage he must pay) when the supply curve moves to the left? The equilibrium price rises. Thus, when an employer practices discrimination in hiring, he not only loses the talents of those he won't hire, but he has to pay a higher wage to those he does hire. Talk about a double whammy—and a richly deserved one, too. If the discriminating employer's costs are higher, what happens to profits? By practicing discrimination, the employer has guaranteed lower profits. By not practicing discrimination, an employer can count on higher profits. Now you can see why some economists urge a *laissez faire* approach to dealing with discrimination: the market will solve the problem. It may take a while for discrimination to end this way, and most people are impatient with the existence of discrimination, but end it will. In the mean time, the good guys are rewarded while the bad guys are punished. It's just as if we were watching a Hollywood movie (or a 16th century morality play).

Core-Info

The three ways of attacking discrimination are:
1. Through personal action
2. Through legislation
3. Through *laissez faire*

LABOR RETIED

There you have it: an introduction to labor, labor unions, income, and discrimination. By now, you should have an appreciation for labor, for what affects the demand for labor, and for the unique conditions that affect its supply. You probably can put labor unions into perspective now with a better understanding of what they have and haven't done and what the concerns are now that they are on the decline. You know a bit about who gets the income in the United States. And, you know about the effects of discrimination and what can be done about it. Labor is the most basic of our resources, and understanding labor is crucial to figuring out how the economy really works.

[6.] For a long time Congress exempted itself and its members from all antidiscrimination laws it enacted for the rest of us. Congress was exempt from following nondiscriminatory practices in hiring, pay, or promotions. If members wanted to, they could discriminate against—or toward—any individual or group they wished. Many people agreed this exemption was unjust, and the laws are finally being changed to outlaw discrimination by our elected representatives.

SUMMARY

- In addition to its price, the two factors that affect the demand for labor are demand for the product and the productivity of labor.
- The supply of labor is affected by attitudes and social trends in the economy.
- The supply of labor curve has three distinct segments which display very different types of individual behavior.
- The three types of labor unions are craft, industrial, and government employee.
- The major weapons of management and labor are lockouts and strikes.
- Unions cannot force wages to rise.
- The three components of an individual's income are income from labor, assets, and government transfers.
- Both social and economic discrimination exist and negatively affect the person who discriminates, the person who is discriminated against, and the economy as a whole.
- The three ways in which we can end discrimination are by personal action, legislation, and *laissez faire*.

KEY TERMS

Backward bending supply curve
Binding arbitration
Closed shop
Collective bargaining
Craft union
Derived demand
Government employee union
Industrial union
Labor union
Lockout
Open shop
Right-to-work laws
Strike
Union shop
Work-to-rule

REVIEW QUESTIONS

1. What are the two factors at work in making the demand for labor a derived demand?
2. Define the term *elasticity of demand for labor* and identify the three factors that affect it.
3. Draw a backward bending supply curve for your own labor. Identify where on the curve you are now and where you think you will be ten years from now.
4. Do all college expenditures help build human capital? What of tuition? Books? Room and board? Library and parking fines? Basketball game tickets?
5. What are the three types of labor unions? Which type is most likely to be involved in your future occupation? Why that type of union?
6. Why do unions and management try to avoid strikes and lockouts? What are some methods they can use to arrive at an agreeable settlement?
7. What are the two types of discrimination that can occur and how are people affected by each?
8. Identify and give an example of each of the three ways we can attack discrimination.

CHAPTER 9 • LABOR, UNIONS, AND THE DISTRIBUTION OF INCOME

PROBLEM-SOLVING PRACTICE

1. Attorney Ted King has a labor supply schedule that looks like the following:

Labor Hours Supplied	Hourly Wage Rate
0	$ 2
0	5
20	10
40	20
60	40
75	100
55	150
50	300
40	500
25	1,000

    (a) Calculate the weekly wage rate Ted King would make based on the hourly wage rate and the hours to be worked.

    (b) Draw Ted King's individual labor supply curve. Why does it take the shape it does?

2. The Bear Brokers are a small stock brokerage firm in a medium-sized, Midwestern city. Bear Brokers was able to hire competent financial clerks at $7 per hour. However, labor market conditions have changed, as represented by the labor market supply and demand schedules for financial clerks in this labor market.

Supply		Demand	
Hourly Wage Rate	Labor Supplied	Hourly Wage Rate	Labor Demanded
$13	100	$ 5	100
11	80	7	80
9	60	9	60
7	40	11	40
5	20	13	20

    (a) Construct the labor market supply and demand curves for financial clerks.

    (b) If Bear Brokers and other brokers tried to offer $7 an hour, what would happen in this labor market?

    (c) Identify the equilibrium wage and labor quantity equilibrium in this market.

    (d) Union organizers are trying to unionize financial clerks in this city. A major benefit of the union, organizers claim would be the union's ability to raise wages to $11 an hour. If nothing else changed, what would happen in this labor market at the wage of $11 per hour?

3. Using supply and demand curves for labor, demonstrate the various ways a labor union might attempt to influence the supply and/or the demand for the workers the union represents.

CHAPTER 10

The Firm

CHAPTER OUTLINE

A. The How of Economics: the Firm
B. Definition of a Firm
C. Controlling the Firm
   1. Internal Control of the Firm
   2. Things That Are Said About Managers
   3. Major Firm Managers
D. The Major Types of Firms
   1. Sole Proprietorships
   2. Partnerships
   3. Corporations
E. Other Ways of Organizing Firms
   1. Labor-Managed Firms
   2. Not-For-Profit Firms
   3. Publicly Owned Firms
F. Firms and Markets
   1. Definition of a Market
   2. Types of Markets and Competition

The purpose of this chapter is to introduce the types of firms that exist, to identify how firms are regulated, and to examine the nature of costs and markets for the firm.

AFTER COMPLETING THIS CHAPTER, YOU WILL BE ABLE TO:

1. Describe the role of managers in the firm and identify the three key management positions.
2. Compare and contrast the three major and three minor classifications of firms and explain the situations in which each type of firm serves best.
3. Explain the concept of market as the locus of activities for firms.

The How of Economics: The Firm

Now is the time to look at how things get done in a capitalist economy. We have looked at basic economics, at supply and demand, and at how consumers operate. The next step is to consider how productive activity is accomplished. (Remember that in pure capitalism government has an extremely limited role to play and is not involved in producing or consuming goods and services.)

Do you remember the four economic questions and how they are answered in capitalism?

***WHAT** is to be produced? Decided by consumers.*
***HOW** are goods to be produced? Decided by firms.*
***WHO** gets the goods? Decided by the prices of the goods.*
***WHEN** are the goods provided? Decided by consumers.*

This chapter explores the mechanism used to decide the second question.

DEFINITION OF A FIRM

Firm
An organization that combines resources to provide the goods and services demanded in an economy.

The definition of a firm is not very complicated: a **firm** is an organization that combines resources to produce the goods and services demanded by consumers. Though it is straightforward, this definition contains a lot of information. The definition of a firm reminds us that consumers are ultimately in control. Firms respond to consumer demand and produce the products and services that consumers want. Firms combine resources in accomplishing this goal. What are the resources that firms combine? What are the four economic resources (or inputs or factors of production) introduced earlier in this book? Land, labor, capital, and entrepreneurship. Firms decide how much land, labor, and capital to use and look for ways to bring entrepreneurship or creativity to bear on the production of goods and services. These inputs are substitutes for each other, and firms combine them in such a way as to maximize production while minimizing cost.

Core-Info

1. Firms are the part of the capitalistic economy that answers the "How?" question of economics.
2. A firm is an organization that combines resources to provide the goods and services demanded by consumers in a capitalistic economy.

CONTROLLING THE FIRM

If firms are responsible for producing the goods and services in the economy, there had better be a good method of regulating and controlling what they do. Out in the marketplace where suppliers and demanders meet, you can find a pretty good regulator in action to efficiently direct both parties toward optimal actions. That regulator is known as price.

Price serves as the regulator of markets. It sends signals to both suppliers and demanders that direct them to adjust their actions to move toward an equilibrium in which goods are provided to those who want them from those who have the ability to produce them.

Price is an efficient regulator of markets. No one has to sit down and calculate a list of correct prices, tell consumers when to buy more or less, or tell producers when to increase or decrease production. Through the interaction of supply and demand (driven by consumer wants and producers' costs), prices automatically move up or down, and consumers and producers respond appropriately.

Internal Control of the Firm

Because price is so efficient and effective as a regulator in the marketplace, some people have tried to use it inside firms as the regulator there. The buyer would purchase the raw materials and sell them to the loading dock. The loading dock would sell the goods to the storeroom. The storeroom would sell the goods to the shop floor. The shop floor would sell the finished products to the sales department. The sales department would sell the goods to the customer. Whew! It makes you tired just thinking about it, doesn't it? If you get tired thinking about it, imagine how tired employees of the firm would get if they tried to actually use prices at all levels within the firm. Prices, which are very efficient as regulators outside the firm, are very inefficient as regulators inside the firm. A different type of regulator is needed to direct the actions of the firm toward the efficient use of resources. That regulator is the manager.

Things That Are Said about Managers

Many things have been said about managers; some couldn't be repeated in this book. Rather than dwell on the negatives, let's focus on the positive things about managers. There are, in fact, four specific things that can be said about managers.

First, managers operate to make production happen at the lowest possible cost given the product to be made. This is true for all managers whether their products are expensive or inexpensive. Once consumers have decided what they want, firms must supply this demand. If the firm hopes to make a profit, it must be careful not to waste anything for all waste comes directly out of profits. With inexpensive products, that is obvious, but what of expensive goods? How many gold filings could a jewelry craftsperson waste before managers should become concerned? The materials that go into the production of an expensive item have a greater cost than those that are used in an inexpensive one. Thus, a high level of care must be exercised by all managers if they hope to make a profit.

Second, managers act to prevent shirking. This statement is almost an outgrowth of the first one; it relates to the fact that very few products are made and delivered to the marketplace by only one person. Batman had Robin, Bonnie had Clyde, and even the Lone Ranger had Tonto to ride into town and check things out for him. It is much more likely that production takes place through the cooperation of teams of workers. One person lays out the fabric, another cuts it, another sets the major seams, another does the final touches, another packages the clothing for shipment. If any person lets down in this chain, the whole team suffers. It is the manager's job to make certain that all workers do their part or the whole organization will pay the price.

Third, managers are motivated by competition for their jobs. Most people believe they could do their boss's job better than he or she is doing it. Unfortunately, the employees who work for those people believe the same thing. Given these strongly held beliefs and the fact that the corporate ladder gets narrower as it ascends, there is a constant pressure below managers that motivates them for their current job as well as a constant pressure within them that motivates them toward their next job. This dual motivation is believed to drive managers forward in their jobs.

Fourth, managers often receive a bonus for the success of their work group. They are made **residual claimants.** As with many economics phrases, this term probably seems incomprehensible until you break it down into its parts.

Residual Claimant
A person who has a right to the profits of a business.

What is a claimant? Someone who has a claim or right to something. What is a residual? Something that is left over. What is left over in business? If a firm is doing well, it has profit left over after it covers all costs. Businesses take in money from selling their products, pay their bills, and have profit left. By making managers a residual claimant, businesses put them in a position to benefit if the company or work group is a success. Tying compensation to profit encourages the manager to be as cost efficient as possible. If the manager knows that a portion of the money saved will go directly into his or her pocket, the manager is thought to be more likely to work hard.

How are managers made residual claimants? A variety of methods have been used. Profit-sharing plans exist in some companies whereby a portion of the profits is divided among the managers (and sometimes the workers as well). Bonus plans, stock option plans, and other incentive schemes have been used to encourage managers to work harder and to be more concerned with efficiency.

Core-Info

Managers are the regulators of the firm. These statements tend to apply to all managers:

1. Managers try to make production happen at the lowest possible cost.
2. Managers act to prevent shirking.
3. Managers are motivated by competition for their jobs.
4. Managers are often residual claimants, sharing in any profits.

Major Firm Managers

The initials that denote the top management posts in most companies are used commonly in news media reports and general conversation these days.

Topping the list is the CEO, the chief executive officer. The chief executive officer is the ultimate authority in the firm. This person is responsible for everything—all production, all planning, all spending and revenue, all legalities. President Truman used to have a sign on his desk that acknowledged these duties when he was the CEO of the country. His sign read, "The buck stops here." The CEO may delegate many duties to others, but he or she is ultimately responsible.

Another top manager is the COO, the chief operating officer. The chief operating officer is responsible for the day-to-day operations of the firm. This person oversees the production of whatever goods or services the firm produces. Typically the COO is not responsible for long-range planning or for watching the money but focuses his or her energy on getting the goods produced as efficiently as possible.

Watching the money is the CFO, the chief financial officer. The chief financial officer is responsible for monitoring the revenues, paying the bills, and accounting for the profit. The CFO is not responsible for seeing that the goods are produced or distributed, only with controlling the monetary aspects of the firm.

Obviously in a small firm, one person is likely to fill all three roles, and that is one weakness of the small business. Each person has a unique set of gifts and abilities. To the extent that each person can specialize and put that skill set to work, the firm can operate more efficiently and effectively.

Core-Info

The three major leaders in a firm are:

1. The chief executive officer (CEO)
2. The chief operating officer (COO)
3. The chief financial officer (CFO)

FIGURE 10.1
Not all businesses are a success—some file for bancruptcy. Fortunately over the past eight years while the total number of firms has increased, the number of failures has decreased.

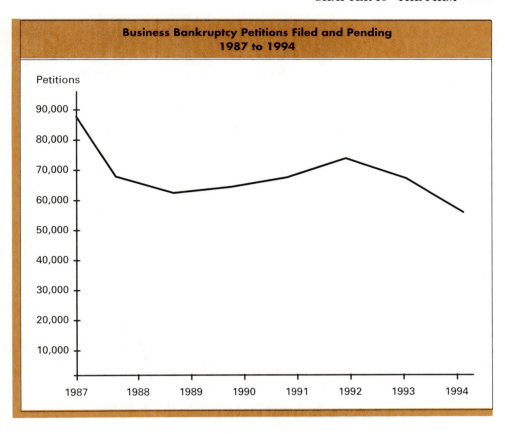

THE MAJOR TYPES OF FIRMS

We will move now to an examination of the firms that these managers manage. Because firms are the vehicle for producing goods and services in the economy, we must understand how they are organized to gain some sense of why they do what they do. The organization of a firm is based on the owner's desires and the advantages and disadvantages of each organizational type. Figure 10.2 provides a summary of business organizations.

Sole Proprietorships

Sole Proprietorship
A form of business owned and operated by an individual.

Sole proprietorships are the most common type of business because they are the simplest type to organize and run. In a sole proprietorship, the owner is the manager of everything. The business is considered to be an extension of the person who owns it, and any profits are reported on the owner's individual income tax return.

Nearly three quarters of all businesses in the country are sole proprietorships, but they generate less than 10 percent of all business revenues. They offer the advantages of allowing the owner to have direct control over the firm, to be his or her own boss, and to get all the profits. On the down side, because the owner is all alone in the venture, it is more difficult to get funds for expansion, she or he must bear all losses, and, most important of all, the owner faces **unlimited liability.** Unlimited liability means that the owner is completely and solely responsible for what happens in the business. If the business loses money, it comes out of the owner's pocket. If the business is sued, the owner is sued personally, and the owner's assets can be attached to meet any creditor's demands or lawsuits that are lost. Obviously this responsibility creates a real risk for sole proprietors. Their home, savings, and future income are at stake when serious business problems occur.

Unlimited Liability
The idea that the owners of a business are completely and personally responsible for debts of certain types of firms.

FIGURE 10.2

Major Types of Business Organizations				
Type	% of Firms	% of Revenue	Advantages	Disadvantages
Sole proprietorship	74	7	Easy to organize Owner gets all Be own boss Direct control	Limited funds to expand Bear all losses Must be good at all Unlimited liability
Partnership	9	3	Easy to organize Easier to borrow Extra skills Shared risks	Profits shared Hard to dissolve Unlimited liability Costs to organize
Corporation	17	90	Easier to raise funds Ownership and control separate A legal "person" Limited liability	No owner control Extra rules and taxes

FIGURE 10.3
Passing new rules on businesses will reach a large number of *small* businesses. On the other hand, if you exempt small businesses from new regulations, you will miss a large portion of the workforce. *Source:* U.S. Bureau of the Census

Number of Establishments and Employees by Employment-Size Class: 1992 (In Thousands)		
Employment-Size Class	Establishments	Employees
Under 20	5,507 (87.2%)	25,000 (26.9%)
20 to 99	678 (10.7%)	27,030 (29.1%)
100 to 499	118 (1.9%)	22,227 (24.0%)
500 to 999	9 (0.1%)	6,270 (6.8%)
1000 or more	6 (0.1%)	12,275 (13.2%)
TOTAL	6,318	92,801

The disadvantages of sole proprietorships have led to a search for other ways to structure businesses. That search resulted in the next form of business, the partnership.

Partnerships. **Partnerships** are very similar to sole proprietorships except they involve more than one owner. In partnerships, two or more persons join to operate a business. Firms often choose to adopt the partnership form because it is in the best interest of all partners to be productive.

Partnerships are the least frequent form of business in the United States. Less than 10 percent of businesses are partnerships, and these businesses generate 3 percent of all business revenues. These businesses are still relatively easy to organize and permit a sharing of the risks (any loss is divided among the partners). Multiple owners contribute varied skills to the ownership team, and it is typically easier to borrow money for expansion. The negative aspects of partnerships include the need to share the profits among the owners and unlimited liability for all owners—including liability for what the *other* owners might do. Finally, partnerships are difficult to dissolve or break up.

As an example of the difficulty of dissolving a partnership, think about a business valued at $10 million and owned by two partners. If one partner wants to leave the business, what must the other do? Come up with $5 million and buy the first one out. Where does he or she get this money? Most likely the firm's bank would lend the remaining partner the $5 million needed—at 10 percent interest. Even as simple interest, this means that the now sole proprietor must pay $500,000 in interest each year just to own his or her own business, and this $500,000 will have to come out of profits. Now you can see the difficulties involved in dissolving a partnership.

Partnership
A form of business similar to a sole proprietorship but owned by two or more individuals.

Again, the disadvantages of the partnership have led to a desire to find another way to organize businesses, one which allows businesses to accumulate capital through multiple owners but which protects the owners from the responsibility for the business itself. That form is known as the corporation.

Corporations. Because they eliminate many of the disadvantages of sole proprietorships and partnerships, **corporations** are the dominant form of business today. While there are numerically more sole proprietorships, corporations earn about 90 percent of all business revenues. Thus, corporations tend to be larger than sole proprietorships or partnerships. However, size is not a requirement one way or the other. Many corporations are very small, and the Ford Motor Company was a sole proprietorship until the 1950s when it adopted the corporate form.

The major advantage corporations have is that they separate ownership from control of the firm. A person can be an owner of the firm through the purchase of **stock.** These owners elect a board of directors, which selects and oversees the management of the firm. The corporation exists on its own, separate from the owners. The corporation can sign contracts. It can sue and be sued. It costs money and time to organize the business, and a corporation faces extra rules and taxes, but it does offer **limited liability.** With limited liability, owners are not responsible and cannot be sued for the actions of the corporation. If the corporation is sued because of some problem and loses the suit, the worst thing that can happen to the stockholders (the owners of the corporation) is that they lose their investment when the firm goes bankrupt. The owner's liability is limited to the amount of his or her investment. A disadvantage to owners is that individually they have no control over what the corporation does. If the corporation pollutes or discriminates in hiring, one stockholder cannot do much to alter the policy.

One new type of corporation that has come onto the scene recently is known as the **S corporation.** This type of corporation is designed for relatively small businesses with 35 or fewer stockholders. These S corporations pay no income tax directly; the earnings of the corporation must be reported as a part of the personal income taxes of the owners.

With all of its advantages for accumulating funds, for protecting the owners, and for ensuring continuity, the corporate form of business is here to stay. With the collapse of the socialist economies, no other type of business form on the horizon challenges the corporation for the foreseeable future.

OTHER WAYS OF ORGANIZING FIRMS

Occasionally businesses are organized for special purposes or to conduct nontypical activities. In these cases, a different form of business organization beyond sole proprietorships, partnerships, or corporations may be necessary.

Labor-Managed Firms

Labor-managed firms are those in which the laborers are the managers. This was the predominant form of business in the former Yugoslavia where workers elected their managers. It has been tried in a limited way in the United States in firms that were about to close; the workers took over in an attempt to save both their jobs and the company. Other similar approaches include membership on the Chrysler Corporation board of directors of a leader from the United Automobile Workers union, profit-sharing plans, and stock purchase plans wherein the workers can directly benefit from the firm's success.

Not-for-Profit Firms

Not-for-profit firms are firms that are organized to provide a service of some sort to people. Examples include churches and synagogues, soup kitchens and homeless

---

Corporation
A form of business that exists independently of the owners.

Stock
A share in the ownership of a corporation.

Limited Liability
The idea that the owners of a corporation are not responsible for the debts of the firm.

S Corporation
A type of corporation designed for small businesses with special tax requirements.

Labor-Managed Firms
A type of firm in which the workers are also the owners and managers.

Not-For-Profit Firms
Firms organized to provide a good or service generally thought to be beneficial to society. These firms do not earn a profit and do not have residual claimants.

What About the Stock Market?

Every day we hear reports like this: "Disney was up a quarter while McDonald's lost an eighth." What we're hearing about, of course, is the performance of the company's stock on the stock markets for the day. Let's look at the stock markets and see why they exist and what they accomplish.

If you own shares of stock, you can sell them to anybody, but how do you find a buyer? What you need is some organized way to let potential buyers know you have stock for sale. That task is accomplished by brokers and stock markets such as the New York Stock Exchange.

Stock markets are places where people can buy and sell shares of stock in various companies. It is a free-floating market in which the price of a stock is determined by what buyers are willing to pay and what sellers want to get for their stock. A lot of factors affect what a stock is worth, including the number of shares of the stock available, sales this year and expected sales next year, profits, the expected health of the overall economy, anticipated government actions and regulations, and a host of other tangible and intangible factors.

The price of each stock is reported in daily newspapers so owners can keep track of their stocks (or their dream portfolio). The stocks of three companies are presented here to illustrate how to read the stock tables. This exercise uses three companies in the automobile industry, Chrysler Corporation, Ford Motor Corporation, and General Motors Corporation. The following is a report taken from a single day's trading activity and displayed as you might see it in your daily newspaper.

A	B	C	D	E	F	G	H	I	J	K
52 Week		Stock	Div	Yld	PE	Sales	High	Lo	Last	Chg
Hi	Lo					100's				
64 7/8	41 1/8	Chryslr	2.40	3.8	10	19476	63 5/8	62 3/4	63 1/8	−1/4
37 1/8	25 3/4	FordM	1.40	3.9	13	33141	35 7/8	35 3/8	35 5/8	−1/4
58 1/8	42 3/8	GnMotr	1.60	2.8	8	18796	57	56 1/8	56 1/2	−1/2

At first glance these data may make little sense. Even after mastering Chapter 2, the table isn't easy to understand. Fortunately, most newspapers include a guide to help you read the stock market reports. The list below provides that information. It may take a little time to work your way through the table, but it is worth it. Once you can read this with ease, you can follow any company that interests you. These data are valuable to stock buyers, stockholders, and job hunters.

A— The highest price the stock has traded at in the past year. Prices are reported in dollars and eighths of a dollar.
B— The lowest price the stock has traded at in the past year.
C— The name of the company.
D— The annual dividend rate paid on the stock.
E— The annual dividend rate divided by the closing price of the stock.
F— The closing price of the stock divided by the company's earnings per share for the past year.
G— The number of shares of stock traded during the day in hundreds of shares.
H— The highest price the stock reached during the day.
I— The lowest price the stock reached during the day.
J— The last price at which the stock was traded.
K— The gain or loss in the price of the stock for the day compared to the previous day's closing price.

shelters, and many private colleges. Not-for-profit firms are different from firms that are designed to make a profit in that there are no residual claimants; no one can share in any difference between what is taken in, often through donations, and what is spent. Any excess may be accumulated over the short run, but it all has to be plowed back into the business.

In economics the term *not-for-profit* is quite different from *nonprofit*. The former term designates a firm that has been organized not to make a profit under the existing tax codes. A nonprofit firm is one like General Motors which, while designed to make a profit, actually lost more than $20 billion in 1992. It was most definitely a nonprofit firm that year.

Publicly Owned Firms

Publicly owned firms are businesses that are owned and operated by the government. Sometimes these firms exist when it makes economic sense for only one firm to exist. This condition is known as a **natural monopoly.** In a natural monopoly, it would be inefficient for more than one firm to exist in an industry. Examples are the water supply systems and electric power providers in a city. Urban areas probably don't need 20 different water companies digging up their city streets to lay or work on pipes. One company will cost much less for consumers even though the result is a monopoly. In these instances, a publicly owned firm is often formed. Sometimes, however, publicly owned firms exist alongside profit seeking companies. The U.S. Postal Service competes with a number of firms for package delivery (although it has a pure monopoly in the delivery of first class mail), and public hospitals and recreation facilities compete with their private counterparts.

The economic problem that publicly owned firms face is that, lacking the profit motive, they tend to be inefficiently run. Without the pressure for maximum profit, and often with a monopoly of some sort, these firms do not find themselves faced with the necessity to operate at maximum efficiency and thus do not.

In America there is a tendency to criticize government workers as being lazy individuals. However, studies have shown that the same supposedly "lazy" workers become quite efficient when they begin to work in a profit-seeking firm. Similarly, formerly efficient workers from the private sector tend to slack off when placed in a government bureaucracy. The system, not the individual, seems to be at fault.

Publicly Owned Firms
Businesses that are owned and operated by the government.

Natural Monopoly
A situation in which it makes sense from an economic standpoint to have only one firm in an industry.

Core-Info

The three major ways in which firms are organized are:
1. Sole proprietorships
2. Partnerships
3. Corporations

Firms also may be organized as:
1. Labor-managed firms
2. Not-for-profit firms
3. Publicly owned firms

FIRMS AND MARKETS

Definition of Market

As their definition states, firms exist to provide the goods and services that consumers want. Firms on the one hand produce goods and services, while consumers on the other hand demand various goods and services. Where these two meet is in the **market.** The market is where sellers and buyers, suppliers and demanders, meet and exchange goods. It is in the market that prices are established through the interaction of supply and demand. When these two are free to move in response to consumer demands and supplier costs, an equilibrium is achieved that provides for a stable economic world.

Market
A place in which buyers and sellers exchange goods and services produced and desired in an economy and which, if allowed to function freely, results in equilibrium.

Core-Info

The market is the place where buyers and sellers, suppliers and demanders, consumers and firms meet.

Types of Markets and Competition

It is easy to see that the number of firms varies greatly from industry to industry. Some industries have a single firm that supplies all of a good. Other industries have a large number of firms. In addition, the level of competition within an industry can be anything from nonexistent to intense. As you would expect, the number of firms in an industry and the level of competition that each faces has a dramatic effect on the operation of the firm. The different types of markets are the subject of the next chapter.

SUMMARY

- The role of managers inside the firm is much like that of prices in the marketplace. They provide direction and guidance. The three top positions in a firm are chief executive officer, chief operating officer, and chief financial officer.
- The three major types of firms are sole proprietorships, partnerships, and corporations.
- The three other ways in which firms may be organized are as labor-managed, not-for-profit, and publicly owned firms.
- Markets are the place where firms sell their products to consumers.

KEY TERMS

Corporations
Firm
Labor-managed firms
Limited liability
Market
Natural monopoly
Not-for-profit firms
Partnerships
Publicly owned firms
Residual claimants
S corporation
Sole proprietorships
Stock
Unlimited liability

REVIEW QUESTIONS

1. Managers are the regulators of the firm. What are four things that can be said about managers?
2. Identify and describe the major types of firms.
3. Explain the advantages and disadvantages of sole proprietorships, partnerships, and corporations.
4. Explain the difference between limited and unlimited liability.
5. Explain the roles of labor-managed, not-for-profit, and publicly owned firms.
6. Describe the concept of natural monopoly.
7. Define markets and explain their roles in the economic world.

PROBLEM-SOLVING PRACTICE

1. Describe the roles of each of the following types of firm managers:
    (a) CEO
    (b) COO
    (c) CFO

2. Explain when you as an owner would prefer each of the following types of business organizations:
   (a) proprietorship
   (b) partnership
   (c) corporation
   (d) worker-owned company
3. In a capitalist market economy, under what circumstances might a publicly owned company be a good option? Name some specific examples of publicly owned companies in the U.S. economy.

CHAPTER 11

Competition and Monopoly

CHAPTER OUTLINE

A. Perfect Competition and Monopoly as Models
B. Perfect Competition: the Dream
   1. The Conditions Required
      a. Homogeneous Product
      b. Large Number of Buyers and Sellers
      c. No Barriers to Entry or Exit
      d. Information Is Perfect and Free
   2. The Frequency of Perfect Competition
C. Monopoly: the Nightmare
   1. The Conditions Required
      a. Unique Product
      b. Single Seller
      c. Barriers Exist to Entry
      d. Information Costs—Imperfect Information
   2. The Frequency of Monopoly
D. The Benefits and Costs of Perfect Competition and Monopoly
E. Supply and Demand in Perfect Competition and Monopoly
F. Summary of Competition and Monopoly
G. Economic Concentration and Its Measures
   1. Aggregate Concentration
   2. Industry Concentration
H. Mergers
   1. The Structure of the Productive Process
   2. Definition of Merger
   3. Types of Mergers
      a. Horizontal
      b. Vertical
      c. Conglomerate
   4. Concerns about Mergers
I. Solutions to the Monopoly Problem
   1. Prohibition
   2. Price Regulation
   3. Government Ownership
   4. *Laissez Faire*
J. From Fiction to Reality

The purpose of this chapter is to introduce the outside boundaries of market structure and to examine the nature of industrial concentration in the United States.

AFTER COMPLETING THIS CHAPTER, YOU WILL BE ABLE TO:

1. Identify and describe the conditions that are required for perfect competition and monopoly.
2. Use supply and demand curves to explain the nature of both the firms and markets in perfect competition and monopoly.
3. Demonstrate the effect of economies of scale on firms and markets.
4. Describe three types of mergers that may occur and explain the impact of each type on the market.
5. Demonstrate four methods that may be used to control the effect of monopolies in the marketplace.

Perfect Competition and Monopoly as Models

Our introduction to economics will move now to the wider arena. Thus far, we have looked at consumers (who answer the "What?" question in capitalism) and have begun to understand what makes them tick. We have also looked at firms (which answer the "How?" question) and have seen how they organize to produce the goods that consumers want. We now need to bring these two actors in the economic drama together on their natural stage—the marketplace.

The **market** is an important place in economics. It is where buyers and sellers, demanders and suppliers get together. Buyers want certain goods and services. They want many things, they have limited incomes, and they have to pay for their goods. In the market, they seek the best set of deals possible to meet their varied needs. Firms, the suppliers, come to the market ready to meet consumers' needs and seeking to make a profit. Regardless of any other motivation that a firm or a manager might have, the company will ultimately go out of business unless it makes a real profit.

As you can see, this marketplace is a critical one for consumers and firms, for demanders and suppliers. Both come to the marketplace seeking to maximize their own welfare—consumers to maximize their satisfaction given their tastes and incomes and firms to maximize their profits given consumers' demands. Because the marketplace is critical for suppliers and demanders, it is critical for all people. After all, people are both demanders and suppliers. They are in the marketplace on both sides of the equation. Sometimes they are suppliers, offering their goods or labor services to buyers for a price. Sometimes they are demanders, looking for goods or labor services to buy. In both cases, how the market is organized, who has power, and how prices are set are all critical. In a free market, consumers have some control over prices, but under certain conditions consumers may have no impact on pricing. An examination of markets and their structure will illustrate when and why this is so.

Markets in a capitalistic system are organized in three basic ways: perfect competition, monopoly, and imperfect competition. This chapter covers the first two of these structures, perfect competition and monopoly. We will defer the discussion of imperfect competition until the next chapter after we have built an understanding of what the extreme or outside conditions are.

In this examination of perfect competition and monopoly, it is important to be aware of three points. First, these two ideas are artificial constructs, straw men if you will. As you will see, neither perfect competition nor monopoly really exist. (In fact, they're as rare as pure capitalism, as you will see in Chapter 14.) Why then do economists build these two ideas and hold them up for examination? Because perfect competition and monopoly define the outside boundaries for markets. Every market, in reality, lies somewhere in between these two extremes. If you can understand the boundaries, the issues that define them, and the advantages and disadvantages of each, you can better understand the real world in between the two extremes.

The second point to note is that perfect competition and monopoly are models. Do you remember the definition of the term *model* from Chapter 1? Models are representations of reality, ways of looking at the world. Models tend to simplify reality so people can look at it and examine it carefully. A model used frequently in this book is that of the law of demand. The law of demand is a model that says the quantity of a good that consumers are willing and able to buy is inversely related to the price of that good. When the price of a good is high, *ceteris paribus* (all else equal), the quantity that people will buy is low. Of course, there is much more to consumers' decisions about how much of any good they will buy. Chapter 6 covered some of these factors: income, tastes, prices of other goods, expectations about tomorrow's prices or incomes, and a host of other factors. In spite of these qualifications, economists persist in using the law of demand model as the primary descriptor of consumer be-

---

Market
The place where buyers and sellers exchange goods and services produced and desired in an economy and which, if allowed to function freely, results in equilibrium.

CHAPTER 11 • COMPETITION AND MONOPOLY

havior. Why? Because models serve two purposes: they help people to understand what is going on today and they help to predict what could happen tomorrow. If one t-shirt store on the beach sells shirts for $8 and the shop next to it sells similar shirts for $11, the law of demand explains why the first store sells more t-shirts than the second. In addition, the law of demand allows people to predict what could happen. For instance, according to the law of demand, if the second store were to reduce its prices, it would sell more t-shirts. Thus, economists use models to better understand the world around them and to look down the road at what might come to pass. This is the case with the models of perfect competition and monopoly.

The third point to be aware of is that these first pages of this discussion already have done something that some economists warn against: using the terms *perfect competition* and *monopoly*. These economists seem to feel that using these terms in the absence of a true perfect monopoly in the real world might be confusing. To quote the immortal Scrooge, "Bah! Humbug!" You may not be able to define the perfect sports car, but you know one when you see one. In the same vein, our definition of monopoly and perfect competition might not be 100 percent correct, but these constructs are certainly close enough to define the outside boundaries of markets and to help bring real-life markets into focus. Thus, we shall use the terms freely in this chapter and throughout the book.

Core-Info

All markets, the places where buyers and sellers determine prices and output, are organized in one of three ways: as perfect competition, as monopolies, or as imperfect competition.

PERFECT COMPETITION: THE DREAM

Perfect Competition
A market model in which there is a very large number of buyers and sellers, entry and exit are possible, the product is homogeneous, and information is free.

The first of two polar opposites is **perfect competition.** Perfect competition is the economist's dream. Under true perfect competition, the greatest amount of goods would be produced at the lowest possible cost. Every resource (land, labor, capital, and entrepreneurship) would be paid its full and appropriate amount. Goods would go to those who really valued them. The economy would adjust quickly and smoothly to every disturbance. Workers would receive their just wage. What a lovely thing perfect competition is—or would be, if it were possible.

As hard as we have tried, achieving perfect competition has been elusive—and will remain so. No matter what we do, we will never get to it. It is not a matter of will; it has to do with the requirements, the conditions that must be met to achieve perfect competition. Let's consider what it would take to get there. You will discover both the advantages of perfect competition and the reasons why it cannot be attained.

The Conditions Required

Four conditions must be met to achieve perfect competition. As if that's not tough enough, these conditions must be met simultaneously. The four conditions for perfect competition are:

1. Homogeneous product
2. Large number of buyers and sellers
3. No barriers to entry or exit
4. Perfect and free information

Let's examine each of the four requirements in turn to see what they mean, why they are important, and what difficulties stand in the way of achieving them.

Homogeneous Product
A product that is completely identical regardless of who produces it such that consumers are indifferent as to where they buy it.

Homogeneous Product. A **homogeneous product** is an identical product. It is precisely the same no matter who makes it, who sells it, or who buys it. There is absolutely no variation in the product whatsoever. Examples of homogeneous products are winter wheat or Saudi light crude oil or West Texas crude. Whether you buy it from your brother, a stranger, or the store down the street, it is precisely the same product. Homogeneous products are not Uncle Ben's Rice or Safeway Rice; they're plain white rice.

If the product is homogeneous, if there is no variation at all, what factor would buyers use to decide where to purchase it? Price is everything with a homogenous good. Why wouldn't it be? The wheat is the same regardless of which farmer sells it. The oil is the same regardless of which well it comes from. If the price charged by one seller is higher than that charged by another, which one would make the sale? The one with the lowest price. This translates into pressure to keep the price down. If one supplier charges more for a product than a second supplier, people will buy it from the second supplier. The first supplier has no choice but to keep its prices down, to push them as low as possible, to sell its product. How low can the price go? The next two conditions for perfect competition help define those limits.

Large Number of Buyers and Sellers. The second condition required for perfect competition is that there must be a large number of buyers and sellers—an infinitely large number of buyers and sellers. Of particular interest is the number of sellers. Perfect competition would require thousands upon thousands of sellers of one homogeneous product. With that many sellers, it would seem as though they would all have to be very small in size, and that is true. In perfect competition, many thousands of small firms would produce an identical product. A 100-acre wheat farm in Kansas would lie in the middle of a thousand other small wheat farms across the midwest.

Because there are so many small firms, no one of them would be large enough to have any impact on price. Whether or not one farm sells its wheat this year won't affect anybody but that farm. With thousands of other farms producing wheat, even if the output on one farm doubles, it won't have much of an impact on the overall supply of wheat; it won't move the supply curve out much at all. If a farm has a terrible growing season and its output falls to zero, again it won't have any significant impact on the overall supply. If the aggregate or overall supply curve doesn't move in or out, then the price doesn't change. Thus, single suppliers can and will have no impact on the price. With thousands of others producing an identical product, one producer cannot have much of an impact on anybody. Each farm sells its wheat at the market price—the price determined by the interaction of all suppliers and all demanders taken together—or stays home. No one would pay more than the market price for anyone's wheat. And, as to selling it for less than the market price, why would anyone want to? Each farm can sell its wheat at the price that is set in the marketplace, so there is no reason to price it for less. What this means is that a firm in perfect competition is a **price taker;** it must take the price that is set in the market by the interaction of all the suppliers and demanders and sell its product for that price. A single supplier's impact in the market is nil. Each supplier has no influence, no impact; it's really not all that important in the overall market.

No Barriers to Entry or Exit. In perfect competition, the product is homogeneous and available from an enormous number of sellers. The third condition, which must exist at the same time as the first two, is the absence of **barriers** to entry or exit in the market. Barriers are restrictions or hindrances, anything that would keep a firm from doing what it wants to. In perfect competition, anyone who wants to can move into the market as a buyer or a seller. If a producer wants to, he or she can stop producing and move on to something else.

What would cause someone to want to produce a particular product? What is the prime motivating factor in business? The opportunity to serve all humankind? Of course not. It is profit! Firms are in business to make a profit. Unless they make a profit, none of their other objectives—hopefully including serving humankind—can be met. It is out of profits that firms can invest, expand, or hire more workers. It is hoped-for profits that serve as the incentive to firms to enter a particular market. Profits act as a magnet, drawing new firms into producing a product. With no barriers to entry in perfect competition, firms will enter as long as there are profits to be made.

Price Taker
The idea that in perfect competition a firm has no control over the price of its product but can sell all it produces at the market price.

Barriers
Anything that would prevent a firm from entering or leaving a market at will.

On the other hand, why would someone want to stop making a particular product? Again, the incentive of profits comes into play. This time, of course, it is the lack of profits—losses—that would convince a firm to get out of the business. If the firm were losing money, it would want to leave the industry to stop losing money and move to an industry where there is money to be made. With no barriers to exit, with no restrictions on leaving, the firm could do this quite quickly.

No barriers to entry: a firm can enter if there is profit to be made. No barriers to exit: a firm can leave if it is losing money. What is the outcome of this freedom of entry and exit? Profits will be zero. As long as firms are making profits in an industry, other firms are attracted to it. When firms are losing money, some of them leave the industry. The net effect is a profit of zero. In perfect competition, firms can fully cover the cost of producing a product, but they make no profit in the deal.

Now is a good time to deal with the issue of profit. The idea of firms making no profit probably doesn't sound enticing. However, it all has to do with how economists define profits. As you have seen, economists and business people don't think alike. To a business person, profit is what is left after the money costs are all covered. Economists define profit a bit differently. When economists calculate profits in a perfectly competitive context, they take the firm's total revenue from selling its product and subtract all costs associated with production. There are three components to these costs. First, there are **fixed costs,** those costs that don't change as output changes or as the firm produces more or less of a good (costs such as mortgage payments, property taxes, contractual salaries, etc.). Second, are **variable costs,** those costs that do change as output changes (such as raw materials, piece-rate labor, etc.). Finally, there is what is called a **normal profit,** a rate of return on the money invested in producing the product that is equal to what the firm could have earned if it had invested in the next best opportunity (another example of opportunity cost). What does not result in perfect competition is any excess profit. Firms pay all of the costs of producing the product (all of the inputs or resources or factors of production are fully paid for), but they don't get anything extra. Everything is paid for and there is no extra or waste. It sounds like an efficient way to run an economy, and so it is. That's one of the real beauties of perfect competition: there is no waste. Nothing is wasted, and resources are not diverted away from where they can be most productive. It may not be inviting to a business person, but it is a great thing to the economy as a whole.

Information Is Perfect and Free. Perfect competition requires an identical product, a very large number of buyers and sellers, and no barriers to entry or exit. This is a nice trio of conditions, but perfect competition cannot exist without a fourth as well: information must be free and perfect. In perfect competition, everybody knows what is going on. Everybody knows what the latest trends are. Everybody knows the latest technologies for producing and selling the product. Everybody knows what the expected demand for the product is going to be. Everybody knows everything, and they find out at a zero cost. Firms need to use no resources to collect all of this incredibly valuable information.

Obviously, this condition is crucial to perfect competition. Without perfect information, firms would not necessarily be aware of opportunities for profit and thus would not move into an industry where firms were earning an excess profit. Without perfect information, not everybody would know the latest techniques for producing the good, and thus some firms would have costs lower than other firms. Without perfect information, some firms would have an advantage over others and could thus in time dominate the market. With perfect information, resources can flow to the place where the return is the greatest, and the economy operates at its maximum potential on its production possibility curve.

The Frequency of Perfect Competition

Thus we have it. There are four conditions that must exist simultaneously in perfect competition. The product is homogeneous; it is identical regardless of who produces it. There must be an infinitely large number of buyers and sellers, so many

---

Fixed Costs
Costs which do not change as the level of production increases or decreases. These costs cannot be changed in the short run.

Variable Costs
Costs which increase when production increases and decrease as production decreases. These costs do change in the short run.

Normal Profit
A return to a firm that includes all costs of production and an amount equal to what could have been earned if the business had invested elsewhere; the opportunity cost of production.

sellers that no one of them has any impact on the price. Firms cover their costs but make no profits. There are no barriers to entry or exit. If there are profits to be made, firms can enter. If there are losses, firms can leave. Profits are zero. Everybody knows everything about everything, and it doesn't cost a cent to find it out. Now do you see why perfect competition can't exist in the real world? All of the required conditions cannot be met. Businesses don't want to operate in a perfectly competitive world where they have no impact, where they are at the mercy of the market, where their profits are zero. Businesses would much rather operate in the world of monopoly, and it is to that world that we now turn our attention.

Core-Info

Perfectly competitive markets produce the greatest quantity of goods at the lowest possible prices. These markets are nonexistent because they must meet four key criteria simultaneously:

1. Homogeneous product
2. Large number of buyers and sellers
3. No barriers to entry or exit
4. Perfect and free information

MONOPOLY: THE NIGHTMARE

As you examine what a monopoly is and how it operates, remember that economists like to keep the principles of their science simple and nicely packaged. If they think that there are natural barriers to something, you can bet that they also think that there are artificial barriers. If you discover that economists think that there are vertical mergers, you would be right to guess that they also think that there are horizontal mergers. The same principles are at work for the monopoly/perfect competition issue. These two market systems are portrayed as exact opposites. They are polar opposites; they define the outside boundaries of economic markets. Thus, it should come as no surprise that the conditions that must exist for monopoly are exactly the opposite of those that must exist for perfect competition. For studying purposes, if you can learn the list of conditions that are required for one market model, all you have to do is turn that list upside down to come up with the four conditions that must exist for the other market model.

The Conditions Required

Monopoly
A market model in which there is a single seller, entry is limited, the product is unique, and information is restricted.

We will examine each of the four conditions that exist in a pure **monopoly.** These conditions are:

1. Unique product
2. Single seller
3. Barriers exist to entry
4. Information is neither perfect nor free

Unique Product. If the first condition of perfect competition is that the product is homogeneous, what would be the opposite condition? A unique product is the first requirement for monopoly.

A unique product is without equal, and buyers can find no substitutes for it. You can either buy this particular product or you can do without. The choice remains yours as a consumer, but you are faced with an either-or decision. Examples of unique products are insulin to a diabetic or Porsche 356s to a collector. There really are no good substitutes. Perhaps the adjective "good" is the key. There are substitutes for insulin or Porsche 356s, but to the diabetic or collector, they are lousy substitutes.

Obviously, economists must be very careful when they insist that there be no substitutes for a product. In reality, there are substitutes for every product; it's just that they either are not very good (as in the case of diabetic shock in the absence of insulin) or they are defined differently. As you have seen, there are, in reality, substitutes for everything. There are substitutes for Safeway white bread (Kroger white bread, A & P white bread, whole wheat bread, and rye bread), for beef (pork, chicken, and lentils), for the telephone (FAX, letters, telegraph, bicycle couriers, carrier pigeons, and two tin cans with a string), for water (milk, orange juice, smelly bodies if people don't take a shower, and brown grass if they don't water their lawns), and for anything else you can imagine. That's why some economists don't like to use the word "monopoly."

The key to the term *monopoly* is to carefully define the product or market without limiting it unreasonably. If you define your product too tightly (Oscar Meyer wieners, for instance), then Oscar Meyer does have a monopoly in the sale of Oscar Meyer wieners. So what? If you define the product too loosely (all forms of intraurban communications, for example) then nobody could have a monopoly over anything. We'll consider this issue a little later, but it is important to remember that it is an area of conflict (and many professional papers) for economists.

Single Seller. The second condition that is required for perfect competition is that there be many sellers, an infinite number of sellers. The opposite condition is one seller, and that is the second requirement for monopoly.

A single seller means only one firm or person has the item for sale. No other seller exists. You can either buy the unique product from this one seller or you can go without. There is absolutely no competition of any kind for this good. Because there is no competition, the firm that produces this product has the possibility of making a profit. While there is no guarantee that the company will make a profit, it does have that possibility. Being the sole seller of this unique product can go a long way toward that goal, but it doesn't guarantee it. To make a profit, somebody must be willing to buy the product at a price greater than the costs of making it. The sole seller of a unique product such as nuclear waste, for instance, probably won't make any money because it will encounter difficulty in selling it at all, much less at a profit. But, if a firm has a product that is desired by consumers and its costs of production are low enough, it might make a profit.

Barriers Exist to Entry. In addition to the existence of only one seller of a unique product, another condition that must exist at the same time in a monopoly is barriers to entry. The limited number of sellers puts the firm that produces the unique product in a position to make a profit. If it does make a profit, that will be a signal to other firms to try to enter the market and make the product, too. Unless there is some way of keeping other firms out of the market, competition will arise and profits will be driven down, as is the case in perfect competition. Thus, barriers to entry are essential to the survival of a profitable monopoly.

One or more natural or artificial barriers must exist if a monopoly is to continue and make a profit. Unless a barrier exists, competitors can enter the market where a profit is being made, and there will no longer be a single seller no matter how unique the product is.

Natural barriers are barriers or restrictions that exist because of how resources are owned or how the product is made. If one firm owns all of a particular resource, it can be said to have a natural monopoly over that good. The DeBeers diamond company is one example. As a firm, the DeBeers company owns approximately 90 percent of the naturally occurring diamonds in the world. If you want a natural (as opposed to a man-made) diamond, you pretty much have to buy it from DeBeers or one of its outlets. Owning all the diamond mines gives DeBeers a natural monopoly.

The other way a natural monopoly can exist is in a decreasing cost industry. A decreasing cost industry is one in which the more of a good a firm produces, the less it costs per unit to make the item. This is known as **economies of scale.** To make a few units of the good is very expensive per unit, but the more a firm makes, the less it costs to make each one. When a factory produces automobiles, for instance, the cost of making the first car is very expensive. The firm must set up a plant, buy a lot of machinery and raw materials, and train the workers. Fixed

Natural Barriers
Restrictions on entry into an industry because of economies of scale or total ownership of a resource.

Economies of Scale
A situation in which the cost of production per unit declines as the number produced increases.

costs—those that do not change as output changes—are very high. As car production increases those fixed costs remain fixed. This means that the average cost of producing cars declines as production goes up. The more the firm makes, the less it costs to make each one. This acts as a natural barrier to anyone else who wants to go into business and compete against the first producer.

There is nothing you can do about natural barriers short of taking all the diamond mines from DeBeers and giving them to a lot of other people to own. Artificial barriers, on the other hand, do not need to exist. **Artificial barriers** are those barriers that are imposed by the government, and there are three different types of these barriers.

The first kind of artificial barrier is the government franchise, with which the government grants to one firm the sole right to produce or sell a product. This form of monopolistic barrier appears alongside interstate highways. Along these limited-access roads are a few gas stations and restaurants. There aren't more of these gas and food outlets because the government has restricted the number that can operate along the highway. The restriction helps speed up traffic and makes travel safer, but it also creates something of a monopoly on the interstates.

A second type of artificial barrier is the government license. A government license permits only those with the proper permit to pursue the occupation. The government licenses doctors and dentists to protect the public from incompetent practitioners. The government licenses funeral directors, television stations, and taxi drivers. In fact, government licensing requirements control a significant number of industries.

Finally, the third type of artificial barrier to entry is that of copyrights and patents. With copyrights and patents, the government grants to the author or inventor the sole right to sell and produce the product for a fixed number of years. The net effect of this is to grant to that person a monopoly. Why would the government grant a monopoly to an inventor or author? What if you had invented a new product, developed a new process, or written a new book? Would you want someone else to come along and copy what you had invented or written and sell it? Probably not. If someone else could do this, what incentive would you have to take the time and energy to try to produce something new? Your incentive would approach zero, and the level of innovation and development of new ideas would fall to almost nothing. This scenario supports the use of copyrights and patents.

As you can see, there is a rationale behind the existence of artificial barriers. While not all artificial barriers are good ones (the government sometimes grants restrictions that are not necessary), many serve a useful function even though they may help to create a monopoly. The problem then becomes to keep the monopolist created by artificial barriers from gaining too much of an unfair advantage over the public.

Information Costs—Imperfect Information. There must be a unique product sold by a single seller and barriers must exist to maintain the market to create and support a monopoly. But even if these three conditions exist at once, a fourth condition is needed to maintain the monopoly. If the fourth condition required for perfect competition is that information must be perfect and free, the opposite must be the case for monopoly, and so it is. In monopoly, information is not perfect and it is not free.

The monopolist is in a special position. As the sole producer of a unique product, the monopolist knows some things that outsiders can't, such as how much it costs to produce the good, what the market really looks like, and how to best sell to existing customers. No outsiders who wanted to enter the market and compete would know this at the outset. They would have to spend time and money to gather this information, and the monopolist would still know more than newcomers. This lack of information can be a formidable barrier in some cases. For instance, the formulae required to produce life-saving drugs—as well as dog food and cosmetics—are well-kept secrets. No outsider can produce AZT, Alpo, or Revlon lipstick without getting the necessary formulae from the manufacturer. This lack of information helps to keep the current producer in the so-called "cat bird seat," and thus we have a monopoly.

Artificial Barriers
Restrictions on entry into an industry that are put in place by government.

The Frequency of Monopoly

That completes the examination of the four conditions that must be met if a monopoly is to exist. Remember, too, that these conditions must exist simultaneously. The product is unique; there are no substitutes. There is only one seller, and this profit-seeking seller will set the price of the product at whatever level is necessary to make the maximum profit possible. There are barriers to entry. When the monopolist can make a profit, it signals other producers to enter the market unless something prevents them from doing so. Information is not free and perfect for everybody. Some people, at least the monopolist, have information that the rest of us don't have. Now do you see why monopoly can't exist in the real world? The conditions that are required for a true monopoly can't exist at the same time. While there is no question that businesses want to have a monopoly position and many try very hard to achieve it, they fall short precisely because of the factors we have just examined.

Core-Info

While the consumer can decide whether or not to buy the product, a firm in monopoly has quite a bit of market power because of four key criteria:
1. Unique product
2. Single seller
3. Barriers to entry
4. Information costs and is imperfect

THE BENEFITS AND COSTS OF PERFECT COMPETITION AND MONOPOLY

Throughout the preceding discussion, we have held up perfect competition as the ideal and monopoly as the worst-case scenario. Perhaps the name calling is a little excessive, but then from an economic standpoint, maybe not. Perfect competition provides the maximum amount of production at the lowest possible cost. The goods are sold for just what it costs to produce them and, if capitalism is at work, they go to the people who value them the most. With monopoly, the opposite happens. Output is lower and the selling price higher than would be the case in perfect competition. The goods produced in monopoly are sold at a price above the full and true cost of producing them.

It sounds as if the deck is stacked in favor of perfect competition, and so it is. In perfect competition, we can achieve **productive efficiency,** the situation where production occurs at the lowest possible opportunity cost of resources, and **allocative efficiency,** the situation where the socially optimal amount of each good is produced in response to peoples' tastes and preferences. On the opposite side of the fence, we find monopoly producing **contrived scarcity** where output is reduced, **"X-inefficiency"** where there is no pressure for low cost production, and **static inefficiency** where price is higher than it needs to be (it is greater than marginal cost).

Are there any arguments in favor of monopoly? In fact there are. The first one results from the existence of barriers. In industries that are declining cost industries (where economies of scale exist) it may make sense for only one firm to exist. Even though this single firm prices its product higher than necessary, it still may be lower than if the industry were forced to break up into smaller components. The other argument in favor of monopolies is the idea of **dynamic efficiency.** The concept of dynamic efficiency is that, because monopolists can (at least potentially) earn a profit, these firms have the funds necessary to invest in innovation and will do so to maintain their position. That is a great theory, but it doesn't work out in reality. In reality, monopolists tend not to innovate, evidently because they do not feel any competitive pressure.

Productive Efficiency
A situation in which production occurs at the lowest possible per unit cost.

Allocative Efficiency
A situation in which the socially optimal amount of a good is produced in an industry.

Contrived Scarcity
The situation in which the quantity of a good produced is less than that which would have resulted from a competitive market.

"X-Inefficiency"
The idea that monopolies may lack the incentive to reduce costs because of a lack of competition.

Static Inefficiency
The idea that monopolies produce too little quantity of a good at too high a price.

Dynamic Efficiency
The idea that monopolies may be more innovative and efficient over time because they may be able to generate the resources for these ends.

Core-Info

In a perfectly competitive market, the benefits accrue to the consumer, and firms find their influence limited. In monopoly, the opposite is true.

SUPPLY AND DEMAND IN PERFECT COMPETITION AND MONOPOLY

Before you look at Figures 11.1 and 11.2, try to envision what the supply and demand curves are likely to look like for firms in perfect competition and for firms in monopoly. This may take some effort, but all the information you need has been covered in the previous discussion.

First, think about how you have drawn supply and demand curves in the past. Then, consider what you know about firms in perfect competition and monopoly.

Here's a hint: you can come up with the supply curve from what you know from our earlier study of supply curves. You can derive the demand curves from the four conditions that are required for firms in perfect competition and monopoly.

Figures 11.1A and 11.1B and 11.2A and 11.2B show for perfect competition and monopoly respectively the supply and demand curves for the whole industry (composed of all buyers and sellers) and for a single seller.

Starting with perfect competition, see if you can derive the curves. The supply curve for the entire industry in perfect competition is what you would expect. When the price that suppliers can receive for their product increases, existing suppliers are willing to increase their output and additional suppliers enter the market (there are no barriers to entry, remember). As a result, a standard, upward-sloping supply curve exists for the industry in perfect competition. Buyers, or demanders, also act predictably. As the price of the good decreases, the quantity that existing demanders purchase increases and additional buyers are attracted into the market. The result is a standard, downward-sloping demand curve. These curves are shown in Figure 11.1A. The equilibrium quantity and price are determined by the intersection of the two curves. Thus, the figure shows an overall level of output that the industry will produce and a market price at which the product will be sold.

Let's now move to a single firm in perfect competition. Figure 11.1B shows the supply and demand curves for one firm, one out of the thousands of other firms in the industry. The supply curve is again relatively straightforward. It is determined by the costs of producing the product, and firms are willing to increase their output, incurring increasing costs, when the price they receive for their output is higher. When the price they receive falls, they reduce their output to reduce their costs. The result is a typical supply curve.

The demand curve for a single firm in perfect competition requires a little bit more thought. You can derive it by applying the four conditions that must exist in perfect competition: homogeneous product, a very large number of sellers, no barriers to entry, and free information. One of these four conditions determines what the demand curve for the firm will look like. Can you figure out which of the conditions is key? It is the second condition, an infinitely large number of sellers.

What is the effect of a large number of sellers? No one seller can have any impact on the price. The seller can sell all of its output at the market price. Whether it sells its regular output, doubles its output, or goes out of business, the market price is not affected. The firm can sell its product at the market price or not. Frankly, the market doesn't care. The demand curve reflects this relationship, the quantity that can be sold at various price levels. As we have seen, the firm can sell all that it wants at the market price. Above the market price, it sells

CHAPTER 11 • COMPETITION AND MONOPOLY   171

FIGURE 11.1A
The industry

FIGURE 11.1B
The firm

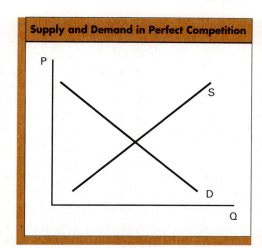
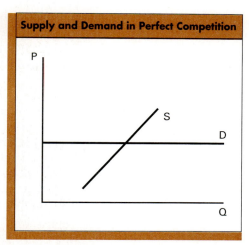

FIGURE 11.2A
The industry

FIGURE 11.2B
The firm

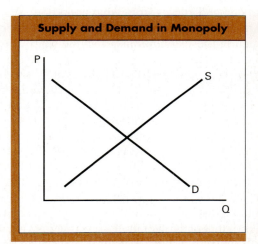
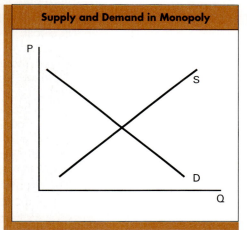

absolutely nothing. There is no reason to sell below the market price (given that it can sell everything at the market price). Therefore, the demand curve for the firm in perfect competition is a straight, horizontal, infinitely elastic line at the market price.

Figure 11.1B shows the result. The price that the firm can receive for its product is fixed by the market. The firm's output, therefore, is determined by its supply curve (which in turn is determined by the costs of production). The firm produces until its costs of production are just equal to what it can receive by selling the product. As long as the marginal revenue is greater than the marginal cost of production, the firm increases its output. If the marginal costs are greater than the marginal revenue, the firm curtails its output. With entry into the market possible as long as any profits are being made, firms expand their output and new firms enter the market. Firms continue to enter until there are no excess profits to be earned. When this occurs, the industry is at equilibrium, and the cost of producing the product equals the full and true cost of production. Buyers pay precisely what it cost to produce the product. It would be impossible to sell the product for less without taking losses. Thus, the market achieves an ideal situation in which the cost to the buyer is the lowest it can possibly be and firms have all their production costs met. If all markets acted this way, the economy would offer the greatest amount of output at the lowest possible cost.

Let's now move to a monopolized market and trace its supply and demand implications. As was the case for perfect competition, the supply curve for monopoly is straightforward. When the price that suppliers can receive for their product increases, existing suppliers are willing to increase their output. As a result, a standard, upward-sloping supply curve exists for the industry in monopoly just as in perfect competition. Buyers, or demanders, act as they always do whether it is monopoly or perfect competition. As the price of the good decreases, the quantity that existing buyers purchase increases and additional buyers also want to buy the product. The result is a typical downward-sloping demand curve. These curves are shown in Figure 11.2A. As was the case in perfect competition, the equilibrium quantity and price are determined by the intersection of the supply and demand curves. Thus, the graph illustrates the overall level of output that the monopolized industry will produce and the market price at which the product will be sold.

Now consider a single firm in a monopolized industry to see if you can derive its supply and demand curves from what you know. What conditions must exist to create a monopoly? Unique product, single seller, barriers to entry, and information at a cost. Which of these conditions affect the supply and demand curves of a single firm in a monopolized industry? Condition number two is the key. By definition, a monopoly is a single seller. There is only one firm in the entire industry. Therefore, the supply and demand curves for the industry are identical to the supply and demand curves for the firm. Figures 11.2A and 11.2B are the same.

These supply and demand curves pose many implications about the workings of a monopoly. A monopolist faces a demand curve that slopes downward and a supply curve that slopes upward. As the monopolist tries to produce more output, its costs rise. At the same time, if it raises its price, it faces a downward-sloping demand curve. Consumers buy less of the monopolist's product as the price rises. Thus, if the monopolist wants to increase its output, it must lower its price. A monopolist cannot raise its price and its output at the same time. The monopolist must choose: higher output at a lower price or a lower output at a higher price. How will it make this decision? It will price its product so as to maximize its profit. Because its demand curve is downward sloping (and marginal revenue is decreasing more rapidly than price), it will always reduce its output below what it would have produced in perfect competition. Because the monopoly takes this action to maximize its profits, prices are higher than they would have been in perfect competition (where there are no profits). Thus, the monopolist will produce a lower output at a higher price, and all of us—with the exception of the monopolist—lose.

SUMMARY OF COMPETITION AND MONOPOLY

Perfect competition and monopoly are very special market conditions. There are peculiar characteristics that markets must meet if they are to be in either of these situa-

Core-Info

> Because there are many firms in a perfectly competitive market, the demand curve for a single firm is completely flat (elastic). Because there is only one firm in a monopolistic market, the supply and demand curves for both the firm and the market are identical.

tions. Perfect competition produces maximum output at the minimum price. In the case of monopoly, output is reduced and price is higher than would have been the case in perfect competition. Even given this latter situation, however, the monopolist does not have control of the market. The consumer remains very much in control and will reduce the quantity demanded if the monopolist raises the price of the product. While this may not make you long for a world full of monopolies, it does offer a measure of reassurance that, even in that worst-case scenario, consumers still are in charge.

> **Core-Info:** The consumer reigns—even in a monopoly.

ECONOMIC CONCENTRATION AND ITS MEASURES

Now that we know something about the advantages of competition and the disadvantages of monopoly, just how monopolized is the American economy? To the extent that monopolies reign, you would expect reduced supplies and higher prices. If competition is the norm, however, the reverse should be the case. There are two ways to determine how competitive the economy is—by measuring aggregate concentration and industry concentration.

Aggregate Concentration

Aggregate Concentration
The measure of the percentage of business assets owned by the largest 100 or 200 firms.

The word *aggregate* just means overall, so measuring **aggregate concentration** means looking at how concentrated or centralized the overall economy is. The method used to determine this is to come up with the percentage of all business assets owned by the biggest firms. We use the biggest 100 and the biggest 200 firms as our measures. The higher the percentage of assets owned by these firms, the more economic power the large companies have. The lower the percentage, the more diffused is economic power in the country. Figure 11.3 presents aggregate concentration ratios for the economy for selected years. What do you see?

It appears as if, after a period of increasing concentration, aggregate concentration has stabilized in recent decades. Today, a little less than half of all business assets are owned by the largest 100 firms, and about three fifths of all assets are owned by the biggest 200. Given that there are a little more than 20 million firms in the United States, that is fairly concentrated, but at least it hasn't gotten much worse in recent years.

Industry Concentration

Industry Concentration
The measure of the percent of an industry's sales controlled by the largest four or eight firms.

The other way to measure how concentrated the economy is is to look at individual industries. To do this, economists measure the percentage of total sales produced by the top selling firms and call it **industry concentration.** Figure 11.4 gives some four-firm concentration ratios (the percentage of total industry sales controlled by the biggest four firms) for a selection of industries.

One would expect that the lower the four-firm concentration ratio the greater would be the level of competition in an industry, and in general this is true. There are some caveats, however, to this general rule. First is the matter of international trade. The amount of competition between American automobile firms is well known, even though four firms control 92 percent of all American production. In addition, of course, Honda, Toyota, Nissan, and Volkswagen all work to increase the competition and account for about a quarter of all car sales in the country. The second caveat is what is called interindustry competition. Cars compete with trains, and aluminum competes with copper. An analysis of competitiveness must include this aspect. A final consideration is localized markets. An industry may not be concentrated in general, but it may be a monopoly in a given local market. Many retail stores enjoy this sort of position,

FIGURE 11.3

Aggregate Concentration Ratios		
Year	100 Largest	200 Largest
1925	34.5	—
1935	40.8	47.7
1950	38.4	46.1
1958	46.0	55.2
1965	46.7	57.1
1980	46.7	59.7
1984	48.9	60.7

FIGURE 11.4

Selected Industry Concentration Ratios	
Industry	Four-Firm Ratio
Motor vehicles and car bodies	92
Cigarettes	90
Cereal breakfast foods	86
Aircraft	64
Petroleum refining	28
Women's dresses	6
Ready-mix concrete	6

Core-Info

To determine how concentrated or competitive the economy and markets are, economists use measurements called aggregate (overall) concentration and industry concentration.

and the same is true for some industries. You must take into account the extent of the market before you make statements about how concentrated an industry is.

MERGERS

One of the most frequently discussed economic phenomena of the past decade is that of mergers. Firms have combined for a variety of reasons, including an attempt to streamline production, a desire to eliminate competition, and goals of pure financial gain. As we discuss mergers, you will learn not only what they are but whether or not they are cause for concern. Some, you shall see, are not threatening and, in fact, may be quite beneficial to the economy. Others are another story.

The Structure of the Productive Process

Nobody owns and controls all phases of the productive process of anything. Not even the massive Ford Motors River Rouge complex controls the entire process from the collection of raw materials to the retail sale to the final consumer. Along the way there are many firms involved in bringing a good to the consumer. Figure 11.5 offers an overview of this process, in this case regarding the production of a loaf of bread.

Definition of Merger

Merger is a fairly simple term although the results can be quite complex. A **merger** is simply the joining of the ownership and resources of two firms into a single larger one. How this takes place and the impacts these mergers can have on the economy are of significant interest.

Merger
The joining of the ownership and assets of two firms into a single firm.

FIGURE 11.5

The Productive Process	
Wonder Bread	**Wholsum Bread**
Grocery store	Grocery store
Distributor	Distributor
Bakery	Bakery
Wholesaler	Wholesaler
Rural co-op	Rural co-op
Farmer	Farmer
Farm supplier	Farm supplier

Types of Mergers

There are three types of mergers that can occur in an economy: horizontal mergers, vertical mergers, and conglomerate mergers.

Horizontal. A **horizontal merger** is a merger between two firms at the same stage of the productive process. In the example in Figure 11.5, two bakeries or two rural co-ops could merge into a single larger unit. This type of merger reduces the amount of competition in an industry and gives the new, larger firm more economic power relative to those it purchases from and those it sells to. This type of merger may well result in increased prices as competition declines.

Vertical. If you think for a second, you can probably guess what **vertical mergers** are. They are mergers between two firms at different stages of the productive process. The bakery joins with the distributor, or the farmer merges with the rural co-op. These mergers may result in more efficient operations and guaranteed markets for firms. They do not decrease industry competition, so they need not be opposed on those grounds.

Conglomerate. The third type of merger is actually the best known type today, **conglomerate mergers.** Conglomerate mergers occur between completely unrelated firms. A bakery and a cigarette firm merge, or an automobile company acquires a movie company. In such cases, the number of firms is reduced, a few firms are getting bigger, and the aggregate concentration ratio may rise, but industry concentration ratios are unaffected. The amount of industry competition remains the same, but the newly merged firm may be able to draw on its expanded managerial and financial resources to compete.

Concerns about Mergers

Obviously, the key concern with mergers focuses on economic power. We probably don't want General Motors and Ford Motors to merge. We may not even want General Motors and Time Warner Communications to merge. In both cases economic power would be increased for the merged firms and could have a negative impact on the economy. What to do? There are several potential solutions to the so-called monopoly problem.

Horizontal Merger
A merger between two firms at the same stage of the productive process.

Vertical Merger
A merger between two firms at different stages of the productive process.

Conglomerate Merger
A merger between two firms producing unrelated products.

Core-Info

The three types of mergers—the joining of two or more firms—are horizontal merger, vertical merger, and conglomerate merger.

The Urge to Merge

The news media regularly carry stories about how greedy businessmen (yes, men) have been merging their firms with other industry giants or have been gobbling up smaller businesses across the land until there is hardly a shred of competition left. That's a bit of an exaggeration as the table below shows.

Over the last eight years for which complete data are available, there were an average of 1,481 major mergers and 216 buyouts. This was offset by an average of 1,378 divestitures where a business or division was sold to another party. Numerically, therefore, merger mania was not significant, although the amount of dollars involved should draw some attention. The "Value of Mergers" row on the chart is measured in billions of dollars; it encompasses some pretty significant sums. The year 1989 was the high point in dollar value of mergers. In that year, the average merger was worth $79.4 million. The total value of the mergers was about 2.8 percent of our gross national product and, if it had been a country, the value of the mergers would have ranked 23rd of the 67 major developed nations.

By way of comparison, in the same time period there have been more than 5 million new business incorporations, an average of 669,750 per year. True, most of these new businesses were small firms and not in the size category of those which were merging, but you get some sense of the relative scale of business activity. Admittedly, that comparison may fall into the "apples and oranges" category, but the data comparisons should help to put mergers into perspective.

Activity	YEAR							
	1985	1986	1987	1988	1989	1990	1991	1992
Number of Mergers	785	1174	1267	1405	1844	2155	1516	1705
Value of Mergers (in $ billion)	82	92	81	111	146	97	73	61
Divestitures	780	1090	1004	1274	1615	1907	1759	1598
Buyouts	154	233	208	291	293	177	171	199
New Incorporations (in thousands)	664	703	686	685	677	647	629	667

SOLUTIONS TO THE MONOPOLY PROBLEM

Economists have proposed four options to deal with monopolies.

Prohibition

The first strategy to deal with monopolies is to prohibit them. Antitrust laws seek to preserve competition by preventing monopolies from ever forming. A strong, activist government filled with lawyers and economists would be needed to monitor firms and markets and to bring suit against businesses where necessary. You can decide whether that would be a good or bad thing.

Price Regulation

The second option is to allow monopolies to exist but to control the prices that they charge. This strategy may be effective in number of cases. Think for a moment about electric utility companies. How many of them would you think are needed to serve your city? Do you want a large number of electric companies, all with their own power plants and each with its own electric lines? Would that even make economic—not to mention visual or ecological—sense? Not likely. Probably the best course would be to authorize a single company to be the monopoly electric utility and then regulate it so it cannot raise its prices out of reach for families with low incomes. In fact, this is the route that most jurisdictions have taken, and utility companies report to public service commissions for approval before they can change their prices.

Government Ownership

The third approach is to have the government take control of monopolies and run them itself, theoretically in the public interest. Government managers can oversee the businesses and control prices and output so that the worst effects of monopolies can be avoided. Unfortunately, unless government managers are residual claimants and have some personal stake in the operation of the business, optimal levels of prices and output may not be forthcoming, and efficiency may not be the central focus.[1]

Laissez Faire

The final option is to do nothing—just leave them alone. Economists who advocate *laissez faire* are *not* in the pocket of big business. Let's think for a minute about monopolies and consider if a hands-off approach may not be a way to regulate them.

There are two possible outcomes from monopolies: they can make profits or they may generate losses. There is no guarantee that monopolies will make profits. The only guarantee of monopoly is that the firm is in the best position to make a profit if one is to be made. If a monopoly is losing money, there isn't much need to regulate it, is there? If it can't make money when it is free to gouge and steal, there is no reason to control its prices. Unless you believe that government bureaucrats can manage the firm more efficiently than the original business owners, regulating the firm will only add another layer of cost to the overall operation. When losses are being incurred, the best option is to leave the monopoly alone.

Monopolies can, however, earn profits. When they do, the temptation to control them can be overwhelming. Here, again, the call is *laissez faire*. If a monopoly is making profits, those profits will serve as an incentive to other firms to try to find a substitute good, a new process, or an alternative product. Once the profits are reduced, the incentive to compete is likewise reduced. Intervening in the market may reduce, not increase, the likelihood of competition, and the outcome might be to support the monopoly's hold on the marketplace.

FROM FICTION TO REALITY

We have just completed a chapter of economic fiction. Neither perfect competition nor monopoly exist, so it has to be fiction, doesn't it? Not completely. While economists may be hard pressed to find many pure examples of either, competition and monopoly do represent the directions that firms and markets take in real life. On rare occasions, with new or completely generic products, markets may even approach these extremes. Finally, these two market models offer a good understanding of the boundaries that exist for markets and why it may be a good idea to be on guard against some types of mergers. That said, let's now move on to a dose of economic reality—imperfect competition.

Core-Info

The four methods that have been proposed to control or deal with monopolies are:
1. Prohibition
2. Price regulation
3. Government ownership
4. *Laissez faire*

SUMMARY

- Perfectly competitive markets are those which produce the greatest quantity of goods at the lowest possible prices. The characteristics of these markets are a homogeneous product, a large number of buyers and sellers, a lack of barriers to entry or exit, and free and perfect information.

---

[1] It may be instructive that many countries which had opted for government control have moved in recent years to privatization, selling to private interests businesses that the government had owned and operated.

- A monopoly is a situation in which a single firm exists, the product is unique, there are barriers to entry, and information costs and is imperfect.
- The supply and demand curves in perfect competition and monopoly take on unique shapes as determined by the four conditions that establish each market type.
- Economies of scale apply to many goods: the more you produce the less it costs to produce each one.
- A merger is the joining together of two or more firms. The three types of mergers are horizontal, vertical, and conglomerate.
- The four possible solutions to the monopoly problem are prohibition, price regulation, government ownership, and *laissez faire* (leaving them alone to solve themselves).

KEY TERMS

Aggregate concentration	Fixed costs	Normal profit
Allocative efficiency	Homogeneous product	Perfect competition
Artificial barriers	Horizontal merger	Price taker
Barriers	Industry concentration	Productive efficiency
Conglomerate merger	Market	Static inefficiency
Contrived scarcity	Merger	Variable costs
Dynamic efficiency	Monopoly	Vertical merger
Economies of scale	Natural barriers	"X-inefficiency"

REVIEW QUESTIONS

1. If perfect competition and pure monopoly do not exist very often in the real world, why do we use them as models in economics?
2. Identify and describe the four conditions that are required for perfect competition to exist.
3. Identify and describe the four conditions that are required for pure monopoly to exist.
4. Who benefits and who suffers if an industry is in perfect competition? If it is in pure monopoly?
5. Explain what is meant by economies of scale.
6. What are the two ways in which economic concentration is measured?
7. What are the three types of mergers that can occur?
8. Describe the four methods that may be used to deal with monopolies.

PROBLEM-SOLVING PRACTICE

1. Draw the supply and demand curves for the firm and the industry for the following situations:
   (a) a breakthrough technology that makes voice-recognition computers available at a low price.
   (b) a Kansas farmer deciding whether or not to produce wheat.
2. Describe the advantage to a firm if it can achieve economies of scale before other firms in an industry.
3. What are some advantages of a conglomerate merger? Identify two firms that have resulted from conglomerate mergers.
4. Describe a situation in which a monopoly might be the most efficient form of market structure.

5. Describe a way in which a firm that faces much competition could move itself into a monopoly position.
6. If barriers prevent an industry from moving to a situation of perfect competition, why would government actively erect barriers in an economy?
7. Explain why it might not be a crucial problem if an industry has a particularly high industry concentration ratio.
8. Describe the advantages to the two firms of undergoing a vertical merger. What could be the disadvantages of a vertical merger?

CHAPTER 12

Imperfect Competition

CHAPTER OUTLINE

A. And Now for Something Completely Different
B. Two Models of Imperfect Competition
   1. Monopolistic Competition
      a. Background for Monopolistic Competition
      b. Conditions Required
   2. Oligopoly
      a. Background for Oligopoly
      b. Conditions Required
C. Understanding Oligopoly
D. How Oligopolists Compete
E. How Oligopolists Raise Prices
   1. Price Leader
   2. Mark-up Pricing
   3. Collusion
F. The Role of Advertising
G. Cartels
   1. Definition
   2. Organizing and Maintaining a Cartel
H. A Final Look at Real Markets

The purpose of this chapter is to introduce the most common form of market today—imperfect competition—and to examine the implications of this market structure for the behavior of firms.

AFTER COMPLETING THIS CHAPTER, YOU WILL BE ABLE TO:

1. Apply the concept of imperfect competition to U.S. markets.
2. Demonstrate the relevance of the oligopolistic model to the economy.
3. Construct a kinked demand curve and use it to explain how most markets function.
4. Explain the concept of "sticky prices" and explain its importance to competition and price adjustments by firms in oligopoly.
5. Describe the nature of and predict the long-run impact of cartels in the market.
6. Demonstrate the two goals of advertising through the use of a product demand curve.

And Now for Something Completely Different

I want you to go on a journey with me, a journey to a place where competitors are few and competition is intense; a place where economic fiction is left behind and ugly reality raises its fearful head. In short, come with me now on a journey to "The Daylight Zone."[1]

Let's face it: the last chapter either wandered around in Never-Never Land or got lost in Oz with Dorothy. It described some sort of economic fantasy land that not only doesn't exist but can't. Consider these facts:

1. The economy is never in a situation with a completely homogeneous, absolutely identical product, nor is it ever in a situation where the product is heterogeneous or unique and without any substitute.
2. The economy has never had an infinite number of sellers and only very rarely is there a single seller of a product.
3. There are generally some sort of barriers to entry that act to keep firms from entering markets. Furthermore, information is neither free nor perfect, another strike against the marvelous model of perfect competition.

Even though neither market model exists in real life, perfect competition and monopoly form the outside boundaries of what markets can be; they illustrate the best and worst possibilities for a market and the economy. Perfect competition would be the economist's paradise. If the economy could ever achieve perfect competition, it would produce the greatest amount of goods at the lowest possible cost. All the resources used to produce the good would be paid for in full, and no one would reap excess profit. The good would be purchased by people who paid just what it cost society to produce it. No waste. No rip-off.

Monopoly, on the other hand, heads in the opposite direction. As the only seller of a unique product, the monopolist has some very real power in the marketplace. It is true that the monopolist faces the industry demand curve and that if the firm wants to increase its sales it must lower its price, but as the only seller it will do this with profits in mind. The monopolist will always price the product so that the profit generated for the firm is the maximum possible given market demand. While this may be the monopolist's idea of ecstasy, it poses a hard choice for consumers. They can either purchase the product at a price above what it cost the firm to produce it or go without. The economic sports score is: Monopolist 1, Consumers 0.

Perfect competition and monopoly define the boundaries against which to measure any market. Every type of market structure you will encounter will fall somewhere between these two extremes. It is this middle ground, the area of reality, that suppliers and consumers meet.

Core-Info: Monopoly and perfect competition provide the boundaries within which the real economy operates.

TWO MODELS OF IMPERFECT COMPETITION

Imperfect Competition
Market models in which the actions of individual sellers can have an impact on price.

The world of economic reality is known as **imperfect competition.** The term was developed about 60 years ago to describe the type of markets that were found to exist in the real world and not in some economist's imagination. The two different types of imperfect competition are monopolistic competition and oligopoly.

---

[1] Apologies to Monty Python for the section title and to Rod Serling and his television series, "The Twilight Zone."

Monopolistic Competition

Monopolistic Competition
A market model with relatively easy entry and exit, a large number of firms, and a similar but differentiated product.

Background for Monopolistic Competition. **Monopolistic competition** was first described by Edward H. Chamberlain, an American economist. Chamberlain coined the term because some of the markets he observed in his research had elements of both monopoly and perfect competition. Neither of the earlier two approaches accurately described what he found as he looked at contemporary businesses.

Conditions Required. As Chamberlain developed his theory, he identified the conditions required for monopolistic competition to exist. These conditions are:

1. A differentiated product
2. A large number of sellers
3. Barriers to entry exist
4. Information costs and is imperfect

For monopolistic competition to exist, the product must be differentiated. A differentiated product is similar in its basic characteristics, but is varied by each seller in an attempt to make it unique. Monopolistic competition also requires a large number of sellers.

Barriers to entry must exist, and information must have a cost and be imperfect. Conditions 3 and 4 come directly from monopoly, and Condition 1 is a variation on the unique-product theme of that market form. Condition 2, on the other hand, comes from perfect competition. While this model has much to commend it, the other model of imperfect competition does an even better job of describing the reality that businesses and consumers face today.

Oligopoly

Oligopoly
A market model for any type of product but with few firms and difficult entry.

Background for Oligopoly. The second model of imperfect competition is that of **oligopoly.** Oligopoly is perhaps the best model for understanding the economy today. The oligopolistic model explains much about how modern prices are set, how firms compete with one another, and why the advertising industry is so big. If you can gain a solid understanding of how oligopoly works, you will have a solid base for dealing with real markets and for making the business decisions that you will face in the coming years.

The theory of oligopolistic markets was developed by British economist Joan Robinson. Robinson's studies of economic markets led her to the realization that the extent of competition was limited but highly intense. She felt, as many economists do, that perfect competition didn't exist and that a different model in which firms regularly earn economic profits was more appropriate.

Conditions Required. As with all other market models, there are four conditions that must exist in oligopoly. These conditions are:

1. Any type of product
2. A few sellers
3. Barriers to entry exist
4. Information costs and is imperfect

The first condition, or requirement, has to do with the type of product. In oligopoly, any type of product is possible. The product can be homogeneous (once you specify the alloy content of steel, for instance it doesn't matter who you buy it from), heterogeneous, or differentiated (automobiles are a good example of a varied product).

The second condition has to do with the number of sellers. In perfect competition, there is an infinite number of sellers who are independent of each other in terms of impact. In monopoly there is a single seller. This single seller is independent of competition as well—there is none. Oligopoly splits the difference—and arrives at reality. In oligopoly there is a limited number of sellers, each of which is

Interdependent
A situation in which the actions of one firm have an impact on other firms in a market.

aware of and affected by the other. in oligopoly, sellers are **interdependent.** What one seller does affects the other few sellers, and they in turn affect the first seller.

The third and fourth conditions are similar to those for monopoly: there are barriers to entry into the market, so profits may be earned by firms, and information is neither free nor perfect.

These requirements seem to square with what you know to be reality, don't they? There really is a limited number of firms or businesses that compete with one another. A hotel in downtown Detroit really doesn't compete with a hotel in the suburbs (much less those in Flint, Bay City, or Sault Ste. Marie), but it does compete, and very strongly, with those few other hotels in its immediate area and price range. Effective barriers keep new hotels from entering this market: downtown land is already in use and would be expensive to acquire, and the construction of a new hotel is exceedingly expensive. In addition, the knowledge required to efficiently manage a hotel is limited and costly to obtain. The oligopolistic model works for hotels in Detroit, barber shops in Boise, and restaurants in your town. Let's take an in-depth look at this model.

Core-Info

The conditions under which imperfect competition—monopolistic competition and oligopoly—exists reflect the reality of markets as they are today.

UNDERSTANDING OLIGOPOLY

Whether you have owned a business or not, it should be obvious that the competitors to any business are really quite limited. To be competitors, businesses must appeal to a similar group of potential customers, must be located in relatively close proximity to each other, and must offer products that are good substitutes for each other. Examples include the six television repair businesses on your side of town, the four discount stores along the same major road, or the three gas stations at the same intersection. These cases with a limited number of competitors resemble reality. The gas stations or discount stores watch each other carefully. When one has a sale or changes its product or service mix, the others notice and must decide how to react in order to remain competitive. They cannot ignore the actions of each other but are linked together in something like an economic "dance" in which they watch and react to each other's every move. They may appear to be spinning by themselves, but just as it is with dancers, each business knows what its competitors are doing at all times and reacts to their actions. Let's use the three gas stations as an example of oligopoly and see how it works.

Figure 12.1 depicts three gas stations at an intersection. These three stations offer a differentiated product (Exxon, Mobil, and Sunoco gasoline) but one which is a good substitute for the gasoline offered by the others. Because of their location, they sell to a similar group of customers and must pay attention to what each other does. As you would expect in a situation like this, the price of gasoline settles down to some level and each gas station sells some amount of gas each week. For the sake of this discussion, let's assume that the three gas stations charge the same amount per gallon (you could assume that they charge slightly different amounts if you want to; the result will be the same). The price the stations charge for gasoline is called the equilibrium price, and the quantity that each sells is its equilibrium quantity. In this example, the equilibrium price is $1.09 per gallon, and the Sunoco station sells 5,000 gallons per week. This equilibrium point as point A can be found in Figure 12.2.

Now let's look at the role of the Sunoco station manager. The manager has been selling gasoline on the corner for some time and, because there is a limited number of stations selling to the customers in the area, has been making an economic profit. Unfortunately, her costs (e.g., labor, utilities, property taxes, bulk gasoline) have been drifting upward in recent months, and her profits have been declining. At some point, it would seem inevitable that she must raise her prices. If gasoline has been selling for $1.09 per gallon, she may decide to increase it to $1.19 per gallon. If she does this, what would her customers do? Most of them would be-

FIGURE 12.1

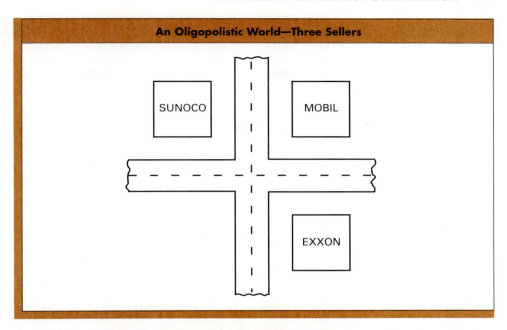

FIGURE 12.2

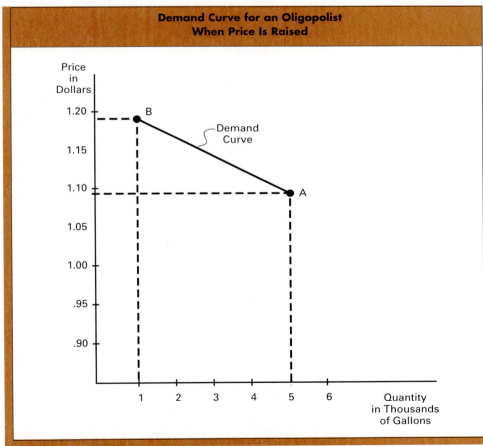

gin to buy their gas at either the Mobil or Exxon station. Even the Sunoco dealer's mother probably would drive by her station to buy at one of the other stations. A few people might continue to buy Sunoco gas—those who ran out of cash and had only a Sunoco credit card, for instance. The rest would drive by to another station.

If the Sunoco dealer raises her price a little bit, she will lose a lot of sales. A small increase in price results in a big decrease in quantity. That sounds very much like a highly elastic demand curve, and so it is. Figure 12.2 shows how the quantity

FIGURE 12.3

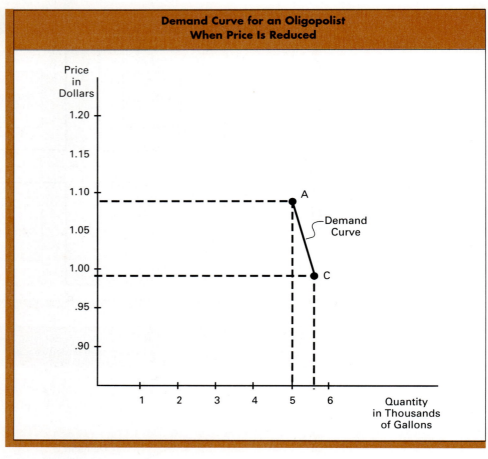

will respond when one in an oligopolistic market increases its price. When the Sunoco dealer raises her price from $1.09 per gallon (where she was selling 5,000 gallons of gasoline each week, at Point A) to $1.19 per gallon, her sales will fall drastically (say to Point B where she now sells only 1,000 gallons per week).

As you can see, if the price is increased by an oligopolist, a big decrease in the quantity sold results. The other competitors can sit still with their prices stable and reap the benefit of the Sunoco dealer's action. She raised her price, and *their* demand increased. That is known as a high **cross elasticity of demand.**

A price hike obviously didn't work, and the Sunoco dealer very quickly reduces her price back to $1.09 per gallon. Unfortunately, she is still faced with declining profits and wants to make more money. If raising the price doesn't work, what about lowering the price? She vaguely remembers something about the law of demand from her economics class in college, something about a price cut resulting in increased quantity demanded. Perhaps that might be the answer to her problems, so she lowers her price from $1.09 per gallon to 99 cents per gallon.

If the Sunoco dealer cuts her price and the other gas stations do nothing, what would happen? Nearly everybody would start buying gasoline at her station. If she alone lowers her price, her sales would skyrocket—and those of the other competitors in this oligopolistic market would collapse. Obviously, they are not going to stand for this. They very quickly react and cut their price to 99 cents. When each station cuts its price, the total sales of all three combined increase a little as buyers now fill up their tanks and a few new customers arrive (but not many people will drive across town just to save a few cents per gallon of gas). Thus, the total sales of all competitors in the oligopoly increase a little, but this increase is shared by all three sellers. A decrease in price results in a very small increase in the quantity sold by the Sunoco dealer. That sounds like an inelastic demand curve, and it is.

This portion of the demand curve for one competitor in an oligopoly is shown in Figure 12.3. If one firm lowers its price below the equilibrium price, all other

Cross Elasticity of Demand
A measurement of the amount by which the demand for one good changes in response to a change in the price of another good.

FIGURE 12.4

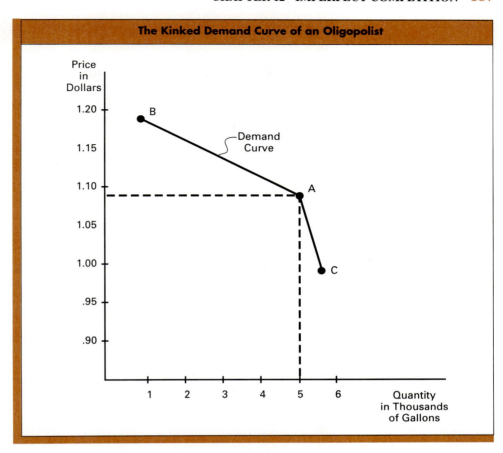

firms will lower theirs as well, and each firm will experience a small increase in the quantity demanded. Again, the Sunoco manager is in trouble. Given the interplay of factors that determine elasticity, her revenues fall.

It is time to join the two half demand curves into one complete demand curve for a single firm in an oligopolistic market. Figure 12.2 shows what happens if price is increased. Figure 12.3 shows what the demand curve looks like if price is reduced. The complete demand curve can be seen in Figure 12.4, and it doesn't look like any demand curve you've seen before.

If price is raised above the equilibrium price, demand is highly elastic. Quantity demanded falls dramatically and revenue decreases. If price is reduced, demand is inelastic. Quantity increases a little bit, but revenue falls again. The demand curve is not a straight line but is bent, or kinked. The supply curve for the gas stations looks like any other standard supply curve; the station is willing to supply more gasoline as the price it receives rises. This supply curve, of course, goes through the equilibrium price and so may be added to the demand curve as in Figure 12.5.

Now the supply and demand curve diagram for one firm in an oligopoly is complete. The demand curve is kinked about the equilibrium point, and the resulting price is highly stable, or sticky. With **sticky prices,** firms tend to maintain prices even in the face of declining profits. Everybody is afraid to be the first to raise prices. On the other hand, when one competitor reduces its price, all other competitors feel compelled to follow suit and reduce theirs. Examples of this sort of behavior abound. When one gas station cuts its price, others do, too. When McDonald's cuts its price on Big Macs to 99 cents, Burger King quickly cuts the price of Whoppers to 99 cents, too. When rebates are announced on the Chevrolet Lumina, Ford will respond with a competitive price reduction of its own on the Taurus. This type of price-matching behavior is quite typical of oligopolized industries and, in fact, is a good indicator that this is the form of market structure that an industry or group of firms is in.

Sticky Prices
The concept that in oligopolized industries prices frequently do not respond to changed cost conditions.

FIGURE 12.5

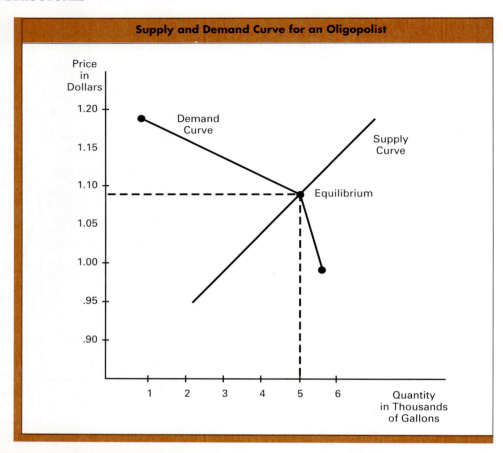

Core-Info

In oligopoly the number of competitors is few, competition is intense, and firms are interdependent. Because of this, each firm has a unique kinked demand curve.

HOW OLIGOPOLISTS COMPETE

It looks as if price, which is generally thought to be the main weapon of rival firms, cannot be used by oligopolists to compete with one another. If someone does try to compete by lowering his or her prices, all competitors will be forced to follow suit, and each will find that their revenues have declined. Yet we know from real-life experience that it is in oligopolistic industries with a few large competitors that competition is most intense. McDonald's vs. Wendy's. Ford vs. Chevrolet. Pepsi vs. Coke. The stories of competition in oligopolized industries are legendary, and oligopolists accomplish this intense competition through **nonprice competition.**

In nonprice competition, firms look for ways to attract buyers to their products without provoking a direct response from other firms in the way that a change in the price would. You can probably think of a dozen strategies that firms use to make themselves and their products more attractive. Here are a few examples:

1. Special services for the customer: car parking or package delivery
2. Advertising: messages to raise awareness about the firm and/or its products
3. New products: an inflatable running shoe or a new type of French fries
4. Special offers: premiums such as getting a shirt and tie at no extra cost with the purchase of a suit
5. Product differentiation: attempts to make the product either really or apparently different from the competition
6. Innovation: new ways to produce the good
7. Bonuses: frequent flyer miles and other "rewards"

Nonprice Competition
The many ways in which firms attempt to increase sales of their products other than price.

Core-Info

Oligopolists compete by using everything but price.

8. Coupons: two-for-the-price-of-one dinners and other cost-saving offers
9. Quality: improvements such as cars with a five-year, 50,000-mile warranty

HOW OLIGOPOLISTS RAISE PRICES

Sticky prices and nonprice competition are fine, but someday an oligopolist has to raise prices. As the prices that the oligopolist pays for its inputs increase, the firm's profit margins decline until they become losses. Unless revenues can be increased, the firm will someday be in trouble.

However, raising prices is a problem in oligopolistic industries. No one wants to be the first—unless they have some assurance that their competitors will follow. If everybody raises prices, then all firms may experience some decline in the quantity demanded, but no one will be hit with a gigantic drop. Oligopolists have found three ways to raise prices: through a price leader, by mark-up pricing, and through collusion.

Price Leader

Price Leader
A market in which a single firm sets its price for a product and all other firms adopt the leader's price.

A **price leader** is a firm that is generally acknowledged by the oligopolistic firms to set the pace for the firms in the market. Sometimes this is the oldest firm with the best track record. Sometimes it is the most modern firm with the lowest costs of production. Sometimes it is the firm with the most dynamic chief executive. Somehow, one firm becomes acknowledged as the price leader. When this firm raises its prices, the other firms go along and raise their prices as well. This price increase is not discussed in advance, and there is no official designation of one firm as the leader. The process just evolves.

Mark-up Pricing

Mark-up Pricing
A market situation in which firms face similar costs and thus adjust the price of their products to reflect any changes in cost.

The second approach to increasing prices that is used by firms in an oligopolistic market is called **mark-up pricing.** In the example of the three gas stations, all of their costs are likely to be quite similar. They hire from the same labor pool. They buy electricity, water, materials, and supplies from the same companies. Even their bulk gasoline prices are similar because of oligopolistic competition on the part of the oil companies. Thus, when one gas station has an increase in its costs, its competitors have an increase in their costs of approximately the same amount, and they all find that their profits are declining. The firms could, if they felt secure about it, mark up their prices by the amount that their costs had gone up, knowing that the other firms would do likewise. This mark-up pricing means that no one firm would gain or lose when compared with the other firms.

Collusion

Collusion
An agreement among firms in an industry not to engage in competition.

The final way that prices could be increased in an oligopolistic industry is illegal in the United States. This approach is called **collusion.** Collusion occurs when executives from different firms in an oligopolistic industry meet and establish when and how much prices will increase. This type of action is considered by law to be "in restraint of trade" and, thus, is illegal. If you follow the price adjustments that a competitor makes, you are not in violation of the law. If you meet with your competitors and discuss what you are thinking of doing, you can go to jail. Collusion may seem hard to detect and thus may be very tempting, but remember that law schools graduate thousands of lawyers each year, many of whom would love to make their mark by prosecuting a price fixer.

Core-Info

When oligopolists have to raise prices which are generally sticky, they do it by following a price leader, through mark-up pricing, or by collusion.

FIGURE 12.6

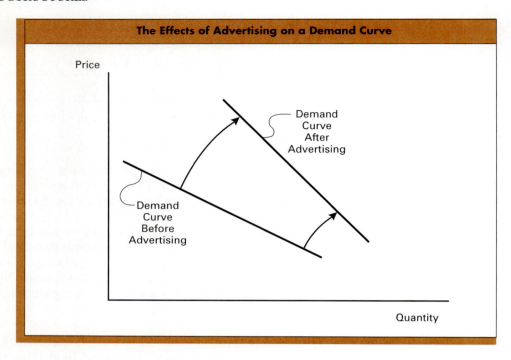

THE ROLE OF ADVERTISING

As we have seen, it is in markets characterized by oligopoly that competition is the most intense. In monopoly, there is no competition because one firm produces a unique product. In perfect competition, there is no competition for precisely the opposite reason: an infinitely large number of firms produces an identical product. In oligopoly, however, competition is fierce. With a limited number of known sellers of the product, what one firm does affects the other firms. Each will keep the other under close scrutiny and will attempt to capture as much of the market as possible. One way to do this is through advertising.

Advertising is any activity that acts to communicate information to a potential buyer in order to stimulate a positive response. Advertising is quite controversial, and feelings about it run deep. Some see it as a way to steal from consumers; Stephen Leacock once said that "advertising may be described as the science of arresting the human intelligence long enough to get money from it." Others view it as a way to inform; Thomas Jefferson is quoted as saying that "advertisements contain the only truths to be relied on in a newspaper." However you may feel about it, advertising is not only here to stay but is a major industry and a fact of live in oligopoly.[2]

From an economic standpoint, firms advertise for two reasons: to increase demand and to reduce the elasticity of demand. The first reason, increasing demand, makes sense. Firms want to get more people to buy their product, and they want their existing customers to buy more than they did before. Increasing demand through advertising moves the demand curve outward to the right. The second reason, decreasing the elasticity of demand, means that, through advertising, firms want to build customer loyalty. Firms want their customer to really want their product, to want it so much that customers will not reduce how much they buy even when prices increase. If firms can make their product inelastic, then revenues actually increase when they raise prices. This decrease in the elasticity of demand means that the slope of the demand curve changes to a steeper slope than the original demand curve. The net effect of both increasing demand and decreasing the elasticity of demand through advertising the product is illustrated in Figure 12.6. The new demand curve is both steeper and farther to the right.

Advertising
Activities on the part of firms to give information to potential consumers so as to increase demand for the product.

[2] The revenues earned from advertising exceeded $4 billion for *each* of the ten largest U.S. advertising agencies in 1991.

Buy Now!

In 1991 Coca Cola spent $367 million on advertising. The company ranked 28th in advertising spending in the country. Total spending for advertising was nearly $38 *billion* that year. Clearly, profit-seeking companies must think that advertising works or they wouldn't do it. Let's take a look at who advertises where to see if we can learn a bit more about the economy.

In 1991, the top five companies in terms of advertising spending were Proctor and Gamble (with more than $2 billion), Philip Morris, General Motors, Sears & Roebuck, and PepsiCo. What sort of market type do these companies operate in? Perfect competition? Monopoly? The answer, of course, is that these leading advertisers have very active competition from, among others, Colgate-Palmolive, RJR Nabisco, Ford Motors, JCPenney, and Coca Cola, respectively. The market type is oligopoly. There is a limited number of firms in the marketplace, each with an identifiable product and each vying for the customer's dollar.

There are no great surprises in terms of the industries which spend the most on advertising. Automobiles lead the way, followed closely by retail and then business and consumer services, food, and entertainment. The amounts, however, are staggering. About $5.3 billion was spent in automobile advertising, and even the pets and pet foods industry, which ranked 27th in spending, laid out almost $200 million in 1991 alone.

More than half of all advertising spending takes place on television. Network, spot, syndicated, and cable television absorb 56.2 percent of all advertising dollars. Newspapers are a distant second with 18.1 percent, followed closely by magazines with 17.2 percent ($6.5 billion, to put its third place finish into perspective).

As you can see, spending on advertising is great. Whether or not it is a "wise" category of spending given all the other needs of society is an open question. You can expect the debate to continue and even to expand as firms in oligopoly look for ways to win new customers in the nonprice competition in which they are engaged.

You might be interested to know that the $37.8 billion spent in advertising is greater than the gross national product of Bangladesh, Chile, Cuba, Egypt, El Salvador, Ethiopia, Ghana, Iraq, Kenya, North Korea, Kuwait, Morocco, Nigeria, Peru, Sri Lanka, Sudan, Syria, and Zaire.

Of further interest is that one major advertiser is the U.S. government. It spent more than a quarter of a billion dollars in advertising in 1991. Who paid for it? And, who says monopolies don't advertise?

Core-Info

Because of the intensity of competition, oligopolists advertise their products to both increase demand and to decrease the elasticity of demand.

CARTELS

Definition

Cartel
A group of firms that bands together to act like a monopoly to increase total profits.

Another concept to introduce in this discussion of imperfect competition is cartels. Cartels could have been discussed in the chapter about monopoly because a **cartel** is defined as a group of firms that acts together as if it were a single firm to reap the benefits of monopoly. The firms in a cartel act as a single seller to control quantity and increase price. They cooperate in order to jointly make a profit and do so by reducing the quantity produced while raising the selling price. They are typically discussed along with imperfect competition because cartels involve a limited number of firms and these firms react strongly to the behaviors of others in their group. The best known examples of cartels today are OPEC (the Organization of Petroleum Exporting Countries) and the Medellin Drug Cartel. Cartels are basically illegal in the United States and exist only in limited and very controlled ways such as the milk marketing boards in some rural districts.

The definition of cartel says it all: it is a monopoly that has been formed from a group of firms that once competed. In a cartel, these firms stop competing and give over control of the decisions about pricing and production to the group as a whole. The group leaders decide how much is to be produced, both overall and by each individual firm, and what the prices will be.

Organizing and Maintaining a Cartel

As you may recall from the discussion of the differences between perfect competition and monopoly, when a monopoly is formed, prices increase and the quantity produced decreases. This is also true in a cartel. The cartel pushes prices up while reducing the amount of the product that is produced. The problem comes in getting former competitors to act together. The cartel tells each firm to raise its price and cut its output. The firms may agree, but they are likely to want someone else in the cartel to make the first move. Even if a firm trusts the others in the cartel, it must be tempted to let them raise their prices, so customers will want to buy from it. The other firms feel the same way. Everybody wants to be the last one to join the cartel. Everybody wants the other firms to join first and raise their prices. As a result, it is very difficult to get a cartel started. If you are the first to join, you lose. If you are the last to join, you win.

But let's assume that you have been able to get the cartel going. Firms are now cooperating by agreeing to raise their prices and keep them at a high level while reducing output. With that agreement in hand, isn't it tempting for one firm to increase its production just a little bit? No one would notice, right? If one firm increases its production while prices are kept high, it should be able to make a lot of extra money. The other firms know that, too. If they can increase their production for a while, they can make some extra profit as well. The temptation is there for everybody to increase their production, and the prize goes to the firm that does it first. If you are the first to cheat, you win. If you are the last to cheat, you lose. As a result, cartels are very difficult to keep going.

While cartels can appear to be powerful, they have some built-in problems. They are very difficult to organize and very difficult to keep going. Cartels tend to break down fairly quickly unless there is some enforcement mechanism in place to deal with those who cheat (you might speculate on the mechanisms that the Medellin Drug Cartel members use to maintain pricing and output decisions). Without enforcement, cartels are generally short-lived and pose little cause for concern. The price of gasoline today is somewhat below what it would have been if the price had increased at the same rate as inflation over the past 20 years. If the United States had thought about the nature of cartels for a minute during OPEC's heyday, we could have relaxed, secure in the knowledge that OPEC would likely lose its effectiveness.

Core-Info

Cartels, which are hard to organize and difficult to maintain, try to act like monopolies in the marketplace.

A FINAL LOOK AT REAL MARKETS

Most businesses in the United States find themselves in an oligopolistic situation. These firms have a few competitors who they consider important and watch carefully. The fact of that competition limits their freedom to adjust prices freely, and most firms resort to a great deal of nonprice competition to enhance growth.

Take a few minutes to think about oligopoly. If you can understand this theory, you will understand the nature of the competition that you and your businesses will face in the coming years. Perhaps with this understanding, your business will be the one that comes out on top.

SUMMARY

- Imperfect competition, not monopoly or perfect competition, is the dominant type of market structure in the economy today.
- The two types of imperfect competition are oligopoly and monopolistic competition.
- Oligopoly is a market type that is characterized by a limited number of interdependent sellers with information limited and entry restricted.
- Firms in oligopoly have a demand curve that is kinked or bent at the point of equilibrium.
- Prices in oligopoly tend not to change in response to changed cost conditions because of intense competition.
- In oligopoly, firms compete through nonprice means such as product innovation, product differentiation, and advertising.
- When oligopolists adjust prices, they do it through following a price leader, by mark-up pricing, or through collusion.
- Cartels are groups of firms that organize in order to act like a monopoly in the market. They are difficult to organize and maintain because it is in each firm's best interest to cheat on the cartel.
- The goal of advertising is to increase the demand and to decrease the elasticity of demand for the product.

KEY TERMS

Advertising	Imperfect competition	Nonprice competition
Cartel	Interdependent	Oligopoly
Collusion	Mark-up pricing	Price leader
Cross elasticity of demand	Monopolistic competition	Sticky prices

REVIEW QUESTIONS

1. What does the term "imperfect competition" mean?
2. What are the four conditions that are required for an oligopoly to exist?
3. What does the term "interdependent" mean to a business firm?
4. If a gas station finds it difficult to compete by lowering prices, what other methods might it use to increase sales?
5. Identify the three methods that oligopolists may use to raise prices and state when each approach might be used.
6. What are the two purposes of advertising?
7. Why is it that cartels are difficult to organize and keep going?

PROBLEM-SOLVING PRACTICE

1. Identify a product for which a kinked demand curve is appropriate. Draw the demand curve and graphically show the effect of a price increase and a price decrease.
2. Prepare a demand schedule and draw the curve for sale of Wheaties at a grocery store. Revise the schedule and curve to show the effects of a new advertising campaign.

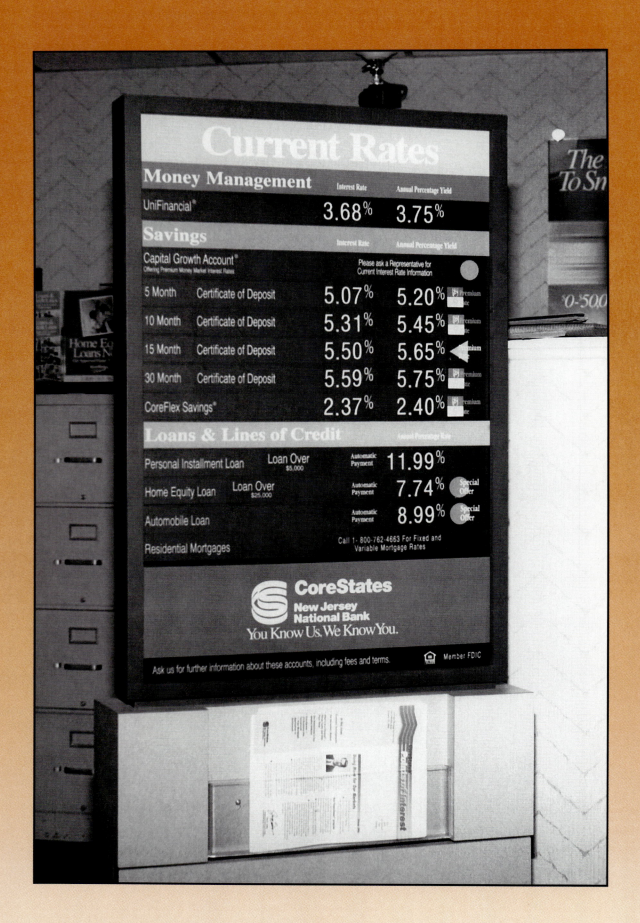

CHAPTER 13

Rent, Interest, and Profit

CHAPTER OUTLINE

A. Factors of Production and Their Returns
B. Rent
  1. Defining the Term
  2. Inframarginal Rent
  3. Pure Economic Rent
  4. Quasi Rent
  5. Monopoly Rent
  6. Rents—a Summary
C. Interest
  1. Capital: the Goods
  2. Capital: the Funds
    a. Time
    b. Risk
    c. Cost of Making the Loan
  3. Overall Interest Rates
  4. The Nominal *vs.* the Real Rate of Interest
D. Profits
  1. Entrepreneurship
  2. Profit as a Residual
  3. Accounting *vs.* Economic Profit
  4. Profit Rates Since 1945
E. By Way of a Summary

The purpose of this chapter is to introduce the returns to the factors of production, or resources, other than labor.

AFTER COMPLETING THIS CHAPTER, YOU WILL BE ABLE TO:

1. Apply the concept of rent.
2. Demonstrate the effect of the four types of rent in the market.
3. Compare nominal and real interest rates and apply the concept to business and individual decisions.
4. Explain the relationship between economic profit and accounting profit as a measure of business success.

Factors of Production and Their Returns

This chapter will finish our look at the factors of production and complete our understanding of their returns. Remember the factors of production that were introduced in Chapter 1? Land, labor, capital, and entrepreneurship. Those four factors of production, also known as resources or inputs, are what suppliers use to produce all goods and services available in the economy. The returns to these factors of production are what suppliers receive when these inputs are used productively.

Take a minute to consider the return on each factor of production. What does labor receive for its efforts? The return is wages. The return to land is called rent. Capital's return, or payment or earning, is known as interest. Entrepreneurship, when successful, receives profits.

Having studied labor, in this discussion we will explore the remaining three inputs to develop a clear understanding of how their returns are determined.

Step back a minute to the discussion on the most dominant of the factors of production, labor. In Chapter 9 we discovered that wage rates are set by the forces of demand and supply in the marketplace. The demand for labor is a function of the demand for the product and labor's productivity. The greater the demand for the product and the higher the productivity of labor, the greater the demand for labor. The supply of labor is a function of the individual's trade-off between income and leisure and results in the odd-shaped, backward-bending supply curve of labor. What follows is a similar analysis of the other factors.

RENT

Defining the Term

The word *rent* has a special meaning in economics. To most people, rent is what they have to pay to use something that belongs to someone else. They rent an apartment to live in, they rent a car on vacation, and they rent a tux for a special evening. Technically, the common usage of the term is no different than its definition in economics, but it certainly doesn't seem that way. Consider the following definition for the term. It sounds more complicated than a monthly rent check, doesn't it?

Rent—A Working Definition

Payment to a factor of production in excess of its opportunity cost.

Rent
Payment to a factor of production in excess of its opportunity cost.

This definition of rent may seem pretty incomprehensible at first glance. Any time you are faced with a definition like this one in economics or any other field, a good course is to pull the words apart a piece at a time to make sense of them.

Payment to—what is received by; what is paid to

A factor of production—any of the four inputs or resources

In excess of—greater than; more than

Its opportunity cost—what is given up to use it

FIGURE 13.1
Each of the four factors of production has its unique return.

Returns to Factors of Production	
Factor of Production	Return
Land	Rent
Labor	Wages
Capital	Interest
Entrepreneurship	Profit

Of the four pieces of this puzzling definition, three are pretty easy to understand: "Whatever is paid to any input that is more than . . . something." The last part of the definition recalls an earlier discussion of opportunity cost. Opportunity cost has to do with what must be given up to use something, with the true cost of using it. In this context, opportunity cost can be interpreted to mean ". . . what it could earn in its next-best use."

Thus, rent is what is paid to any input that is more than you would have had to pay to it. While the definition is correct and closer to understandable, perhaps a few examples will help clarify its meaning.

There are four different types of rent. Each of these examples or types adheres to the basic definition, but each is slightly different in its application. As you look at these types of rent, keep in mind its basic definition and see how it applies in each case.

Inframarginal Rent

Again, your best course is to consider this term in pieces. "Infra" means below or under. "Marginal" means at the margin or the end or last. An example should help to spell out the definition.

A school district needs to hire new teachers. If the district offers a low wage, it will have difficulty in attracting teachers. At a high wage, it can attract more. At a salary of $10,000, only a few prospective teachers would apply. A salary of $15,000 would bring in a few more applicants. At a salary of $20,000, the district would attract the prospects who were willing to work for $10,000 and $15,000 as well as additional candidates. If the salary were higher, even more would be attracted to teach in the school district. The issue here, of course, is the supply of teachers. Measuring the number of applicants at each salary level lays out the supply schedule for new teachers. The supply schedule shows the various prices offered (wage rates, in this case) and the related quantities that would be available.

As you know, any supply schedule can be easily converted into a supply curve. Figure 13.2 illustrates the supply curve of new teachers that the school district would face.

The supply curve shows that as the school board offers more money, as it increases its wage offer, it will attract more new teachers to the district. It will not pay these teachers differing wage rates, however; it will pay all starting teachers with the same amount of education and experience the same salary. The salary is fixed regardless of what the teacher is willing to accept. If the fixed starting salary is $23,000, this is the equilibrium wage, and its intersection with the supply curve provides the equilibrium number of teachers that would be employed at that wage rate.

Herein lies the concept of inframarginal rent. As you have seen, a few teachers are willing to work for $10,000. These teachers will be paid $23,000, or $13,000 more than is required to convince them to teach. Some other teachers are willing to work for $15,000. These teachers will also be paid $23,000, or $8,000 more than their minimum requirement. (Remember "payment to a factor of production in excess of its opportunity cost"?) Some more teachers are willing to work for $22,500, but these, too, will be paid $23,000. Finally, some teachers are willing to take the job at a salary of $30,000. They won't accept the positions for the $23,000 salary. All of those teachers who were willing to work for less than $23,000 will nonetheless be paid that fixed starting salary. These laborers receive a payment that is greater than what they were willing to accept. That is **inframarginal rent.**

You can see inframarginal rent in the area A-B-C on Figure 13.2. This area shows how much these new teachers are receiving above what they would be willing to accept. Like those teachers, *you* receive inframarginal rent on your job. Don't believe it? Would you quit your job if your salary was cut by one cent per year?

Inframarginal Rent
That portion of a payment to a factor of production such as labor in excess of what it would have been willing to accept.

FIGURE 13.2

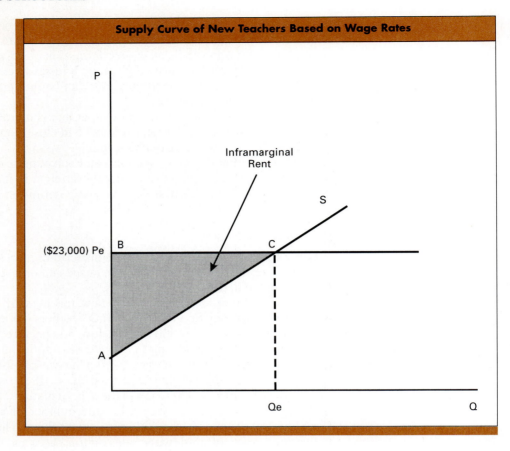

Supply Curve of New Teachers Based on Wage Rates

Most people would keep working, and so they are paid more than they would have to be paid. They are receiving rent. Would you quit if your salary was cut $1 per year? $100 per year? $1,000 per year? At some point (soon, if you haven't already) you would say, "Enough. I quit." The salary required to keep you on the job is wages. The amount that you receive above that is inframarginal rent. Thus, you are a rent receiver as well as a wage earner in the economy.

Pure Economic Rent

Pure Economic Rent
Any payment made to a factor of production that is fixed in supply.

The next example of rent is **pure economic rent.** In this case, pure economic rent is any payment made to a factor of production or anything that is fixed in supply. Again, an example may help to clarify the definition.

Think for a minute about the supply curve for something that is fixed in supply. What would such a supply curve look like? The quantity is fixed; it never changes. It might be the supply of all land in the United States, the supply of Rouault paintings, or the supply of Michael Jordans. There is a limited number or amount of each. Thus, the supply curve is a straight, vertical line. This supply curve is shown in Figure 13.3.

As you can see, the supply of Rouault paintings is fixed. Some Rouault paintings could be destroyed, but no more can be produced. Georges Rouault died in 1958, so the number of his paintings will never increase. What determines the price that will be paid for these paintings? If supply is fixed, only the demand for these paintings affects the price. If the demand for Rouault paintings is shown by the demand curve D1, then the price paid will be P1. If Rouault becomes popular and the demand for his works increases, then the demand curve might shift outward to D2. When this happens, the price for his paintings will rise to P2. If people tire of Rouault's use of color and broad, post-impressionistic work, the demand might

FIGURE 13.3

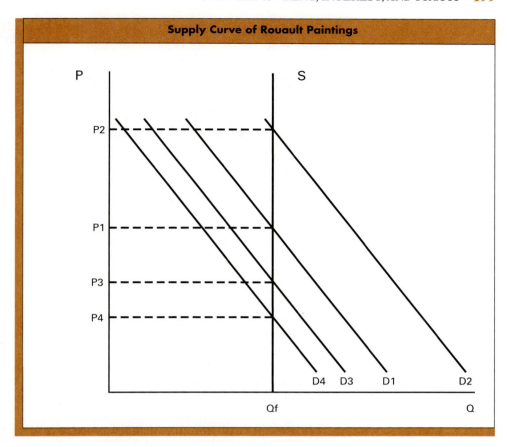

fall to D3. When this happens, the price will fall to P3. And, should the bottom drop out of the market for Rouault's works and the demand falls to D4, the price will fall even further to P4.

You will note that there is neither an increase in the quantity supplied of Rouault paintings that results from an increase in demand nor a decrease in the quantity supplied when demand falls. Under ordinary circumstances, with goods that are not fixed in supply, an increase in demand will increase both the price and the equilibrium quantity. The price will rise and suppliers will make more of the good available. Likewise, a decrease in demand will drop both the price and the quantity supplied. Less would be available and at a lower price. This is not the case with a good that is fixed in supply. In this case, the quantity cannot change; only the price can change.

The supply of Rouault paintings will not change regardless of the demand and no matter how much people are willing to pay. The quantity is fixed. Whatever is paid for one of these works of art is more than you would have to pay to get it to be a work of art. The alternatives for a Rouault canvas are zero. Therefore, anything paid for a work of art is rent, pure economic rent, and the same is true for anything else that is fixed in supply.

Quasi Rent

The third type of rent is quasi rent. This type of rent is an odd bird as you will quickly see. Do you remember the discussion about firms in perfect competition? How much profit do they earn? In perfect competition, firms sell their output for just what it costs to produce their product, so they earn no profit. The price they receive is equal to the marginal cost of producing the good. Firms can pay for all of their inputs, but they make no profit.

Let's assume that a firm, say a wheat farm, is operating in perfect competition. In this situation, the farm earns no profits but continues in business year after year producing its wheat at a price set in the marketplace. If the President, either because of declining ratings in popularity polls or out of a real concern for hungry people in underdeveloped countries, decides to ship tons of wheat overseas this year, what would happen to the overall demand for wheat? Demand would increase. What would happen to the price that wheat would sell for (the equilibrium price) if the demand for wheat rose? The price would also rise. This means that farmers, who planted their wheat in anticipation of receiving the previous price, are now paid more for each bushel than they anticipated. The price they receive is more than the marginal cost of producing the wheat. For this year only, farmers make a profit. Their revenues are greater than their costs. Thus, farmers are paid more for their wheat than they would have accepted. In the short run—as long as the President's polls lag or his concern for the starving continues—these farmers would receive profits, and these profits are known as **quasi rents.** When the demand returns to normal, these quasi rents disappear.

Monopoly Rent

From your understanding of quasi rents, you should be able to guess what **monopoly rents** might be. They are payments made to a monopolist that are more than the minimum the firm would accept.

The discussion of monopoly noted that monopolists are in a position to have an impact on the market. Monopolists attempt to make a profit by seeking a price that maximizes this opportunity. Whether they are successful or not in generating profits, they price their product above the level that would have been established in perfect competition. The price they charge is higher than it needs to be, and the monopolist can reap a profit because of it. Thus, profits received by monopolists are rents, and are called, appropriately, monopoly rents.

Rents—a Summary

Is the concept of rent clearer now? Look again at the definition: rent is payment to a factor of production in excess of its opportunity cost. Can you see how that applies to each of the four types of rents outlined here? Inframarginal rent is what wage earners receive over and above the minimum they would accept. Pure economic rent is any payment made to a resource that is fixed in supply. Quasi rents are the short-run profits that are earned by firms that ordinarily operate in perfect competition. And monopoly rents are the profits that monopolists receive because of their control in the marketplace. Each of these rents is an excess payment, and each is like an extra cost that is unnecessarily paid.

Quasi Rent
The short-run profits earned by firms in perfect competition when demand unexpectedly increases.

Monopoly Rent
The profits earned by monopolists that exceed the normal profits earned by firms in perfect competition.

Core-Info

Rent is a return to a factor of production in excess of its opportunity cost. In other words, it receives more than is required to get it to do its job.

INTEREST

Heed this warning as you start this section: Take it slow. If you don't, you're likely to get confused. In discussions to date, we have stressed that "capital" does not mean money. In economics, capital is productive goods, which suppliers use to produce other goods. This section relaxes that rigid definition a bit. Now the term capital can mean either the physical goods used to produce other goods or the money suppliers accumulate to purchase capital goods.

CHAPTER 13 • RENT, INTEREST, AND PROFIT   201

Capital: The Goods

Capital goods are productive goods. Suppliers build them and use them to build other goods. In economics, this is known as **round-about production.** Suppliers produce punch presses and back hoes not so they can have more punch presses and back hoes but so they can have more bicycle wheels with spoke holes and more drainage ditches. The total amount of capital goods available is known as the **capital stock.** Adding to the capital stock is known as **capital formation.** Using up, wearing out, or depleting the capital stock is known as **capital consumption.**

You can think of a country's capital stock in much the same way as you think about your bank account. The amount of money you have in your account is available to be productive for you. Putting money into your account is like adding more capital equipment to the capital stock. Taking money out of your account is like consuming or depleting the capital stock. Any year in which you add more money to your account than you take out of it leaves you in a better position going into the next year than you were before. Any year in which you withdraw more money from your account than you put in it leaves you in a worse condition. So it is with the economy. Adding to the capital stock (when capital formation is greater than capital consumption) makes the country potentially more productive than before; it moves the production possibility curve farther out. If the reverse happens and capital stock decreases, the production possibility curve moves inward and the overall size of the economy is diminished.

The bank account example can illustrate another point about the capital stock. How can you add to your bank account this year? If you want to save money, you must spend less on consumer goods. You must forego consumption this year to save for next year. The same is true for the economy. If suppliers want to add to the capital stock, they must shift some production away from producing goods for consumption today and produce some goods that will be productive tomorrow. This shift lowers the standard of living today but produces the potential for a higher standard of living in the future.

Capital: The Funds

The other definition of capital is money. This is the definition that most of you brought with you to this course. People say they have to accumulate capital if they want to start a business or buy a car, and so they set out to save or borrow enough money to do what they want.

As with everything else in life, this saving or accumulating process has a cost, and the cost is the **interest** that people have to pay. Why is interest charged on money that people borrow? If you loaned someone $100, would you rather be repaid today or a year from now? Most people would choose to be repaid today rather than wait a year for the same amount. If you have to wait for a year to get your money, you would probably want to be paid extra for the inconvenience and the opportunities lost because you didn't have your funds. That's what interest is. It is a payment to offset the opportunities lost because people didn't have access to their money. Interest is also the payment that people receive when a bank or other entity has the use of their money for a time. Interest deals with what is known as people's "time preference" for money: they would rather have it today than have to wait until tomorrow to get it.

Everybody knows, however, that there is not one single interest rate in the market but dozens of rates. There is the **prime rate,** which is the rate charged by banks to their best corporate customers. There are mortgage rates, auto loan rates, and rates charged by people who are willing to loan you money from the back seat of their cars and who *always* collect. The interest rates charged by these sources vary significantly. What causes this variation? Three factors affect interest rates: time, risk, and the cost of making the loan.

Round-About Production
The production of capital goods today so that increased quantities of consumer goods can be produced tomorrow.

Capital Stock
The total amount of capital, or productive goods, that exists in an economy at a given time.

Capital Formation
An increase in the quantity of capital stock in an economy.

Capital Consumption
A decrease in the quantity of capital stock in an economy.

Interest
The cost of money.

Prime Rate
Generally, the lowest interest charged by banks of their best customers.

Time. In general, the longer the time period of the loan, the higher the interest rate that will be charged. A couple of factors play into this. First, the longer the time period, the more opportunities to use the money the lender must forego. Second, the longer the time period, the greater the uncertainty about the overall economy and of the borrower's continuing ability to repay.

Risk. The greater the risk the lender faces regarding loan repayment, the higher the interest rate will be. Let's say that you want to borrow $10,000 to start a new small business. At the same time, General Motors wants to borrow $10 million to buy some new equipment for its Saturn Division. Even though General Motors lost $23 billion in 1992 and you did not, which business would you guess is seen by the lender as being more risky? You pose the greater risk. General Motors has a history of paying its bills on time and of not going out of business. You may have paid your Visa account on time, but your business does not have a track record and thus will appear to be much more risky to a banker. Because you are seen to present a greater risk of not repaying the loan, the lender will charge you more to borrow money than General Motors. This practice may appear to give established businesses an advantage over newcomers, but it really is determined by the risk that a lender estimates.

Cost of Making the Loan. The more it costs to make a loan, the more the lender charges the borrower. Let's return to the example of you and General Motors both wanting to borrow money from the same bank. Think about the process that you will have to go through to borrow money. You must complete a loan application. The loan officer reviews your application for completeness and appropriateness. If she feels that your loan has merit, the loan officer passes it on to an assistant who runs a credit check on you and contacts your references if necessary. Once that information is assembled, it goes back to the loan officer who reviews the documents and presents the file to the Loan Committee for approval. If everything is O.K., your loan comes through. The cost of this process is fairly high in terms of the person-hours involved.

What must General Motors do to borrow the money it needs? Some vice president at General Motors calls the vice president at the bank with the news that GM needs $10 million. The bank's vice president is likely to promise that the money will be transferred into GM's account that afternoon. The cost of making the loan to GM is quite low. Thus, GM will probably pay a lower interest rate than you must. Is this unfair? Not really. From an economic standpoint, the resources involved in making the loan to GM were much fewer than in making the loan to you.

What can you do about this seeming inequity? Borrow money for as short a period as possible. Reduce the risk that the lender will face in loaning you money. Pay your bills on time and keep your credit record clean so the lender sees that you are a good risk. Establish a good working relationship with your banker so that the loan process itself can be handled quickly and at a minimum of cost to the lender.

Overall Interest Rates

We have seen how interest rates get set at the microeconomic level. What about at the macroeconomic level? What determines the overall level of interest rates in the economy? It should come as no surprise that supply and demand are at the core of this equation.

Figure 13.4 presents the supply and demand curves for loanable funds. The quantity of money is shown on the horizontal axis, as would be expected. The cost of money (price) is interest, so the interest rate is shown on the vertical axis. The demand curve shows that the lower the interest rate, the more money people are

FIGURE 13.4

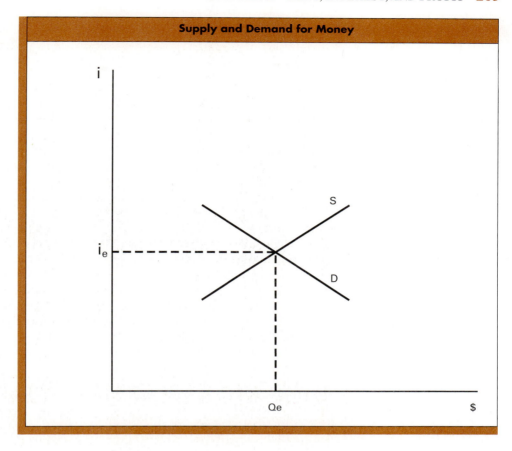

willing to borrow. The higher the interest rate that people must pay to borrow, the less they want to borrow. Suppliers, on the other hand, operate in just the opposite way. The higher the interest rate, the more money they are willing to loan to borrowers. When interest rates fall, on the other hand, lenders are more reluctant to make loans available to borrowers. The interaction of supply and demand establishes an equilibrium interest rate (i_e in Fig. 13.4) in the market and an equilibrium quantity of funds that will be loaned to borrowers.

The Nominal vs. the Real Rate of Interest

The interest rate that borrowers see on paper may not be the real interest rate after all. The real rate may be much lower than the rate that is quoted to consumers. The interest rate that is quoted is called the **nominal interest rate.** The nominal interest rate is whatever rate is stated by the lender, say 10 percent. The **real interest rate** reflects the actual, true cost of the loan in terms of what is given up.

Let's say a friend loans you $100 for one year at 5 percent interest. After one year, you repay the $100 principal plus $5 in interest for a total of $105. It looks as if your friend gets the money back plus, doesn't it? That is true as long as there isn't any inflation during the year. If there is inflation, however, the result is a general increase in the level of prices and a general decrease in the purchasing power of the dollar. In that case the money you give your friend at the end of the year will not buy as much as it would have at the beginning of the year. If bread sold for $1 per loaf at the beginning of the year, your friend could have bought 100 loaves with that money. If during the year the rate of inflation is 5 percent and the price of bread goes up by this percentage, then bread sells for $1.05 per loaf, and the

Nominal Interest Rate
The stated, market-determined rate of interest.

Real Interest Rate
The true cost of borrowing determined by subtracting the rate of inflation from the nominal rate of interest.

How Much Will It Cost Me to Borrow?

Interest is the cost of money. As with any price, it acts as a rationing device. To this end, the interest rate serves a dual function: it rewards those who are willing to save and invest their money so others may use it, and it is a cost to those who want to borrow. The key interest rate that people watch and that is reported daily in the news is the prime rate. The prime rate is the interest rate that banks charge their best corporate customers, those businesses in the most sound financial position and which have the best repayment record. Thus, the prime rate is generally the lowest interest rate that is available for borrowing.

The table below shows the prime rate for the 15 years from 1980 to 1994. As you can see, the rate has varied from 6.00% to 18.87%. That is quite a spread from lowest to highest, a full 12.87%. The effect of this great volatility would be tremendous on corporate investment decision making. Many of the investments that businesses make take place over a number of years. A decision is made today and an investment is begun while the money to fund it is acquired over the life of the project. If the cost of making the investment will vary significantly, decision-makers must receive a higher rate of return to cover the increased risk.

Fortunately, the actual cost to businesses of borrowing is not the prime rate but the real rate of interest. As you have seen, the real rate of interest is the nominal rate minus the rate of inflation. When the real rate of interest is calculated for the same 15 years, a different picture emerges. The real interest rate varies much less, ranging from 1.76% to 8.75%, still a significant variation, but at 6.99%, one that causes fewer problems for business decision makers. In fact, the actual average interest rate to businesses was 5.51%, not the 10.42% that the prime rate would lead you to expect. This is likely why the 92-month expansion period of the mid-1980s was the second longest in American history as business investment increased rapidly.

Year	1980	1981	1982	1983	1984	1985	1986	1987
Prime Rate	15.26	18.87	14.85	10.79	12.04	9.93	8.33	8.21
Inflation Rate	13.5	10.3	6.1	3.2	4.3	3.5	1.9	3.7
Real Int. Rate	1.76	8.57	8.75	7.59	7.74	6.43	6.43	4.51
	1988	1989	1990	1991	1992	1993	1994	Average
	9.32	10.87	10.01	8.46	6.25	6.00	7.15	10.42
	4.1	4.8	5.4	4.2	3.0	3.0	2.6	4.91
	5.22	6.07	4.61	4.26	3.25	3.00	4.55	5.51

$105 repaid to your friend at the end of the year will purchase only 100 loaves, the same amount that could have been purchased 12 months earlier. Your friend earns nothing for loaning you the money. Clearly, if a lender plans to make any money, it must earn a rate of return that is greater than the rate of inflation. Thus, a lender must take into account the rate of inflation when setting the interest rate for a loan. The formula for this is:

Real Interest Rate = Nominal Rate – Rate of Inflation

If the nominal interest rate (the rate that is quoted to a borrower) is 10 percent and the rate of inflation is 5 percent, then the real interest rate is 5 percent. Five percent is the true cost to the borrower of the loan, and it is also the rate that the lender actually earns. When you borrow money, you must take into account the rate of inflation to calculate the real cost of the loan.

Core-Info

Interest is the return to capital goods, those goods used to produce other goods and services. Interest is also what is received as a payment for deferred consumption.

PROFITS

Profits are the hoped-for result of entrepreneurship. There is no guarantee about profits. If you add an acre of land to production, you can pretty much predict what the result will be in terms of increased output. The same is true for labor and capital: add one unit of either to the mix of inputs and you can guess in advance what the change will be. This is not the case with entrepreneurship.

Entrepreneurship

As you may remember from the discussion of entrepreneurship in Chapter 1, this input is the risky one. There is no guarantee that, when you take a risk and become entrepreneurial, you will find fame and fortune. You may just as likely fall flat on your face and lose all your money. An entrepreneur is someone who perceives an opportunity, accumulates the necessary resources, bears a risk, and seeks a profit. If the entrepreneur guesses right and applies the right combination of resources to the problem, a profit may result. However, a loss could just as easily be the outcome, as the thousands of business failures each year attest.

Profit as a Residual

Profit, you will recall, is a residual. Profit is what is left over after all the costs are accounted for, whether the costs are paid in cash or not. Profit is what is left over even if the bills aren't paid in an accounting sense.

Accounting vs. Economic Profit

There are two types of profit, so there are two ways in which profit is calculated. The first type of profit is accounting profit. Accounting profit is calculated by subtracting the actual dollar costs (explicit costs) incurred in production from the total revenue received from selling the goods. The formula for accounting profit is:

Accounting Profit = Total Revenue − Explicit Costs
AP = TR − EC

This is an important measure of the results of a business. Both the Internal Revenue Service and the firm's managers are critically interested in the amount of dollar profit, or accounting profit, that the firm generates.

Thus, a firm does its best to generate an accounting profit and dutifully pays its business taxes to please the IRS. But, all the while, this measure of business profit is by far less important to a firm's long-term success than that other measure of profit, economic profit. As opposed to accounting profit, economic profit takes a much broader view of what constitutes a successful operation. Economic profit doesn't just take into account the dollars that are earned or the dollar cost alone. Economic profit looks at the total or true cost involved in producing the good. Economic profit is calculated by subtracting the total value of all resources used in the production of the goods from the total revenue obtained by selling the goods. The equation for economic profit, therefore, is:

Economic Profit = Total Revenue − Total Costs
EP = TR − TC
EP = TR − (EC + IC)

where: Total Cost = Explicit Costs + Implicit Costs
Explicit costs are actual dollar costs
Implicit costs are the dollar value of resources used but not paid for in dollars.

This profit measure is critical to the firm. There is much more to be concerned about than just dollars (as important as they are), so firms must pay attention to the true costs involved in producing the product. Just because a firm records an accounting profit doesn't mean it really made a profit. It may have

FIGURE 13.5
Source: Department of Commerce, Bureau of Economic Analysis

Profit Rates in the United States (all figures in billions except profit rates)					
	1950	1960	1970	1980	1990
Net national product	$241.1	$414.5	$800.5	$2121.4	$4459.6
Corporate profits	$ 37.7	$ 49.9	$ 69.4	$ 182.7	$ 319.0
Profit rate	15.6%	12.0%	8.7%	8.6%	7.1%

earned a dollar profit solely because it didn't pay for all the resources that it used to produce the product. If a business received some free resources that it used as inputs to the product or if it didn't pay its owner a salary, then there were opportunity costs involved that must be included before the firm can determine if it really covered all its costs.

Just knowing the difference between the two types of profits gives a firm a significant advantage in the long run over its competitors who only pay attention to their dollar profit. Only if you earn an economic profit are you really breaking even. If you only earn an accounting profit, you may make money today, but you will not likely be able to continue to do so when you have to pay the full cost of production some day in the future.

Profit Rates Since 1945

What of profit margins in the United States? What do U.S. firms earn on average? Profit margins vary significantly from industry to industry and from year to year. The restaurant industry, for instance, has an average profit margin of just 3.8 percent. The automobile industry, which usually does fairly well overall, has fallen on hard times in recent years, and all of the American manufacturers and most of the foreign producers have been operating at a loss. General Motors, for instance, lost $23 *billion* in 1992 alone. Figure 13.5 shows the overall profit rate for corporations in the United States over the past 40 years. Most people hold the general belief that corporations are becoming more and more profitable over the years and, at first glance, that might seem to be the case. Corporate profits are 8½ times larger than just 40 years ago, rising from $37.7 billion to $319 billion. On the surface it would seem that corporations are doing much better than in the past. However, the economy has not been static during this time period. While it had business cycles of ups and downs, the economy has been generally growing over those years. In fact, the economy in 1990 was 18½ times as large as it was in 1950. Therefore, the economy is growing faster than corporate profits. The result is that the overall corporate profit rate has been steadily declining. Whereas corporations had a profit rate of 15.6 percent of net national product in 1950, by 1990 this had fallen to just 7.1 percent.

Core-Info

Profit is the return to entrepreneurship and is what is left after costs have been deducted from revenues. Economic profit is the profit that remains after all costs, cash and otherwise, have been subtracted.

BY WAY OF A SUMMARY

In this chapter, you have seen that all factors of production have a return. The term *rent* has a special definition in economics; it means something like paying more for something than you should in terms of the resources actually used to produce the product. Interest is the return to capital, and you discovered that there are two interest rates of concern, the nominal rate and the real rate. The rate of inflation makes the difference between the two. Finally came a reminder that of the two types of profit, accounting profit and economic profit, only the latter includes the full and true cost of producing the good.

SUMMARY

- Rent is any return to a factor of production that is in excess of its opportunity cost, the minimum it would accept to induce it to go to work.
- The four types of rent are inframarginal rent, pure economic rent, monopoly rent, and quasi rent.
- Interest is the return to financial capital.
- Profits are the residual when costs are subtracted from revenues. Accounting profit only considers the money actually spent whereas economic profit subtracts all of the costs of production.

KEY TERMS

Capital consumption	Monopoly rent	Quasi rent
Capital formation	Nominal interest rate	Real interest rate
Capital stock	Prime rate	Rent
Inframarginal rent	Pure economic rent	Round-about production
Interest		

REVIEW QUESTIONS

1. Identify the four types of rent and give one example of each type.
2. What does the term "round-about production" mean in an economy?
3. Why is the prime interest rate generally the lowest available in the market place?
4. What are the three factors that affect interest rates?
5. How is the overall rate of interest determined?
6. Describe the difference between nominal and real interest rates.
7. What are the two measures of profit? How is each type of use to a manager?

PROBLEM-SOLVING PRACTICE

1. A developing country had a capital stock worth $10 billion at the beginning of the year. During the year there was capital formation of $2 billion and capital consumption of $1 billion. What is the capital stock at the end of the year? Draw production possibilities curves for the beginning and end of the year.
2. The following chart gives the prime rate and the rate of inflation for selected years in an emerging nation. Calculate the real interest rate for each year.

	Prime Rate	Rate of Inflation
1990	10%	2.3%
1991	15%	7.8%
1992	19%	15.0%
1993	22%	20.1%
1994	15%	3.0%
1995	10%	2.0%

3. What is the role of profits in a capitalist market economy?

PART 4
ECONOMIC ORGANIZATION

Chapter 14: Economic Systems

Chapter 15: Government and Taxes

Chapter 16: The National Economy

Chapter 17: Money, Banks, and the Interest Rate

Chapter 18: Economic Growth, Development, and Inflation

Chapter 19: The Global Economy

CHAPTER 14

Economic Systems

CHAPTER OUTLINE

A. Scarcity Yet Again
B. Definition of Economic Systems
C. Economic Systems *vs.* Political Systems
D. Characteristics and Types of Modern Economic Systems
  1. Characteristics
  2. Types
E. Capitalism
  1. Definition of Capitalism
  2. Conditions Required for Capitalism
     a. Private Property is Protected
     b. Free Enterprise
     c. Competitive Markets
     d. Limited Role for Government (*Laissez Faire*)
  3. Effects of Capitalism
F. Socialism
  1. Definition of Socialism
  2. Conditions Required for Socialism
     a. The Issue of Property
     b. The Issue of Enterprise
     c. The Issue of Competition
     d. The Role of Government
  3. Effects of Socialism
G. Mixed Economies
H. Concluding Thoughts

The purpose of this chapter is to introduce capitalism and socialism, the two basic economic systems in the world, and to help you understand the characteristics and effects of each.

AFTER COMPLETING THIS CHAPTER, YOU WILL BE ABLE TO:

1. Describe the three characteristics of modern economies.
2. Explain the differences between economic systems and political systems.
3. Compare and contrast capitalism and socialism through their required characteristics.
4. Predict and summarize the differential outcomes of capitalism and socialism.

Scarcity Yet Again

Scarcity is a way of life. Scarcity is the *way of life for humankind. Even in the super-rich United States, scarcity is at the foundation of the economy. Somehow we must produce and distribute all the goods and services we want and need. But the reality is that we can't have everything we want. Even the super rich can buy only one airline or one ski resort at a time. Even their resources are scarce.*

People try to deal with the problem of scarcity as best they can. On a personal level, they work to make things and trade with other people. Both work and trade add to wealth, but the amount that is added is restricted by people's limited abilities, limited energy, and limited knowledge of other people with coincident wants.

If people are going to get more and more of the goods and services they want, they need to get organized. People need other people and what they can do if everyone is to get more and more. This is the purpose of economic systems: they organize consumers and suppliers so the economy can produce and distribute all the things people want.

DEFINITION OF ECONOMIC SYSTEMS

Economic System
That part of the social system that answers the four economic questions; the part of the social system that has to do with the use of resources.

An **economic system** is that part of the social system that answers the four economic questions: What? How? For Whom? When? That definition may sound like a tautology, (a needless repetition) but it's not. Somehow each society must answer those four key questions. The mechanism it employs for answering the questions is known as its economic system.

> **Core-Info**
>
> Societies organize economic systems because all groups and nations must deal with the reality of scarcity.

ECONOMIC SYSTEMS *VS.* POLITICAL SYSTEMS

Political Systems
That part of the social system that has to do with how power is utilized.

It is important at this point to differentiate between economic systems and **political systems.**
- Economic systems have to do with how people use resources.
- Political systems have to do with how people use power.
- Economic systems have to do with who's got the goods.
- Political systems have to do with who's got the guns.

Economic systems, as you will see, include capitalism and socialism. Political systems, on the other hand, include liberal democracies and totalitarian states. The United States is a democratic capitalism. Albania is a totalitarian socialism. Sweden, until very recently, was a democratic socialism (it is now joining the capitalist camp). There are no totalitarian capitalisms (ten extra points to the person who can tell the instructor why this is the case).

> **Core-Info**
>
> Economic systems have to do with how societies deal with their resources; political systems have to do with how societies deal with power.

CHARACTERISTICS AND TYPES OF MODERN ECONOMIC SYSTEMS

Every society has some sort of economic system: there is some mechanism for producing and distributing goods and services among the members of the group. In small early or primitive societies, a barter system is generally used. People produce what they need and a bit more and trade the excess with others. The problems with barter are numerous and well known, so a better system is required if an economy is going to grow.

Characteristics

While every society has some sort of economic system in place, modern economies are different. Modern economies are not just larger versions of primitive or tribal economies. In fact, there are three characteristics in particular that define a modern, developed economy:

1. Large amounts of capital
2. Specialization
3. Use of advanced technology

Just as levers, pulleys, and wheels can multiply the physical work that a person can do, physical capital multiplies the economic work people can do. The more capital people have, the more they can multiply the individual's output. Modern economies have vast sums of capital per worker in all segments of the economy.[1]

A high degree of specialization is also a way of life for modern economies. Mass production and automation are typical. Most workers do not produce a complete product but perform a portion of the overall job. By specializing, of course, workers often find boredom along with bounty, producing much but facing a highly routinized job.

The final characteristic of all modern economies is the use of advanced technology. Not only is a lot of capital directed to specialized applications, but the techniques employed use the latest technologies and are highly productive.

Types

The two types of modern economic systems are capitalism and socialism. These are presented as polar opposites in much the same way as pure competition is contrasted with monopoly. As with pure competition and monopoly, these systems don't exist in their pure form in real life. The two economic systems are portrayed as opposites for the same reasons that market systems are. By showing the extreme positions, you can more easily understand the reality which lies between.

Core-Info

Modern economic systems are characterized by large amounts of capital, specialization, and the use of advanced technology.

CAPITALISM

Capitalism
An economic system in which the resources are owned by and economic decisions are made by individuals.

Capitalism has emerged in the last decade as *the* predominant economic system in the world. While most western nations have pursued a capitalistic economy in one form or another for the past two centuries, the rest of the world is now scrambling to adopt the model, frankly with quite mixed success. After we examine the two types of systems, we will look at some of the reasons for the difficulties the former socialistic economies are facing.

---

[1] This means *all* segments. The U.S. economy has more capital per worker in agriculture than per manufacturing worker.

Definition of Capitalism

Capitalism is an economic system in which the productive resources are owned by individuals and the economic decisions are made by individuals. Using the term *individuals* is not meant to remove businesses from the discussion but to signify the absence of government involvement. People as economic beings are the key. Whether alone or voluntarily combined into businesses, people and people alone are the central and sole focus in capitalism.

Conditions Required for Capitalism

How would you know if you were in a capitalistic economy? What would you look for if you landed in a strange country and wanted to know whether it was capitalistic or not? Fortunately, that is an easy question to answer. There are four characteristics of a capitalistic economy. All four must be present for the economy to be truly and fully capitalistic. If one or more is absent or restricted, then the economy deviates from the model and is not purely capitalistic. The four characteristics of a capitalistic economy are:

1. Private property is protected
2. Free enterprise
3. Competitive markets
4. Limited role for government[2]

Private Property is Protected. This characteristic is absolutely central to capitalism. Without private property, capitalism cannot exist. Unless your right to private property is protected, there is nothing else to talk about. Physical property is to be protected and intellectual property is sacred. What you own—your store, your land, your tools, your house—must be safeguarded. The same is true for ideas. Inventions, art works, books, and music are all to be protected. Capitalists know that without this protection, all of the capitalistic economy goes out the window.

Why is private property so sacred to capitalists? The key word here is incentive. Unless your property is absolutely protected, what incentive will you have for working hard to produce more goods and services—and jobs—in the economy? If, after all your hard work someone could come along and take your possessions, why would you want to work again? Obviously, you wouldn't, and the whole economy would suffer. With your property protected, you have the incentive to work hard, to accumulate capital, and to invest. Everybody benefits.

Free Enterprise. Free enterprise takes your right to private property one step farther. With free enterprise you are free to decide how to use your property—as long as you don't violate other people's private property rights. Laborers can choose where they want to work. Employers can choose who they want to hire. Businesses can decide what they want to produce. Consumers can decide what they want to buy. Investors can decide where they want to put their money. Each person is given free reign as to what they will do—as long as they do not violate someone else's property rights. This means that people can buy a gun, but they don't have the right to use it to rob you. This also means that in true capitalism there can be no discrimination. In a real capitalistic economy, discrimination based on race, gender, religion, or other characteristic would not and could not exist. Why is this so? Economic discrimination means paying people differently based on some nonrelevant factor. Employers who practice discrimination pay

---

[2] In this discussion of capitalism and socialism, the text will take the position of one who believes in each respective model. The discussion will be passionate in an attempt to convince you that this approach is right and the other is wrong.

some people less than market wage for their work. Another word for that practice is theft. Discrimination is theft and as such is the taking of another's property, a violation of the fundamental requirement of capitalism. Thus, in a real capitalistic economy, there can be no discrimination.

Competitive Markets. The third characteristic of capitalism is competitive markets. In a true capitalistic economy, no one can dominate the market. True capitalism is founded fervently in competition. Capitalists believe that competition produces an improved product, lower costs, lower prices, more jobs, *and* more profits! Real capitalism requires something very closely approximating perfect competition: a large number of buyers and sellers (especially the latter) and free entry and exit. In perfect competition, there are so many sellers that no one can have any impact on the price or the market. When an economy reaches this point, it is very close to truly competitive markets that are required in capitalism.

Limited Role for Government (*Laissez Faire*). The final requirement for capitalism is a limited role for government. The French term for this is ***laissez faire,*** which means to leave to do, to leave alone. To a good capitalist, the role of government should, in fact must, be limited to protecting the nation from attack and to three other tasks: making certain that private property is protected, guaranteeing truly free enterprise so people can use their personal and physical property in any way they want (except to take away another's private property, of course), and assuring that markets are and remain truly competitive. Other than these duties, the government should stay out. True capitalists want governments as limited as possible because they believe that the individual level is the proper locus for decision making. Capitalists believe that no one knows more about what you want than you do. *You* know what is important to you and how you value things. You can weigh the costs and benefits of all the decisions you must make, and you can make those decisions better than anyone else. What is true of the individual is also true of the business person. Managers and firms can and should decide for themselves how to produce and distribute the products that consumers want with no interference from some outside influence. Government should leave businesses alone—as long as businesses don't violate any of the three conditions required for capitalism.

Effects of Capitalism

Capitalism is the dominant economic system in the world today. Capitalism is not perfect, but it does have one major advantage: it grows. The growth rate among the more fully capitalistic economies of the world has been between 2.5 and 3.5 percent per year for the past century. Even on a per capita basis (taking into account the increase in population), the growth rate has been between 1.7 and 2.4 percent per year. Following the "rule of 70s," capitalistic economies have been doubling in their production of goods and services *per person* every 35 years. Thus, the benefits of capitalism are potentially great.

That capitalism is productive has rarely been questioned. The main criticism of capitalism has been that it is unfair, efficient without equity. Some people have argued that capitalism generates a lot of goods, but that these goods are not fairly distributed. Obviously, the word "fairly" is a normative word and thus is open to a variety of interpretations. What is "fair" to you may be grossly "unfair" in someone else's opinion. Let's see if we can move the issue to positive grounds. What is the income distribution in capitalism? The distribution of income in the United States has been quite consistent over the past half century. There are rich and there are poor and their pieces of the pie have been relatively constant: the richest 20 percent get about 41 percent of the income while the poorest 20 percent receive about 5 percent. Anyway you look at it, that is quite

Laissez Faire
The public policy of government not interfering with or regulating the market.

The Rule of 70

The rule of 70 gives us a handy device for understanding what the growth rate means. The rule shows the relationship between the growth rate and the length of time it will take an item to double. All you have to do is divide the number 70 by the one to get the other. An example should help. Let's say the economy is growing at the rate of 2.5 percent per year. Dividing that number into 70 yields 28; the economy will double in size in 28 years. If the economy could grow at a 3 percent rate, it would double in 23⅓ years. Conversely, for the economy to double in 20 years, it must grow at a 3.5 percent rate.

How significant is the difference between a 2.5 percent and a 3 percent growth rate? It is tremendous. The following table traces the pattern of doubling at each growth rate, beginning with an initial starting point of $100.

2.5% Growth (28-year doubling)		3% Growth (23⅓ year doubling)	
Start	$ 100	Start	$ 100
Year 28	200	Year 23⅓	200
Year 56	400	Year 46⅔	400
Year 84	800	Year 70	800
Year 112	1600	Year 93⅓	1600
Year 140	3200	Year 116⅔	3200
		Year 140	6400

At a 2.5 percent growth rate, the economy will become 32 times as large in 140 years. At the slightly higher growth rate of 3 percent, the economy will become 64 times as large in the same time period. Small difference in the growth rate, big difference in the outcome. The saying must be true: "Little things mean a lot."

Core-Info

Capitalism is an economic system in which individuals are central. The characteristics of capitalism are the protection of private property, free enterprise, competitive markets, and a limited role for government.

---

unequal. The richest quintile receives eight times as much as the poorest quintile. Maybe the criticism of capitalism is deserved: maybe capitalism is unjust. Let's withhold final judgment until after the discussion of socialism, but for now, put this issue down as a concern about capitalism.

SOCIALISM

Socialism is the other major type of economic system in the world. In the past, socialism was a very strong rival of capitalism for the heart and mind—and resources—of nations. In the past decade, however, socialism has fallen on hard times. Few unquestioning adherents remain, and those who persist tend to be aging leaders of truly backward nations. What has happened? A short time ago socialist leaders were predicting that they would bury capitalism. Now, just the reverse is happening. Let's examine socialism and see if the seeds of socialism's destruction are to be seen within the system.

Definition of Socialism

When looking at socialism, it is convenient to think of it as the complete opposite of capitalism. Therefore, while capitalism is an economic system in which the productive resources are owned by individuals who also make the economic decisions, socialism is an economic system in which the economic resources are owned by the government which also makes the economic decisions. Government is the prime mover and decision maker in the economy. It is not that individuals are not important in socialism: they are. The important issue is how

---

Socialism
An economic system in which the resources are owned by and economic decisions are made by the government.

FIGURE 14.1

The percent of a nation's gross domestic product that is a part of the governmental sector is one measure of where on the capitalism-socialism continuum the country is. *Source:* Organization for Economic Cooporation and Development, Paris

Tax Revenues as a Percent of Gross Domestic Product – 1992	
Country	Percent
Sweden	50.0
Denmark	49.3
Luxembourg	48.4
Finland	47.0
Netherlands	46.9
France	43.6
United Kingdom	35.2
United States	29.4
Japan	29.4
Australia	28.5
Turkey	23.1

to make the best decisions for the overall economy and thus help the most people. While capitalism relies on the combined individual decisions of people to direct the economy, socialism looks to a centralized decision-making group within government for this guidance.

Conditions Required for Socialism

The best way to understand socialism is to look at it in the same way we examined capitalism. Thus, we will consider how socialism views private property, free enterprise, competitive markets, and the role of government. As you will see, socialism's approach is the exact opposite of that of capitalism. (Remember: this text will now take the position of a committed socialist as it portrays its characteristics.)

The Issue of Property. The capitalists are absolutely wrong. Productive property belongs to everyone. Some individuals may have been given temporary custody, but property belongs to all people and should be used to the benefit of everyone. What you earn with your labor is yours, of course, but nothing else.

The Issue of Enterprise. With the issue of free enterprise, capitalists again are way off base. Free enterprise entails using productive property (which really belongs to all people, after all) to benefit individuals. Since when did one person become the center of the universe? Individuals may know what is best for them and perhaps their children, but do they know what is going on on the other side of town? How about in the rural poverty areas of the country? Individuals may know what is needed today, but what about tomorrow? Long after the people here today are gone, the state will remain. Taking care of individuals today is important, but so is making sure that the needs of people 100 years from now are met. Only the state can make the decisions to use labor or machines in the best way for the overall economy. All a business looks out for in capitalism is its profits. Only the state has the length and breadth of vision to make the economic decisions that are best for the whole country. That's why socialism is best. Oh, and by the way, that argument about discrimination? Look at the evidence. Discrimination flourishes in capitalistic economies.

The Issue of Competition. As far as competition goes, even many capitalistic economists talk about how competition leads to waste. How many different brands of hand soap do you really need? A little different perfume, a little different color, and a different package are all that separate one brand from another. Oh, yes, and a *lot* of advertising. All advertising does is to convince people to buy

"It Was the Best of Times; It Was the Worst of Times."

The path from totalitarian socialism to the start of a democratic capitalism has been filled with detours and potholes for Russia. Life expectancy has fallen, inflation has soared, and the ruble has all but collapsed. Could anyone have expected essential services to decline and organized crime to rise? Maybe so. Remembering that politics has to do with power, economics has to do with resources, and that both interact to form the social system, we can look at the chart below and see why Russia has encountered the difficulties it has.

Five characteristics shape the way a nation and government deal with the social issues its people face. The first area is *recognition of the problem*. Are the channels of information to the government open and complete? Can government officials see the broad picture? How quickly does the government learn of a problem? The second area is *responsiveness to need*. To whom are local government officials responsible? Who do they answer to? The third area is the *ability to decide*. Can decisions be made quickly or are there multiple layers of government that must be involved in the process? The fourth area is the *ability to implement*. Does the government have control over individuals and can it move resources as it wishes? The last area is the *ability to assess results*. Is there a mechanism for getting feedback from local officials and those affected to decision-makers at the top?

If you review these five areas and look for patterns in them, you begin to see where totalitarian socialism (a command approach) and democratic capitalism (a freedom approach) have their strengths and weaknesses, and you can see why Russia is in trouble. The freedom approach has its strengths where information and concern are the issue. The command approach has its strengths where action is the issue. Before the recent Russian revolution, people had little impact on the government, and local officials were responsible to party leaders in Moscow, but the government could act when it wanted to. In the new Russia, people have much more input than before and local officials are elected by the people they serve, but the government cannot direct resources with the same force that it could apply just a few years ago. Can you see why there is such despair in Russia? Then people had no voice, but things got done. Now they can speak, but nothing happens. You can begin to understand why many Russian citizens think they would like to return to the "good old days." Going back is not the answer. Going ahead, with all its difficulties, is the only way.

Social Problem Issue	Political/Economic System Type	
	Totalitarian Socialism	Democratic Capitalism
Recognition of the problem	Slow	Fast
Responsiveness to need	Low	Moderate
Ability to decide	Fast	Slow
Ability to implement	Strong	Moderate
Ability to assess results	Fair	Good

things they wouldn't buy otherwise; if that isn't the definition of waste, what is? Rather than waste resources on competition, socialists keep the economy in sharp focus by eliminating competition and having all goods and services produced by state agencies.

The Role of Government. Obviously, we socialists have a very different view of the role of government. We contend that government is not only a force for good but is the means for preventing what would be the negative excesses of capitalism from ruining the economy. Government should own the resources, make the decisions, and provide the goods when and where they are needed. Government not only has the right but the responsibility to do this.

Effects of Socialism

What are the outcomes of socialist economies? As we examine socialism in the areas of productivity and income distribution, let's assume that the last decade during which socialist economies collapsed is an anomaly.[3] In general, how well has socialism done with economic growth? It has not fared as

---
[3] Many economists would disagree and insist that the past decade is the norm for socialism and defines reality.

well as capitalism. The average per capita growth rate for socialist economies has been about 0.5 percent lower than that of capitalist states. Again, one-half percent may not sound like much, but apply the rule of 70s to see what the difference would be over the long run. If capitalist economies grew at the rate of 3 percent per year while socialist economies grew at the rate of 2.5 percent per year, the 0.5 percent difference in growth rate makes a tremendous difference in just a century. Thus, socialist economies tend to be less efficient than capitalist economies.

What is the reason for the difference in efficiency? The key issue seems to be incentive. In a capitalistic economy, individuals have an incentive to attempt to improve themselves. If they try and are successful, they reap the rewards. If they try and fail, they lose, but optimism usually induces them to keep trying. In a capitalistic economy, people can start a new business, develop a new product, try a new process, or anything else they think will produce success.

And what of the issue of justice? A comparison of the distribution of income may be a bit of a surprise. The popular press has often compared capitalism and socialism with statements indicating that the former offers efficiency while the latter offers equity. What is the income distribution in socialism? Again, there are rich and there are poor. This time the richest 20 percent get about 37 percent of the income while the poorest 20 percent receive about 6 percent. However you want to look at it, it is still quite unequal. The richest quintile receives more than six times as much as the poorest quintile. The difference between rich and poor is not quite as great as it is in capitalism, but it is still substantial. When you combine income distribution with the sizes of the two economies, the choice becomes a lot easier. (Quick: Which would you rather have—5 percent of a 20-ounce steak or 6 percent of a 15-ounce steak?)

Thus, the income distributions are quite similar for both capitalism and socialism. Interestingly, these percentages hold for almost all developed economies of whatever type. In the case of underdeveloped economies, however, the dispersion is much greater and the economies tend to be much less equal. Capitalism is the more productive type. Which would you choose? Probably the same one as most of the nations of the world.

Core-Info

Socialism is an economic system in which the government is the central decision maker. Socialism's characteristics are the direct opposite of those of capitalism.

MIXED ECONOMIES

The truth, of course, is that there is no such thing as pure capitalism or pure socialism in the world. The closest we get to the pure varieties are, perhaps, Hong Kong and Albania, respectively. Most of the economies live in a less than pure world, one of **mixed economies.** A mixed economy is one that displays characteristics of both capitalism and socialism. The United States, for instance, is a mixed capitalism. The predominant form of economic organization is capitalism, but there is a significant role for government. In the United States, government provides the schools and roads, regulates business and communications, takes big tax payments, and funds welfare checks. Similarly, the old socialist economies were, in reality, mixed socialisms. Individuals had their own gardens and some small businesses and made some selections of their own goods. In addition, a flourishing black market provided the goods and services that consumers really wanted.

Mixed Economies
Economic systems that contain significant elements of both capitalism and socialism.

Core-Info

All economies of the world are mixed economies with aspects of both capitalism and socialism included.

CONCLUDING THOUGHTS

The past decade has written the conclusion to this chapter. Capitalism rules. As capitalistic economies have become dominant and socialistic economies have receded from the world stage. Mixed capitalistic economies have survived. Two schools of thought explain what is happening here. Some economists say capitalism has survived because governments have been a part of the process to provide the adjustments necessary to prevent the economy from collapsing. Other economists contend that capitalism has survived *in spite of* government involvement, that it would be a great idea if somebody tries pure capitalism someday.

Until someone comes up with a better system, capitalism will likely be the continuing dominant economic force. Socialist economies can be expected to continue their transition toward capitalism, and therein lies the challenge for the next decade. In the old socialist economies, while incentives were low and government decision-makers were not particularly responsive to consumers' wants, governments did have the ability to impose economic order. With control of production, markets, and the currency, governments could react to crises with speed and determination if they desired. There no longer exists a centralized economic engine to provide the drive required for the transition period. Until the capitalist approaches become a part of the people and the institutions of the old socialist economies, problems can be expected to continue. It is essential that capitalistic economies provide more than just the model and encouragement if crises of world proportion are to be avoided.

SUMMARY

- The three characteristics of all modern economies are large amounts of capital, specialization, and the use of advanced technology.
- Economic systems are concerned with how societies utilize their resources. Political systems are concerned with how power is used in societies.
- Capitalism is an economic system in which individuals and businesses own the resources and make the economic decisions. The four characteristics of capitalism are protection of private property, free enterprise, competitive markets, and limited government involvement in the economy.
- Socialism is an economic system in which government owns the productive resources and is the central decision maker. The four characteristics of socialism are the exact opposite of those of capitalism.
- Capitalism has proven to be more effective than socialism because of its understanding of the role of motivation and incentive and its focus on the individual as opposed to the state.

KEY TERMS

Capitalism *Laissez faire* Political systems
Economic systems Mixed economies Socialism

REVIEW QUESTIONS

1. What is the difference between economic systems and political systems?
2. Explain the three characteristics that define a modern, developed economy.

3. What are the four characteristics of a capitalistic economy?
4. What is the major advantage that proponents put forward in favor of a capitalistic economy?
5. What are the four characteristics of a socialistic economy?
6. What is the major advantage that proponents put forward in favor of a socialistic economy?
7. What is the definition of a mixed economy?

PROBLEM-SOLVING PRACTICE

1. Identify the four possible combinations of economic and political systems and write three descriptive sentences about each of the four combinations.
2. How does socialism, either in theory or in practice, differ from capitalism? Compare and contrast how capitalism and socialism deals with each of the following:
    (a) property
    (b) enterprise
    (c) competition
    (d) the role of government
3. The United States has been called a mixed capitalism. Give three examples that show that it is capitalistic in nature and three examples that show that it is a mixed capitalism.
4. Describe how capitalism and socialism differ in terms of output, freedom, and the ability to address problems.

CHAPTER 15

Government and Taxes

CHAPTER OUTLINE

A. Why Government?
B. The Role of Government
   1. Government in Socialism
   2. Government in Capitalism
C. Market Failure
D. Causes for Government Intervention in Capitalism
   1. Antitrust and Monopoly Regulation
   2. Externalities
      a. Definition
      b. Negative Externalities
      c. Positive Externalities
      d. Possible Governmental Responses
   3. Public Goods
      a. Definition
      b. Applicability
   4. Common Ownership
      a. Definition
      b. Solutions
   5. Income Redistribution
      a. The Concern
      b. Redistribution Approaches
      c. Issues in Income Redistribution
   6. Economic Stabilization
E. A Final Look at Government
F. Paying for Government: Taxes
   1. Defining Taxes
   2. Issues about Taxes: Efficiency and Equity
      a. Efficiency
      b. Equity
   3. Types of Taxes
      a. Income Taxes
      b. Sales Taxes
      c. Excise Taxes
      d. Customs Duties
      e. Property Taxes
      f. Estate and Gift Taxes
      g. Capital Gains Taxes
   4. The Effect of Taxes
   5. Tax Shifting and Tax Incidence
   6. Tax Progressivity
      a. Proportional Taxes
      b. Progressive Taxes
      c. Regressive Taxes
   7. A Final Look at Taxes
G. Budget Deficits and Debt
   1. Budget Deficits
      a. Defining Budget Deficits
      b. The Size of the Budget Deficits
   2. Budget Philosophies
      a. Annually Balanced Budget
      b. Cyclically Balanced Budget
      c. Functional Finance
   3. Causes of Debt
   4. The Size of the Debt
   5. Effects of Budget Deficits and Debt
      a. Erroneous Concerns
      b. Legitimate Concerns
H. Now What?

The purpose of this chapter is to expand your knowledge of the role of government in a capitalistic economy and to introduce the economics of taxation and government deficits.

AFTER COMPLETING THIS CHAPTER, YOU WILL BE ABLE TO:

1. Explain the concept of market failure as a rationale for government involvement in the marketplace.

2. Describe the five roles for government in capitalism.

3. Differentiate between taxes and fees and describe how tax shifting affects tax incidence.
4. Apply the concept of tax progressivity to government taxation programs.
5. Describe the three ways in which societies address the concern for a balanced budget.
6. Explain the impact of government budget deficits on individuals, business, and the economy.

Why Government?

That is a good question. Why government, indeed? Until the previous chapter, we had been talking about consumers, workers, firms, and investors as if they existed all by themselves. Chapter 14 finally introduced economic systems and the issue of government involvement.

The next step is to look at government and its role in economic systems. The role of government differs significantly, depending on whether the economic system is capitalistic or socialistic. This chapter will define that role more fully and explore how citizens pay for whatever amount of government they decide to have.

THE ROLE OF GOVERNMENT

The role of government is highly varied in economic systems. In some, it is all pervasive. In others, it is all but absent. This discussion of government's role emphasizes capitalism for two reasons. First, that is where we live. Not only is the U.S. economy predominantly capitalistic, but most of the rest of the world is joining in. The second reason is that the role of government in capitalism is most interesting. Capitalism posits a *laissez faire* government, but everyone is quite aware of the magnitude of government, at least every April 15 when taxes are due. The whys and wherefores of government in capitalism provide an interesting study.

Government in Socialism

The role of government is socialism? This one is easy: government is pervasive. In socialism, government is at the center of the economy. Government owns the economic resources, government makes the production decisions, government controls markets, and government decides who will benefit. In socialism, the role of government need not be discussed because government is involved in everything. There has been much discussion about how government should carry out its duties in a socialist state, but whether it should be involved is not an issue.

Government in Capitalism

The role of government in a capitalistic economy, as compared with socialism, is open to much debate. In a purely capitalistic economy, the role of government is extremely limited. Government is to protect private property, make certain that enterprise remains truly free, and help markets to remain competitive. Beyond that, capitalism says government should stay out.

And yet, there are many calls for government involvement in capitalistic economy. "We need a new road." "America needs health care for all." "We need better schools." "Food stamps are a necessity today." Every place you turn, someone is claiming that government should become involved in one aspect or another of economic life.

Rather than analyzing each of the individual calls for government involvement, the strategy here is to step back from these individual demands to the general types of demands that are made. The call for food stamps, for example, is a call for a transfer of income from the more wealthy to those with lower incomes. In this chapter you will examine the latter issue, income redistribution, rather than the individual program. You can easily insert the program or the issue at the end of the discussion.

FIGURE 15.1
Federal government spending touches all areas of life. Today a decreasing portion of the federal budget is being spent on defense and an increasing portion on other areas such as education, health, welfare, and interest on the debt. *Source:* Budget of the United States Government

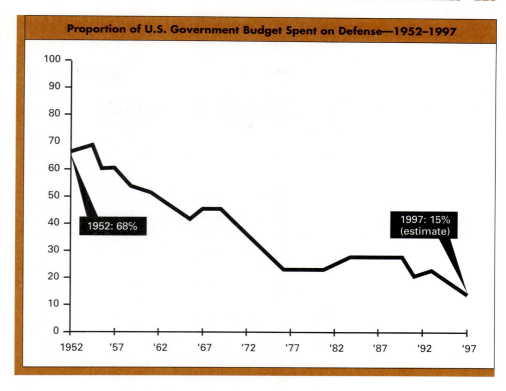

Core-Info

The role of government is very limited in capitalism; it is all pervasive in socialism.

MARKET FAILURE

If markets are working properly, the greatest amount of goods will be produced at the lowest possible cost. Employment and incomes will be high and cost and waste will be low. Of course, the "if" in "if markets are working properly" is a big "IF." Sometimes they don't.

What does that mean, markets aren't working properly? The answer is both simple and hard to measure in reality. The answer to what constitutes **market failure** is twofold:

Market Failure
A situation in which the socially optimal amount of a good or service is not produced by the private sector.

1. When the optimal amount of a good or service is not fully produced by the private market; and
2. When the costs of production or consumption are not fully (properly) accounted for.

It is one thing to define the problem but quite another to measure it. What does the term *optimal* mean? Who defines it? Is optimal the absolute maximum that could be produced, or should some constraints be permitted? What do you mean that costs are not "properly" accounted for? Who does the accounting? Does this accounting cover explicit costs or implicit costs or both?

The other issue regarding market failure is whether the prescribed correction entails direct control of the market or a lesser degree of help to keep it on track. In nautical terms, should the government trim the sails of a ship that is underway or should it set the course and steer the ship? There is a big difference, and the calls for both approaches have been strident of late.

There are six reasons why people might want government involvement in the market. Remember in your classroom discussion that there will likely be a great deal of difference among fellow students about the proper role for government. It does tend to become an emotional issue. Try to place the discussion on a positive basis (as in "factual," not "optimistic") to start so you can determine how and whether you think government should be involved from an economic standpoint. Look at the probable benefits. Examine the probable costs. Then decide. (Those steps would also be a good guide to follow after the course is over.)

Core-Info

> Market failure is said to exist when the optimal amount of a good or service is not produced by the market or when all costs of production are not accounted for.

CAUSES FOR GOVERNMENT INTERVENTION IN CAPITALISM

That there should be some government involvement in capitalism is fairly well accepted. Deciding how much and in what areas is when debates arise. This section will explore the six areas in which there have commonly been calls for government intervention:

- Antitrust and monopoly regulation
- Externalities
- Public goods
- Common ownership
- Income redistribution
- Economic stabilization

We shall examine these six issues in this order because it takes us from the areas with the greatest amount of agreement to the areas of least agreement. Remember as this discussion progresses to try to keep thinking positively.

Antitrust and Monopoly Regulation

Everybody but the monopolist agrees that monopolies should be limited. Monopolies *always* do two things: they always raise prices and they always reduce output. They always do this because it is in their self-interest. This is not a moral issue; you would do the same thing in the same situation. However, it is a problem for the economy. To the extent that monopolies exist, the output is lower than would be the case in perfect competition, prices are higher, and there is a difference between the cost of the product and the price paid by consumers. That difference becomes the monopolist's profit.

The role of government, therefore, is to regulate monopolies. Two strategies can be used: prevent monopolies from forming or regulate those that are permitted to exist. The first option is pretty straightforward. If the government can prevent monopolies from getting started, it can keep the benefits of competition and capitalism flowing. This is a legitimate role for government. The second option is less obvious. There may be instances where a monopoly is preferable to the alternative. Does a big city need 13 water companies all running their pipes under the streets, all competing for big businesses, and none overly interested in supplying less developed areas? The efficient solution is a single water company supplying an entire region, but this means that a monopoly would be formed. If a water monopoly starts, people would expect higher prices and less service. To prevent this, the government may allow the monopoly to exist but regulate it to reduce the tendency for monopolistic behavior. Only government with its coercive power can do this. That is why most people see monopoly regulation as a legitimate function for government in a capitalistic economy.

Externalities

The second area of possible government intervention is known as externalities. Again, there is general agreement that government involvement is appropriate where externalities exist.

CHAPTER 15 • GOVERNMENT AND TAXES

Externalities
The benefits or costs of an individual's or business' actions that the person or firm does not receive or pay for.

Definition. The term **externalities** means *unintended outcomes.* When an individual does something, sometimes others are affected. Something external to the original intent results. This is an externality. Externalities are the benefits or costs of an action that are borne by someone else. You do something; someone else is affected. This concept does not apply to the interaction of suppliers and consumers: one side sells, the other buys. Those are voluntary actions. The buyer could choose not to be part of the effect. An externality is the involuntary involvement on one person's part in another's actions. Perhaps some examples can help clarify this concept.

Negative Externality
The cost that one individual bears as a result of the actions of another.

Negative Externalities. The first kind of externality is known as a **negative externality.** With negative externalities, one person acts and another pays. One person's actions exact a cost from someone else. Pollution is a prime example of a negative externality. A car company is in business to make cars and to make a profit. As a part of making cars, it produces some pollution. Some waste water is dumped into the streams and some sulfur dioxide is vented into the air. That is not an intended outcome: the firm is not in business to produce pollution. The result of its pollution, however, is that people must purify the water before they can use it and the air they breathe is contaminated. People bear the costs of the car maker's pollution.

Most economists agree that government has a legitimate role in stopping pollution. Why? In this discussion, the ethical, moral, and environmental problems of pollution are not the central issue. Why from an economic standpoint in a capitalistic economy should the government act to stop producers from polluting the environment? The key is that when someone pollutes, others must pay a price. The polluter is taking their money against their will. That violates the first and most basic rule of capitalism: private property is protected. By preventing pollution or by forcing the polluter to pay for cleanup, the government keeps polluters from stealing from others. Government action in this situation helps to support the capitalistic system, not to override it.[1]

Positive Externalities
The benefit that one person receives as a result of the actions of another.

Positive Externalities. Positive externalities are actions by one individual that benefit others. This concept does not apply to benefits that people pay for. If you purchase a wonderful car from a manufacturer, that is not a positive externality. A positive externality is a benefit that people receive without having to do anything and for which the person who provides the benefit receives no gain. These are also known as "spill-over" benefits.

Some examples of positive externalities can be supplied by the auto manufacturer. Assume that the manufacturer is considering building a new assembly plant in your state. What would be the positive impacts if this were to happen? First, construction would occur. Then, jobs would be created at the factory. More jobs would be created because the plant is there. The factory workers would earn an income and then be taxed and spend money in the community. The taxes would help pay for schools, roads, and welfare costs. The private spending would go to grocery stores, clothing shops, home builders, appliance dealers, and many others. The earnings received by the factory workers would be multiplied as they spend their money, for there would be new jobs at the grocery stores, these people would earn money to spend, and so on. This is known as the **multiplier effect.** One extra dollar of earnings is multiplied as it is passed on through the community through repeated spending.

Multiplier Effect
The overall outcome of a change in one variable that includes the cumulative effects of additional increases or decreases caused by that change.

Possible Governmental Responses. What should government do about these externalities? In the case of negative externalities, government actions should probably

---

[1] An interesting question has been posed by economist Ronald Coase: "Why is it that you have a right to clean air and I don't have a right to pollute?" Consider this issue purely on the basis of civil rights. Laws against pollution limit the rights of one person in order to give rights to another. Why does the one have priority over the other? (Before you question Coase's sanity, consider that he is a Nobel Prize winner in economics.)

be to "internalize the externalities." The goal of government involvement is to ensure that those who cause costs pay for them. The government can employ four techniques:

- Elimination
- Regulation
- Negotiation
- Adjudication

Elimination means that no negative externalities are permitted. The government would prohibit firms from creating pollution in the first place. This is a simple solution on the surface, but the cost may be much higher than the benefit. Could your house operate on a no pollution basis? No carbon dioxide could be emitted, no garbage could be taken to the curb, no toilet waste down the sewer. All polluting materials would have to be recycled internally. The cost of this approach would be astronomical. The same reality holds true for outlawing all industrial waste and pollutants, although elimination may be necessary for highly toxic chemical or biological agents.

Regulation means to put controls on negative externalities. Rather than eliminate them entirely, regulation would limit the amount of effluents that could be released. Laws could specify so many parts per million in the water or air, for example. Scientific studies could determine the level of danger of the proposed pollutant, and the amount that could be released into the air or water could be set. Any pollution above the set level would be prohibited.

Negotiation means that the individual responsible for the externality and those affected get together and work it out among themselves. If a business wants to dump effluent in a river, it could work out an arrangement with representatives in that jurisdiction that satisfies both sides. The business might be permitted to dump a certain amount of effluent and then agree to pay for cleanup if it exceeds the agreement. Under this arrangement, either the business will clean up the pollution or those affected will have the resources to do it.

Adjudication is the last of the options for dealing with negative externalities. Adjudication means that any dispute goes to court. If the polluter and its neighbors can't work something out, they appear before the judge and plead their case. What this option boils down to is an attempt to establish property rights: who has the right to do what with regard to this pollution? This may be the ultimate question in capitalism, for it goes straight to the first and major criterion of that economic system.

But what of positive externalities? Is there a role for government here? The role is less obvious and direct in this area. In the case of negative externalities, somebody is injured and his or her property is being taken away. Government should act to prevent this. With positive externalities, somebody benefits. Its citizens may want their government to encourage the creation of positive externalities. Government can offer tax breaks to big corporations if they locate their plants in the community, for example. After all, landing a new corporate facility translates into additional jobs and more tax revenue for the community. This approach may also be used to encourage redevelopment of blighted urban areas. Tax incentives are often used by big cities to lure businesses into declining neighborhoods to spark a renaissance and create both jobs and hope in the community.

Thus, government does have a role in dealing with externalities. If it acts appropriately, government can help to make those who would create negative externalities bear their own costs and can help to create incentives to those who can create positive externalities and benefit the community as a whole.

Public Goods

Thus far we have focused mainly on private goods. Private goods are those which provide benefits only to those who pay for them. Your car gets you to and from school and work. Your backpack provides the benefit of keeping textbooks and notepads in some semblance of order. No one else benefits from your car or backpack. You are willing to pay for your car and backpack because you are the one who benefits. Other people do not benefit, so they don't have to pay. Public goods are quite different from private goods, and this is why we need to consider them as a special case.

Public Good
A good which, when made available to one consumer, is available to all consumers; a good which is not exclusive in use.

Definition. Whereas private goods exclusively benefit the person purchasing and consuming them, the benefits from **public goods** are not exclusive. Once public goods are made available to one person, they are available to all. No one can be denied access to or benefits from a public good. One person's consumption of a public good does not diminish another's ability to consume the same good.

Applicability. The definition of public goods may sound strange, but they are quite common. The street light in front of your house is a public good as is the B-2 bomber overhead. Once the street light goes in, it benefits you, your neighbors, and everyone who uses the street at night. Even those who pay no local taxes benefit from that street light through reduced crime in the neighborhood and easier walking at night. The same is true for the bomber. Your house is protected from potential enemies even if you paid none of the taxes that built the bomber. Therein lies the problem. There is very little incentive to pay for public goods. Whether people pay or not, they benefit. The result is what is known as "free riders," those who would attempt to get the benefit of a public good without paying for it. No rational person would voluntarily pay for a public good. Everyone may want those goods and services, but paying for them is a very different matter. Everyone wants someone else to pay for them. If people are to have public goods where the benefits are not exclusive to those who pay, government must be involved.

It is important to differentiate between public goods and goods that are publicly provided. *Public goods* are those that are not exclusive in use. *Publicly provided goods* are those provided by the government. Not all goods provided by the government are public goods; many are private goods. Ever play golf on the city links? Private good. Tie your boat up at the city marina? Private good. Attend a public college? Private good. In each case, the benefits of the good are exclusive to the person using it. No one else benefits from your golf game, your boat, or your college education. These goods are provided by the government but benefit individuals. They are private goods.[2]

Remember that public goods can be produced by private firms (but generally are not) and private goods can be produced by the government (and frequently are). The question is not who produces them but how are they consumed. Because the benefits of public goods are received by all, mostly government is involved in their provision.

Common Ownership

In capitalism, private property is central. Where property rights have been established, everyone is pretty clear about what should be done. The owners are responsible for their property and no one else can interfere with it. When property is not private, those issues are not so clear, and that is what common ownership solutions seek to remedy.

Definition. Common ownership is the situation where property rights have not been assigned. Anyone can use—and abuse—the property. When everybody owns a resource, nobody owns it or has any incentive to take care of it. This concept applies to the whales in the ocean, the alleys of the cities, and large underground oil reserves. Let's take the whales as an example. Nobody owns them. Whales are available for anybody to catch if they want. All that is required is to have the right equipment and go out and harvest all you can. Everybody has that opportunity. The tendency, therefore, is to try to get as many whales as you can as fast as you can before everybody

---

[2] You may want to note just who is likely to use these publicly provided goods. Do many poor people play golf, own boats, or go to college? Not many. Many publicly provided goods are in reality transfers of income from average citizens to the more wealthy.

else does. There is no incentive to conserve. On the contrary, there is every incentive to overfish the waters, and overfish is what everybody will do. At the same time, there is no incentive to replace the whales that have been harvested. If the ocean belonged to a business, it might replace the whales it killed so it would have some to take tomorrow. Since it is everyone's ocean, any whales one fisherman helps to grow might be harvested by someone else, so all fishermen are loathe to spend their resources on replacing them. And so it goes with all resources that are owned in common.

Solutions. The solutions to the common ownership problem are relatively simple. There are three that come to mind:
- Agree to cooperate
- Designate a single owner
- Impose government regulation

Obviously, if people can all agree that it is in their long-term interest to cooperate and rationally use the commonly owned resource, everyone is better off. The simplest and often most effective solutions come when people resolve the problem themselves. In concert, they can deal with the ways in which the resource is to be used and how it will be maintained and replenished.

If people can't or won't cooperate, they can designate a single owner for the resource. The United Nations could be assigned the responsibility for caring for the whales. With a single owner identified, there is an incentive for that owner to try to maintain the resource appropriately.

Finally, management of the resource can be accomplished by government regulation. In the whaling example, each government could agree to limit the harvest of whales by its nation's fleet. If fishing rights can be allocated or if technology can be controlled (no dynamite fishing, for example), the resource can be maintained. The same governmental regulation approach can be applied to all resources that are owned in common.

Income Redistribution

Income Redistribution
Taking resources from one individual and giving them to another.

The Concern. Income redistribution? Does that mean someone would take your money and give it to someone else? We are now moving into the much more controversial areas for government involvement in capitalism. From here on out, the arguments become more intense and really separate the liberals from the conservatives.

Taking money or resources from one person and giving it to another is precisely what income redistribution involves. This is not something that is done voluntarily. Of course some Americans are exceedingly generous in their giving. In fact millions of dollars are given each year to churches and temples, to the United Way and the Combined Federal Campaign, to the Boy Scouts and animal protection groups. Some give and some do not. If everybody is to participate in transferring the billions that the government transfers ($23 billion for Food Stamps, $322 billion for Social Security, for example), coercion will likely be necessary.

Redistribution Approaches. There are two basic tools used to redistribute income: taxes and transfers. Taxes are money subtracted from your income. Once taxes are applied, your income is lower than it would be otherwise, so taxes can be considered negative income. By adjusting tax rates or taxing different things, the government can effectively transfer income from one person or group to another. If airline tickets or luxury dinners are taxed, the cost is borne mainly by wealthy people. If city bus travel or grocery store food is taxed, poor people will bear the burden. Varying tax rates to tax high incomes at a higher rate than low incomes again effectively redistributes income. However, as you will find shortly, the tax burden often falls on people other than those who are supposed to pay the bill.

Transfers
Money or goods received by an individual from the government for which the individual did not pay.

The second means for redistributing income is through transfers. **Transfers** are resources that are provided to an individual (generally by the government) for which no payment is made. These transfers can be made in cash; unemployment assistance, welfare payments, and college tuition grants are examples. Transfers may also be made in kind, such as food stamps, subsidized housing, and free medical care at the college clinic. As a result of these transfers, recipients have more resources available than they did before. The wealth of the recipient has been increased as a result of the transfer.

Issues in Income Redistribution. The previous paragraphs focused on one of the major problems with income redistribution: the unwillingness of most people to do it. Another earlier example cited public golf courses, marinas, and colleges in which resources go from poor to rich when the government redistributes income. Many government programs unwittingly have resulted in the transfer of resources from the general taxpayer to the wealthy. Subsidized art museums, subsidized college loans, and city-funded sports arenas with luxury boxes all result in higher real incomes for upper income citizens. If this is something people want to do, if they think, for example, that it is good for all citizens to have access to art museums (even if the poor do not use them) or if they think that the luxury boxes will attract businesses to locate branches in town, these transfers may be the answer. However, people who support these amenities should be aware that they require the transfer of money from the poor to the rich.

All government programs have a redistributive impact. All programs result in resources moving from one person—the taxpayer—to another person—the program participant. As a result, it is absolutely essential to very carefully examine the probable impact of any tax or spending proposal before it is implemented. Once programs are implemented, it is very difficult to eliminate them or even to change their direction.[3] Both the benefit recipients and the people in charge of the program (whose income would be eliminated if the program were stopped) have a vested interest in continuing a government program.

Economic Stabilization

The last area of possible government involvement in capitalism is that of **economic stabilization.** An unstable economy makes everybody nervous, and nervous people don't spend on consumer goods or invest in new plant and equipment. If the economy is relatively stable and predictable, then consumers and business people alike can go about their economic lives in the ways that they feel will best add to their welfare. The result will likely be active participation in the economy. When the economy is unstable, when interest rates are widely variable, when unemployment and incomes are going up and down, when foreign exchange rates are fluctuating, people must spend time and resources trying to determine what future course to set rather than focusing on making decisions about production and consumption.

The issue of stability in the economy is not a simple one. Some economists firmly believe that the government should not attempt to adjust interest rates, unemployment rates, or prices. In fact, these economists insist that it is precisely these so-called stabilization attempts that upset the economy. Economists who believe this point out, with some justification, that prices, interest rates, and employment levels serve to send signals to businesses and consumers to adjust their behavior and that in the absence of these signals, the economy becomes even more destabilized. Government involvement is seen as interference in the natural workings of the market and, as such, a move away from the capitalist system that promises the greatest amount of goods at the lowest possible prices.

Economic Stabilization
The attempt by government to keep the economy from growing or contracting too rapidly.

Core-Info

There is a legitimate role for government in capitalism in making certain that private property is protected, that markets are not monopolized by force, and that freedom exists for all. Beyond these three tasks, how involved government should be is a highly normative question.

[3.] Witness the recent debates about reducing the rate of increase of Social Security payments to recipients.

A FINAL LOOK AT GOVERNMENT

There is a role for government in capitalism. The proper interaction of government with a capitalistic economy can help to keep that economy on the most productive path. This is obviously a good result. If the economy can be encouraged along its capitalistic path, output can continue to grow at its maximum, and the benefits of this growth can be passed on to all members of society.

The picture for government is not perfectly clear, however. Some problems with government are inherent in its makeup. In fact, three problems bedevil government's involvement in the economy:

1. The government may not learn about problems promptly, and that lag time is compounded the larger the economy is and the more governmental layers there are.
2. Government often has difficulties in acting or responding once problems are discovered. Bills must be drafted and voted upon, money must be found and allocated, administrations must be directed to act, plans must be implemented, and programs must become functional.
3. Government decision makers do not bear the costs of their decisions (taxes are paid by the citizens) but do reap some benefits from their decisions. Politicians gain re-election, and bureaucrats can count on job security. When people benefit from something but do not bear the costs, they are likely to do a lot of it whether or not it needs to be done.

These three factors make it very difficult for government to be effective in addressing real problems in the economy, a problem that is compounded if government operates in a reactive mode (responding to problems once they have been presented). Even if government is proactive and anticipates problems, the cost-benefit issue still makes it very problematic for government to function in a capitalistic economy without becoming intrusive. We shall examine this issue further when we look at macroeconomics in depth in the next few chapters.

Core-Info

Even when government involvement in the market may be appropriate, problems arise with timing and the fact that the bureaucrats who write and enforce the laws do not bear the costs of the laws but receive benefits from their existence.

PAYING FOR GOVERNMENT: TAXES

All this government has to be paid for somehow. If there is to be government at all (and all but the most absolute libertarians agree that there should be at least some), then we must acquire the resources to pay for it. That is how taxes enter the picture. The only source of money to pay for government is the individual. *YOU* pay taxes. Not businesses, not landlords, not any organization but the individual. As you examine how taxes are raised to pay for all the government services people seem to want today, it is essential to keep this simple truth in mind. Many politicians and people in the popular press would have you think otherwise.

Defining Taxes

What is a tax? This is not as simple a question as you might think. Taxes are not necessarily all payments to the government. Many payments to government are not taxes but payments for goods or services or fines imposed by courts. The sewer and water bill paid to the city or county is not a tax. A park entrance fee is not a tax. Parking meter charges are not taxes. The fine you paid for driving 68 mph in a 55 mph zone is not a tax. These are all fees or fines and do not qualify as a tax.

A tax has special characteristics. A **tax** is a nonvoluntary payment made by a firm or household to a government agency for which no good or service is directly received. If there is a direct *quid pro quo,* the payment is not a tax even if it is re-

Tax
A compulsory payment by an individual or business to a government for which no direct benefit is received.

quired. If payment is voluntary, it is not a tax even if the money goes to serve the public. Both conditions must be met if a payment is to be considered a tax.

Issues about Taxes: Efficiency and Equity

Many of our discussions have focused on efficiency and equity as key issues. This is especially a concern in the case of taxes because money is taken from people by force for programs and services they may or may not support. Taxes must be considered to be both efficient and equitable by the majority of taxpayers.

Efficiency. Efficiency in taxation has to do with how expensive it is to collect the tax. When taxpayer compliance is high and collection is easy, taxes are considered to be efficient. On the other hand, if a high degree of taxpayer evasion makes collection difficult or expensive, the tax is considered to be inefficient. An efficient tax is certainly a key goal of tax policy.

Equity. Equity has to do with fairness. Where taxes are considered to be fair, people are more likely to voluntarily comply and the level of satisfaction is greater. The two types of equity are called horizontal equity and vertical equity, and the ideal is taxes that are both horizontally and vertically equitable.

Horizontal equity means the equal treatment of equals. People in identical situations should pay the same tax. If people's incomes are the same, their taxes should be the same, for example.

Vertical equity has to do with the *unequal* treatment of *unequals*. People who are in different circumstances should be treated differently, according to this principle. If your income is higher than another person's, your tax should be higher.

Types of Taxes

A variety of taxes may be used to separate people from their money. The tax chosen is determined by assumed effect and degree of fairness it has on people. None of the taxes described in the following paragraphs is strictly applied. Each tax has some exemptions and qualifications that keep it from fully applying to the item in question.

Income Taxes. Income taxes are based on income that is earned. They may be taxes on the earnings of individuals or taxes on corporate profits. If they are taxes on individuals, they can be either income taxes such as those due on April 15 each year, or they may be Social Security taxes that are collected from the individual and the employer. The net effect of individual income taxes is to reduce the income available to the earner. Federal income tax rates vary from zero to 39.6 percent depending on income. State income tax rates vary from no taxes in some states to 11 percent in California.

Corporate income taxes are quite different from individual income taxes. While corporate income taxes are deductions from the profits of firms, the net effect is increased prices as the taxes are passed on to consumers. Thus, corporate income taxes are really a form of sales tax. Federal corporate income tax rates reach 35 percent for large, successful firms.

Sales Taxes. Sales taxes are based on expenditures for a given item. These taxes are typically a fixed percentage of the selling price of the good in question. The effect of sales taxes is to raise the price of the item to the consumer. State sales taxes vary from zero in a number of states to 7 percent in Mississippi and Rhode Island.

Excise Taxes. An excise tax is based on the quantity, not the value, of a good sold. The gasoline tax is an excise tax. A fixed amount is added to the price of each gallon sold. These taxes vary from 7.5 cents per gallon in Georgia to 26 cents per gallon in Connecticut and Rhode Island. The federal tax is in addition to this. As seen in Fig. 15.2, the impact of the gasoline tax is much greater on low-income families than high-income families.

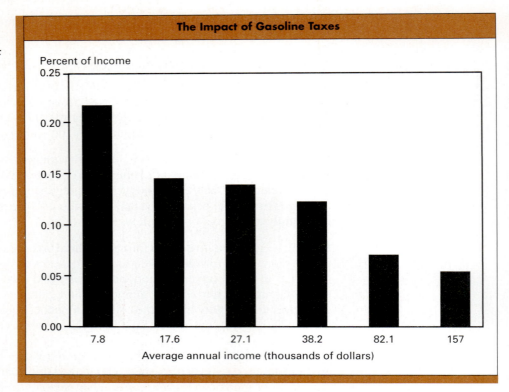

FIGURE 15.2
Percent of Income Paid in Gasoline Taxes. *Source: Economic Trends,* Federal Reserve Bank of Cleveland, June 1996, p. 7.

Customs Duties. The United States collected nearly $18 billion in customs duties last year. Customs duties are taxes that must be paid when a foreign-made good is brought into the country either by an importer or by a traveler. These duties effectively raise the price of the good to the purchaser. The tariff rates vary by type of good imported.

Property Taxes. Property taxes are taxes that are based on the assessed value of property owned by an individual or firm. These taxes are the largest single source of revenue for state and local governments. Per capita property tax collections vary from $171 in Alabama to $1,475 in Washington, D.C. Property taxes on individuals are really wealth taxes and then only on a portion of the wealth held. Property taxes on firms are passed on to consumers in the form of higher prices, so they are effectively sales taxes.

Estate and Gift Taxes. Estate and gift taxes are levies on funds that are given by one person to another. These taxes affect both gifts given during the lifetime of an individual and bequests at death. Significant exemptions are available to allow funds to be given to children, passed on to surviving spouses, or given to charities. However, if the net amount to be passed on exceeds $3 million, the marginal tax rate reaches 55 percent. Approximately $11 billion was collected through federal estate and gift taxes last year.

Capital Gains Taxes. Capital gains taxes are levies placed on the increase in the value of an asset such as a home, stocks, or artwork. When a property or an asset is sold for more than the purchase price, a tax is applied. The tax rate has been reduced in recent years from a high of 49.1 percent in 1976 to the current 28.0 percent in an effort to encourage investors.

The Effect of Taxes

The goal of taxes is to collect money from people. The effect of taxes is to influence people's decision making at the margin which is where it counts. Taxes are monies that people pay if they engage in certain behaviors (such as earn income, spend money, or hold an asset). Thus, people can be expected to change their behaviors as

Tax-Free Property Available

Here's got a poser for you (that's what the British call a good question; it is pronounced with a long "o"). Should the property owners in Sun City and Sun City West, Arizona, pay taxes to support the local public schools?

About 50 percent of all public elementary and secondary school funds are derived from local property taxes. Property taxes are levied on the value of the homes and businesses in the school district. These taxes apply whether or not you use the parks, own a car, or have children in the schools on the idea that all citizens benefit from the expenditures that result (parks, roads, and education). In Sun City, however, residents pay no taxes to support public schools.

The Sun City areas of Arizona have two special characteristics: one or more adults in the home must be at least 50 years of age, and no children under the age of 18 may be a part of the family. Thus, Sun City residents do not, cannot, and will not ever have children to send to the public schools and thus do not (directly) use them. Would it be fair, then, for them to pay school taxes?

Before you answer, consider two families who do not live in Sun City. First, mine. I am over 50, have no children under 18, and live in another state. Should I pay school taxes? What of a second family that has the same characteristics (50-plus, no kids) but lives in Glendale in the same school district as the Sun City senior? Should that family pay school taxes?

Chew on it for a while. Tax equity is rarely an easy issue.

---

a result of all taxes. While very few people will radically alter their behavior because of taxes, people will make marginal changes: they will work fewer hours, buy fewer goods, travel a little less, or do a little less of whatever is being taxed. The cumulative effect of these changes can be great, and the fact that the individual changes may be small does not mean that the effect should be dismissed.[4]

Basically, taxes have two major overall effects:

- Taxes shift money from the private sector to the public sector (the programs supported by these taxes may shift money back to the private sector, but that is a separate issue).
- Taxes drive a wedge between the price paid for something and the cost of producing it.

In the first case, taxes take money from people and firms in the private sector, the central place that earnings are generated in a capitalistic economy. These monies have been earned in the private sector and would have been spent in the private sector where market signals of price and profit, supply and demand would direct them toward their optimal uses. Once these resources have been taken outside the private sector, the freedom of individuals to choose how they will be spent is curtailed. This may be a goal of the tax: cigarette and alcohol taxes are designed to reduce consumption—or at least punish those who choose to consume. However, this effect also occurs when reduced consumption is not a goal.

In the second case, the impact of a tax is to add to the cost of the item taxed. Employment is taxed by income taxes. Books are taxed by sales taxes. Bequests are taxed through estate taxes. Taxpayer behavior is modified as a result. Depending on the relevant price elasticities (how much people decrease their activities as prices are increased), you can expect shifts in behavior and an attempt to avoid the tax through means that are legal or illegal. The higher the tax rate, the more effort you can expect will be put into tax avoidance.

Tax Shifting and Tax Incidence

Tax Shifting
Passing on the burden of a tax from the person on which it was imposed to another person.

Because taxes are a cost, people try to avoid them. One of the result of these efforts is known as **tax shifting.** In tax shifting, the burden of the tax is moved from one person to another. Let's say the city decides to tax landlords who are charging college students high rents. When the property tax bill on your apartment building increases, what do you think would happen? Your rent would increase as well. Landlords would

---

[4.] A tax that has no impact on the production or consumption decisions of people is called a neutral tax. Economists are hard pressed to find one.

Let's Raise Gasoline Taxes

People often get fired up about the tax on gasoline. Most who complain about it claim that it is too low. These critics point to gasoline prices in Europe or Asia that are double and triple those in the United States as a rationale for increasing taxes and prices here. Since an increase of gasoline taxes is likely in the near future, let's look at the tax to see what effect it has.

There are two particular roles for taxes. By raising prices, taxes serve as an incentive (a disincentive, really) to consumption. Taxes also are used to redistribute income. How are these two roles applied in the case of the gasoline tax?

As to the incentive aspect, the gasoline tax is an excise tax and is added to the dealer cost to yield the price to the consumer. The final price of gasoline is therefore higher as a result of the tax, and consumption of gasoline is discouraged. How much it is discouraged or decreased is determined by the price elasticity of demand for gasoline. Studies have shown that gasoline is relatively inelastic; the consumption of gasoline decreases less than the increase in price (on a percentage basis). Thus, an increase in the gasoline tax is not a particularly effective way to decrease consumption, encourage conservation, and improve the environment.

What of the distributional effect of the gasoline tax? This effect presents another problem. As Figure 15.2 shows, the gasoline tax is a highly regressive tax. Poor people pay a higher percentage of their incomes than rich people do. Thus, the poor and middle class bear a much greater burden from the gasoline tax than do the wealthy.

This is not to say that the government should never raise the gasoline tax. It may want to discourage consumption even if the impact is not great. In addition, the ability to pay principle is not the only way to judge a tax. It may be just as fair to judge the gasoline tax on the benefits principle, and then a per gallon tax that effectively approximates the number of miles driven (hence, the use of the highways) may be the appropriate tax. Finally, the government may just want to raise some revenue, and the gasoline tax is a relatively easy way to do that.

Whatever people finally decide about the gasoline—or any other—tax, they need to be certain that they have examined its true impact on the product, the behaviors of consumers, and the distribution of income. Of course, the government can raise the tax, but its proponents should understand who will be affected.

Tax Incidence
The final resting place of a tax; the person who actually pays the tax as opposed to the person on which the tax was levied.

shift the burden of the tax from themselves to their tenants. Even though the landlords write the checks to city hall, their tenants actually pay the tax. The **tax incidence,** or final resting place of the tax, is on the tenants. The burden of many taxes is shifted just like this in fairly obvious ways.

In some cases, tax shifting is not so obvious. In the tax reform program of 1990, the federal government decided that the rich weren't paying their fair share and had to be taxed. The bureaucrats and politicians wanted a method that would affect only the rich, and they settled on an additional tax on luxury items. After all, only the rich purchase Chris Crafts and private airplanes; only the rich purchase expensive Winnebagos and jewelry. If they were to tax these items, the government officials reasoned, surely they would sock it to the wealthy without affecting people in the lower and middle incomes. They taxed expensive cars, boats, RVs, aircraft, and jewelry. Now it is question and answer time.

QUESTION: What did the imposition of the new tax do?
ANSWER: It raised the price of the goods to any would-be purchaser.

QUESTION: And what do people do when they are faced with higher prices?
ANSWER: Reduce their purchases, of course, and that is precisely what the rich did. The rich decided that they could survive for another year or two with the old cabin cruiser and that the RV had at least another long trip in it.

QUESTION: What happens to the production of boats, RVs, and aircraft when sales fall?
ANSWER: Manufacturers stop producing the items.

QUESTION: What happens to those who assemble the items when production falls?
ANSWER: They are laid off.

QUESTION: Who really paid the tax?
ANSWER: The middle and lower middle class workers paid this tax through their lost jobs. The rich, who cut their purchases of these big-ticket items by more than 50 percent, shifted the tax to those less well off.

FIGURE 15.3

Tax Rate Progressivity						
Income	Proportional Tax		Progressive Tax		Regressive Tax	
	Rate	Amount	Rate	Amount	Rate	Amount
(1)	(2)	(3)	(4)	(5)	(6)	(7)
$ 10,000	20%	$ 2,000	15%	$ 1,500	25%	$ 2,500
$ 50,000	20%	$10,000	20%	$10,000	20%	$10,000
$100,000	20%	$20,000	25%	$25,000	15%	$15,000

Tax shifting is a complicated process, and it is absolutely critical that every new tax be examined for its total impact before it is implemented. If it is not, the result may be a tax as ill-directed in its final impact as the luxury tax of 1990.[5]

Tax Progressivity

Who pays, how much, and how it is determined are key issues in taxation. Most people think that current income is the best measure of the ability of an individual to pay taxes. The impact of taxes is generally measured against the income of the individual. This leads to the whole issue of progressivity. This discussion will refer to Figure 15.3 which portrays three different taxpayers.

There are three measures of how taxes can be related to the income of an individual. Taxes can be proportional to income, progressive, or regressive.

Proportional Tax
A tax that applies the same rate to all levels of income.

Proportional Taxes. A **proportional tax** is one which requires that individuals pay the same percentage of their income in taxes. In Figure 15.3 three taxpayers have incomes of $10,000, $50,000, and $100,000. The effect of a proportional tax is shown in columns 2 and 3. The tax rate is fixed at 20 percent, and 20 percent is taken from each taxpayer's income. As income goes up, so too does the amount of the tax. The concern for vertical equity is met (higher income people pay more than lower income people). As long as the tax is applied across the board, horizontal equity also is met.

Progressive Tax
A tax for which the tax rate increases as income increases.

Progressive Taxes. A **progressive tax** is one in which the tax rate increases as the individual's income rises. Columns 4 and 5 in Figure 15.3 show that the taxpayer with a $10,000 income pays 15 percent whereas the person with the $100,000 income pays 25 percent. The vertical equity condition is met by a progressive tax and, as long as all people with the same income are taxed equally, horizontal equity concerns likewise are met.

Regressive Tax
A tax for which the tax rate decreases as income increases.

Regressive Taxes. With a **regressive tax,** the tax rate decreases as income increases. Columns 6 and 7 in Figure 15.3 show this case. A person with a $10,000 income is taxed at a 25 percent rate whereas the wealthier person with a $100,000 income is taxed at a 15 percent rate. Note that the concern for vertical equity can still be met with a regressive tax. The rich person still pays more tax than the poor person. The burden on the wealthier person, however, is significantly lighter.

The extent to which taxes are progressive or regressive is often not obvious at first glance. See Figure 15.4 for a graphic presentation of the different ways of measuring taxes. In fact, two taxes that everyone pays are solidly regressive: they take more from the poor than from the rich. Can you guess which ones they are? They are the Social Security tax and the state sales tax.

[5.] A final note about this tax. Those workers who lost their jobs stopped paying income and social security taxes and were eligible for unemployment compensation and other income assistance. Not only did the tax not raise much revenue (the rich weren't buying the items that were taxed), but welfare costs were increased to boot. When the government finally realized that the tax was counterproductive and canceled it three years later, it refunded to the rich any taxes that had been paid. Talk about pouring salt into a wound.

FIGURE 15.4
When taxes are judged on the ability to pay principle, the tax rate is compared to the taxpayer's income. If the tax rate rises as income rises, the tax is progressive. If the tax rate declines as income rises, the tax is regressive. If the tax rate remains the same regardless of income, the tax is proportional.

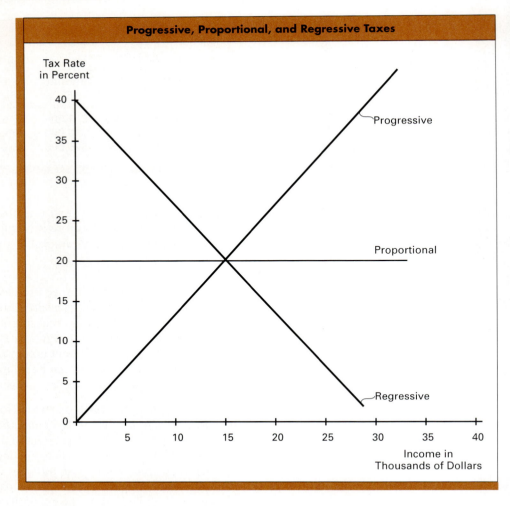

FIGURE 15.5

Sales Tax: Effective Rates			
Income	Spending	Tax @ 5%	Actual Tax Rate
$ 10,000	$10,000	$ 500	5%
$100,000	$80,000	$4,000	4%

The Social Security tax is pretty obviously regressive. People are taxed at 15.3 percent of their income; they pay half and their employer "contributes" half (guess where it comes from!) on the first $57,600 earned. Those who earn $10,000 pay 15.3 percent. Those who earn $30,000 pay 15.3 percent. Those who earn $50,000 pay 15.3 percent. Those who earn $100,000 pay 15.3 percent on the first $57,600 and nothing on the remaining $42,400. This is a regressive tax: the poor and middle income classes pay a higher percentage than the wealthy.

The second regressive tax that most everyone pays is the state sales tax. Figure 15.5 helps to demonstrate this. This figure shows two families, one poor and one wealthy. The poor family earns $10,000 and spends all of it trying to make ends meet. The wealthier family earns $100,000 and can save and invest $20,000 while spending $80,000. Sales taxes are applied against spending, so the poor family pays $500 in taxes while the wealthier family pays $4,000. The tax rate based on income decreases as the income rises because of differing spending patterns. The tax still meets the vertical equity condition (higher income people pay more tax), but the tax rate and burden decrease as incomes climb. Some

Income Tax Rates Cut!

What a lovely headline to read—our income tax rates have been cut. It does happen from time to time. Mostly, however, tax rates have been, or at least have felt, relatively high. 'Twas not always so, however, as a quick review of history will show.

Americans are so accustomed to paying income tax that it frequently comes as a surprise to people to learn that the tax is of relatively recent origin. For the first 200 years of U.S. history there were very few taxes as such. Duties were levied on imported goods and there were excise taxes on a limited number of things including liquor, tobacco, and sugar, but by-and-large few funds were collected. The Civil War changed all that. The nation needed a significant amount of money, and it turned to the income tax. A progressive tax was established—no tax below $600 in income; 3 percent for incomes between $600 and $10,000; a higher rate for the really wealthy. That lasted until Congress repealed the tax in 1868. An income tax was reinstituted in 1894, but the Supreme Court declared it unconstitutional in 1895. From then until the passage of the 16th Amendment to the Constitution in 1913, no income tax existed.

When the income tax became law in 1913, Congress set rates that were designed to exempt most Americans from having to pay—only the wealthy were hit. The tax rate was low, the personal exemption was high, and the income brackets were elevated. (It is probably significant to note that the average annual income at this time was less than $600, so most people still paid no tax.) Actual tax rates are shown in the table below.

As with the old proverb about the camel getting his nose in the tent, once the income tax was in place, the rates began to climb. The following table presents the income tax rates for the 1994 year. They look significantly different, don't they? The difference is even more marked when we compare the current tax rates with the 1913 tax as expressed in 1994 dollars, as shown in the next table. Whereas only a few people filed income tax returns in 1913, today the Internal Revenue Service receives and processes over 200 million returns each year.

So there you have it. Our income tax is a relative newcomer to the financial arena. Most of us pay it and, while some other country's tax rates may be higher, the U.S. income tax is significantly more pervasive than originally envisioned.

1994 Income Tax Rates

Tax Rate	Income Level
15%	up to $22,750
28%	$ 22,750–$ 55,100
31%	$ 55,100–$115,000
36%	$115,000–$250,000
38%	over $250,000

(A $6,250 combined exemption/deduction for single filers and $11,250 combined exemption/deduction for a married couple.)

1913 Personal Income Tax System

Tax Rate	Income Level
1%	up to $20,000
2%	$ 20,000–$ 50,000
3%	$ 50,000–$ 75,000
4%	$ 75,000–$100,000
5%	$100,000–$250,000
6%	$250,000–$500,000
7%	over $500,000

(A $3,000 exemption for single filers and $4,000 for a married couple.)

1913 Personal Income Tax System in 1994 Dollars

Tax Rate	Income Level
1%	up to $298,507
2%	$ 298,507–$ 746,269
3%	$ 746,269–$1,119,403
4%	$1,119,403–$1,492,537
5%	$1,492,537–$3,731,343
6%	$3,731,343–$7,462,687
7%	over $7,462,687

(A $44,776 exemption for single filers and $59,701 for a married couple.)

states try to get around this problem by exempting certain types of goods such as food or prescription drugs, but the difficulty remains.

A Final Look at Taxes

"In this world nothing can be said to be certain except death and taxes."[6] The issue of taxes will arise again, both in and out of this book. As you have seen, the

---

[6] This familiar quote was contained in a letter from Ben Franklin to Jean Baptiste Le Roy on November 13, 1789.

extensive and sometimes hidden impact of taxes necessitates an analytical approach. The effects of taxes are far-reaching and can alter the way people behave. Unless the government wants to repeat the problems of its luxury tax, it must proceed with great caution and not be swept up by rhetoric or surface appearances. If we can slow down and think before we act, we can help to lead our economy into a new, more rational age.

Taxes are compulsory payments by an individual or business to a government. Taxes are complex in nature and affect people's behavior, and care must be taken to determine how the burden may be shifted from one person to another.

BUDGET DEFICITS AND DEBT

The sky is falling! The sky is falling! Deficits are skyrocketing, interest payments are out of control, and the debt is crushing us. Woe is us.

Was Chicken Little an optimist? What about those politicians who repeat Chicken Little's cries? Are they right? Is the debt out of control? Will it end our economic way of life? Are we mortgaging our children's futures and leaving them with an unbearable burden?

No.

Budget deficits are a popular issue for politicians to shout about every couple of years, but they are such an insignificant issue that it is hardly worth losing sleep over. But because deficits are in the news, you need to know what they are all about and why they are not such a great concern. The first step is to examine the annual budget deficit to see how it comes about and what its effects are. The next stop is the accumulated debt and related interest payments to see how they affect the economy.

Budget Deficits

Budget Deficit
A situation that exists when the government spends more money than it collects in taxes.

Defining Budget Deficits. **Budget deficits** are related to the annual budget cycle and can be thought of in much the same way as an overrun in a household budget. When income is less than expenditures, you may run a tab on the Visa account. So, too, with the federal government. When tax revenues are less than expenditures, the result is a deficit. On a personal level, if you want to stop running deficits, you either have to earn more money or spend less. The same is true for the federal deficit. The way out of the deficit situation is to either raise taxes or cut government spending.[7]

The Size of the Budget Deficits. The U.S. government has run budget deficits in each of the past 20 years. Politicians, Democrats and Republicans alike, have found it in their best interest to spend more on programs than the taxes they assessed. It is almost as if they were trying to buy the affections of voters.

What makes budget deficits a growing concern is that the size of the deficit has been growing. Recent annual deficits have exceeded $200 billion, so the numbers are beginning to be impressive even to politicians who are dealing with other people's money.[8]

[7.] Actually it is a bit more complicated than that. It all depends on the reasons for the deficit and the stage of the business cycle. If, for instance, the government runs a deficit in a recession, lowering taxes may stimulate the economy to grow and result in more taxes collected in the long run.

[8.] As Senator Everett Dirksen once said, "A billion here and a billion there and it begins to add up." If your rich uncle died and left you a stack of $100 bills totaling a billion dollars and you began spending those $100 bills at the rate of one per minute every hour all day and night until you ran out, it would take you more than 19 years to spend it all.

FIGURE 15.6

		Deficit		Total Debt		Interest Paid	
Budget Deficits, Debt, and the Size of the Economy[9] **(In Billions of Dollars)**							
Year (1)	GNP (2)	Amount (3)	% GNP (4)	Amount (5)	% GNP (6)	Amount (7)	% GNP (8)
1950	$ 288	$ 6	2.1	$ 257	89.2	$ 6	2.1
1960	$ 515	($ 1)	(0.2)	$ 291	56.5	$ 9	1.7
1970	$1,016	$ 3	–	$ 381	37.5	$ 19	1.9
1980	$2,732	$ 74	2.7	$ 909	33.6	$ 75	2.7
1990	$5,463	$221	4.0	$3,206	58.7	$265	4.9

A summary of the situation is shown in Figure 15.6. As a comparison to annual deficits, the country's annual gross national product (the dollar value of all goods and services produced in the economy) has been included.

After all, a $10,000 Visa bill means a lot less to someone like Donald Trump than it does to a factory worker who earns $20,000 a year. As can be seen in Column 3, the deficit has risen from about $6 billion in 1950 to $221 billion in 1990. On the surface, that is a mammoth increase. However, the economy also has been growing all those years. When the deficit is compared to the gross national product, you can see that the effective deficit has less than doubled.

Budget Philosophies

There are three different approaches to handle the federal budget, and each plays itself out in differing deficit philosophies. Each approach starts from a very different premise, and each has extremely vocal proponents.

Annually Balanced Budget. The annually balanced budget means keeping revenues and expenditures in balance each year. This approach is generally supported by those who want to keep the government from growing and who prefer a more capitalistic economy. The annually balanced budget effectively removes the government as an agent of fiscal economic adjustment for whether there is a boom or a recession, the budget must remain in balance. In fact, as you will see in a future chapter, a completely balanced budget will intensify the size of the business cycle, increasing expansions and making recessions worse.

Cyclically Balanced Budget. The cyclically balanced budget recognizes that there is no reason why the economy should be examined on a 12-month basis. Business cycles frequently last two or three years with periods of expansion followed by periods of decline. In the recessionary years, the government can spend money and help to restore the economy to health. In years of expansion, the government can curtail its spending and so not add to inflationary pressures. Over the long term, however, the budget must be balanced so that total expenditures equal the taxes collected. The problem, of course, is that if the upswings and downswings are not equal, it may be impossible to balance the budget.

Functional Finance. Functional finance says a balanced economy, not a balanced budget, should be the goal. What the country needs is an economy operating at full employment with stable prices. Under this approach, the goal of the federal tax and budget process should be to help the economy remain stable overall, and the government should use deficits or surpluses as necessary to achieve this. Functional finance

---

[9] Don't try to make much sense of the debt and deficit numbers you find in the newspapers: they can appear in a variety of ways depending on the dates and definitions used.

FIGURE 15.7

Revenues and expenditures by state governments vary widely and are affected by local attitudes, prices, and industry-base.
Source: U.S. Bureau of the Census

State Government Revenues and Expenditures: 1993

	Revenues			Expenditures	
Rank	State	Amount	Rank	State	Amount
1	Alaska	$10,303	1	Alaska	$8,253
2	Hawaii	4,151	2	Hawaii	4,365
3	Wyoming	3,940	3	Rhode Island	3,541
4	Delaware	3,625	4	Wyoming	3,528
5	New York	3,470	5	New York	3,391
U.S. Average		2,534	U.S. Average		2,506
46	Georgia	2,039	46	Georgia	2,037
47	Florida	2,015	47	Tennessee	2,020
48	Tennessee	1,989	48	Florida	2,017
49	Texas	1,980	49	Texas	1,948
50	Missouri	1,974	50	Missouri	1,875

recognizes that the economy is growing and that deficits or surpluses this year will in all likelihood be larger than last year's. It contends that deficits aren't all that bad.

Causes of Debt

Budget deficits cause **debt.** If expenditures are greater than revenues, if the government spends more than it collects in taxes, it accumulates debt. The causes of budget deficits that result in debt are three-fold:

- Wars—During wars the country needs extra revenue to finance the fighting, so rather than raise taxes (and discourage people from working) or print lots of extra money (and cause inflation), the government generally runs deficits.
- Recessions—When the economy is in a recession, tax revenues fall but welfare and other expenditures increase, and a deficit results.
- Intentional Decisions—There have been times in the economic past when Congress decided to give tax cuts to people that were not matched by budget decreases (or any expected increase in tax revenues due to increased incomes). These choices have resulted in structural deficits.

The Size of the Debt

Columns 5 and 6 of Figure 15.6 and Figure 15.8 illustrate what has happened to the level of federal debt over the past 40 years. It is 12 times what it was in 1950! While that is true, the overall burden of the debt is considerably less today than in the good old days. Now the debt is just over half of the annual gross national product. Then it was very close to 90 percent. Today's debt burden should be quite a bit more manageable. And it would be, except for one thing: interest rates have really gone up over the past decades. Whereas the average interest rate was in the 3%–4% range in 1950, it climbed to more than 21 percent in the 1970s. The result has been a significant interest expense as a part of the federal budget each year. Columns 7 and 8 show us that, while interest payments have increased by a factor of 40 in the past four decades, the portion of gross national product dedicated to meeting these payments has just a little more than doubled. That's a lot of money, but not as big a burden as it might seem.

Effects of Budget Deficits and Debt

Erroneous Concerns. What does the size of the deficit and especially the debt really mean? There are a couple of misconceptions to clear up. One, the country is not going bankrupt. Unlike common folk, the government has the option of print-

Debt
The total amount of money owed by the government to individuals as a result of spending in excess of receipts.

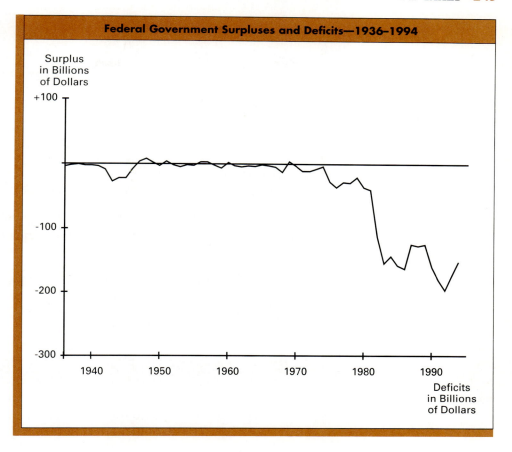

FIGURE 15.8
With very few exceptions, the U.S. government has spent more than it has taken in every year since 1938.

ing money any time it wants to. If it decides to get rid of the debt, it can just run the presses down at the Bureau of the Mint and print sheets of $10,000 bills until there are enough to cover the debt. Of course, inflation and other problems would arise if this solution were adopted, but it could be done.

The other point is that we are not burdening our poor children with an unbearable debt. Yes, they will have to pay the debt, but to whom will they pay it? To themselves, of course. Nearly 90 percent of the federal debt is held by Americans. This means that taxes are going to pay the interest on your government savings bond—from one citizen to another. And why was this debt that the children face incurred? To fight wars and keep the country free, to pay for highways and dams, and to fund college scholarships and loan programs. Much of the money spent was an investment in the future. As such, it makes sense that the children of today should help pay.

Legitimate Concerns
What are the real issues about the debt? One effect may be the redistribution of income from the poor and middle income classes to the rich. If it is the higher income classes who buy and hold government bonds, and interest payments to them come from the general tax funds, then money shifts from the average to the above average income group. (Note that these people have provided a service and deserve to be paid. The concern is solely over the redistributive effects.)

A second issue is with the so-called "crowding-out effect." If the government is entering the market to borrow billions of dollars, it is increasing the demand for funds. When the demand for something is increased, what happens to the price? The price increases. And what is the price for money? Interest. The government demand for borrowed funds increases the market interest rate, and this means that some people who would have borrowed funds at a lower interest rate are crowded out of the market because of the increased cost. The result is an increase in the size of the public sector and a decrease in the size of the private sector.

FIGURE 15.9

When we speak of *government* we generally mean the U.S. government, but there are a few other governments as this table shows. In fact, 14 states contain over 2,000 governments each with Illinois leading the way with 6,810 governments in 1992.
Source: U.S. Bureau of the Census

Number of Governmental Units, by Type: 1942 to 1992						
Type of Government	1942	1952[10]	1962	1972	1982	1992
Total	155,116	116,807	91,237	78,269	81,831	86,743
U.S. Government	1	1	1	1	1	1
State government	48	50	50	50	50	50
Local governments	155,067	116,756	91,186	78,218	81,780	86,692
County	3,050	3,052	3,043	3,044	3,041	3,043
Municipal	16,220	16,807	18,000	18,517	19,076	19,296
Township and town	18,919	17,202	17,142	16,991	16,734	16,666
School district	108,579	67,355	34,678	15,781	14,851	14,556
Special district	8,299	12,340	18,323	23,885	28,078	33,131

[10] Adjusted to include units in Alaska and Hawaii which adopted statehood in 1959.

A final concern has to do with incentives. If the government raises taxes to make the interest payments, this could act as a disincentive to those who are employed or who invest. If people work or invest less, it will hurt the economy in the long run. While it is not likely to have a major impact, any effect in this direction at the margin is enough to cause concern.

Core-Info

The effect of budget deficits on the economy is relatively small, and the way in which they are measured and reported can greatly affect how large they appear to be.

NOW WHAT?

This chapter has covered a lot of ground. Government has a legitimate role in capitalism. Government spends a lot of money on programs of all sorts. We pay a variety of taxes, some of which may be counterproductive to the equity that we wish to achieve. Taxes do not cover the full cost of government. Each year we have been spending more than we have collected in taxes, and the deficits and debts have been increasing steadily. The debt merits attention, not because of the panic reactions of some news media and politicians, but because there may be some long-run and equity concerns that require correction.

SUMMARY

- When markets do not produce the optimal amount of a good or service or when all costs of production are not accounted for, there may be a legitimate reason for government intervention in the economy.
- Government's role in pure capitalism is limited to making certain that private property is protected, that markets are not monopolized by force, and that economic freedom exists for all.
- Taxes are monies that are taken from an individual or business by a government and for which no direct return is received. Taxes may be shifted to people other than the individual on which it was originally levied, so tax incidence must be carefully assessed.
- Income is generally considered the most appropriate basis for measuring the impact of a tax. Progressive taxes take an increasing percentage as income rises. Regressive taxes take a decreasing percentage as income rises.
- The three philosophies of federal budgeting are the annually balanced budget, the cyclically balanced budget, and functional finance.
- The impact of budget deficits is relatively small in the economy. Most of the debt is owed by Americans to Americans and not to foreign nations.

KEY TERMS

Budget deficit	Multiplier effect	Regressive tax
Debt	Negative externality	Tax
Economic stabilization	Positive externality	Tax incidence
Externality	Progressive tax	Tax shifting
Income redistribution	Proportional tax	Transfers
Market failure	Public good	

REVIEW QUESTIONS

1. Define the concept of market failure, and explain why we might want government intervention in a capitalistic society.
2. Describe the six areas in which there have been calls for government intervention.
3. Describe the four techniques that the government can employ in order to deal with "externalities."
4. When is a payment to government not considered to be a tax?
5. State and briefly explain the different types of taxes described in this chapter.
6. What are the two major overall effects of taxes? Differentiate between tax shifting and tax incidence.
7. There are three measures of how taxes can be related to the income of an individual. Briefly explain the three measures and provide an example of each.
8. Budget deficits are situations that exist when the government spends more money than it collects in taxes. There are three different approaches to how we might handle the federal budget. Briefly explain these approaches.
9. Describe some of the causes of the budget deficits that result in debt.

PROBLEM-SOLVING PRACTICE

1. What do economists mean by the term externalities? Explain and give examples of:
   (a) negative externalities
   (b) positive externalities
2. Identify and define six different types of taxes. How do each of these taxes rate on the following issues?
   (a) efficiency
   (b) equity
   (c) the progressive/regressive scale of taxation
3. After reading this chapter, how would you evaluate the federal budget deficit in the U.S.? Consider each of the following:
   (a) the potential bankruptcy of the U.S. federal government
   (b) economic stabilization policies
   (c) crowding out
   (d) the burden of the national debt on our children
   (e) income distribution

CHAPTER 16

The National Economy

CHAPTER OUTLINE

A. The Big Picture
B. National Accounting
 1. Expenditures *vs.* Income Approaches
 2. Uses for National Accounts
C. Gross National Product *vs.* Gross Domestic Product
D. Difficulties in Using National Accounts
E. Aggregate Demand and Aggregate Supply
 1. Aggregate Demand
  a. Price and Quantity Relationship
  b. Factors Affecting the Slope
  c. Factors That Affect the Curve: Nonprice Determinants
 2. Aggregate Supply
  a. Price and Quantity Relationship
  b. Shape of the Curve
  c. Factors that Affect the Curve: Nonprice Determinants
F. Macroeconomic Policy
 1. A History of Macroeconomic Policy
 2. The Purpose of Policy Adjustments
  a. Classical Policy
  b. Keynesian Policy
  c. Intermediate Policy
  d. Monetarist Policy
  e. Rational Expectations Policy
G. Current Debates in Macroeconomic Policy

The purpose of this chapter is to introduce some of the basic issues in the national economy such as aggregate supply and demand, and to explain the types of macroeconomic policies that are possible.

AFTER COMPLETING THIS CHAPTER, YOU WILL BE ABLE TO:

1. Explain the usefulness of national accounts for decision making.
2. Demonstrate the difficulties of comparing national accounts between nations.
3. Draw the relevant aggregate demand and aggregate supply curves and describe the factors that affect each.
4. Compare the five approaches to macroeconomic policy.

The Big Picture

If you've been keeping score, the tally for discussions to date is Microeconomics 7, Macroeconomics 1. We focused on microeconomics first not because it is inherently more important but because it is closer to home. It's at the microeconomic level that we live our daily lives. Decisions about how to spend money, set taxes, and plan for business are all done at the micro level. However, these decisions are not made in a vacuum. We all live in the wider society, and our actions take place within a macroeconomic context. Changes in the overall economy can have a dramatic impact on the outcome of local decisions. Knowing how the overall economy functions is essential if we are to accomplish good personal and business planning. It is to macroeconomics, therefore, that we now turn.

All microeconomic actions take place within a macroeconomic setting. The whole economy encompasses individual decisions; in fact, the economy can be thought of as a circle. Figure 16.1 provides a view of the **circular flow** of the economy. In this view, there are two operating sectors in the economy, households and businesses.[1] Households buy goods and spend money in the product market.

Households also provide inputs (land, labor, capital, and entrepreneurship) for which they receive money income in the form of rent, wages, interest, and profit. Businesses buy resources in the resource market and incur costs. Businesses also produce goods and services in the product market for which they receive revenue.

As you can see, households and businesses are both suppliers and demanders. In the product market, households are demanders and businesses are suppliers. The interaction of the two determines product prices. In the resource market, households are suppliers and businesses are demanders. The interaction in this market determines resource prices. In all of this is the usual scarcity. The wants of both sectors are always growing, and economic decisions must be made carefully.

---

[1] Businesses produce goods and services while absorbing resources. For this simple model, government can be thought of as a part of the business sector, producing goods and services and absorbing resources.

Circular Flow
The pattern in which resources, funds, and goods and services circulate within the economic system.

FIGURE 16.1

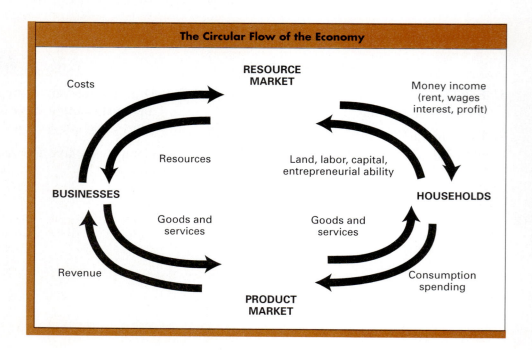

The Circular Flow of the Economy

Core-Info

The economy operates in a circular pattern, with resources, funds, and goods and services flowing between businesses and households and between the resource market and the product market.

NATIONAL ACCOUNTING

Don't worry: you don't need to be an accountant to understand this section. However, this introduction to the basics of national accounting will help you to figure out what all those big economic numbers really mean.

National accounts are like personal or business accounts; they provide a way to measure economic health. If things are going well for the country, these accounts hold the clues to that success so it can be repeated next year. On the other hand, if things are going badly, these accounts should help to locate the problem so it can be corrected before things get worse. National accounts offer an evaluation of the current status, the data behind trends that are taking place, and information needed to make more effective policy decisions.

A critical component in national accounting is the **gross national product (GNP).** Gross national product is generally considered one of the best measures of economic health. The gross national product is the total market or dollar value of all final goods and services produced by the economy in a given year. Just as you learned the definition of rent, you should consider this definition one word at a time. "Total" means the overall sum. "Market value" involves the quantities of each good or service multiplied by its price. This shows society's evaluation of the worth of the output. "Final goods and services" means items purchased for final use and excludes goods (called intermediate goods) used in the production of other goods. "Produced" means that it measures output, not sales. If items are added to inventory but are not purchased, they nonetheless involve economic activity this year. "By the economy" means all parts of the economy, whether the firm's plants are in California or Calcutta.

A few things are specifically excluded from gross national product. Intermediate transactions are one example. Only final sales to a consumer are included, not transactions that occur along the way. The GNP also excludes nonproduction (*not* nonproductive) transactions. Nonproduction transactions are purely financial transactions for which goods are not produced. Public and private transfer payments (welfare and unemployment benefits, bequests, and college scholarships), securities transactions (sales of stocks and bonds), and secondhand sales are all excluded because, while they might be very beneficial to those involved, no final good or service is produced as a result.

You can probably already anticipate some problems with this measure. Gross national product goes up if prices go up, for instance. Does inflation mean the country is automatically better off? Probably not. Gross national product also goes up if a firm produces more goods overseas. Is the U.S. economy better off because General Motors produces more Holdens in Australia? Not much. Ultimately, economists also depend on a slightly different measure that focuses on real changes that affect this country's households and businesses. Stay tuned.

Expenditures *vs.* Income Approaches

As you saw in the depiction of the circular flow of the economy, there are two ways to think of what is happening in the economy. You can take an expenditures approach or an income approach. Since in a closed economy, all spending

---

National Accounts
The records of the income on expenditures of an economy that allow an assessment of its performance.

Gross National Product
The total market or dollar value of all final goods and services produced *by* the economy in a given year.

is equal to all earnings by someone, both will provide the same final result: they are just two different ways of looking at the situation. Either route ends up with the same answer.

The expenditures approach adds all final spending in the economy in a year. The equation that shows this best is:

$$GNP = C + I + G + X_n$$

where: GNP = Gross national product
C = Consumption expenditures by households
I = Gross private domestic investment
G = Government purchases of goods and services
X_n = Net exports (goods made here and sold abroad minus goods made abroad and sold here; i.e., exports minus imports)

The expenditure approach to national income accounting gives us a full picture of how people and businesses spend their money. This is a product market analysis of the economy. The income approach to gross national product examines how it is earned. It works on the resource side of the equation. The equation for this approach is:

$$GNP = Wages + Rents + Interest + Profits$$

where: GNP = Gross national product
Wages = Payments to employees including benefits
Rents = Payments for the use of property resources
Interest = Payments for the use of capital
Profits = Payments to owners of businesses

Which approach should you take in analyzing gross national product? It depends on the data you can get and the questions you want to answer. Both approaches provide the same final result. The path is all that differs.

Uses for National Accounts

Just as many people evaluate their income and spending patterns every so often, analyzing the same patterns in the national economy uncovers plenty of useful information. Economists who use the expenditures approach assess today's spending patterns to decide if they are on the right track. For instance, if a very high percentage of the GNP comes from consumption spending and a small portion comes from investment spending, you can infer that tomorrow's economy will not be significantly larger than is today's. If the reverse is true and investment spending is very high, you can conclude that the economy will likely be much stronger tomorrow. One way or the other, this analysis can help policy makers decide whether to encourage changes in spending patterns. On the other hand, the income approach to gross national product is useful in assessing how the benefits of the economy are distributed among the various groups. If the wages portion of the package is decreasing while rents and profits are increasing, policy makers may decide to help change that direction in favor of those who directly labor. Whatever course is set, knowledge of the national accounts supports the ability to make informed choices and to bring change in the desired direction.

Core-Info

National accounting allows us to examine the operation of the overall economy. The accounts may follow the expenditures or the income approach.

GROSS NATIONAL PRODUCT VS. GROSS DOMESTIC PRODUCT

Gross national product includes the value of all goods that are produced by an American company in its overseas plants. It also excludes all goods produced in American plants by foreign firms. Thus, under the gross national product approach, Honda Accords produced in Ohio by American workers using American parts are added to the accounts of Japan. On the other hand, Manhattan shirts produced in Malaysia by Malaysian workers are added to the American GNP. When international trade is a very small portion of the economy, this practice has little impact. When international trade constitutes a significant portion or where a large imbalance in trade exists (more exports than imports or vice versa), an approach that acknowledges these limitations is needed. **Gross Domestic Product (GDP)** is that approach. Gross domestic product is the total market or dollar value of all final goods and services produced within the economy in a given year. Whatever is produced within a nation's borders (less any imports used in the process) is included, regardless of who owns the company. Because this approach more accurately reflects the actual activity of a nation's economy, it has generally been reported most frequently in recent years.

Gross Domestic Product
The total market or dollar value of all final goods and services produced within a nation's borders in a given year.

Core-Info

Gross national product measures the final output of goods and services *by* the economy whereas gross domestic product measures the final output of goods and services *within* the country's borders.

DIFFICULTIES IN USING NATIONAL ACCOUNTS

Gross national product and gross domestic product numbers convey a lot of information, but not everything citizens need to know about their economy. Just as economics is not everything in people's personal lives, so it is for the nation. The welfare of a nation needs a more inclusive view than just GNP or GDP. Thus, we must take into consideration a number of factors when we analyze national income statistics. This is true when we are looking at the United States, and it is even more critical when we make international comparisons.

If national income statistics are to be effectively utilized as measures of a nation's welfare, a number of adjustments and considerations must be made:

1. Nonmarket transactions—When a homeowner calls a plumber to repair a leaky pipe, that transaction increases the GNP. If the homeowner fixes the leak without calling in a professional, there is no addition to GNP. Where the nonmarket sector is large, as in less developed countries, GNP data may underestimate the level of economic activity that is occurring.

2. Product quality—An increase in product quality is not reflected in gross national product unless it adds to the price of the product. The introduction of televisions with remote controls, automobiles with side impact protection, or wrinkle-free shirts does not increase GNP although people's lives are measurably better because of those improvements.

3. Leisure—As you may recall from our discussion of the backward bending supply curve of labor, people rationally choose leisure over additional income and the goods it would provide. In fact, it has been shown that, as economies develop, workers always add to their leisure time and decrease the number of hours worked. This choice of leisure results in a decrease in the gross national product.

4. Type of output—If an industry produces a product that creates toxic waste, are we better off as a nation? The GNP certainly would go up. If people decide to clean up

But Are We Better Off?

The U.S. economy is incredibly productive. The gross national product per capita has grown from $4,959 in 1970 to $22,276 in 1990 and per capita personal consumption expenditures have increased from $3,152 to $15,048 in the same time period. Even when accounting for the effect of inflation, per capita personal consumption expenditures have increased from $8,842 to $13,093. As a result of the expanding economy and the opportunities it provides, many factors are looking up as shown in the following table.

Improvements Since 1970

	1970	1990
Households with two or more vehicles	29.3%	54.0%
Homes with color television sets	33.9%	96.1%
Size of a new home in square feet	1,500	2,080
Life expectancy in years	70.8	75.4

Unfortunately not all is rosy. Although many measures show lifestyle improvement in the past two decades, other data support a contradictory viewpoint. The next table highlights a few impairments, and they bring into question the overall direction of society, if not the economy.

Downward Trends Since 1970

	1970	1990
Divorce rate per 1,000 population	3.5	4.7
Births per 1,000 unmarried women	10.7	28.0
Rapes per 100,000 females	30.4	80.5
Prisoners per 100,000 population	96.7	295.0
Consumer price index for medical care	34.0	162.8
Scholastic Aptitude Test verbal score	460	424

How do you weigh the obvious and significant economic success enjoyed by the vast majority of Americans against the declines that the second set of statistics portrays? It is not an easy question, and it points very quickly to people's value systems. That is where the normative discussion takes over. The positive data from the tables can take the analysis only so far. After you examine the data, you must make some very fundamental decisions about society.

Good luck as you decide.

---

the pollution and build equipment toward that end, are we better off as a nation? Again, GNP would increase. Clearly what people make is as important as the fact that they make it. Similarly, if people are afraid of crime and buy security locks for their doors and guns for protection, the gross national product will be the better for it.

5. The distribution of output—You have seen from the outset that how income is distributed is important. An economy with a very few wealthy families and a lot of poverty may have the same gross national product as an economy with a fairly equal, albeit low, income distribution. However, the former would certainly not meet the equity criterion for judging economic systems.

6. Population factors—If the nation's gross national product increases by 2 percent per year, the economy is growing. If the population is growing by 3 percent per year, however, the nation is falling behind on a per capita basis. Any analysis must view all gross national product data with an eye to both the current population and its rate of growth.

The key then is to take these six factors into consideration when evaluating gross national product figures and to be particularly aware of them when making international comparisons. This comprehensive approach will make the data most useful as you try to understand the overall economy.

Core-Info

National accounting data must be used carefully because a number of aspects of an economy such as leisure, nonmarket transactions, and quality are not measured.

AGGREGATE DEMAND AND AGGREGATE SUPPLY

The discussion in Chapter 5 on supply and demand went a long way in describing how the individual works. It showed how businesses and consumers interact to determine the prices and quantities of individual goods and services. You now should be able to follow trends in price and quantity for individual goods and understand the causes of the changes you observe. That understanding is essential at the individual level, but now it is time to expand our perspective. We must understand why the overall price level is sometimes steady and why there are periods of inflation. We need to know why there are business cycles with periods of growth interspersed with times of recession. Toward this end, we need to understand aggregate demand and aggregate supply.

Aggregate demand and aggregate supply involve a summation of the general supplies and demands for goods and services. As you would expect when talking about supply and demand, prices and quantities are involved. In fact, as you look at the overall supply of goods and the overall demand for goods, price and quantity take on special meaning.

Aggregate Demand (AD)

Aggregate Demand has to do with the overall demand for goods and services in the economy. The aggregate demand curve shows the total quantity of goods and services that will be produced in an economy at each price level. As the overall price level changes, how does the overall demand for goods and services react? At the aggregate level, the demand curve may look like that for an individual good, but the causal factors are quite different.

> **Aggregate Demand**
> The total quantity of goods and services that will be demanded in an economy at each price level.

Price and Quantity Relationship. As price rises on the individual level, the quantity demanded decreases. The same is true for a nation. As the overall level of prices increases, the overall quantity of goods and services demanded decreases. Figure 16.2 provides a graphic depiction.

As expected, the aggregate demand curve slopes downward from upper left to lower right just like the demand curve for a single good. The reasons for the slope, however, are quite different. The standard income and substitution effects do not apply here because the curve encompasses all goods, not a single good. Thus, consumers cannot buy anything else as prices change, and as all prices change, so do all incomes in an equivalent manner.

Factors Affecting the Slope. The curve does slope as expected, however, for three reasons. First is the foreign purchases effect. As the general price level rises, goods cost more relative to foreign goods so people import more (buying fewer domestic goods) and foreigners buy fewer U.S. goods. Second is the wealth effect. As prices rise, people's accumulated wealth decreases in value; it can now buy fewer goods, so people are willing to buy less. Finally there is the interest rate effect. As prices rise, people need to use more money to buy the same goods. Thus, the demand for money increases. Because the price of money is the interest rate, the interest rate rises as the demand for money increases. As the interest rate rises, people borrow less to buy goods and businesses borrow less to invest in new capital. Thus, the demand for goods decreases. Therefore, all three factors contribute to the downward slope of the aggregate demand curve.

Factors That Affect the Curve: Nonprice Determinants. In the same way that factors affect demand (as opposed to the quantity demanded) for individual goods, nonprice factors affect the aggregate demand curve. The first of these factors is consumer spending. As consumers change their attitudes about how much of their income they should spend, the curve will shift outward as they spend more and inward as they spend less. The second factor has to do with business

Figure 16.2

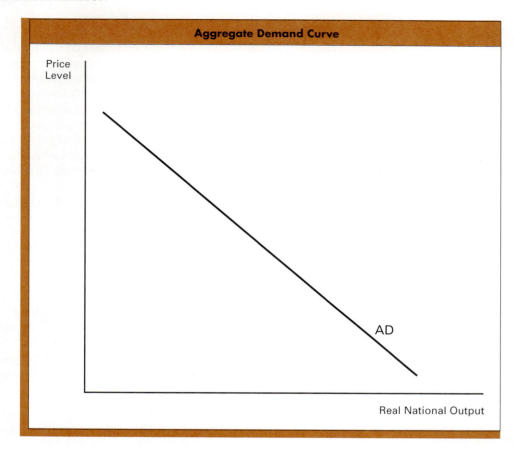

investment. If business expectations about future profits change or if the supply of money changes, if business tax rates fall or if new technologies arrive on the scene, businesses will alter their investment decisions and the aggregate demand curve will shift. The third factor affecting the location of the curve is government spending. If the government decides to change the amount of goods and services it purchases (*not* change transfer payments), the aggregate demand curve will shift. Finally there is the net export effect. As foreign incomes or international trade policies change, the quantities imported from the United States will change, resulting in a change in aggregate demand. Similarly, as the strength of the dollar relative to other currencies changes, people will change their purchases of American goods.

Aggregate demand is a fairly simple concept, but complexity builds when all factors that affect it are considered. If you know the basic factors that affect the curve's slope and position, you can think logically about them and explain how each affects overall demand.

Core-Info

Aggregate demand is the total quantity of goods and services demanded in an economy at each relevant price level. There is an inverse relationship between the price level and aggregate demand.

FIGURE 16.3

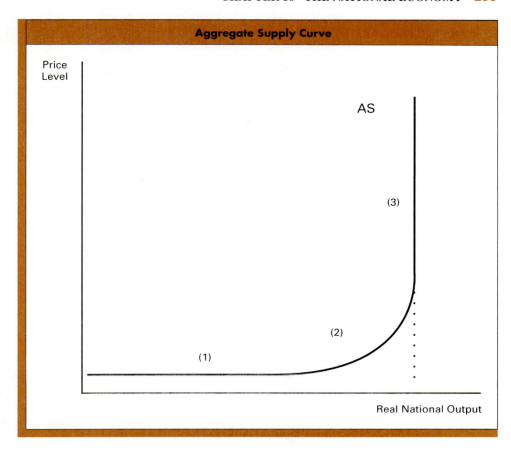

Aggregate Supply (AS)

The other side of the supply and demand relationship is **aggregate supply.** The aggregate supply curve shows the total amount of goods and services that will be produced in an economy at each price level. As was the case for the price and quantity supplied of individual goods, a positive relationship exists between the overall price level and the total amount of goods and services produced, or real national output.

Price and Quantity Relationship. Figure 16.3 provides a graphic summary of the aggregate supply curve. While similar to the usual supply curve, this curve has a somewhat different shape. It does slope upward to the right, however, because at higher price levels, more output is likely produced by businesses. The shape of the curve, however, is very much the center of controversy.

Shape of the Curve. As Figure 16.3 shows, the aggregate supply curve has three distinct sections. The first section of the curve (1) is known as the **Keynesian range** (named after Lord Maynard Keynes, a British economist who, in the midst of the Great Depression of the 1930s, produced his *General Theory;* he felt that this section represented all of the aggregate supply curve). This section of the curve assumes that there is much unemployment and unutilized capacity and that output can be increased significantly without affecting the overall price level. The second section of the curve (2) is called the **intermediate range.** In this area some industries are at full capacity and some have unutilized capacity. Some labor shortages and production bottlenecks exist, but

---

Aggregate Supply
The total quantity of goods and services supplied in an economy at each price level.

Keynesian Range
That portion of the aggregate supply curve that assumes the existence of unemployed recourses such that output can be increased without affecting the overall price level.

Intermediate Range
That portion of the aggregate supply curve that assumes that any increase in national output will be accompanied by an increase in the aggregate price level.

Classical Range
That portion of the aggregate supply curve that assumes that the economy is operating at full capacity and that any increase in demand will result only in an increase in the price level, not in the quantity of goods produced.

the economy has opportunities for expansion. If businesses are to expand, they must buy up the now increasingly scarce resources, so the general price level will rise as output increases. Finally comes the **classical range** in which the economy is operating at full capacity. If one industry wishes to expand, it must bid resources away from other industries by offering more money. If the industry is successful in doing so with the economy at full capacity, the net result will be the same level of output but at higher prices. The three sections together comprise the aggregate supply curve. Because of the implications of its unusual shape, this curve is the focal point of much debate among economists and politicians. Liberal economists tend to see the economy as forever in the Keynesian range and thus in need of help from the government. Conservative economists tend to see the economy as always in the classical range and contend that all government intervention will do is increase prices. Both camps have been right; both have been wrong.

Factors That Affect the Curve: Nonprice Determinants. The position of the curve is determined by a variety of nonprice factors. The first of these is changes in input prices. As input prices increase, production costs rise and supply is reduced. Input prices are affected by domestic resource availability, the prices of imported resources, and market power. The second nonprice factor affecting aggregate supply is changes in productivity. As productivity increases, the economy can produce more goods per unit of input. As the cost per unit produced decreases, the aggregate supply curve shifts to the right. The third nonprice factor affecting aggregate supply is changes in the institutional environment. If government adds new regulations to businesses, costs increase and the aggregate supply curve shifts to the left. Similarly, the curve shifts if business subsidies are instituted or if new taxes are imposed. The position of the curve is determined by all of these nonprice factors acting together.

Aggregate supply is a fascinating subject. The aggregate supply curve involves many different issues and thus offers a great deal of food for thought.

Core-Info

Aggregate supply is the total quantity of goods and services supplied in an economy at each relevant price level. In general, there is a direct relationship between the price level and aggregate supply, but the aggregate supply curve is composed of three distinct sections.

MACROECONOMIC POLICY

The reason for even thinking about aggregate supply and aggregate demand has to do with **macroeconomic policy.** If the economy is not progressing at a satisfactory rate, many people feel the need to intervene to get it back on track. Understanding aggregate supply and aggregate demand and how they interact provides the tools for knowing how, when, and to what extent to become involved in making adjustments.

A History of Macroeconomic Policy

Macroeconomic policy is not a new phenomenon. For centuries divinely appointed kings, power-mad dictators, and elected governments have all tried to shape the economies of their countries. Until the rise of nation-states, economic policy tended to focus on how well the castle's agricultural lands were doing. Then came a stage called mercantilism. In this phase, governments attempted to manipulate their economies so

Macroeconomic Policy
The attempt by the government to move the economy toward full employment and stable prices by affecting aggregate supply, aggregate demand, or the supply of money.

they could amass and hoard as much gold as possible. When capitalism hit its stride at the beginning of the 19th century, governments began practicing a policy of *laissez faire,* leaving the economy alone to fend for itself. (When governments needed to intervene in something during this period, they generally did it by mucking about in the economies of their colonies—rarely to the benefit of the colonies.) The Great Depression of the 1930s left 25 percent of the work force unemployed. This led to a new wave of concern for macroeconomic policy making to help ameliorate the severity of the crisis. Even with the recent round of conservative economics in Washington, the federal government remains a very active player in the American economy.

The Purpose of Policy Adjustments

The purpose of government involvement in the market is to help the economy to operate as close as possible to full employment without incurring a round of inflation. By using a series of tools to affect aggregate demand or aggregate supply, macroeconomic policy can help to make the adjustments necessary to achieve these ends. As we examine these adjustments, it is important to remember a lesson that was learned in the 1960s and 1970s. At that time economists believed very strongly in their ability to get the economy to full employment and keep it there through the use of macroeconomic policy. The economists were wrong. What they learned the hard way was that they can help provide direction to the economy and may be able to foster changes, but they cannot micro-manage the economy so that it remains always in that blissful state of full employment with no inflation. Economic tools are neither sophisticated nor sensitive enough to make this happen. That said, much can still be done at certain times to help the economy on an upward path.

Figure 16.4 brings both sides of the macroeconomic puzzle together in one graph. Aggregate supply and aggregate demand as described previously come

FIGURE 16.4

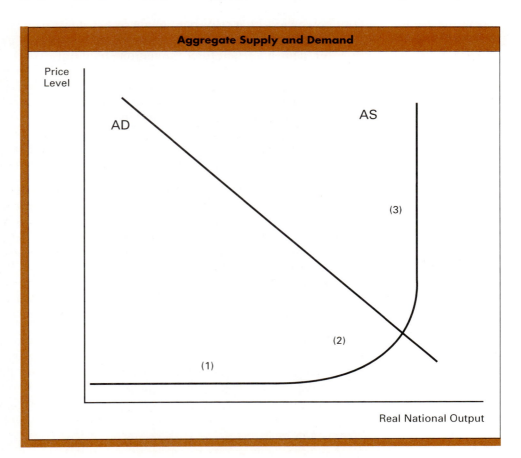

together at an equilibrium point that shows the level of aggregate or total output that will be produced and the general price level that will prevail. (If you think of this equilibrium price as something like the Consumer Price Index [CPI] which tracks the general price level, you won't be too far wrong.)

Given the two graphs that are now brought together, economists can examine potential policy approaches to use if the equilibrium is not what they want. Which approach to follow will be determined by the economists' understanding of how flexible the economy is and how much faith they have in its ability to adjust.

Classical Policy. The first policy approach that can be taken is known as **classical policy.** This approach assumes that the economy naturally operates at full employment, is flexible, and will adjust automatically without interference. It bases this belief on what is known as **Say's Law,** named for French economist Jean Baptiste Say. Remember the circular flow of the economy from the beginning of the chapter? That's it. Making goods yields the income to buy the goods. Buying goods yields the money to make goods. Any disequilibrium that takes the economy away from full employment will result in a decrease in the price level which will induce people to buy more goods; thus, the economy will fairly quickly return to full employment.

This policy approach assumes the nation is operating in area (3) of the aggregate supply curve. It contends that the economy will stay there if government can keep out of the way. Any government interference will only add to the price level; the economy is already at full employment. Stimulating increased demand through government spending is definitely not the answer.

Keynesian Policy. The second policy approach that people follow is essentially the opposite of the classical approach. This is known as the **Keynesian policy** approach. This approach contends that wages and prices are not flexible downward, that they may increase but don't decrease. Monopoly firms keep prices high and monopoly unions keep wages high even in the face of declining demand. Therefore, the nation shouldn't expect the price level to drop to help restore the economy to full employment, which doesn't exist, anyway! For the Keynesians, the economy is perpetually operating below full capacity, somewhere along section (1) of the aggregate supply curve. This being the case, government actions can stimulate the economy to expand its aggregate output. This approach insists it can do this without pushing prices up. Stimulating increased demand through government spending is definitely the answer in Keynesian policy.

Intermediate Policy. It is fairly easy to pick holes in both the classical and Keynesian policy approaches, especially when they are taken to their (il)logical extremes. This has led many economists to agree on an **intermediate policy.** This policy assumes that the intermediate range (2) of the aggregate supply curve is more likely to be correct. In this range, economists recognize that aggregate output and price level are directly related and that more goods can and will be produced as the price level rises. In this range, there is room for some government involvement to stimulate demand and help expand the economy, but it does affect the general price level.

Monetarist Policy. So far we haven't talked about money. The monetarist policy advocates would argue that the foregoing discussion was mostly wasted, that money is the answer. **Monetarist policy** assumes that through appropriate control of the money supply, the economy may be adjusted to achieve full employment. Adjusting the money supply is quick, flexible, and isolated from some of the petty political squabbles that surround fiscal policy. The monetarists contend that ad-

---

Classical Policy
The macroeconomic approach of *laissez faire* based on the belief that the economy is self-correcting and that it naturally moves toward full employment.

Say's Law
The belief that in a closed economy, the act of creating goods creates income equal to the value of the goods produced.

Keynesian Policy
The macroeconomic approach of direct government intervention in the economy based on the belief that aggregate output can be increased without affecting the price level.

Intermediate Policy
The macroeconomic approach of limited government intervention in the economy based on the belief that an increase in output will be accompanied by an increase in prices.

Monetarist Policy
The macroeconomic approach of government adjustment of the money supply as the key tool for economic stability.

justing the money supply affects investment, exports, and imports as well as the demand for goods and services. The monetarists, who tend to be from the classical school of thought, think that government involvement is not required to spur the economy to full employment.

Rational Expectations Policy. The final macroeconomic policy approach is called **rational expectations policy.** This approach assumes that consumers are rational, that they think, and that they act on their expectations. If consumers think a stock is going to fall in value, they sell today and prices will fall. If consumers believe that the price of an item will rise, they buy now, and their purchases cause prices to go up. Government policy, which takes time to implement, therefore often reinforces the problems that consumers had anticipated. A specific example: if consumers believe that government is going to push interest rates up in an effort to reduce demand by borrowers, they will borrow money today, driving up interest rates to the expected level. If government then pushes interest rates up, the rates will be too high and will greatly curtail business and consumer willingness to borrow, sending the economy into a recession. Another example: if businesses expect that government will provide a tax break for new investment during an economic recession, they will delay investing in their businesses until the tax break is enacted, prolonging the recession and delaying the recovery. The prescription by rational expectations policy economists is to provide as much information to consumers and businesses as possible and to stay out of their way. Rational people act in ways that help to stabilize the economy because it is in their best interest. Government involvement in the market is ill-advised at best, counterproductive at worst. An informed *laissez faire* is the answer.

> **Rational Expectations Policy**
> The macroeconomic approach that acknowledges that businesses and individuals will act on their anticipations of government intervention in the economy and in so doing render those interventions ineffective.

Core-Info

The goal of macroeconomic policy is to help the economy function at full employment without inflation. Depending on one's philosophy concerning the nature of the economy, there are five different sets of policy tools that can be applied to assist the economy in meeting the overall goal.

1. Classical policy
2. Keynesian policy
3. Intermediate policy
4. Monetarist policy
5. Rational expectations policy

CURRENT DEBATES IN MACROECONOMIC POLICY

You could probably guess over which issues debate is raging currently. How flexible are wages, anyway? Economists know they can move up, but can they move down as well? Are corporate downsizing, part-time and contract work, and job redefinition examples of downward flexibility, or are they a different phenomenon? Is money all it is cracked up to be? If the money supply were allowed to increase by a fixed percentage every year, would all economic problems vanish as is claimed by the monetarists? Is government macroeconomic involvement really counterproductive all the time? It appears on the surface as if it has had some success in the past. With a domestic economy that is tightly linked to international markets, can one nation practice a *laissez faire* approach when other national governments intervene regularly? Stay tuned. You are developing the tools needed not only to understand the questions but also to help to frame the answers for the next century.

SUMMARY

- National accounts provide a picture of the economic health of the nation. These summaries can use either an expenditures approach or an income approach. Both provide the same final figures.
- National income data are not directly comparable between nations or within the same nation over a period of years because varying amounts of nonmarket transactions exist, product quality may change, the desire for leisure varies, the type of output is not reflected in the accounts, national accounts do not reflect a changing population size, and the distribution of output may be as important as the size.
- Aggregate demand is the total demand for goods and services in the economy. A graph displaying aggregate demand includes overall output and the overall price level.
- The four components of aggregate demand are consumer spending, business investment, government spending in goods and services, and net exports.
- Aggregate supply is the total supply of goods and services that will be produced in an economy at each price level. The supply curve has three distinct segments that reflect varying views of the concept.
- The three factors that determine aggregate supply are changes in input prices, changes in productivity, and changes in the institutional environment.
- The government often becomes involved in macroeconomic policy. The goal of this involvement is to help the economy to achieve full employment without incurring inflation. The type of policy pursued is determined by the underlying economic (and political) beliefs of the policy maker.

KEY TERMS

Aggregate demand
Aggregate supply
Circular flow
Classical policy
Classical range
Gross domestic product
Gross national product
Intermediate policy
Intermediate range
Keynesian policy
Keynesian range
Macroeconomic policy
Monetarist policy
National accounts
Rational expectations policy

REVIEW QUESTIONS

1. Why does a nation care about its gross national product?
2. What items are excluded from the measure of a nation's gross national product?
3. What is the difference between gross national product and gross domestic product? When is this difference important?
4. What are the four factors that affect the level of aggregate demand?
5. What are the three factors that affect the level of aggregate supply?
6. What does the intersection between the aggregate supply and aggregate demand curves show?
7. What is the purpose of government involvement in the market place?
8. What are the five macroeconomic policy approaches?

PROBLEM-SOLVING PRACTICE

1. Describe some ways in which the gross national product of the United States could decline while people in the country became better off.
2. Based on recent income and interest rate statistics (look them up if necessary), draw the aggregate supply curve for the United States.
3. Describe how the rational expectations theory of macroeconomic policy is related to the rational self-interest theory stated about consumers and businesses.

CHAPTER 17

Money, Banks, and the Interest Rate

CHAPTER OUTLINE

A. Money Matters
B. Money
  1. The Definition of Money
  2. The Functions of Money
    a. A Medium of Exchange
    b. A Measure of Value
    c. A Store of Value
  3. The Supply of Money
    a. M1 = Currency and Checkable Deposits
    b. M2 = M1 + Near Monies
    c. M3 = M2 + Large Time Deposits
  4. The Demand for Money
    a. Transactions Demand
    b. Asset Demand
    c. Total Demand
  5. The Market for Money
C. The U.S. Financial System
  1. A Brief History of Banking in the United States
  2. The Federal Reserve System
    a. The Role of the Federal Reserve
    b. The Structure of the Federal Reserve
    c. Activities of the Federal Reserve
    d. The Creation of Money
  3. Banks
    a. Definition
    b. Types and Roles
    c. Deregulation and Its Effects
D. Interest Rates
  1. The Definition of Interest
  2. Factors That Affect Interest Rates
    a. Supply and Demand for Money
    b. Expectations
  3. The Effects of High and Low Interest Rates
E. The Banking Industry Today—and Tomorrow

The purpose of this chapter is to introduce money and its functions, to offer an overview of the factors which affect the supply of and demand for money, and to introduce the role of the central bank.

AFTER COMPLETING THIS CHAPTER, YOU WILL BE ABLE TO:

1. Explain the three functions that money serves in an economy and describe how each applies to individuals and businesses.
2. Describe the three measures of the supply of money.
3. Graphically present and discuss the two factors that affect the demand for money.
4. Describe the impact of the Federal Reserve Bank on the economy.
5. Predict the effect on the economy of the creation and destruction of money.
6. Describe the role and effects of interest rates.

Money Matters

You may have noticed the play on words. This chapter is devoted to money matters: banking, checking accounts, interest rates, little things like that. It also admits, finally, that money really does matter. A lot of economists preach that money isn't as important as the real *factors of the economy, but of course they don't make these pronouncements for free. Money really does matter, and it is to this critical issue that we now turn.*

MONEY

The Definition of Money

You know from previous discussions that an economy can operate on the barter system. People can exchange goods with one another without the use of money. However, this becomes a real problem for any economy beyond a local, tribal operation. What is needed to help an economy to function and to grow is money. Money, therefore, can be thought of as a tool for the economy.

What is money anyway? **Money** is anything that is accepted by both parties as money. Throughout history, primitive peoples have used things such as bones, gems, boulders, and gold. One tribe today is so primitive that it uses little green pieces of paper with pictures of dead white males on them as money. It may be hard to imagine, but people in this tribe are willing to accept these little green pieces of paper in exchange for a day's labor, and stores are willing to accept them in exchange for goods. It is as if they actually believed that these little green pieces of paper were worth something.

The Functions of Money

In addition to honoring heros from the past and giving counterfeiters something to duplicate, money serves three major functions in the economy. Any one of these would make money a useful tool; that it accomplishes all three tasks makes it of great value.

A Medium of Exchange. Money serves as a medium of exchange. Money allows people to trade the goods they produce for the goods that others make. Because they can trade, money allows people to specialize, to produce one product very efficiently, and to trade for the other things they need. Specialization allows the economy to grow as people generate a surplus. This function of money allows geographic separation between two trading partners. You probably have never met the farmer who produces the oranges you buy. He or she is out there somewhere, but a level of impersonality arises in the economy through the use of money. In sum, money as a medium of exchange allows a great variety of goods to be produced and traded in an efficient manner.

A Measure of Value. Money serves as a measure of value. When barter is the rule, people must calculate the price of each good in terms of every other good. One fish = 2 loaves of bread = 1/30 of a soothing root prepared to ease a toothache. Money provides a single price system that makes the assessment of relative value much simpler. You can measure with money prices; you know that one fish costs $2, a loaf of bread costs $1, and a dental check-up costs $60. The same ratio applies as in the barter economy, but you don't have to calculate each price every time you want to make a purchase. This feature of money allows people to compare the relative worth of different goods, to more easily pay debts that are owed, and to calculate the size of the gross national product.

A Store of Value. The third function of money is to serve as a store of value. Money allows people to accumulate wealth. Dairy farmers who want to accumulate wealth for the future would find that difficult in a barter economy. They can't really

---

Money
Anything that is accepted by both parties in trade.

save their own output. Milk won't store for any length of time, and even cheese will eventually go bad. The farmers must convert their output into something they can store, something such as gold, jewels, or money. This function of money also works well for the overall economy. Because people can accumulate wealth, individuals and businesses can make investments and stimulate economic growth.

All in all, money is a good thing. It enables people to exchange more goods by reducing the cost of exchange (no calculations each time they make a trade). If something costs less, people buy more, so exchange is encouraged through the use of money. They also can specialize more. And, they can accumulate for investment. All of these lead to increased personal and national wealth.

> Money is anything that is accepted by both parties in trade. Money serves as:
> - A medium of exchange
> - A measure of value
> - A store of value

The Supply of Money

What is money? Anything people say is money. While that may technically be a correct definition, it is pretty loose. If we are to understand what money really is in today's economy, we need to tighten the definition a bit.

Three types of money exist in the economy. Economists call these M1, M2, and M3. Each classification of money yields a different perspective on the supply of assets readily available to our economy.

M1
All currency, both coins and paper, and checkable deposits.

M1 = Currency and Checkable Deposits. The basic type of money for the average consumer is M1. **M1** includes all currency, both coins and paper money, and checkable deposits (bank deposits on which checks can be written). Checkable deposits permit the maximum of convenience and safety; deposits are insured and transmittal is protected. This type of money is the easiest to get your hands on; it is immediately accessible to its owner. Coins comprise about 3 percent of M1, paper money is another 28 percent, and checkable deposits make up the remaining 69 percent.

M2
M1 and highly liquid financial assets.

M2 = M1 + Near Monies. The second type or category of money is called **M2** and consists of M1 plus highly liquid financial assets. These latter are money market funds, savings deposits, and small time deposits (under $100,000) that are quickly, although not immediately, accessible to the owner.

M3
M2 and large time deposits.

M3 = M2 + Large Time Deposits. M3 is the most expansive definition of money. It encompasses M2 plus large time deposits (over $100,000) held in commercial banks and thrift institutions and institutional money market funds.

Notably absent from this discussion are credit cards. Even though people are encouraged to "think of it as money," a credit card is *not* money but a way of getting a loan. Having credit cards readily available does not increase the supply of money but may, in fact, reduce the demand for currency as people substitute credit card purchases for cash purchases.

Finally, one additional type of asset must be included in the discussion of money. Nonmoney liquid assets also exist in the economy. Savings bonds, Treasury securities, and commercial paper are included in liquid assets. These assets are not immediately accessible (they have a fixed due date some time in the future), but they are extremely secure and individuals and businesses may borrow against them.

If numbers are added to these words about money, the result is Figure 17.1. Figure 17.1 provides a breakdown of the components of the overall money supply

FIGURE 17.1
Source: Board of Governors of the Federal Reserve System

	United States Money Supply—1994		
	Type of Money	Amount in Billions	Percent of Total
	Currency and travelers checks	$ 362	8.4
PLUS	Checkable deposits	+ 785	18.3
EQUALS	M1	$1,148	(26.7)
PLUS	Near monies	+ 2,465	57.3
EQUALS	M2	$3,613	(83.9)
PLUS	Large time deposits	+ 689	16.0
EQUALS	M3	$4,302	(100.0)

as of 1994. As you can see, highly liquid assets (near monies) are the largest portion of the overall money supply and currency is the smallest. About 90 percent of the currency is in the form of paper money and 10 percent is in coins. What doesn't appear on the table is the fact that about 90 percent of the dollar volume of transactions is by checks. This percentage will be decreasing as electronic funds transfers continue to expand.

A final comment about Figure 17.1 has to do with nonmoney liquid assets. This collection of savings bonds, Treasury securities, and commercial paper totaled about $981 billion in 1994, which brings the total financial asset amount to $5,283 billion.

While in the short run the supply of money may be considered to be fixed, it is not fixed for all time. As you will see shortly, a number of factors determine the overall supply of money, and these factors can do much to affect the overall economy.

Core-Info

The money supply consists of three components:
- M1 = Currency and checkable deposits
- M2 = M1 + highly liquid financial assets
- M3 = M2 + large time deposits

The Demand for Money

As *The Hobbit's* Gollum would say, "We wants money." And we do. Businesses and individuals both want and need money to survive and to grow. There are two distinct types of demand for money, transactions demand and asset demand.

Transactions Demand (Dt). To survive in a nonbarter economy, people need money to buy goods. That is what is known as **transactions demand.** Given their tastes and preferences, the amount of money that people will need for transactions demand is determined by the size of the economy. The larger the economy, the greater is the transactions demand for money.

Asset Demand (Da). In addition to a need for money to make transactions, there is a cost to holding money. Money does not earn interest, investments do. Therefore, an opportunity cost is involved in having money on hand. If interest rates are high, the demand for money is low as people invest their funds where they can get a return. If interest rates are low, people will hold onto their money rather than face the risk involved and have to deal with the inconvenience of having money tied up. Therefore, the **asset demand** for money is inversely related to the

---

Transactions Demand
The demand for money in order to buy goods. It is directly related to the size of the economy.

Asset Demand
Money held rather than invested. It is inversely related to the interest rate.

FIGURE 17.2

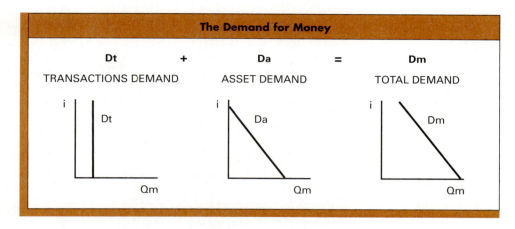

interest rate. The higher the interest rate, the lower the asset demand for money. The lower the interest rate, the higher the asset demand.

Total Demand (Dm). To determine the total demand for money, economists add the transactions demand to the asset demand.

Figure 17.2 presents all three pieces of the demand for the money equation. As can be seen, the transactions demand is a fixed amount based on the size of the economy and people's spending and saving habits. This is fixed in the short run. The asset demand varies based on the interest rate and is inversely related to it; the higher the interest rate, the less money people want to keep on hand. The **total demand** is the sum of the asset demand and the transactions demand. These may be obtained by adding the two curves horizontally just as you would sum up individual demand curves to get the total demand for a product.

Total Demand
The sum of the asset demand and the transactions demand.

Core-Info

There are two specific types of demand for money:
- Transactions demand—money needed to buy goods
- Asset demand—money held rather than invested

The total demand for money is the sum of transactions demand and asset demand.

The Market for Money

As with any commodity, the market for money is determined by the interaction of the supply of money with the demand for money. You can see this relationship in Figure 17.3. Here, the fixed (in the short run) supply of money is seen as a vertical line. The quantity of money supplied does not change regardless of what the interest rate is. The total demand for money curve has been overlaid on the supply of money curve. The intersection of the two curves yields the overall interest rate that will exist in the market. If the economy grows and additional funds are needed to conduct daily transactions, the demand for money curve would move outward to the right and the interest rate would rise. If extra money is printed by the government and dumped on the market, the supply of money curve would also move outward to the right and the interest rate would decline. Yet again, supply and demand rule.

THE U.S. FINANCIAL SYSTEM

A Brief History of Banking in the United States

It is no surprise that people want money. The problem is that people want money so much that they will do almost anything to create it. In a barter system, this is

FIGURE 17.3

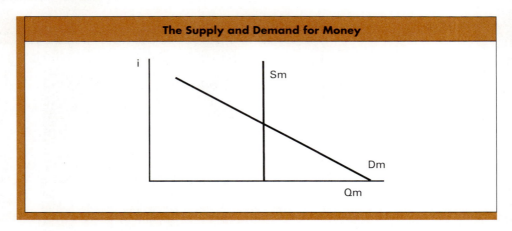

no problem. People exchange goods for goods, so the creation of additional goods to exchange benefits the creator and the economy. With money, things change. People will create money in an attempt to obtain more goods. Since money is not inherently of worth, the creation of money itself does nothing to benefit the economy; it only benefits the creator. Unless there are some controls on the creation of money, therefore, rampant inflation results as people make more and more of it until it becomes worthless. Governments, which have the power to coerce people into their ways of thinking, have taken control of the money supply for most of recorded history.

The use of gold for exchange has been common for millennia. For whatever reason, people like gold and have been willing to accept it in exchange for goods with some useful value. A number of problems are associated with uncontrolled gold, however. Carrying it about to make transactions is unsafe, and lugging large quantities to make large purchases is very difficult. In addition, few people can really distinguish between pure gold and adulterated gold. To get around this, some goldsmiths with storage vaults began to issue pieces of paper to people who deposited their gold with them. Thus began the basics of a paper money system.

Until recent years, most economies with exchangeable currencies have operated with a specie-backed currency, a currency that is linked to a nonmonetary commodity such as gold or silver. One dollar, for instance, might be defined to be equal to $1/35$ of an ounce of gold. When other nations linked their currencies similarly (one British pound might be defined as equal to $1/7$ of an ounce of gold), this gave people an established international exchange system. This linkage was followed in general from 1821 to 1973. The problem with this approach, of course, is that the amount of money in circulation is controlled by an outside factor that is not linked to the economy itself. If the production of gold is low (as was the case in the 1870s and 1880s) or if nonmonetary uses of the specie increase, the money supply grows very slowly and the economy experiences a general deflation. If, on the other hand, there are discoveries of new gold, a period of rapid money growth and inflation results. Clearly, control over the currency needs to extend beyond merely linking it to some external standard. The United States accomplished this through the Federal Reserve System, a body that is independent of government and which theoretically can operate without undue political or momentary pressures and can look to the long-run stability and growth of the economy.

The Federal Reserve System

Federal Reserve System
The system that oversees banking operations and controls the money supply.

The Role of the Federal Reserve. The role of the **Federal Reserve System** (affectionately known as "the Fed") is great. It encompasses all aspects of the money supply of the nation. Through its actions, the Federal Reserve supervises member banks, serves as the government's fiscal agent, holds deposits of mem-

CHAPTER 17 • MONEY, BANKS, AND THE INTEREST RATE 269

FIGURE 17.4
Through its board of governors and 12 Federal Reserve Banks, the Federal Reserve System either directly or indirectly controls the nation's banks on behalf of businesses and households.

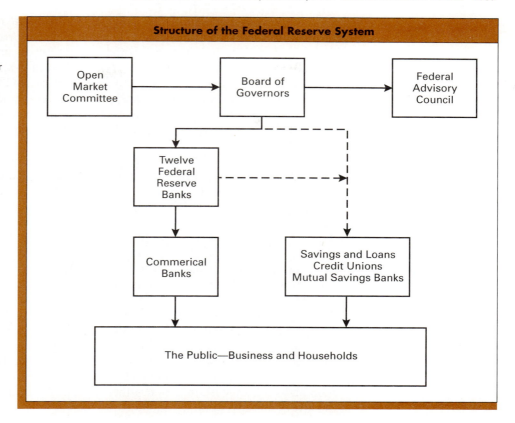

ber banks, provides a means for the collection of demand deposits (checks), and controls the money supply.

The Structure of the Federal Reserve. The Federal Reserve is to be independent of politics. Frankly, the goal is to keep the President and Congress from meddling too greatly in the economy. The Federal Reserve is managed by a seven-member Board of Governors appointed by the President and confirmed by the Senate. These governors have 14-year terms to allow them to accumulate a great deal of experience on the job, to provide for continuity across the years, and to insulate the Board from short-term political pressures.

The Federal Reserve is divided into 12 districts, each with a central bank. These banks are owned by the private sector but controlled by the federal government. The central banks loan to member banks, hold member bank deposits, and issue currency.

Activities of the Federal Reserve. The activities of the Federal Reserve System can be thought of as tools. The Federal Reserve is in place to facilitate the monetary sector of the economy and to help provide overall balance as needed to assure continued long-term growth. The tools of the Federal Reserve fall into three areas: major tools, minor tools, and moral suasion.

There are three major tools of monetary policy: open market operations, the reserve requirement, and the discount rate.

Open market operations—**Open market operations** are the buying and selling of government bonds by the Federal Reserve. If the Federal Reserve buys government bonds from member banks or from individuals, it puts more money in the hands of the sellers, the money supply is increased, and the interest rate falls. The economy can then move toward expansion. The reverse happens if the Federal Reserve sells government securities that it owns.

Open Market Operations
The buying and selling of government bonds by the Federal Reserve from member banks to control the money supply and interest rate.

Reserve Requirement
The portion of a bank's deposits that the bank is required to keep on hand and which it is unable to lend to customers.

Reserve requirement—The **reserve requirement** is the portion of a bank's deposits that the bank is required to keep on hand (to save). The remaining portion is available to loan to borrowers. If the Federal Reserve raises the reserve requirement, banks must hold onto more of their deposits and lend less to borrowers. This will cause the economy to contract (or not grow as rapidly). If the Federal Reserve lowers the reserve requirement, banks are required to hold less money on hand and can lend out more of their deposits to borrowers. This will cause the economy to grow. This is an extremely powerful tool of the Federal Reserve and is adjusted very infrequently.

Discount rate—Member banks can borrow money from the Federal Reserve. As with any loan, they pay interest for the privilege. This interest rate is called the **discount rate.** If the discount rate is low or falls, banks are encouraged to borrow money from the Federal Reserve to make more loans available to their customers. When more loans are made, the economy can expand. If the discount rate is high, banks tend to borrow less and the economy's growth is slowed. The discount rate has varied from 1 percent to more than 13 percent since 1947.

Discount Rate
The interest paid by banks on money borrowed from the Federal Reserve.

In addition to the major tools at the disposal of the Federal Reserve, there are two minor ones. The Federal Reserve can change some requirements of the stock market (in particular the margin requirements), and it can alter consumer credit regulations. These two tools act indirectly, but they can affect the direction of the overall economy.

The final monetary tool at the disposal of the Federal Reserve is called **moral suasion.** Moral suasion means convincing others that your way of thinking is correct. It generally implies a bit of threat if the suggestion is not followed. The Federal Reserve can use moral suasion to convince member banks to follow certain paths if they wish to avoid further regulation, for instance. Moral suasion can be a very effective tool.

Moral Suasion
The means—generally a compelling argument or a veiled threat—by which member banks are convinced by the Federal Reserve to follow a certain path.

The Creation of Money. A major function of the Federal Reserve System is to control the creation of money. As you have seen, an expanding money supply may help an economy to grow, but a money supply that grows too rapidly can lead to inflation. The economy needs a level of stability and predictability in this area as it does in the other critical areas if it is to prosper. The Federal Reserve System helps to provide this stability.

Fractional reserves—The major way in which money is created is through a **fractional reserve system.** When a customer deposits money in a bank, the bank has two choices: it may lend the money to a borrower or it may keep the money in its vaults. If the bank hoards the money, nothing happens. The money may be safe but it earns no interest. If the bank lends all of the money to another customer, then effectively two people have control of the one deposit. The depositor has control and can withdraw the money any time he or she desires and the borrower can use the money as he or she sees fit. The money has in effect been multiplied. Money has been created.

Fractional Reserves
The means by which banks are required to maintain only a portion of a deposit and may lend the remaining portion to customers.

Reserve ratios and multipliers—The reserve is the amount of money (the percent of the bank's deposits) which the bank must keep on deposit in its own vaults or those of the central bank and which it cannot lend to another customer. The **reserve ratio,** therefore, is:

Reserve Ratio
The minimum percent of a bank's deposits that must be kept in the bank's vault and which may not be loaned.

$$R = \text{Reserve ratio} = \frac{\text{Required reserves}}{\text{Total deposits}}$$

The usual percentage as established by the Federal Reserve is 20 percent. This means that each bank must retain at least 20 percent of each deposit and can lend no more than 80 percent. Thus, the bank can multiply the initial deposit by lending what it can to another customer. Money is created in this manner. This process cumulates as subsequent customers deposit their funds and other customers borrow money.

By this method, the entire banking system, guided by the Federal Reserve, which establishes the required reserve ratio, can multiply the initial deposit so

FIGURE 17.5

Fractional Reserves and the Money Multiplier

Initial deposit ——— $100
Required reserve (20%) — $ 20
Available for lending ——— $ 80
    Loaned and borrowed ——— $80
    Required reserve (20%) ——— $16
    Available for lending ——— $64
        Loaned and borrowed ——— $64
        Required reserve (20%) ——— $12.80
        Available for lending ——— $51.20
            Loaned and borrowed ——— $51.20
            Required reserve (20%) ——— $10.24
            Available for lending ——— $40.96
                Loaned and borrowed ——— $40.96
                Required reserve (20%) ——— $ 8.19
                Available for lending ——— $32.77
                    Loaned and borrowed ——— $32.77
                    Required reserve (20%) ——— $ 6.55
                    Available for lending ——— $26.22
Etc.

that the economy grows. Figure 17.5 shows this effect. With a required reserve ratio of 20 percent, an initial deposit of $100 is divided into $20 to be kept in the bank's vault and $80 to be loaned to a customer. When this $80 is borrowed, the customer can either save the money or can spend it in which case the merchant deposits it in a bank. The second bank is required to retain 20 percent of this deposit, so $16 is kept and $64 is loaned. The process will continue *ad infinitum* as the funds are loaned and deposited, loaned and deposited over and over again.

The net result of the fractional reserve system is that the banking system creates money. An equation, called the **money multiplier** helps to show how much the initial deposit (also called an "injection") will be multiplied. That equation is:

Money Multiplier
The fraction, 1 divided by the required reserve ratio, which shows how much an initial deposit can be multiplied by a bank.

$$\text{Monetary multiplier} = \frac{1}{R} = \frac{1}{\text{Required reserve ratio}}$$

Using the example from Figure 17.5, the money multiplier would be:

$$\text{Monetary multiplier} = \frac{1}{R} = \frac{1}{.20} = 5$$

Thus, with a reserve ratio of 20 percent, the money multiplier is 5; that is, a $1 deposit in a bank will result in the creation of $4 additional dollars in the economy. With this, the economy can grow. If you want to create even more money so the economy can grow even more rapidly, you can reduce the reserve ratio. If the reserve ratio were 10 percent, for instance, the money multiplier would be 10 and the money supply would greatly increase.

The reverse would also be true, however. Money can be taken from the economy. The same money multiplier that expands the money supply when there is an injection or addition to the banks will result in a decrease in the money supply when there is a leakage. If consumers do not trust banks and begin to hoard their cash, for instance, banks deposits are reduced and the overall money supply contracts. (NOTE: Consumers who fear that bad times are coming and take their money out of the bank in advance *actually cause* the bad times to come.)

The Hidden American Dollar

Dollars are really quite useful, aren't they? People use them as one way, the main way really, to pay bills and to save for tomorrow. Americans are not the only people who find dollars useful. A recent study by the Federal Reserve Bank of Cleveland has found that the majority of U.S. currency ($260 billion out of the $375 billion in U.S. coins and bills) is held by foreigners.[1] Before you panic, read on.

The chart below shows the percentage of U.S. currency that has been held by foreigners over the past 35 years. You will note a steady increase until today when more than two thirds of all dollar bills are in the hands of non-Americans. Not surprisingly, the reasons why the percentage has risen steadily, then flattened in the past few years, has to do with the basic factors involved in the functions of money. As you remember, money serves three functions: it is a medium of exchange, a measure of value, and a store of value. For Americans, the first two factors predominate, and they hold money mostly for transactions purposes. Foreign dollar holders, on the other hand, keep American currency primarily because of its role as a store of value.

Foreigners find American money attractive because of its universal acceptability and its security. As to the dollar's acceptability, not many people are willing to accept the Birr or the Kyat, the Koruna or the Kwacha, the Loti or the Manat, the Pa'anga or the Tenge in exchange for real goods.[2] "Dollar," however, apparently has a *nice* ring to it.

A number of factors are involved in security. One factor is inflation. The U.S. average rate of inflation since 1980 has been 5.9 percent per year. By way of contrast, Italy's inflation rate was 16.3 percent per year between 1975 and 1980, and Spain's was 12.2 percent per year between 1980 and 1985. For further perspective, in 1994 the inflation rate in Kenya was 29 percent, in Peru 24 percent, in Senegal 32 percent, in Turkey 106 percent, and in Romania 136 percent. Holding dollars, which decreased in value by only 2.6 percent in 1994, made much more sense for people in these countries than holding their own currencies. In addition, political instability abroad has increased the attractiveness of dollars to business and political leaders who might have to make a quick exit if the opposite party wins. Finally, the possibility of currency debasement and recalls make holding some currencies extremely risky.

Why, after 30 years of steadily increasing demand for American dollars, has there been a flattening of the curve in the past five years? Demand cooled for the same reason that people had preferred U.S. currency in the first place—the perception of stability. Not long ago, the U.S. Treasury announced that it would redesign the $100 bill to help prevent counterfeiting. Despite the fact that the Treasury has spent millions of dollars and has set up toll-free hotlines to convince people around the world that the old $100 bill will be accepted forever, some people have feared the worst and have not wanted to hold dollars.

Are foreign currency holdings of this magnitude a problem? Theoretically, everybody holding U.S. dollars could try to cash them in at the same time and bring inflationary pressure to the economy (more money available to purchase the same amount of goods), but this is highly unlikely. The real impact is that foreign dollar holders are in effect making an interest-free loan to the United States. Dollar bills are a debt of the U.S. government, and if foreigners hold dollars, the U.S. does not have to pay interest on the amount held. The net effect, therefore, is a reduced interest bill for the U.S. government and a reduced tax bill for U.S. taxpayers. It has been estimated that the tax burden is between $15 and $20 lower because of foreign currency holdings.

Thus, when anybody asks you where all our money has gone, you can say, "to a far, far-away land"—and be thankful.

Year	Estimated Percent of U.S. Currency Held Abroad
1960	39
1970	41
1975	45
1980	52
1985	61
1990	68
1995	69

1. Carlson, John B., and Keen, Benjamin D. "Where Is All the U.S. Currency Hiding?" *Economic Commentary*, Federal Reserve Bank of Cleveland (April 15, 1996).
2. Currency units from the nations of Eritrea, Myanmar, Slovakia, Zambia, Lesotho, Turkmenistan, Tonga, and Kazakhstan, respectively.

The Federal Reserve System applies controls to make fractional reserve banking and the money multiplier work to the economy's overall benefit. When times are good, banks have a tendency to lend everything they can as rapidly as possible to earn as much profits as might be available. This can lead to an overstimulation of the economy. When times are bad, banks tend to cut back on their

Core-Info

The Federal Reserve serves to regulate banks, bring stability to the economy, and create money. The Federal Reserve regulates and stabilizes by maintaining standards, open market operations, the reserve requirement, and the discount rate. Through the fractional reserve approach, money may be created or destroyed.

lending because of the added risk of default on the part of borrowers. This can lead to a recession in the economy. Profit-seeking banks can exacerbate the business cycle. The Federal Reserve System can help to keep this tendency in check.

Banks

Definition. The term *bank* is vague and has become more vague today. Generally speaking, a **bank** is a financial institution that receives deposits, makes loans, and provides other financial assistance. With the expansion of money management services by a number of different types of institutions, the term is extremely difficult to pin down. Are stock brokerage firms that accept monthly deposits from your paycheck and let you write requests for funds on pieces of paper that look very much like checks banks or are they something else? The term *bank* has definitely expanded in recent years.

Types and Roles. Whatever those new institutions are, there are three main types of what we traditionally call banks. The first is the **commercial banks.** Commercial banks take deposits from businesses and individuals and lend the money back to these groups for the purchase of business capital and durable goods such as automobiles. The second type of bank is the **savings and loan** institution. These businesses accept deposits and use them in particular to finance home mortgages. Finally, **credit unions** are businesses in which groups of members, usually people who work for or belong to the same organization, deposit their funds and then can borrow money to finance purchases.

Twenty-five years ago, only commercial banks were authorized to have checking accounts, but they could not pay interest on the balances. In a competitive move, savings and loans developed NOW (negotiable order of withdrawal) accounts, and credit unions developed share draft accounts. These accounts were similar to checking accounts but, because these institutions were outside the commercial banking system, they could pay interest. Today, since deregulation, all types of banks are permitted to make checking accounts available to their customers.

There are some 25,537 banking institutions in the country. All are regulated either directly or indirectly by the Federal Reserve. (While savings and loan institutions are not members of the Federal Reserve System, they must meet the same requirements as commercial banks.) With more than 70,000 banks and branches plus automatic teller machines, you are never more than a few miles away from access to the international banking community. Figure 17.6 lists the type of banks and their assets in the United States. The size of the numbers alone makes them important.

Bank
A financial institution that receives deposits, makes loans, and provides other financial assistance.

Commercial Bank
A financial institution that takes deposits from businesses and individuals and loans the money back to these groups for the purchase of business capital and durable goods.

Savings and Loan
A financial institution that accepts deposits and uses them to finance home mortgages.

Credit Union
Membership organizations in which members' deposits are loaned to members for various reasons.

FIGURE 17.6
Source: Board of Governors of the Federal Reserve System

Banks in the United States—1993		
Type of Institution	Number	Assets (in billions)
Commercial banks	10,958	$3,706.2
Savings institutions	2,262	1,000.9
Credit unions	12,317	277.2
TOTAL	25,537	$4,984.3

Deregulation
The removal of many restrictions and regulations.

DIDMCA
(Depository Institutions Deregulation and Monetary Control Act) The Act by which Congress deregulated financial institutions in the United States.

Deregulation and its effects. Bank managers are like managers anywhere else: they are always trying to make a profit. Banks earn profits when the money they receive in interest payments from loans exceeds their operating expenses plus the money they must pay in interest to their depositors. Thus, banks are always looking for new ways to generate business. The earlier example of checking account changes is a good illustration. Because a lot of resources are wasted by businesses in trying to work around regulations, the banking industry was deregulated in 1980 under the Depository Institutions Deregulation and Monetary Control Act **(DIDMCA).** This act brought a greater equality to commercial banks, savings and loans, and credit unions. All three types of banking institutions can now offer checking accounts and credit cards and make real estate and commercial loans.

The whole banking industry is a bit of a house of cards. In the example in Figure 17.5, if the banks have loaned all of their excess reserves and one of the borrowers defaults, the result can bring a major disruption to the whole chain. When a series of bad banking decisions leads many borrowers to default, the entire banking system can be thrown into a crisis as illustrated by the savings and loan industry in the 1980s. During that boom time, savings and loan officials loaned great sums of money to borrowers to purchase real estate. When a recession hit and real estate values fell, many borrowers were forced to declare bankruptcy. The result was that banks did not have sufficient funds to pay their depositors, and many failed. In 1988 alone, 221 banks with assets of more than $52 billion failed, and another 1,406 banks with assets of more than $350 billion were declared to be "problem banks." The U.S. government—actually of course the taxpayers—paid billions of dollars over the past ten years to clean up the mess. Recent changes in banking regulations should preclude a return of those great difficulties.

Core-Info

A bank is a financial institution that receives deposits, makes loans, and provides other financial assistance. The three basic types of banks are commercial banks, savings and loan institutions, and credit unions. Because of deregulation, they all compete with one another.

INTEREST RATES

The Definition of Interest

Interest
The cost of money.

The definition of **interest** is simple: it is the cost of money. For borrowers, interest is the cost of having money and the goods it will provide today rather than waiting until the future. For lenders, interest is what they receive to induce them to give up the use of their money now and wait until the future to have access to it. Interest, therefore, displays time preference. People would rather have money today than to wait and have it at some date in the future. If they are to delay having their money, they expect some compensation.

FACTORS THAT AFFECT INTEREST RATES

You have already studied the factors that affect interest rates at the microeconomic level. The three factors are risk, the cost of making the loan, and time. The riskier the loan, the higher the rate of interest will be. The higher the cost of making the loan relative to the amount of the loan, the higher the interest rate will be. The longer the term of the loan, the higher the interest rate. At the macroeconomic level, the general interest rate, not the rate of interest on individual loans, is the key. Therefore, the three microfactors are replaced by two: the supply and demand for money and expectations. The Federal Reserve can attempt to establish an interest rate in the money market, but unless it is supported by these two factors, it will not last long.

Supply and Demand for Money

If the supply of money is plentiful and there is much available to be loaned, the interest rate will be low. Similarly, if the demand for money is low and no one is interested in borrowing, the interest rate will be low. If the supply of money is tight or the demand for money is high, however, the interest rate will be high. Figure 17.3 displays this relationship quite clearly.

Expectations

In addition to the supply of and demand for money, expectations play a part in establishing the general interest rate. You don't have to subscribe to the rational expectations theory to know that consumer and business expectations can affect the economy. If consumers expect interest rates to climb in the future, they will borrow today while interest rates are low rather than pay higher rates in the future. This expectation will increase the demand for borrowed money and drive up the interest rate. If, on the other hand, people feel that interest rates will be lower next year than they are this year, they will delay borrowing money to make purchases until the interest rate has come down. Expectations, therefore, are very much a part of establishing the general interest rate, and once again, individuals and their beliefs and preferences are in charge.

The Effects of High and Low Interest Rates

The interest rate has a profound effect on the economy. A high interest rate discourages borrowers but encourages savers and lenders. A low interest rate encourages current borrowing and discourages saving and lending. Encouraging or discouraging individuals and businesses from borrowing to make purchases or from investing can dramatically boost or stifle the economy. When the multiplier effect is added, each dollar of discouraged investment results in a much larger decrease in the strength of the economy.

> Core-Info
>
> The rate of interest in the market is ultimately determined by the supply and demand for money coupled with peoples' expectations about the future.

THE BANKING INDUSTRY TODAY—AND TOMORROW

The banking industry has undergone a dramatic change in recent years. From a highly regulated and almost backward industry, the banking sector has leapt into the 21st century. With its new found freedom to act, the banking sector has been expanding its influence and has been competing very effectively with other portions of the financial sector. With the introduction of electronic banking at ATM machines in supermarkets and through home computers, the industry is likely to continue its strong growth well into the future.

Yes, money does matter. You were right all along.

SUMMARY

- Money is whatever people are willing to use in exchange. It has varied from stones to gold to paper currency.
- The three functions that money plays in the economy are as a medium of exchange, a measure of value, and a store of value.

- The three types of money are called M1 (currency and demand deposits), M2 (M1 plus near monies), and M3 (M2 plus large time deposits).
- The total demand for money is composed of the transactions demand, a fixed amount given the size of the economy, and asset demand, inversely related to the rate of interest.
- The role of the Federal Reserve Bank is to supervise member banks, to serve as the government's fiscal agent, to hold the deposits of member banks, to provide a mechanism for the collection of demand deposits (checks), and to control the supply of money.
- Through the existence of a fractional reserve monetary system and by controlling the reserve ratio, the Federal Reserve Bank can control the supply of money with relative ease.
- Interest rates serve to ration money to people with a strong current time preference. Those who believe they have good investment opportunities will pay interest to have funds available today.

KEY TERMS

Asset demand for money
Bank
Commercial bank
Credit union
Deregulation
DIDMCA
Discount rate
Federal Reserve System
Fractional reserves
Interest
M1
M2
M3
Money
Money multiplier
Moral suasion
Open market operations
Reserve ratio
Reserve requirement
Savings and loan
Total demand
Transactions demand for money

REVIEW QUESTIONS

1. Money can be thought of as a tool for the economy. Discuss the three major functions of money in the economy.
2. Identify and define the three types of money as classified by economists.
3. Explain the two distinct types of demand for money.
4. What are the major functions of the Federal Reserve Bank?
5. What are the three major tools of monetary policy?
6. What is the relationship of fractional reserves to the creation of money?
7. What are the major reasons for bank deregulation?
8. What are the factors that affect the overall rate of interest?

PROBLEM-SOLVING PRACTICE

1. If a significant proportion of U.S. cash is out of circulation in foreign countries, what are the implications for U.S. monetary policy?
2. Present a graphical analysis of the following:
   (a) the supply of money
   (b) the transactions demand for money
   (c) the asset demand for money
   (d) the economic determination of the interest rate

3. The money supply is controlled through the reserve requirement.
   (a) Define reserve requirement.
   (b) If the reserve requirement is 10% and there are reserves of $200 million in the banking system, what is the maximum amount of bank deposits that could exist?
   (c) If the reserve requirement is changed to 5% with the same level of required reserves in the banking system, what is the new maximum value of bank deposits the banking system could have?
   (d) Calculate the money multipliers for Parts (b) and (c).

CHAPTER 18

Economic Growth, Development, and Inflation

CHAPTER OUTLINE

A. Economic Growth
  1. The Definition of Growth
     a. Expansion
     b. Growth
  2. Business Cycles
     a. Definition
     b. Causes
     c. Effects
  3. Sources of Growth
  4. Measuring Growth
  5. The Effects of Growth
B. Economic Development
  1. Definition
  2. Characteristics of Underdevelopment
     a. Low Per Capita Income
     b. Large Agricultural Sector
     c. Low Savings Rates
     d. Rapid Population Growth
     e. Limited Specialization of the Work Force
  3. The Desirability of Development
     a. Per Capita Income Increases
     b. Population Growth Rate Decreases
     c. Other Benefits
  4. Measuring Development
  5. The Keys to Economic Development
  6. Sources of Economic Development
     a. Quantity of Inputs
     b. Productivity Improvements
  7. The Special Role of Government
  8. The Effects of Economic Development
C. Inflation
  1. Definition
  2. Types of Inflation
     a. Demand Pull
     b. Cost Push
  3. The Effects of Inflation
     a. Anticipated Inflation
     b. Unanticipated Inflation
D. A Final Look at Growth and Development

The purpose of this chapter is to introduce the issues that surround economic growth, the business cycle, and inflation in the economy.

AFTER COMPLETING THIS CHAPTER, YOU WILL BE ABLE TO:

1. Describe the causes of the business cycle and summarize the cycle's impact on the economy.
2. Identify the characteristics of underdevelopment and describe the impact of underdevelopment on an economy.
3. Document the factors that affect economic growth.
4. Describe the two types of inflation.
5. Analyze the differential impact of anticipated and unanticipated inflation on worker lifestyles.

Economic Growth

So far, many of our discussions have approached economics as a static activity. We have looked at supply and demand, we have examined business firms, and we have considered the money supply. All of this has been accomplished as if we were taking a still photograph. The next step is to grab a video camera and take a moving picture. We need to look at an economy on the move and examine economic growth and development.

The Definition of Growth

Once again it pays to be careful with terminology. Some economists differentiate between economic expansion and economic growth. They see the differences as follows:

Expansion. Expansion means to add to the use of current resources. In this model, the economy adds land (by finding new sources of raw materials or using materials that were not used before), adds labor (by increasing the size of the labor force either through population growth or by changing working patterns), or adds capital (by increasing the stock of physical or human capital or both).

Growth. Growth in this model means increasing productivity, operating more efficiently with the resources that producers use or increasing the degree of specialization and technological change.

This discussion, rather than differentiate between the two, will treat both expansion and growth as economic growth. **Economic growth** will be defined as an increase in the gross national product per capita; an increase in real output.

> **Economic Growth**
> An increase in the gross national product per capita; an increase in real income.

Business Cycles

As you examine economic growth, it is important to differentiate it from changes in the economy solely due to the business cycle.

Definition. The **business cycle** is the recurring ups and downs in the economy that take place over time. An economy naturally goes through periods of expansion followed by a peak followed by a recession, a trough, then an expansion again. These business cycles have occurred in the U.S. economy ever since its beginning. The business cycle can be thought of as an exaggerated seasonal swing that shows up in the retail markets during Christmas or new car introduction time. Business cycles occur over longer periods than these.

> **Business Cycle**
> The recurring ups and downs in the economy that take place over time.

Causes. There is no one fixed theory as to why business cycles occur. Sometimes they are related to wars, with an expansion during wartime followed by a recession when the war ends and military spending decreases. In addition, technological innovation can lead to an expansive period as people go into the marketplace to buy the new automobile, television, or other new product. Certainly governments have caused business cycles by creating too much money and causing expansions or by restricting the supply of money and causing a recession. However, the major cause of the business cycle is believed to be aggregate demand, in particular consumer spending. When consumer spending is high, businesses can expand their current operations and purchase capital goods for future expansion. When consumer spending declines, businesses typically stop all capital acquisition, and the economy declines as a result.

Effects. The effects of the business cycle vary significantly among consumers and industries. While all areas of the economy are hit by a downturn, some industries and their workers feel the effects more severely. Industries which produce capital goods and consumer durable goods such as automobiles are typically most affected. Businesses and consumers can delay these purchases until after the recession ends, and so are likely to do so. Consumer nondurables such as food and basic clothing are generally less affected because consumers cannot postpone their purchases until next year. When the upturn comes, nondurable purchases grow very little but durable goods purchases expand significantly. Finally, as the industries face decreases in demand, they will lay off workers, so those employed in durable goods manufacture will typically face a period of unemployment during a recession, compounding the effects of the recession on the family and the nation.

Sources of Growth

As you might expect, there are two basic sources of economic growth: supply and demand. Supply factors affecting economic growth include the quantity and quality of natural and human resources, the stock of capital goods, and technological change. Demand factors include the full employment and efficient use of resources. Taken singly or in concert, supply factors can help to push the production possibilities curve outward. Demand factors, on the other hand, can push a nation out to the production possibilities curve if it has been operating inside the curve rather than on its surface.

Measuring Growth

Economic growth has been defined as an increase in the gross national product. The growth rate compares the economy's position this year to its status last year. This calculation is laid out in the equation that follows. To calculate the growth rate, subtract last year's gross national product from this year's gross national product and divide the result by last year's amount. The result is the percentage by which the economy is larger than last year's gross national product.

$$\text{Growth rate} = \frac{GNP2 - GNP1}{GNP1}$$

The Effects of Growth

Economic growth is important in an economy. Growth increases the standard of living for the nation; the per capita income rises. Growth allows the nation to meet new demands, such as the demand for additional health care or for improved highways. Growth permits a nation to begin new programs such as space exploration. Finally, growth today allows an economy to grow in the future without having to sacrifice consumer goods today.

Core-Info

Economic growth is not the normal ups-and-downs of the business cycle but a general, sustained increase in the gross national product per capita.

ECONOMIC DEVELOPMENT

Economic growth in a developed country is one thing. Economic development in a poor country is something very different. Whereas the annual per capita income in the United States is more than $24,000, the annual per capita income in Bangladesh is about $200. Regardless of how much you want to argue that much of the Bangladeshi economy operates outside the market, that people there have chosen leisure rather than work, or that they are happy with their simple lifestyles, $200 per year isn't very much. In fact, it is abject, crushing poverty on a scale that U.S. citizens can't begin to imagine. While the United States has very real poverty in the rural south and in urban centers, it is nothing to compare with the poverty experienced in Bangladesh, Sudan ($196), Kenya ($189), Nepal ($139), Tanzania ($86), Mozambique ($74), or Ethiopia ($66). The fact is that the per capita incomes in a number of these nations are actually *declining*. Finally, it may be instructive to know that the national income of the United States is significantly greater than that of all developing nations combined.

FIGURE 18.1
Source: International Bank for Reconstruction and Development and the U.S. Bureau of the Census

Comparative International Statistics—1993			
Country	Per Capita Income	Population Growth Rate	Life Expectancy
Bangladesh	$ 200	2.6	55.5
Sudan	$ 196	3.3	54.7
Kenya	$ 189	3.7	52.4
Nepal	$ 139	2.4	53.1
Tanzania	$ 86	3.0	42.5
Mozambique	$ 74	2.5	49.0
Ethiopia	$ 66	2.8	50.0
United States	$24,580	0.9	76.0

Economic Development
The process of increasing skills, capital, and productivity to permanently increase the rate of economic growth.

Underdevelopment
A situation of national poverty characterized by an economy with low per capita income and savings rates, a large agricultural sector, rapid population growth, and a limited specialization of the workforce.

Vicious circle of poverty
The economic trap in which poor nations are held because of the conditions of underdevelopment.

Definition

Economic development is defined as the process of increasing labor and entrepreneurial skills, adding quantities of physical and human capital, and improving overall productivity so that the rate of economic growth per capita is permanently increased. This is not an easy process, as you will see, and it takes a high level of sustained commitment on the part of the citizens to make it occur.

Characteristics of Underdevelopment

Underdevelopment is a complex set of factors that affect a nation's economy. A number of characteristics are typical of underdeveloped nations. Among these are:

Low Per Capita Income. The level of per capita income is extremely low in underdeveloped countries. In fact most currently underdeveloped countries have had per capita incomes at essentially the same level for decades.

Large Agricultural Sector. The major productive sector in the economy is typically the agricultural sector. Earlier discussions in this book noted that agriculture is the first sector to develop in a nation with the manufacturing and service sectors coming into dominance only as an economy matures. Whereas in the United States only 3 percent of the labor force is engaged in agriculture, more than two thirds of most underdeveloped nations' labor forces work in that sector.

Low Savings Rates. Because per capita incomes are so low, the savings rate is likewise very low. It is unrealistic to expect that families who live on subsistence incomes can save money to be used by businesses to invest and help the economy to grow.

Rapid Population Growth. In addition to low incomes, most underdeveloped nations are saddled with very high birth and population growth rates. The factors related to these rates are social phenomena such as assuring that some children will live to maturity to carry on the family name, having family members to work in agriculture, and granting status to the family.

Limited Specialization of the Work Force. The final characteristic of underdeveloped countries is that the labor force is not as specialized as in the more developed economies. With a relatively unspecialized work force, the benefits of efficiency and exchange that are the foundation of the developed economies are lost.

These characteristics of underdeveloped countries lead to what is called the **"vicious circle of poverty."** Low incomes, high birth rates, low savings rates, large agricultural sectors, and low specialization all compound to help lock an economy in a perpetually underdeveloped state.

FIGURE 18.2
Economic development is not a nicety but a necessity for many nations. Per capita incomes are appallingly low in some countries. In a number of underdeveloped countries, real incomes have actually declined in the past decade making a bad situation even worse.

| The Poorest of the Poor: Gross National Product per Capita in 1993 Dollars ||||
Country	1985	1990	1993
Ethiopia	$ 70	$ 73	$ 66
Mozambique	61	70	74
Tanzania	78	85	86
Nepal	122	136	139
Kenya	198	214	189
Sudan	175	174	196
Bangladesh	175	190	200
Uganda	188	205	214
Madagascar	287	280	249
India	226	275	282
United States	$22,240	$24,290	$24,580

Figure 18.1 provides a quick comparison of the United States with a series of underdeveloped nations. Data for per capita income, the population growth rate, and life expectancy at birth show just how dramatic the differences are. High population growth rates mean that the underdeveloped countries must work very hard just to keep from slipping backward, and the low life expectancies in these nations mean that the productive life of the labor force is relatively short (in addition to the obvious concerns that these life expectancies imply for health care issues).

Core-Info

Economic underdevelopment traps the people of many nations in a cycle of low per capita income, a reliance on agriculture, a low savings rate, rapid population growth, and limited labor specialization.

The Desirability of Development

Economic development is a mixed blessing, of course. Old ways are broken down and family structures are changed forever. Rural areas decline and urban areas grow. Technology arrives and an unsullied environment departs. And yet, everyone wants economic development. Two key results of economic development make it all worthwhile:

Per Capita Income Increases. The amount of resources per person increases with economic development. People have more money with which to take control of their lives. Now, with increased funds, families can choose more education for a child, luxuries such as radios and bicycles, or a leak-proof roof over their house. Not only is the nation's long-term improvement assured with economic development, most individual families also find themselves significantly better off.

Population Growth Rate Decreases. The second benefit to economic development is the fact that the population rate decreases. High population rates are the effect—not the cause—of underdevelopment. As soon as economic development arrives, families begin to curtail the number of children they have. It is true that the cost of raising children goes up with economic development, but even more important is the fact that children are no longer needed to work the fields or to serve as their parents' "social security" program.

Other Benefits. Other benefits resulting from economic development include improved health care for the citizenry, widespread education and training opportunities, legal and political protections for individuals and businesses, and the opportunity to pursue spiritual and artistic endeavors more freely.

Measuring Development

As you would expect, it is tough to measure economic development. While the concept of gross national product per capita is fairly clear, what is not so clear is how to make the necessary international—and even intertemporal—comparisons that are required. Peoples' needs and tastes are different. A higher income is required in Minneapolis because of the relatively expensive housing than is needed in Manila where the climate is much kinder and gentler. In addition, much of the underdeveloped nation's economy does not go through the market, so an accurate measurement is difficult. As an economy develops and an increasing portion does go through the market and measurement is possible, we may overestimate the growth simply because the economy is being more accurately measured.

The Keys to Economic Development

There are a number of keys to achieving a sustained level of economic development. An efficient agricultural sector is essential. Until the agricultural sector can produce a surplus that permits the nation to feed itself while using fewer farm laborers, development will be difficult at best. Increased savings and investment rates are required. Without this, the adoption of new technologies will be impossible and the economy will remain mired in its past. The development of human capital is required. More efficient, productive, trained workers are needed to participate in and lead the new technologies that will be introduced. Undergirding all of this must be an effective price system that operates to efficiently allocate resources where they can be the most productive and an institutional setting that permits development to happen. Unless both the people and the government actively desire economic development, it will not happen.

Sources of Economic Development

Edward Denison has completed a major study of the sources of economic growth in the United States from 1929 to 1982.[1] The results can provide guidance for econ-

FIGURE 18.3
The portion of a consumer's budget that is spent on food is often a measure for economic development: the lower the percentage, the more developed the country is felt to be. *Source:* U.S. Department of Agriculture

Spending on Food and Alcoholic Beverages as a Percent of Total Consumer Spending—1991

Country	Food	Alcoholic Beverages
United States	8.3	1.3
Canada	10.8	2.8
United Kingdom	11.5	2.6
Netherlands	11.7	1.5
Sweden	15.3	3.0
Finland	15.4	4.4
Denmark	15.5	3.2
France	16.3	1.9
Ireland	20.5	11.6
Thailand	23.0	4.1
Columbia	27.3	4.1
Greece	33.4	3.1
Venezuela	34.3	1.9
Philippines	52.6	NA
India	53.1	0.8

---

[1] Denison, Edward F. *Trends in American Economic Growth, 1929–1982.* Washington: The Brookings Institution, 1985.

FIGURE 18.4

Sources of Growth in the United States, 1929–1982		
Increase in Quantity of Inputs		51%
Labor	32	
Capital	19	
Productivity Improvements		49%
Technological advance	28	
Education and training	14	
Economies of scale	9	
Improved resource allocation	8	
Legal and human factors	−9	
TOTAL		100%

omists as they seek to help underdeveloped countries compete more effectively on the international scene. It is interesting to note that the causes of economic growth are almost evenly divided between increasing the quantity of inputs and increasing the quality of those inputs as shown in Figure 18.4.

Quantity of Inputs. More people in the labor force joined by more capital per worker has caused just over half of U.S. economic growth in the last 50 years. The increasing population combined with the growth in female participation in the labor force has more than offset the decreased work week and increased school age requirements.

Productivity Improvements. The qualitative factors such as technology and education account for the other half of the country's economic growth. New manufacturing technologies and management techniques have been supported by an increasingly educated labor force, and even the reduction in discrimination has helped to improve resource allocation.

Interestingly, the U.S. economic growth rate has been slowed by a number of institutional and human factors. Expanded government involvement in the market through increased business regulation, environmental controls, and expanded health and safety standards have reduced growth as have labor-management disputes and increased crime and theft.

The Special Role of Government

Developed nations are typically blessed with economic knowledge, relative stability, a solid **infrastructure,** and the rule of law. Unfortunately, these foundations that Americans too often take for granted are frequently missing in underdeveloped countries. Government, therefore, has a special obligation to help provide the beginnings of these supports to foster economic development. While the more conservative economists would encourage these governments to play a very secondary role in the developing nation's economy, they will usually allow for a variation of the "infant industry" argument that is used to endorse trade barriers. During the initial period of development, government may need to play a more active role than in later stages.

Governments should be active in maintaining the rule of law. With bribery, corruption, and violence endemic to many developing nations, governments must provide a climate that both eliminates these threats and decreases the need to spend resources for domestic protection. Governments may also need to be involved in helping the private sector to develop the infrastructure that is necessary for economic growth. Without paved roads, clean water, reliable power, and a minimum of health care, development cannot occur. Government may need to serve as a source or generator of investment funds. With very low per capita incomes, a nation

Infrastructure
A system of physical capital including high-speed roads, assured energy sources, and an effective health care system essential for economic development.

Core-Info

The advantages of economic development are that per capita incomes increase and the population growth rate decreases. Development takes place through an improvement in the quality and quantity of inputs when the government provides an atmosphere of stability and security.

The Effects of Economic Development

When all is said and done, economic development is to be desired because it provides a nation with an expanded set of options in concert with its increased per capita income level. Options are now available for both an improved quality of life and an expanded quantity of life. People eat better, have better health care, are better educated, live safer lives, and have greater material possessions as a result. When these advantages begin to accumulate, the economy not only breaks out of the vicious circle of poverty but enters an upward spiral of prosperity.

INFLATION

Inflation. Just the very mention of the word gives economists the willies. Inflation is an enemy that can steal people's savings and destroy whole economies. It is essential to understand it to keep in under control.

Definition

Inflation
An increase in the general level of prices.

Inflation is defined as a rising level of general prices. This does not mean that all prices are rising the same amount or even that all prices are rising. Some may be decreasing while the general price level rises.

Inflation is measured in much the same way as is an economy's growth—by comparing adjacent years and dividing by the base year. The rate of inflation may be calculated as follows:

$$\text{Inflation Rate} = \frac{\text{Price level in year 2} - \text{Price level in year 1}}{\text{Price level in year 1}}$$

If the price level this year is 132 and last year it was 125, our inflation rate is:

$$\text{Inflation Rate} = \frac{132 - 125}{125} = 5.6\%$$

Inflation appears to have changed somewhat in recent decades. Previously, the price level rose during wartime, then fell following the war. Today this increase-followed-by-a-decrease pattern seems to have ceased. Prices are not overly flexible in a downward direction, and thus there tends to be a ratchet effect of increases, then a leveling, followed by further increases.

Types of Inflation

Two types of inflation occur, demand pull and cost push. While they both result in increasing prices, the causes are quite different.

Demand Pull Inflation
Inflation caused by an increase in aggregate demand.

Demand Pull. As you would expect, **demand pull inflation** begins on the demand side of the equation with an increase in aggregate demand. This operates in much the same manner as demand for an individual good. At the micro level, an in-

That Great Give-away Program—Foreign Aid

First, rest assured that this title is facetious. As you examine foreign aid, you will see how much the United States gives, what it goes for, and what its effect is on the U.S. economy.

Since the end of World War II, the United States has provided about $439 billion in foreign economic and military assistance to countries and institutions around the world. That's a lot of money by anybody's definition. However, when it is broken down as it has been in the following table and examined, this assistance can be seen in a new perspective.

First, of the $439 billion, more than $151 billion (34.5 percent) was for military aid. Theoretically, at least, this was an investment by the United States to stop the spread of communism and protect our way of life. You may want to argue that it was unnecessary to spend this much money to defeat communism, but if that was its purpose, it can hardly be seen as a give-away program.

Second, for both military and economic assistance, much of the funds made available to other countries was in the form of tied aid. Tied aid is aid that has strings attached. The most frequent string is that the money is given in the form of credits and is only available to be used to purchase American made goods and services. Thus, tied aid is a significant benefit to the U.S. business community from whom the purchases will be made.

Finally, while the United States has provided a great deal of money in foreign aid in past years, it is far from the most generous nation. The table that follows provides specific information on the amount of aid provided and the percentage of the country's gross national product for selected nations in 1995. As can be seen, the United States ranked fourth in the world behind Japan, France, and Germany in total dollars spent on foreign aid. In fact, Japan spent almost twice that of the United States. When the size of the nation's economy is taken into consideration, the United States ranks dead last of all major industrialized countries in the percentage of gross national product allocated to helping other nations. As a percent of GNP, Denmark gives four times as much as Japan and almost ten times as much as the United States.

There you have it. The United States *has* given a significant amount of money to foreign aid, but that amount has slipped in recent years. The impact on the U.S. economy is minimal at worst and at best provides jobs for American workers.

U.S. Foreign Economic and Military Aid Programs
1946 To 1993 in billions

Economic Aid—Total—$287,850	
Loans	63,253
Grants	224,598
Military Aid—Total—$151,715	
Loans	39,877
Grants	111,837
TOTAL AID————$439,565	

Source: U.S. Agency for International Development

Foreign Aid Donations by Selected Countries, 1993

Nation	Rank	Amount in Billions
Japan	1	$14.5
France	2	$ 8.5
Germany	3	$ 7.5
United States	4	$ 7.3
Netherlands	5	$ 3.1
Canada	7	$ 2.1
Denmark	9	$ 1.5

Nation	Rank	Percent of GNP
Denmark	1	0.97
Netherlands	4	0.80
France	5	0.55
Canada	6	0.39
Germany	13	0.31
Japan	15	0.28
United States	21	0.10

Source: Organization of Economic Cooperation and Development

crease in demand yields an increase in prices and an increase in the quantity produced. The extent to which both of these outcomes are true is determined by the relationship of the aggregate demand curve with the aggregate supply curve. In the Keynesian range of the aggregate supply curve, there is no increase in prices, only an increase in output. Obviously, this is not inflation. (Note also that this is rarely the case.) If the aggregate supply and demand curves intersect in the intermediate range, the result will be the same as occurs at the micro level. Finally, if the curves

FIGURE 18.5
Source: Bureau of Labor Statistics

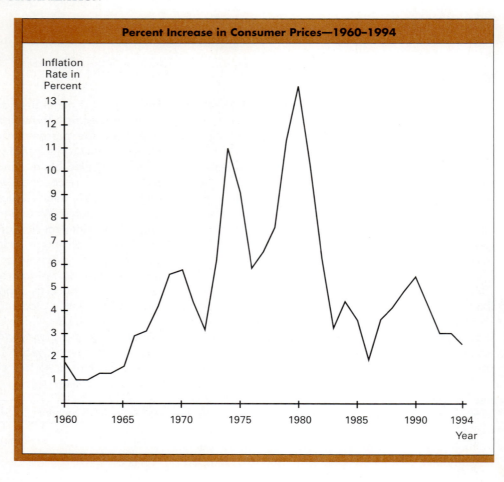

Cost Push Inflation
Inflation caused by an increase in production costs.

intersect in the classical range, the result is only inflation and no increase in output. Demand pull inflation continues unabated as long as demand remains high.

Cost Push. Cost push inflation operates on the other side of the equation. In this case, firms are faced with increased production costs due to exogenous (external) factors including high wage settlements in union-management disputes or unanticipated input prices such as crude oil cost increases. As firms find their costs rising, they see profits decline. In order to prevent a further erosion of profits, firms pass on the higher costs to customers in the form of higher prices. Cost push inflation burns itself out as higher prices result in decreased demand and decreased incomes to buy.

The Effects of Inflation

While all people face higher prices as a result of inflation, some people are more affected than others. Much depends upon whether or not inflation is correctly anticipated.

Anticipated Inflation. When inflation is anticipated, people can take actions in advance to protect themselves as much as possible. Labor unions can build cost of living adjustments (COLAs) into wage agreements (thereby guaranteeing that, once inflation starts, it will continue), and long-term contracts can be signed to borrow money.

Unanticipated Inflation. When inflation is not anticipated or when people cannot make adjustments, they can be seriously hurt by it. Fixed-income recipients are definitely hurt. With incomes locked in, an increase in the general price level means that real purchasing power decreases. This is true of social security recipients, landlords with tenants with long leases, workers with fixed wage contracts, welfare recipients, and mortgage holders. Those who benefit from inflation are those who are on the opposite side of those who are hurt: businesses with contracts for the purchase of labor or materials at fixed prices, tenants, mortgagees, and anyone owing debts. Those who owe money come up a winner because they can pay back their debts with inflated money, money of lower value. Take a moment to consider this dialogue.

Question: Who is the biggest debtor in the world?
Answer: The U.S. government.
Question: Who benefits from inflation?
Answer: Debtors.
Question: Who will benefit most from inflation and who is likely not to mind too terribly if inflation becomes a way of life, money incomes rise, tax collections go up, and they can pay back their debts with inflated money?
Answer: It makes me wonder just how serious the nation's leaders really are about controlling inflation.

Whatever government's real motivations may be, inflation is likely to be with us into the future. Demand pull will continue. Demand is increasing, and it is doing so in an uneven way. Even during sluggish economic periods, the demand for some items increases rapidly. Computer sales during the 1992 mini-recession are one example. Cost push will continue. Costs are likely to be driven up by all people. Few are willing to settle for lower wage increases even if this may help the economy. Fortunately for most people, inflation is both a blessing and a curse: your income may be locked in by a contract with your employer, but your mortgage payment is also fixed. It's hard to know whether to celebrate or weep.

Core-Info

Inflation is a general increase in the price level. Its two types are demand pull and cost push. Anticipating inflation can help you to beat its negative effects.

A FINAL LOOK AT GROWTH AND DEVELOPMENT

Economic growth is very much a desired process. An economy that provides real increases in per capita income is a blessing to all parties. As long as inflation can be kept under control, increases in income allow people to enjoy life more fully in both material and spiritual ways. That's not a bad outcome for a day's work.

SUMMARY

- Business cycles are the regular ups and downs of the economy caused by wars, government action, or changes in aggregate demand.
- Underdevelopment is characterized by low per capita income, a large agricultural sector, a low savings rate, and rapid population growth. Underdevelopment oppresses individuals and nations as they cannot provide the necessities of life.
- Economic growth is fostered by either increasing the quantity of inputs or improving the quality of those inputs.
- The two types of inflation are demand pull inflation and cost push inflation. In demand pull inflation, excessive demand pulls prices upward. In cost push inflation, increased resource prices drive final prices up for the consumer.

- Debtors win during inflationary times; creditors lose. If inflation is anticipated, people can make adjustments to the amount of debt they have to take advantage of it. If inflation is unanticipated, people with fixed incomes and credit extended will suffer.

KEY TERMS

Business cycle
Cost push inflation
Demand pull inflation
Economic development
Economic growth
Inflation
Infrastructure
Underdevelopment
Vicious circle of poverty

REVIEW QUESTIONS

1. Differentiate between economic growth and economic expansion.
2. Explain what is meant by the "business cycle." What are the causes and effects of business cycles?
3. Economic growth can be defined as an increase in the gross national product. Explain how to calculate the growth rate; include the equation in your answer.
4. Explain what is meant by "economic development." State the two key results of economic development.
5. What are some of the keys and sources to achieving a sustained level of economic development?
6. Inflation is a rising level of general prices. Discuss how inflation is measured, as well as the different types of inflation.
7. Identify some of the effects of inflation.

PROBLEM-SOLVING PRACTICE

1. Compare the rate of economic growth for four countries between Year 1 and Year 2. The GDP figures for each country are in billions of dollars.

Country	Year 1	Year 2
A	$4,000	$4,100
B	3,000	3,500
C	2,000	2,200
D	4,000	4,040

    Rank the countries by the rate of growth of GDP between Year 1 and Year 2.

2. A study of a nation showed that it had long-term economic growth based on the following sources:

Sources of Growth		
Increases in quantity of input		60%
Labor	30%	
Capital	30%	
Productivity improvements		40%
Technological advances	10%	
Economies of scale	15%	
Improvements in resource allocation	10%	
Legal and human factors	(−5%)	
Education and training	?	
		100%

(a) Based on the above data, how much of the national economic growth the nation should be attributed to education and training?

(b) How would the answer to part (a) change if legal and human factors played no role at all and were eliminated as a category?

(c) What value would education and training have if legal and human factors went from −5% to +5%?

3. The following chart presents the price index of a nation.

	Price Index
Year 1	110
Year 2	114
Year 3	118
Year 4	120
Year 5	130

(a) Calculate the rate of inflation for Year 2, Year 3, Year 4, and Year 5.

(b) Calculate the average rate of inflation over the time period Years 2 through 5.

CHAPTER 19

The Global Economy

CHAPTER OUTLINE

A. Gaining a Perspective
   1. International Trade
   2. Politics *vs.* Economics
      a. Power *vs.* Resources
      b. Political and Economic Variations
B. The Good Old Days
   1. In the Beginning
   2. Tribalism
   3. Mercantilism
   4. Colonialism
   5. Capitalism and Socialism
C. The Present
   1. The Fork in the Road
   2. Tariffs and Trade
   3. Common Markets
      a. The United States
      b. The European Economic Community
      c. COMECON
      d. NAFTA and Others
   4. Multinational Firms
   5. The Language of Trade
   6. "Resistance Is Useless"
D. Tomorrow
   1. Revolution, Not Evolution
   2. The Communications Revolution and the Service Sector
   3. The Increased Mobility of Human and Financial Capital
   4. The Triumph of Economics over Politics (or, "Economics: the Integrating Approach")

The purpose of this chapter is to introduce the basic ideas of the global economy and, by giving an historical perspective, to look into the future.

AFTER COMPLETING THIS CHAPTER, YOU WILL BE ABLE TO:

1. Differentiate between political and economic approaches in analyzing nations.
2. Summarize the development of the general economic approach in history.
3. Analyze the impact of current trends in the global economy on the United States.
4. Predict the future of the global economy.

Gaining A Perspective

Throughout this textbook we have addressed global issues as a part of the ongoing discussion. In this chapter, global economics will be the sole focus. We shall see just how tightly interrelated the nations of the world are and how the United States fits into the overall picture.

An understanding of international economics does not require acquisition of a new set of tools. The old tools of marginal analysis, cost, and supply and demand will be directly applicable. We will apply these tools to global issues rather than local concerns.

International Trade

As you have learned, there are two reasons why people or nations engage in trade: differing resources and comparative advantage. Some nations have resources that other nations lack. Trade is obviously the answer here. If Americans want Saudi oil or Honduran bananas, they need to trade with those nations. On the other hand, some products can be made in many locations. In this case, comparative advantage rules, and Americans produce goods when they can do it relatively cheaply and buy goods when others hold that advantage.

The advantages of trade are obvious. First, people can acquire resources and goods that they don't have locally. Second, they can get things at a lower cost than would be possible if they were to make the goods themselves. Finally, people can specialize and use their labor and capital to produce goods and services at a lower cost for themselves and for others around the world.

International trade is very much a way of life in the United States, and its importance is growing. Exports and imports (things going out and things coming in, respectively) can be either goods or services. Goods can include raw materials, agricultural products, and manufactured goods. Services can include banking, insurance, tourism, and education. Figure 19.1 provides an overview of the ten top commodity imports into the United States in 1994. As can be seen, eight of the top ten products are manufactured goods and two are materials. The top ten U.S. commodity exports to other nations are shown in Figure 19.2. Interestingly, the number one U.S. export is agricultural products. How can this be? The United States is the largest industrial economy in the world, and an early chapter noted that the U.S. economy is predominantly service-oriented. So how can agricultural products be the greatest export? It has to do with the physical size and fertility of U.S. agricultural lands. While only 3 percent of the U.S. work force is engaged in farming, the agricultural sector is highly mechanized and uses great quantities of chemical fertilizers and pesticides. Thus, it can produce great quantities of food for domestic consumption and have extra left over for export abroad.

FIGURE 19.1

Source: U.S. Department of Commerce

Top Ten U.S. Commodity Imports—1994	
Commodity	Value in Millions
Vehicles (new cars)	$59,177
Electrical machinery	57,750
Data processing equipment	52,058
Crude oil	38,479
Clothing	36,748
Telecommunications equipment	32,418
Agricultural products	25,955
General industrial machinery	21,330
Vehicle parts	19,609
Power generating machinery	19,543

FIGURE 19.2

Source: U.S. Department of Commerce

Top Ten U.S. Commodity Exports—1994	
Commodity	Value in Millions
Agricultural products	$44,936
Electrical machinery	44,454
Data processing equipment	30,867
General industrial machinery	21,816
Vehicle parts	21,314
Power generating machinery	20,345
Specialized industrial machinery	19,677
Airplanes	18,803
Scientific instruments	16,475
Telecommunications equipment	15,872

FIGURE 19.3

Source: U.S. Bureau of the Census, *U.S. Merchandise Trade*

Leading Buyers of U.S. Products (Exports)—1994	
Country	Value in Millions
Canada	$114,441
Japan	53,481
Mexico	50,840
United Kingdom	26,833
Germany	19,237
South Korea	18,028
Taiwan	17,078
TOTAL	**$512,670**

FIGURE 19.4

Source: U.S. Bureau of the Census, *U.S. Merchandise Trade*

Leading Sellers of Products to U.S. (Imports)—1994	
Country	Value in Millions
Canada	$128,948
Japan	119,149
Mexico	49,493
China	38,781
Germany	31,749
Taiwan	26,711
United Kingdom	21,730
TOTAL	**$663,768**

The United States trades with almost all nations of the world. From Afghanistan ($5 million in imports from the United States in 1994) to Zimbabwe ($102 million in exports to the United States) and everywhere in between, the United States is economically linked. Figure 19.3 lists the top seven buyers of U.S. exported goods. Figure 19.4 identifies the top seven exporters to the United States. Do you notice any similarities? Interesting, isn't it, that the same nations appear on both lists? The same is true for most nations of the world. Truly, our economies are highly linked, and a disruption in any nation will quickly be felt across the world.

A summary of commodity exports from and imports to the United States since 1950 is presented in Figure 19.5. As you can see, for a long time U.S. exports of goods to other countries exceeded imports of goods from them. Since the early 1980s, however, the balance has shifted, and the United States now imports more than it exports. Is this a problem? Stay tuned.

FIGURE 19.5
U.S. Exports and Imports of Goods

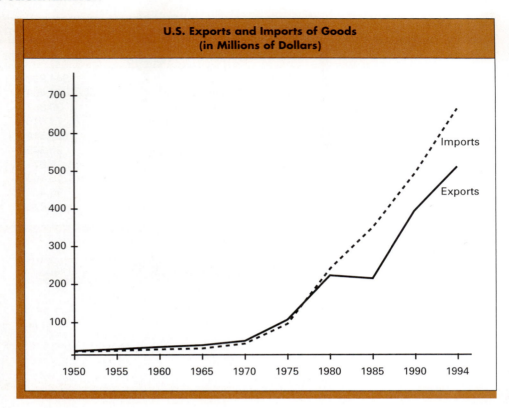

While international trade is increasing and most of the world favors it, there are detractors. Some people and nations would raise barriers against trade for a variety of reasons. Some feel that it is necessary to protect domestic industries or local workers by keeping them in areas where goods could be purchased more cheaply abroad. Unfortunately, this is much the same as being forced to buy a car from a dealer in your neighborhood which charges $1,000 more for its vehicles than a dealer in another town. It is not a good use of resources, and there are better ways to help the local workers and businesses.

The ways in which governments act to restrict trade are through prohibitions, quotas, tariffs, and NTBs (nontariff barriers). Prohibitions are just what the word means—you cannot buy or sell the good. The United States has placed prohibitions on cigars from Cuba, computers to Russia, and clothing from factories which use child labor. A quota is a limitation in the quantities of goods that may be imported. These quotas may be mandatory or "voluntary." The United States has had quotas on the imports of foreign shoes, beef, and cars. Tariffs are taxes placed on the import of goods. The goods are free to be imported, but the price will be raised by the amount of the tariff. These tariffs are borne of the law of demand which recognizes that people will buy less of a good when prices are high than when they are low. Nontariff barriers (NTBs) are other restrictions or rules that are placed on foreign goods or services. Licensing requirements for importers, product safety regulations, and commodity conformity laws are among the NTBs that have been used.

Tariffs have been a way of life for the United States from its very beginning. Figure 19.6 shows what the average level of tariffs on imported goods has been for the past 175 years. For most of our history, tariffs against foreign goods have been very high. With few exceptions, tariffs levied on foreign goods have averaged about 50 percent of their value. Since 1947, however, with the establishment of the General Agreement on Tariffs and Trade (GATT), tariffs worldwide have fallen dramatically. Not too surprisingly, the world has had an economic boom of unprecedented proportions in the half-century since.

FIGURE 19.6
U.S. Trade Tariffs

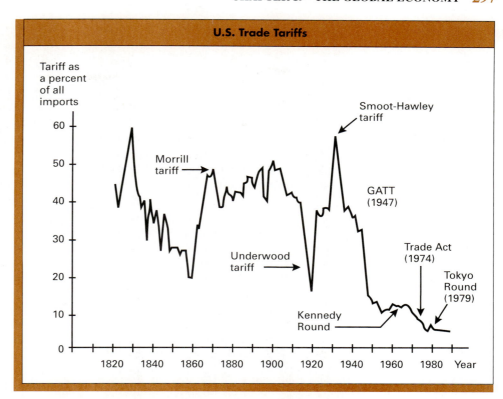

Core-Info

International trade is large and growing. It takes place because of differing resources and comparative advantage and benefits both trading partners.

Politics vs. Economics

Power vs. Resources. As was noted in a previous chapter, there is a significant difference between politics and economics. Politics is concerned with power. Who rules and gets to make decisions, who votes and who cannot are the stuff of politics. Economics, of course, deals with resources and their use. What things are going to be produced, how they will be made, and who will get them when are the issues of economics. It is easy to confuse the two and to begin to talk of them as if they were the same.

Political and Economic Variations. There are two major types of political systems: liberal democracies and totalitarian states. In liberal democracies, the people hold the power and make the basic decisions about how that power will be applied. They may elect representatives and may even allow a king or queen to hold a position, but the final decisions rest with the citizens. Totalitarian states take many forms. In them, power is held by the government and is used as the government sees fit. Dictatorships, tribal states, and police states are all forms of totalitarian governments. Totalitarian governments may act in what they perceive to be in the best interest of the people, but it is the government which makes the decisions, not the people themselves.

Like political systems, economic systems take two basic forms, capitalism and socialism. In capitalism, the resources are owned by the people and economic decisions are made by the people. Government's role is to facilitate the decisions

How Not to Succeed in Business

A popular Broadway musical inspired a movie with the same title, "How to Succeed in Business without Really Trying." Both versions humorously portray how a low-level employee schemes his way to the top of the Worldwide Wicket Company. With Korea, you can see just the opposite: how to move a country from at least potential success to abysmal failure.

For hundreds of years, Korea was an integrated nation with both the northern and southern portions sharing in growth. The country was ethnically and religiously uniform. Much of the mineral wealth and most of the industry was located in the north. The nation became divided into North Korea and South Korea in 1948, and since that time the two nations have become increasingly divergent with South Korea developing and North Korea stagnating.

North Korea has chosen a highly socialistic path for itself. Industry and farms have been collectivized, there is little opportunity for individual enterprise, and religious and political repression is the rule. Military forces and aggressive international behavior have become an integral part of its national persona. South Korea has chosen a capitalistic model of development with individual enterprise encouraged. While South Korea's record on political freedom leaves something to be desired, annual surveys of freedom have shown it to be far ahead of the North.

The following table presents the results of the two paths to development. The North with its larger land area and greater natural resources has not been able to keep pace with the South. One likely reason—in addition to the rigid socialist model of development followed—is the North's expenditures on the military. With a smaller population, the North has twice as many persons in the military as the South and spends six times as much of its gross national product for their support. It has built or purchased more tanks, aircraft, and ships for its defense forces and thus has had less to spend for roads, factories, and productive equipment. As a result, North Korea has a lower—and relatively decreasing—per capita income and far fewer civilian goods than does the South.

There may be legitimate reasons for North Korea to spend great sums of money on its military. Perhaps the North feels truly threatened by South Korea and its American ally. Second, not all military spending is wasteful: jobs are created and civilian benefits can result. Finally, the military can provide useful technical training for its members. However, by diverting resources from other uses, military spending is, by and large, a drag on economic development.

The differences should not be lost on Americans or other nations seeking to grow economically. The choices citizens make have real implications. While the U.S. active military force has been declining steadily since 1970 and spending is less than 4 percent of gross national product, it does involve $268 billion in resources annually that could be used for other things. Once again, the choice is ours to make.

	North Korea	South Korea
Population (1993)	23,486,550	45,553,882
Land area	47,399 sq. miles	38,330 sq. miles
Active armed forces	53 per 1,000 pop.	16.8 per 1,000 pop.
Military expenditures	23% of GNP	4% of GNP
Tanks	4,200	1,960
Fighter aircraft	360	132
Submarines	25	2
Television sets	1 per 67 persons	1 per 4.8 persons
Radios	1 per 4.8 persons	1 per person
Telephones	1 per 20 persons	1 per 2.3 persons
Infant mortality	27 per 1,000 births	21 per 1,000 births
GNP per capita (1993)	$1,513	$6,285
GNP per capita (1978)	$590	$880

made by individuals and businesses. In socialism, economic resources are owned by the government, and the government decides how these resources will be used. The role of the individual is to participate in the fulfillment of the government's plan to operate the economy. Socialist economies may be organized with the best interests of the people at heart, but the government makes the economic decisions.

Core-Info

Political and economic systems differ. The former deals with power and the latter with resources.

Democratic Capitalism
A national system wherein individuals hold both the economic and political power.

Democratic Socialism
A national system wherein individuals hold political power and decide that the government should own the major productive resources.

Totalitarian Capitalism
A national system wherein individuals would hold the economic power but the government would hold all political power. Such a system could not exist.

Totalitarian Socialism
A national system wherein the government holds both the economic and political power.

Tribal Economies
Small scale, early economies with limited specialization, infrequent trade, and a barter system.

Mercantilism
An economic system which attempted to maintain an excess of exports over imports and to accumulate gold.

Colonialism
An economic system in which colonies existed for the benefit of the mother country through the provision of raw materials and as markets for finished products.

Political and economic systems coincide in a state, and there are four possible combinations that *could* exist: **democratic capitalism, democratic socialism, totalitarian socialism,** and **totalitarian capitalism.** The final combination, totalitarian capitalism, is impossible, of course. Government cannot hold all power while the people have power over all resources at the same time. The other three combinations are possible, and the United States, Sweden, and China are examples, respectively.

In coming to terms with our global economy, we will take an historical approach. Seeing how the world economic system has evolved will yield some good insights into where it is headed and how to make it grow to the benefit of all.

THE GOOD OLD DAYS

In the Beginning

Most people believe that the earliest economic systems were exceedingly simple. People were hunters and gatherers for an extended period of time. Economic organization and specialization was all but nonexistent, and people collected what they needed for the day from what was available about them.

Tribalism

Tribal economies were the next to develop. In **tribal economies,** rudimentary specialization began to take place. The warriors, priests, and farmers had their individual jobs, and often the division between the sexes began. Trade between tribes was fairly limited, and formal economic systems of production and exchange were not necessary because of the size of the economy.

Mercantilism

Mercantilism was the first modern economic school of thought. It lasted from the 16th to the 18th century and focused on maximizing a nation's wealth, then considered to be reserves of gold and silver. International trade was tightly regulated, and the goal was to achieve what was believed to be a favorable balance of trade. When goods were sold to other nations, the exporting country received gold in return. When a nation imported goods, however, it had to pay for these goods out of its gold stock. Exports, therefore, were seen to be good; imports were seen to be bad. The accumulation of gold by the state was seen to be the highest good.

The seeds for mercantilism's destruction are evident. First, by cutting off imports, a nation deprives itself of goods it does not have naturally and of the benefits of comparative advantage. Further, if gold is accumulated, it results in an expansion of the money supply which produces generalized inflation. Unless the economy can expand as the money supply increases, many people suffer greatly as prices rise exponentially.

Colonialism

Colonialism was an outgrowth of mercantilism. Colonies were, for the most part, very tightly linked to the mother country to the benefit of the latter. Colonies were seen to be sources of raw materials for home industries and buyers of finished products from the home country. High tariffs were imposed on goods imported into the colonies from other countries, and colonies were taxed to support the home country.

What existed was, effectively, economic slavery. Colonies had outlets for their products and received military protection, but the cost in lost freedom was high, and one by one colonies have been gaining independence from the mother countries and have been forging out on their own.

Capitalism and Socialism

Capitalism and socialism are generally seen to be opposites, but in fact they both derived from modern industrial states. Capitalism was the first to develop and arose out of the weaknesses of mercantilism. National leaders realized that the accumulation of gold and silver was the wrong approach to a nation's wealth. The first to tread this path were the Physiocrats in France in the late 18th century. The Physiocrats believed that, rather than gold and silver, a nation's wealth was derived from its land and this wealth was the goods that people possessed. Where the mercantilists wanted to limit trade, the Physiocrats believed that trade should be as free as possible. When Adam Smith adopted the Physiocrats' ideas, he expanded the resource base beyond agriculture and land to include the labor of the workers and managers in factories, farms, and shops.

This is not to say that governments followed their creative economic thinkers, however. In fact, most governments remained strongly protectionist and only in recent years has the trend been toward the general lowering of trade barriers worldwide.

THE PRESENT

The Fork in the Road

There are two major economic issues at present: the collapse of socialism in most of the eastern countries and the globalization of economics. Socialism, as a viable economic system for large economies, has been found wanting. Because of its internal structure and lack of an incentive system through prices, it has been too inflexible to respond to a dynamic world economy. Slowly but surely, the socialist economies are moving toward a capitalistic approach. With globalization, the nations face two choices: to move forward and reap the benefits of international trade or retreat into isolationism and protectionism and fall behind as a nation. In each country are those who call for restrictions on trade and who would take their fellow citizens back to a protectionist past. While this approach might appear to protect domestic jobs, it is at best a short-run solution with extremely high long-run costs. Protectionism is not the answer to an increasingly globalized economy.

Tariffs and Trade

For the past 50 years, tariffs have been moving downward on a worldwide scale. Since the ratification of the **General Agreement on Tariffs and Trade (GATT),** nations have actively worked to reduce their tariffs against other nations. One of the most useful tools in this effort has been the use of **most favored nation status.** Under this approach, any tariff reduction granted to one nation will automatically extend to all other "most favored" nations. This reduces the cost of negotiating tariff reductions and, when the cost of something declines, more of it occurs.

Common Markets

One of the real areas of growth in recent years has been that of common trading pacts. A **common market** is an association of nations formed to remove trade barriers. Nations have been discovering the advantages of specialization and trade and have been moving toward more economic alliances. By expanding their free trade zones, more countries have been able to benefit from the principle of comparative advantage.

General Agreement on Tariffs and Trade (GATT)
A multilateral treaty system that lowers trade barriers among nations.

Most Favored Nation Status
An international trade agreement whereby any concessions offered to one country will be automatically granted to all other nations.

Common Market
A union of national economies by which trade barriers are erased and resource flows among countries is encouraged.

The Global Economy

If your only source of information were the daily newspapers, you might conclude that global economic integration is a phenomenon of the last decade of the 20th century. In fact, it is not. While there has been an acceleration in global activity in recent years, the phenomenon has been going on for decades. The automobile industry provides a good example.

The first automobile was built in the United States in 1896. It was the product of Henry Ford's Dearborn, Michigan, garage. By 1903 the Ford Motor Company was building cars in Canada. Assembly took place in Britain in 1911. By 1920, Fords were being produced in 20 countries. General Motors followed suit and purchased Vauxhall in Great Britain in 1925 and Germany's Opel in 1929. Very soon after the invention of the automobile, American manufacturers became international in scope.

International linkages have continued to this day. As can be seen in the table below, American manufacturers have established significant relationships with foreign firms, from holding a minority interest to outright ownership.

True global economics takes place in two directions, however. As U.S. automobile manufacturers have been expanding overseas, so too have foreign manufacturers. Attracted by the size of the U.S. market and its skilled labor force, many foreign car companies have built plants and have begun to assemble cars here. Examples range from Volkswagen's ill-fated effort in 1978 to more successful recent ventures, including BMW's production of the Z-3 in South Carolina in 1996. A sampling of the early foreign auto plants in the United States can be seen below.

The manufacture of automobiles in the United States by foreign companies and the production of automobiles in foreign countries by U.S. firms is not the whole picture of the global auto market. In addition there are the exports and imports of cars produced in other countries, the shipment of auto parts ($21.2 billion in exports and $19.6 billion in imports in 1994), and the import and export of raw materials for automobile production. Truly, the automobile industry provides a good view of the global economy.

Foreign Auto Manufacturers

Firm	State	Year Begun
Volkswagen	Pennsylvania	1978
Honda	Ohio	1982
Nissan	Tennessee	1983
Toyota	Kentucky	1983
Mazda	Michigan	1984
Mitsubishi	Illinois	1984

Ford Motors		General Motors		Chrysler Motors	
Make	Pct. Owned	Make	Pct. Owned	Make	Pct. Owned
Aston Martin	75	Isuzu	25	Maserati	49
Jaguar	100	Lotus	100	Mitsubishi	12
Kia	10	Opel	100	Lamborghini	100
Mazda	75	Saab	50		
		Suzuki	5		
		Vauxhall	100		

The United States. If you stop to think about it, the United States is the original common market. When the United States was founded more than 200 years ago, the colonies, each with their unique historical and cultural background, were independent economic units. The nation's founders realized the benefits of free internal trade and wrote into the Constitution prohibitions against interstate tariffs or barriers to the movement of people and capital. Along with its great natural resources, long shoreline, and inland waterways, the nation's free trade policies allowed states to specialize and to trade with other states and resulted in the greatest economic entity ever.

European Economic Community (EEC)
An association of European nations established to lead to the complete elimination of all trade barriers between themselves.

Council for Mutual Economic Assistance (COMECON)
An organization of ten communist-bloc countries to coordinate economic and technical development policies among themselves. It was disbanded following the fall of the Soviet Union.

North American Free Trade Agreement (NAFTA)
An agreement between Canada, Mexico, and the United States to lower trade barriers between themselves.

Multinational Firm
A business organization that operates in more than one nation.

The European Economic Community. The **EEC,** or Common Market, grew out of the Treaty of Rome in 1957. The goal was to lower trade and other barriers among the members while establishing common tariffs against nonmembers. The free movement of labor, capital, and services across the national boundaries of members was also one of its original aims. Six nations joined the EEC at the outset and an additional six have become members since then. Much progress has been made toward economic integration, and a common currency is a distinct possibility in the near future.

COMECON. The **Council for Mutual Economic Assistance** was founded in 1949 by ten communist countries. It was established to counter the Marshall Plan which the United States used to help rebuild western Europe following the devastation of World War II. Dominated strongly by the Soviet Union, it sought to coordinate the economic and technical development policies of its members. COMECON was disbanded in 1991 when independence came to Eastern Europe and the Soviet republics, but it was replaced by another union, the Organization for International Economic Cooperation.

NAFTA and Others. Individual nations have been negotiating expanded economic integration. Beginning with the U.S.–Canadian Free Trade Agreement in 1988 and continuing through the **North American Free Trade Agreement (NAFTA)** in 1993, both Democratic and Republican presidents have shown their commitment to an expansion of the free trade zone for American imports and exports. As you saw in Figures 19.3 and 19.4, Canada and Mexico are major trading partners with the United States. By further removing barriers between the three nations, these agreements have created the single largest economy in the world.

Multinational Firms

Another phenomenon, not surprising in light of the greater internationalization of the world economy, is the growth of multinational firms. **Multinational firms** are those with a headquarters in one nation and a significant presence in another. As Figure 19.7 indicates, these firms have grown at a rate of 10 percent per year in the past decade. This international linkage allows corporations to take advantage of varying costs in different nations and to utilize local resources as they become available. Both the parent company and the host country benefit as a result.

The Language of Trade

World trade has been facilitated through the use of a common language—English. Because of Great Britain's empire (on which, it was said, the sun never set), the English language was taken by merchants and local political leaders around the globe. The result was that the language has been unofficially accepted as *the* international language. Most signs are printed in English, airline pilots use English

FIGURE 19.7
Source: Bureau of Economic Analysis, U.S. Department of Commerce

Total Assets of U.S. Multinational Firms (in Millions)		
Year	U.S. Parent Companies	Foreign Affiliates
1982	$2,741,619	$751,486
1984	3,060,031	759,994
1986	3,792,001	931,293
1988	4,363,441	1,206,326
1990	4,951,048	1,559,038
1992	5,579,798	1,761,998
1993	6,084,571	2,053,469

when communicating with control towers, and trade documents are translated into English. At a time when the United States is debating whether or not to adopt English as the standard language of the land, the world has already adopted it to facilitate international exchange.

"Resistance Is Useless"

When the giant and ruthless Vogons speak in *Hitchhiker's Guide to the Galaxy,* they generally say, "resistance is useless." So it is in economics. The world economy is becoming increasingly globalized, and there is little that any group or political leader can do to stop it. There may be short-term pull-backs on the part of some nations (Albania and Iran are prime examples), but globalization will continue into the future. The goal of the United States should be (note the change to the normative from the positive) to seek to take advantage of the trend and to use it to further national and personal objectives. Individually Americans will be presented with increasing opportunities to be involved in the global economy. Nationally they will have the chance to benefit from trade and the relationships this engenders.

TOMORROW

Revolution, Not Evolution

The world is entering a revolutionary period. Growth has become exponential rather than arithmetic, and the ability to rely on natural resources or a favorable location are past. Even China, which has long resisted Western ideas, is adopting a more capitalistic approach to its economy (see Figure 19.8). Both individuals and nations must be prepared to ride the crest of the wave or they will be overwhelmed by the rapidity of the changes.

Core-Info

The major world issues today are the collapse of socialism and the globalization of economics. The move toward universal capitalism and common trading areas will soon link the world.

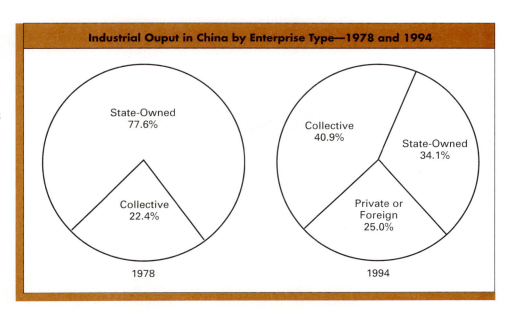

FIGURE 19.8
As China has struggled to improve its economy, it has begun a major shift away from state-owned businesses to a reliance on the private—if regulated—sector. *Source:* 1995 Statistical Yearbook of China

The Communications Revolution and the Service Sector

World growth will occur in the communications and service sectors. With the major changes in communication that have occurred and the decreases in the cost of communication, people and resources can be mobilized instantly to take advantage of global opportunities. If the sun never set on the British Empire in the past, it never sets on today's interlinked global stock markets. Shares of stock, commodity futures, and money may be traded 24 hours per day. Teleconferencing allows people to quickly and easily meet with others to resolve problems. The growth of computer networks allows individuals in one nation to communicate with people, firms, and libraries around the world.

The greatest growth in the world economy, therefore, can be expected in the service sector. As emerging nations enter the industrial stage of development, they will pass through it rapidly en route to real prosperity. Some nations may even be able to leap from simple undeveloped colonial outposts to world leaders as Singapore has shown. In addition, the growth of services will allow nations to increase their foreign trade. As Figure 19.9 shows, service exports from the United States have multiplied by more than 22 times in the past 30 years alone. Similar increases can be expected for the United States and other nations in the coming decades.

The Increased Mobility of Human and Financial Capital

As travel costs decline, more and more people are willing to visit other countries and to accept jobs there. As human capital flows to where it can best be utilized, the economies of the world benefit and grow and resources are used more efficiently. Similarly, the electronic revolution in banking has facilitated international capital flows. Funds can flow instantaneously to places where they can be used most effectively. The result of both phenomena is that the global economy is becoming more efficient, and output per unit of input is rising.

The Triumph of Economics over Politics (or "Economics: the Integrating Approach")

Where political systems and personal prejudices have sought to divide nations and pit people against people, economics has succeeded in breaking down the barriers. Increasingly we interact with people from other lands. We do this directly through travel to other countries and meeting foreign travelers in our own cities, and we do it indirectly through the purchase of goods with foreign connections. The net result is, hopefully, a greater opportunity for peace. Now, more than ever, we really do need each other.

FIGURE 19.9
Source: Bureau of Economic Analysis, U.S. Department of Commerce

| Service Exports by the U.S. (in Millions) ||
Year	Amount
1965	$ 8,824
1970	14,171
1975	25,497
1980	47,584
1985	73,155
1990	147,819
1994	198,716

U.S. Higher Education—Our Hidden Export

We are always looking for ways to increase our exports. By selling more abroad, we add jobs for American workers and generate increased incomes at home. Naturally we think of manufactured goods (cars, computers, and cardigans) and agricultural products (cattle, corn, and cotton), and these are products much in demand overseas. But the United States is becoming a service economy. How can we export services? Its not as hard as you might think.

The United States exported nearly $200 billion in services in 1994. Passenger fares by internationals on American aircraft, insurance policies purchased by foreigners, and research and development work contracted to American firms all generated substantial revenues. But perhaps the most important U.S. service export is higher education. International students come to the United States with their money, exchange it for a college education, and return to their home countries.

There are two aspects to the U.S. export of higher education. The first is financial. The table below shows that the United States is increasingly becoming the country of choice for international students. Each of these students faces the same costs that resident American students face: tuition, fees, books, room, food, entertainment, clothing, transportation, and so forth. For just the first two items alone (tuition and fees) the average at all American colleges (two-year and four-year; public and private) was $10,594 in 1994. Just multiplying this figure by the number of foreign students enrolled yields expenditures of $4.757 billion dollars. When all related expenses are added in, the total expenditure by foreigners in American colleges is $10 billion per year, and $10 billion is a sizeable export.

The other aspect to international students studying in the United States is that, through exposure to American culture and people, relationships are established that can last a lifetime. Given that those international students who are studying in the United States are the elite from their home countries, the bonds that are forged while they are in college in the United States may ultimately result in improved relationships between their countries and the United States when they return to their homelands.

All in all, higher education may be the best long-run export that the United States has.

Year	Foreign Student Enrollment
1980	286,000
1985	342,000
1990	387,000
1994	449,000

Source: Institute of International Education.

SUMMARY

- Economics is the study of how resources are utilized. Politics is the study of how power is applied. There is a world of difference.
- The world's economies have grown from small, localized systems to increasingly international enterprises. Along the way, governments have attempted to control the economies in ways they thought were beneficial to the nation. Mostly, the approaches focused on limiting trade and acquiring gold, and were incorrect.
- At the business firm level, there has been such a rapid growth in multinational firms that the United States now measures gross domestic product rather than gross national product.
- As a nation, the United States is increasingly exporting services of all types.
- At the international level, in recent years most nations have participated in attempts to reduce tariffs and have tried to forge new economic common markets to eliminate trade barriers.
- International trade will continue to expand, barriers will continue to fall, and the world will be a better place because of it.

KEY TERMS

Colonialism
Common market
Council for mutual economic assistance (COMECON)
Democratic capitalism
Democratic socialism
European economic community (EEC)
General agreement on tariffs and trade (GATT)
Mercantilism
Most favored nation status
Multinational firm
North American free trade agreement (NAFTA)
Totalitarian capitalism
Totalitarian socialism
Tribal economies

REVIEW QUESTIONS

1. What are two reasons why people or nations participate in trade?
2. Identify some ways in which governments act to restrict trade.
3. What is the purpose of a quota?
4. Describe the difference between politics and economics.
5. Identify the two major types of political systems.
6. What are the two basic forms of economic systems?
7. What are the two current major economic issues?
8. Explain the idea of multinational firms.

PROBLEM-SOLVING PRACTICE

1. Without looking back at this chapter, see if you can answer the following:
   (a) What are the three products that top the list of U.S. exports?
   (b) What are the three products that top the list of U.S. imports?
   (c) What are the three countries to which the United States has the highest level of exports?
   (d) What are the three countries from which the United States has the highest level of imports?
2. Describe the benefits of trade between nations.
3. What has been the historical pattern of the United States regarding free trade and tariffs?
4. Briefly describe each of the following as it relates to international trade:
   (a) common markets
   (b) NAFTA
   (c) multinational firms
   (d) European Economic Community
   (e) COMECON

PART 5
A SUMMARY

Chapter 20: Economics: a Final Look

CHAPTER 20

Economics: a Final Look

CHAPTER OUTLINE

A. We Made It!
B. Key Ideas in Economics
   1. There Is No Free Lunch
   2. Costs Are More Than Dollars
   3. Trade Benefits All
   4. The Market Works (Mostly)
C. Is Economics All?
   1. People May Not Live by Bread Alone, but Everything Has Its Price
   2. Two Economists Yield Three Theories
D. Efficiency and Equity One More Time
E. Edmund Burke Revisited

The purpose of this chapter is to remind you of some of the key ideas in economics and to help you to conclude this course on a positive note.

AFTER COMPLETING THIS CHAPTER, YOU WILL BE ABLE TO:

1. Summarize the major economic cost, trade, and the market.
2. Demonstrate the centrality of economics for individuals and businesses.
3. Explain the relationship and linkage of equity and efficiency in business and individual decisions.

We Made It!

Now that you've come to the end of this book, would you agree that it wasn't so bad after all? Whatever you thought about economics before you began, you know more now and should feel more comfortable about economic issues. If you have developed a little of both knowledge and comfort, then the book and the course have been successful.

You have probably discovered that economics is just another organized way of thinking about the world. Much the same as psychology, physics, mathematics, and theology provide a structure and a language for describing reality from their particular viewpoint, so too does economics. Economics focuses on scarce resources and how they are used to meet human needs. The effective use of economic ideas should help people to live in ways that make better use of these resources to better address the needs of individuals and the group.

In these directed meanderings, you have wandered through diverse areas of relevance: what money is and how it is created; the nature of capitalism and socialism and their strengths and weaknesses; types of business organizations and markets; and why the American economy is a corporation-based capitalism and what advantages this approach has for its citizens. Now that you have examined many of the details, let's conclude with a review of the overall ideas that should stay with you for the next few decades.

KEY IDEAS IN ECONOMICS

What are the key ideas that should form the basis of your economic thinking as you consider personal finance and business decisions and national and world issues? Here are the central tenets of economics.

There Is No Free Lunch

Nobel Prize winner Milton Friedman was surely correct in giving one of his books on economic policy that title.[1] If you learn nothing else from this book, you should always remember that everything has a cost. You have to give up something to get something else. That reality sums up the definition of opportunity cost.

Costs Are More Than Dollars

Dollars are important, as you are no doubt critically aware, but if all you worry about is dollars, you will likely end up making very bad decisions. Economics is concerned about the use of resources, and these resources are defined as land, labor, capital, and entrepreneurship. Money is of concern precisely because of the real resources it represents and not for itself. You must always focus on the resources that are used or given up when you think about the cost of anything so you will understand what it really takes to do the job. Looking at only the dollars involved provides a partial picture at best and may seriously mislead at worst.

Trade Benefits All

Each individual has different gifts and abilities. Each state and country has different natural resources and types of human and nonhuman capital. No human today would voluntarily take on the role of a 20th century Robinson Crusoe (and even he had Friday with his differing abilities) and try to produce everything for him or herself. Neither should any state or country attempt to produce everything it needs within its own borders. Both the individual and the country should specialize in what it can do

---

[1.] Friedman, Milton. *There's No Such Thing as a Free Lunch.* LaSalle, Ill.: Open Court, 1975. It is worth noting that Friedman also published this book under the title *An Economist's Protest* with Thomas Horton Publishers.

best (where its comparative advantage lies) and trade with others for what it lacks. This does not mean that some individuals aren't hurt by a reduction of trade barriers between countries, but the net benefit to society greatly outweighs the cost.[2]

The Market Works (Mostly)

The market economy is a wondrous thing. It regulates itself toward an optimal level if it is left free to work things out. All of the regulation and control the economy needs is provided by the impersonal forces of supply and demand. Individuals acting in their own self-interest, adjusting the quantities supplied and demanded in response to prices, act in ways that benefit not only themselves but all of us. The beauty of it all is that it all happens at no cost. The socialists didn't believe in the free market; they felt that the market had to be regulated in the interests of society, and you can see where it got them. The world may never attain some global optimum by the free and unfettered market. Some homeless people may be bypassed, and the government may need to ride herd on some money-grubbing capitalists, but by and large, citizens can lean back, relax, and let the economy have its head.

Core-Info

> The main ideas of economics are that everything has a cost, that costs are more than dollars, that trade benefits everybody, and that the market is an exceptional and efficient regulator.

FIGURE 20.1

Fastest Growing and Declining Occupations Percentage Change 1992–2005	
Fastest Growing	
Occupations	Percent Change 1992–2005
Home health aides	138.1
Human services workers	135.9
Personal and home care aides	129.8
Computer engineers and scientists	111.9
Systems analysts	110.1
Physical and corrective therapy assistants and aides	92.7
Physical therapists	88.0
Paralegals	86.1
Occupational therapy assistants and aides	78.1
Electronic pagination systems workers	77.9
Fastest Declining	
Central office and PBX installers and repairers	−35.6
Shoe sewing machine operators and tenders	−38.4
Computer operators, except peripheral equipment	−39.3
Portable machine cutters	−40.1
Station installers and repairers, telephone	−50.3
Central office operators	−50.3
Directory assistance operators	−50.6
Peripheral EDP equipment operators	−60.2
Signal or track switch maintainers	−74.6
Frame wirers, central office	−75.3
Average of all occupations	**21.8**

---

[2] The level of ignorance concerning the benefits to the United States of expanded international trade was clearly shown in late 1993 in the debate over the North American Free Trade Agreement (NAFTA).

IS ECONOMICS ALL?

People May Not Live by Bread Alone, But *Everything* Has its Price

That's a silly question, isn't it? Of course economics is everything. (You expected to hear otherwise after all of this effort?) People may not live by bread alone, but everything, including but not limited to bread, has its price. Human existence is characterized by shortages. People must deal with them and make difficult decisions about what they are willing to give up to get the things they really want. Even though things are not always what they seem—imposing rent controls hurts renters, for instance, and reducing the supplies of illegal drugs helps drug dealers—economics can help you to make sense of it all.

Two Economists Yield Three Theories

Is economics everything? Of course not. If you put two economists in a room to discuss something, they will come up with three theories. Economics is certainly a science, and one of increasing precision, but it is a science that deals with human aspirations and reactions. It is laden with emotionally charged views of the way things should be and how people can best get them. Until the very end of time, people will continue to debate with each other as to the best courses of action, but now you can enter the debate armed with the tools of economic analysis so you can add light to the heat of the discussion.

EFFICIENCY AND EQUITY ONE MORE TIME

Efficiency
Doing something at the minimum resource cost.

Equity
Doing the right thing.

Remember in all of your economic analyses and discussions that **efficiency** (doing something at the minimum resource cost) and **equity** (doing the right thing) go hand in hand. There is nothing worse than an economy that worships efficiency without a concern for justice and equity. Adolph Hitler and Joseph Stalin come to mind as leaders who belong in the "Efficiency Hall of Shame." Along the same lines, too much concern for equity at the expense of efficiency can lead to a waste of resources and an overall output that is much lower than would have been possible otherwise. Utopian communities, American communes, and socialist economies fall into this camp.[3]

Core-Info

In economics—as in life—efficiency and equity are the two keys that must be addressed as equal partners if we are to live like human beings.

EDMUND BURKE REVISITED

Was Edmund Burke right? Remember his opinion of economics, cited in the preface? Has the Age of Economists diminished the glory of Europe, or is economics of value? Does this science add something to life? One goal of this text is to demonstrate that economics does make some sense and that you can make better decisions once you are armed with basic economic principles. With your new-found awareness of benefit-cost analysis and your knowledge of supply and demand, you are equipped to take on the world.

Good luck!

[3.] As you have seen, socialist economies in reality are no more equitable than are capitalist economies; they just produce fewer goods to distribute.

So What?

What does it all matter, anyway? At the end of the day what difference does all this macroeconomics, microeconomics, price, and income work do for you? The table here may provide some clues.

While people all hope to find meaning in their work—and it can be a very long work week if they don't—they all work for money. The table presents comparative average earnings as measured in gross national product per capita for ten nations. As can be seen, the United States ranks second on this list, a long way behind Japan but significantly ahead of Germany, Canada, and France, numbers 3, 4, and 5, respectively. In fact, the GNP per capita in the United States is 9.69 times that of the Brazilian economy.

Of course, income isn't everything. Other living factors must be taken into account. One factor of major concern is that of prices. In countries where prices are high, incomes don't go very far. Where prices are low, however, a lower income may provide all that is needed. The last two columns of the table address this issue. Columns 4 and 5 report how many hours the average worker must work to make enough money to purchase a standard market basket of food items. As you can see, the United States again ranks second. This time, however, Canada holds the highest rank (the least amount of work time required to purchase the food) while Japan slips to a distant sixth. In fact, the average Japanese worker must work 2 hours and 22 minutes longer than the average American to purchase the same package of food. (You might want to tell your mother your salary if you take a job in Tokyo, but you probably shouldn't mention the prices.) The gap between Brazil and the United States narrows considerably. Brazilians must work 4.88 times as long as Americans to purchase the same goods, about half of the gap that GNP per capita would indicate.

What is the lesson here? Don't accept raw numbers without looking behind them. Income isn't everything. There are many ways of measuring things. A final point is that we really are very fortunate in the United States.

International Living Comparisons

Country	GNP/Capita		Work Time Required *	
	Amount	Rank	Hours	Rank
United States	$22,276	(2)	2:35	(2)
Brazil	$ 2,300	(10)	12:37	(10)
Canada	$19,400	(4)	2:31	(1)
France	$18,300	(5)	5:20	(7)
Germany	$19,943	(3)	2:42	(3)
Italy	$17,600	(6)	4:42	(5)
Japan	$29,774	(1)	4:57	(6)
Mexico	$ 3,200	(8)	7:19	(8)
South Africa	$ 2,600	(9)	7:53	(9)
United Kingdom	$15,900	(7)	3:52	(4)

* Hours of average work time required to purchase a standard market basket of food.
Source: U.S. Department of Agriculture, *Food Review*, September–December 1994.

KEY TERMS

Efficiency   Equity

REVIEW QUESTIONS

1. Explain the study of economics in relation to resources.
2. Discuss the key ideas regarding cost.
3. Support the statement, "Trade benefits everybody."
4. Explain how the market works.
5. Differentiate between efficiency and equity. Discuss why the two concerns go together.

PROBLEM-SOLVING PRACTICE

1. Based on your understanding of economics, evaluate the meaning of the expression, *there's no such thing as a free lunch*.
2. What do we mean when we say the market works (mostly)?
3. Now that you have studied and mastered economics for a semester, was Edmund Burke right? (If you have no idea what this question means, return to the preface of the book.)

Glossary

NOTE: The numbers following the definition of the terms indicates the chapter(s) in which the term is fully described and applied.

Accounting Costs Costs as determined by an accountant—actual money costs, or explicit costs. 7

Accounting Profit Money profits calculated by subtracting explicit costs from total revenue. 7

Advertising Activities on the part of firms to give information to potential consumers so as to increase demand for the product. 12

Aggregate Concentration The measure of the percentage of business assets owned by the largest 100 or 200 firms. 11

Aggregate Demand The total quantity of goods and services that will be demanded in an economy at each price level. 16

Aggregate Supply The total quantity of goods and services that will be supplied in an economy at each price level. 16

Allocative Efficiency A situation in which the socially optimal amount of a good is produced in an industry. 11

Artificial Trade Barriers The restrictions imposed by government to restrict trade. 4

Artificial Barriers Restrictions on entry into an industry that are put in place by government. 11

Asset Demand Money held rather than invested. It is inversely related to the interest rate. 17

Backward Bending Supply Curve of Labor The oddly shaped supply curve of labor that reflects the fact that people will work fewer hours when the wage rate rises significantly compared with the wage they are used to. 9

Bank A financial institution that receives deposits, makes loans, and provides other financial assistance. 17

Barriers Anything that would prevent a firm from entering or leaving a market at will. 11

Barter The exchange of one good for another without the use of money as a medium of exchange. 1

Binding Arbitration An arrangement in which labor and management agree that a third party will determine the outcome of any dispute. 9

Budget Deficit A situation that exists when the government spends more money than it collects in taxes. 15

Business Cycle The recurring ups and downs in the economy that take place over time. 18

Capital The term applied to those resources, made by people, that includes machines and equipment that can be used to produce other goods and services; capital goods do not directly satisfy human wants. 1

Capital Consumption A decrease in the quantity of capital stock in an economy. 13

Capital Formation An increase in the quantity of capital stock in an economy. 13

Capital Stock The total amount of capital, or productive goods, that exists in an economy at a given time. 13

Capitalism An economic system in which the resources are owned by and economic decisions are made by individuals. 14

Cartel A group of firms that bands together to act like a monopoly in order to increase total profits. 12

Ceteris Paribus A Latin term that means *all else being equal.* 1

Circular Flow The pattern in which resources, funds, and goods and services circulate within the economic system. 16

Classical Policy The macroeconomic approach of *laissez-faire* based on the belief that the economy is self-correcting and that it naturally moves toward full employment. 16

Classical Range That portion of the aggregate supply curve that assumes that the economy is operating at full capacity and that any increase in demand will result only in an increase in the price level, not in the quantity of goods produced. 16

Closed Shop A labor/management arrangement in which workers must be members of a union before they can be hired by an employer. 9

Collective Bargaining The process by which labor and management meet together to negotiate wages and working conditions. 9

315

Collusion   An agreement among firms in an industry not to engage in competition.   12

Colonialism   An economic system in which colonies existed for the benefit of the mother country through the provision of raw materials and as markets for finished products.   19

Commercial Banks   A financial institution that takes deposits from businesses and individuals and loans the money back to these groups for the purchase of business capital and durable goods.   17

Common Market   A union of national economies by which trade barriers are erased and resource flows among countries is encouraged.   19

Comparative Advantage   The idea that each economy has a relative advantage in producing some goods in terms of the amounts of other goods that will be given up in their production.   4

Complements   Pairs of related goods in which an increase in the price of one good results in a decrease in the demand for the other good.   6

Conglomerate Merger   A merger between two firms producing unrelated products.   11

Consumer   An individual who purchases and uses a final good or service in the economy.   8

Consumer Goods   Goods and services which directly satisfy human wants.   1

Contrived Scarcity   The situation in which the quantity of a good produced is less than that which would have resulted from a competitive market.   11

Corporation   A form of business that exists independently of the owners.   10

Cost   Anything that is given up to obtain something else; a result of scarcity.   1, 7

Cost Push Inflation   Inflation caused by an increase in production costs.   18

Council for Mutual Economic Assistance (COMECON)   An organization of ten communist-bloc countries to coordinate economic and technical development policies among themselves. It was disbanded following the fall of the Soviet Union.   19

Craft Unions   Groups of workers organized around a common skill who attempt to restrict the supply of labor in order to drive up wages.   9

Credit Unions   Membership organizations in which members' deposits are loaned to other members for various reasons.   17

Cross Elasticity of Demand   A measurement of the amount by which the demand for one good changes in response to a change in the price of another good.   6, 12

Debt   The total amount of money owed by the government to individuals as a result of spending in excess of receipts.   15

Demand   The desire for a good or service that is backed by the consumer's willingness and ability to purchase.   5

Demand Curve   The graphic representation of the relationship between possible prices of a good and the quantities that people are willing and able to purchase at each price.   5

Demand Pull Inflation   Inflation caused by an increase in aggregate demand.   18

Demand Schedule   A tabular listing of possible prices of a good and the quantities that people are willing and able to purchase at each price.   5

Democratic Capitalism   A national system wherein individuals hold both the economic and political power.   19

Democratic Socialism   A national system wherein individuals hold political power and decide that the government should own the major productive resources.   19

Dependent Variable   A variable that is affected by another variable.   2

Deregulation   The removal of many restrictions and regulations.   17

Derived Demand   The idea that the demand for labor is determined by the demand for the products it produces.   9

DIDMCA (Depository Institutions Deregulation and Monetary Control Act)   The act by which Congress deregulated financial institutions in the United States.   17

Differing Resources   The fact that some resources are either completely absent or in extremely limited supply in some economies.   4

Diminishing Marginal Utility   The idea that as individuals consume more units of a good or service, they derive less additional satisfaction from each subsequent unit.   8

Discount Rate   The interest rate paid by banks on money borrowed from the Federal Reserve.   17

Dynamic Efficiency   The idea that monopolies may be more innovative and efficient over time because they may be able to generate the resources for these ends.   11

Economic Development   The process of increasing skills, capital, and productivity to permanently increase the rate of economic growth.   18

Economic Growth   An increase in the gross national product per capita; an increase in real income.   18

Economic Profit   The amount by which total revenues exceed the total cost (explicit plus implicit costs) of producing something.   7

Economic Questions   The four basic questions that every economic system must answer.   1

Economic Stabilization   The attempt by government to keep the economy from growing or contracting too rapidly.   15

Economic System   That part of our social system that answers the four economic questions; the part of our social system that has to do with the use of resources.   14

Economics The science that studies how scarce resources are allocated to meet competing and unlimited wants and how human beings satisfy their material wants and needs.   1

Economies of Scale A situation in which the cost of production per unit declines as the number produced increases.   11

Efficiency Doing things right; getting the maximum output for the minimum input.   1

Elastic A situation in which there is a relatively large change in a variable in response to a change in another variable.   6

Elasticity The measure of the relative responsiveness of one variable to a change in another variable.   6

Elasticity of Supply A measure of a supplier's response to a change in the price he or she can receive by providing the good or service.   6

Entrepreneurship The creative resource in economics that combines other resources in new and unique ways to produce goods and services.   1

Equilibrium A situation in which the quantity supplied is equal to the quantity demanded for a good or service. The price at which this occurs is known as the equilibrium price, and the quantity is called the equilibrium quantity. This can occur only when prices can move freely.   5

Equity Doing the right thing; including a sense of justice and fairness in decision making.   1

European Economic Community (EEC) An association of European nations established to lead to the complete elimination of all trade barriers between themselves.   19

Explicit Costs The actual dollar or accounting cost associated with obtaining something.   1, 7

Externality The benefits or costs of an individual's or business' actions that the person or firm does not receive or pay for.   15

Extrapolation To project or make guesses about the future based on what is known or has already happened.   3

Fallacy of Composition The faulty reasoning that assumes that what is true for a part is necessarily true for the whole.   1

False-Cause (*Post Hoc*) Fallacy The mistaken linking of cause and effect; mistaking correlation for causation.   1

Federal Reserve System The system that oversees banking operations and controls the money supply.   17

Firm An organization that combines resources to provide the goods and services demanded in an economy.   10

Fiscal Year The 12-month accounting period over which data are collected.   2

Fixed Costs Costs which do not change as the level of production increases or decreases. These costs cannot be changed in the short run.   11

Fractional Reserves The means by which banks are required to maintain only a portion of a deposit and may lend the remaining portion to customers.   17

Free Goods Those goods that are available to meet all human demand at a zero price. There are none.   1

General Agreement on Tariffs and Trade (GATT) A multilateral treaty system that lowers trade barriers among nations.   19

Government Employee Unions Groups of government workers organized in an attempt to drive up wages and affect working conditions through negotiation.   9

Gross Domestic Product (GDP) The total market or dollar value of all final goods and services produced within a nation's borders in a given year.   16

Gross National Product (GNP) The total market or dollar value of all final goods and services produced by an economy in a given year.   16

Homogeneous Product A product that is completely identical regardless of who produces it such that consumers are indifferent as to where they buy it.   11

Horizontal Merger A merger between two firms at the same stage of the productive process.   11

How The economic question that deals with the decisions about the means by which goods and services will be produced in an economy.   1

Imperfect Competition Market models in which the actions of the individual sellers can have an impact on price.   12

Implicit Costs The opportunity cost of resources that is used in obtaining something and for which there is no explicit payment.   1, 7

Income Elasticity of Demand A measure of how responsive consumers of a good are as their income changes.   6

Income Redistribution Taking resources from one individual and giving them to another.   15

Independent Variable A variable that is believed to influence the value of a second variable. A causal variable.   2

Industrial Union A group of workers organized around the product. This type of union attempts to drive up wages through market power.   9

Industry Concentration The measure of the percent of an industry's sales that are controlled by the largest four or eight firms.   11

Inelastic A situation in which there is a relatively small change in a variable in response to a change in another variable.   6

Infant Industry Argument The argument that trade in some goods should be restricted because the industry is young and unable to compete effectively on the world market.   4

Inflation An increase in the general level of prices.   18

Inframarginal Rent That portion of a payment to a factor of production such as labor in excess of what it would have been willing to accept. 13

Infrastructure A system of physical capital including high-speed roads, assured energy sources, and an effective health care system essential for economic development. 18

Interdependent A situation in which the actions of one firm will have an impact on other firms in a market. 12

Interest The cost of money. 13, 17

Intermediate Policy The macroeconomic approach of limited government intervention in the economy based on the belief that any increase in output will be accompanied by an increase in prices. 16

Intermediate Range That portion of the aggregate supply curve that assumes that any increase in national output will be accompanied by an increase in the aggregate price level. 16

Keynesian Policy The macroeconomic approach of direct government intervention in the economy based on the belief that aggregate output can be increased without affecting the price level. 16

Keynesian Range That portion of the aggregate supply curve that assumes the existence of unemployed resources such that output can be increased without affecting the overall price level. 16

Labor The term applied to the category of resources that includes the mental and physical work done by human beings. 1

Labor Unions Groups of workers who join together in an attempt to affect wage rates and working conditions. 9

Labor-Managed Firms A type of firm in which the workers are also the owners and managers. 10

Laissez-Faire The public policy of government not interfering with or regulating the market. 14

Land The term applied to the category of resources that is given by nature; natural resources. 1

Law of Demand The concept that the price of a good or service and the quantity purchased are inversely related. If the price rises, the quantity demanded falls. 5

Law of Supply The concept that the price of a good or service and the quantity produced for sale are directly related. If the price rises, the quantity supplied increases. 5

Limited Liability The idea that the owners of a corporation are not responsible for the debts of the firm. 10

Lockout A weapon used by management in which it refuses to permit labor union members to work at their jobs and earn income. 9

M1 All currency, both coins and paper, and checkable deposits. 17

M2 M1 plus highly liquid financial assets. 17

M3 M2 plus large time deposits over $100,000. 17

Macroeconomic Policy The attempt by the government to move the economy toward full employment and stable prices by affecting aggregate supply, aggregate demand, or the supply of money. 16

Macroeconomics The study of the economy as a whole. 1

Marginal Analysis The idea that people compare the added cost incurred in obtaining something with the added benefit to be received from consuming the good. 7

Marginal Benefit The additional benefit received by obtaining one more unit of a good. 4, 7

Marginal Cost The extra cost involved in producing or acquiring one more unit of output. 4, 7

Marginal Revenue The additional revenue that will be received by selling one more unit of a good. 7

Marginal Utility The additional satisfaction that an individual receives by consuming one more (or the last) unit of a good or service. 8

Market The place where buyers and sellers exchange goods and services produced and desired in an economy and which, if allowed to function freely, results in equilibrium. 1, 5, 10, 11

Market Failure A situation in which the socially optimal amount of a good or service is not produced by the private sector. 15

Mark-up Pricing A market situation in which firms face similar costs and thus adjust the price of their products to reflect any changes in cost. 12

Mercantilism An economic system which attempted to maintain an excess of exports over imports and to accumulate gold. 19

Merger The joining of the ownership and assets of two firms into a single firm. 11

Microeconomics The study of individual decision makers, both people and businesses, within an economy. 1

Mixed Economies Economic systems that contain significant elements of both capitalism and socialism. 14

Model A simplified view of the world that helps to illustrate one aspect of reality. 1

Monetarist Policy The macroeconomic approach of government adjustment in the money supply as the key tool for economic stability. 16

Money Anything two parties agree is money. Money serves as a medium of exchange, a measure of value, and a store of value. 1, 17

Money Multiplier The fraction, one divided by the required reserve ratio, which shows how much an initial deposit can be multiplied by a bank. 17

Monopolistic Competition A market model with relatively easy entry and exit, a large number of firms, and a similar but differentiated product. 12

Monopoly A market model in which there is a single seller, entry is limited, the product is unique, and information is restricted. 11

Monopoly Rent The profits earned by monopolists that exceed the normal profits earned by firms in perfect competition. 13

Moral Suasion The means—generally a compelling argument or a veiled threat—by which member banks are convinced by the Federal Reserve to follow a certain path. 17

Most Favored Nation Status An international trade agreement whereby any concessions offered to one country will be automatically granted to all other nations. 19

Multinational Firm A business organization that operates in more than one nation. 19

Multiplier Effect The overall outcome of a change in one variable that includes the cumulative effects of additional increases or decreases caused by that change. 15

National Accounts The records of the income or expenditures of an economy that allow an assessment of its performance. 16

National Defense Argument The argument that trade in some goods should be restricted because the industry or good is vital to the survival of the nation. 4

Natural Barriers Restrictions on entry into an industry because of economies of scale or total ownership of a resource. 11

Natural Trade Barriers The exchange costs involved in doing trade. 4

Natural Monopoly A situation in which it makes sense from an economic standpoint to have only one firm in an industry. 10

Negative Externality The cost that one person bears as a result of the actions of another. 15

Nominal Interest Rate The stated, market-determined rate of interest. 13

Non-price Competition The many ways in which firms attempt to increase sales of their products other than price. 12

Non-Tariff Barriers Government-established rules and requirements that effectively limit foreign trade. 4

Normal Profit A return to a firm that includes all costs of production and an amount equal to what could have been earned if the business had invested elsewhere; the opportunity cost of production. 11

Normative The approach to science—and economics—that deals with values, judgements, and opinions, not facts. 1

North American Free Trade Agreement (NAFTA) An agreement between Canada, Mexico, and the United States to lower trade barriers between themselves. 19

Not-For-Profit Firms Firms organized to provide a good or service generally thought to be beneficial to society. These firms do not earn a profit and do not have residual claimants. 10

Oligopoly A market model for any type of product but with few firms and difficult entry. 12

Open Market Operations The buying and selling of government bonds by the Federal Reserve from member banks to control the money supply and interest rate. 17

Open Shop A labor/management arrangement in which workers can not be forced to join a union as a condition of employment. 9

Partnership A form of business similar to a sole proprietorship but owned by two or more individuals. 10

Perfect Competition A market model in which there is a very large number of buyers and sellers, entry and exit are possible, the product is homogeneous, and information is free. 11

Physical Sciences The systematic study of the physical world around us. 1

Political System That part of the social system that has to do with how power is utilized. 14

Positive The approach to science—and economics—that describes or deals with data, facts, and reality. 1

Positive Externality The benefit that one person receives as a result of the actions of another. 15

Price Ceiling A government regulation by which a maximum legal price is established for a good or service. Sales above this price are prohibited. 5

Price Elasticity of Demand A measurement of how responsive the quantity demanded is when the price of a good or service changes. 6

Price Floor A government regulation in which a minimum legal price is established for a good or service. Sales below this price are prevented by the government's willingness to purchase all goods or services at this price. 5

Price Leader A market in which a single firm sets its price for a product and all other firms adopt the leader's price. 12

Price Taker The idea that in perfect competition a firm has no control over the price of its product but can sell all it produces at the market price. 11

Prime Rate Generally, the lowest interest charged by banks of their best customers. 13

Production Possibilities Curve A curve that shows all possible combinations of two goods that can be produced with a given set of resources, fixed technology, and full employment. 4

Productive Efficiency A situation in which production occurs at the lowest possible per unit cost. 11

Progressive Tax A tax for which the tax rate increases as income increases. 15

Prohibitions Government-established restrictions in all trade in a good. 4

Proportional Tax A tax that applies the same rate to all levels of income. 15

Public Good A good which, when made available to one consumer, is available to all consumers; a good which is not exclusive in use. 15

Publicly Owned Firms Businesses that are owned and operated by the government. 10

Pure Economic Rent Any payment made to a factor of production that is fixed in supply. 13

Quasi Rent The short-run profits earned by firms in perfect competition when demand unexpectedly increases. 13

Quotas Government-established restrictions as to the amount of a good that may be traded. 4

Rational The concept that individuals always act in ways that maximize the satisfaction they receive from the things they do. 8

Rational Expectations Policy The macroeconomic approach that acknowledges that businesses and individuals will act on their anticipations of government intervention in the economy and in so doing render these interventions ineffective. 16

Rational Self-Interest The view of human behavior that states that all human decisions involve a weighing of the costs and benefits perceived to be associated with them in order to maximize the outcome. Economists use this approach in explaining all human actions. 1

Real Interest Rate The true cost of borrowing determined by subtracting the rate of inflation from the nominal rate of interest. 13

Regressive Tax A tax for which the tax rate decreases as income increases. 15

Rent Payment to a factor of production in excess of its opportunity cost. 13

Rent Controls A form of price ceiling in which a maximum rental amount is established for an apartment. 5

Reserve Ratio The minimum percent of a bank's deposits that must be kept in the bank's vault and which may not be loaned. 17

Reserve Requirement The portion of a bank's deposits that it is required to keep on hand and which it is not able to lend to customers. 17

Residual Claimant A person who has a right to the profits of a business. 10

Resources The things that are used to produce and distribute goods and services in an economy. These include land, labor, capital, and entrepreneurship. They are also known as factors of production. 1

Right-To-Work Laws Laws that prohibit any requirement for a worker to join a union. 9

Round-About Production The production of capital goods today so that increased quantities of consumer goods can be produced tomorrow. 13

S Corporation A type of corporation designed for small businesses with special tax requirements. 10

Savings and Loans A financial institution that accepts deposits and uses them to finance home mortgages. 17

Say's Law The belief that in a closed economy, the act of creating goods creates income equal to the value of the goods produced. 16

Scarcity The idea that all resources are limited and inadequate to meet all human wants. 1

Shortage The amount by which the quantity demanded exceeds the quantity supplied at a price that is below the equilibrium price. 5

Social Sciences The systematic study of all aspects of human relationships. 1

Socialism An economic system in which the resources are owned by and economic decisions are made by the government. 14

Sole Proprietorship A form of business owned and operated by an individual. 10

Static Inefficiency The idea that monopolies produce too little quantity of a good at too high a price. 11

Sticky Prices The concept that in oligopolized industries prices frequently do not respond to changed cost conditions. 12

Stock A share in the ownership of a corporation. 10

Strike A weapon used by labor in which workers collectively withhold labor services. 9

Substitutes Pairs of related goods in which an increase in the price of one good results in an increase in the demand for the other good. 6

Sunk Cost Any cost that has been previously incurred and which is irretrievable. 7

Supply The willingness and ability of a producer to make a good or service available for sales to consumers at a variety of prices. 5

Supply Curve The graphic representation of the relationship between possible prices of a good and the quantities that producers are willing and able to produce at each price. 5

Supply Schedule A tabular listing of possible prices of a good and the quantities that producers are willing and able to produce at each price. 5

Surplus The amount by which the quantity demanded is less than the quantity supplied at a price that is above the equilibrium price. 5

Tariffs Government-established taxes on imported goods. 4

Tax A compulsory payment by an individual or business to a government for which no direct benefit is received. 15

Tax Incidence The final resting place of a tax; the person who actually pays the tax as opposed to the person on whom the tax was levied. 15

Tax Shifting Passing on the burden of a tax from the person on which it was imposed to another person. 15

Total Cost The sum total of all resources that are used whether or not there is a direct money cost involved. The total of both explicit and implicit costs. 7

Total Demand The sum of the asset demand and the transactions demand. 17

Total Utility The total amount of satisfaction that an individual receives from all the units of a good or service consumed in a given period of time. 8

Totalitarian Capitalism A national system wherein individuals would hold the economic power but the government would hold all political power. Such a system could not exist. 19

Totalitarian Socialism A national system wherein the government holds both the economic and political power. 19

Transactional Costs The costs involved in "making the deal" so trade can happen. 4

Transactions Demand The demand for money in order to buy goods. It is directly related to the size of the economy. 17

Transfers Money or goods received by an individual from the government for which the individual did not pay. 15

Transportation Costs The costs involved in shipping the goods involved in trade. 4

Tribal Economies Small scale, early economies with limited specialization, infrequent trade, and a barter system. 19

Underdevelopment A situation of national poverty characterized by an economy with low per capita income and savings rates, a large agricultural sector, rapid population growth, and a limited specialization of the work force. 18

Union Shop A labor/management arrangement in which workers must join a particular union after being hired by an employer. 9

Unlimited Liability The idea that the owners of a business are completely and personally responsible for debts of certain types of firms. 10

Utility The satisfaction received by an individual from consuming a good or service. 8

Variable Something that changes or is changed. 2

Variable Costs Costs which increase when production increases and decrease as production decreases. These costs do change in the short run. 11

Vertical Merger A merger between two firms at different stages of the productive process. 11

Vicious Circle of Poverty The economic trap in which poor nations are held because of the conditions of underdevelopment. 18

What The economic question that deals with the decisions about which goods and services will be produced in an economy. 1

When The economic question that deals with the decisions whether the goods and services produced in an economy will be received in the present or the future. 1

Who (for Whom) The economic question that deals with the decisions about the individuals or groups that will receive the goods and services produced in an economy. 1

Work-to-Rule A weapon used by labor in which workers collectively only do the work that is absolutely required by the terms of their contract. 9

X-Axis The horizontal axis of a graph. 2

"X-Inefficiency" The idea that monopolies may lack the incentive to reduce costs because of a lack of competition. 11

Y-Axis The vertical axis of a graph. 2

Index

Page numbers in *italics* indicate illustrations.

A

Aburdene, Patricia, 36
advertising
   effects on a demand curve of, *190*
   by oligopolies, 190–91
   role of, 190–91
   spending on, 191
aggregate concentration, 173–*74*
aggregate demand, 253–54, *254*, *257*
aggregate supply, 255–56, *255*, *257*
   classical range of, 256
   factors affecting, 256
   intermediate range of, 255–56
   Keynesian range of, 255
allocative efficiency, 169
antitrust regulations, 226
artificial barriers, to trade, 168
Asian-Americans, relative income of, *41*. See also minority groups
asset demand (Da), for money, 266–67
automobile industry, *27–28*, 80, 301

B

backward bending supply curve, 129–31, *130*
bankruptcy, business, *153*
banks/banking
   definition of, 273
   deregulation of, 274
   future of, 275
   history of, 267–68, 275
   roles of, 273
   types of, 273
   in the United States (1993), *273*
barter, 10. See also exchange
binding arbitration, 134
blacks
   discrimination against, 143
   employment/unemployment of, 8, 40, *40*
   relative income of, 41, *41–42*. See also minority groups
budget, federal
   deficits and debt, 44–45, *44–45*, 240–44, *241*
   philosophies about, 241
   surpluses and deficits (1936–1994), *243*
Burke, Edmund, 312
business cycle, 280–81

C

capital
   human, 131–32, 304
   financial, 304
   as resource/factor of production, 7–8, *196*
capital consumption, 201
capital formation, 201
capital funds, 201–203
capital goods, 8, 201
capitalism
   causes for government intervention in, 226–32
   competitive markets in, 215
   conditions required for, 214–15
   definition of, 213–14
   democratic, 218, 299
   as economic system, 297–99
   effects of, 215–16
   free enterprise in, 214–15
   history of, 300
   limited government role in, 215, 224, 232
   markets in, 162
   private property in, 214
   totalitarian, 299
capital stock, 201
cartels, 191–92
ceteris paribus (all else being equal), 5, 69, 162
charitable giving, distribution of, *10*
charts. See graphs, charts, and data tables
chief executive officer (CEO), 152
chief financial officer (CFO), 152
chief operating officer (COO), 152
China, industrial output in, *303*
circular flow, of economy, 248, *248*
classical macroeconomic policy, 258
classical range, of aggregate supply curve, 256
closed shop, 133
collective bargaining, 133–34
collusion, 189
colonialism, 299–300
COMECON (Council for Mutual Economic Assistance), 302
commercial banks, 273
common markets, 300–302
common ownership, 229–30
communications revolution, 304
comparative advantage, in trade, 56, 58

323

competition
  in capitalism, 214–15
  imperfect, 162, 181–93
  monopolistic, 183
  monopoly and, 162–73
  nonprice, 188
  between oligopolies, 188–89
  perfect, 162–66, 169–72, *171*
  in socialism, 217–18
complements, elasticity and, 94
concentrated costs, in trade, 60
conglomerate merger, 178
consumer
  behavior, 114–16
  debt, 115
  decisions (utility), 117–21
  prices (1960–1974), *288*
  as rational, 115–16
  role of, 114
  saving, *120*
  spending, *116*, 120–21
contrived scarcity, 169
copyrights, 168
corporations, 155, *206*
cost(s)
  accounting, 103
  concept of, 102
  explicit, 9, 103, 205
  fixed, 165
  implicit, 9, 103
  labor, 25, 58
  marginal, 53, 108
  sunk, 107
  total, 103–105
  transactional, 59–60
  transportation, 59–60
  understanding, 101–109
  utility and, 118–21
  variable, 165
cost push inflation, 288
craft unions, 132
credit unions, 273
cross elasticity of demand, 94, 186
currency, demand for U.S., 272

D
data, importance of, 18
demand, 68–73
  aggregate, 253–54, *254, 257*
  asset, 266–67
  cross elasticity of, 94, 186
  definition of, 68–69
  derived, 126–27
  factors affecting, 71–*72*
  law of, 5, 69–71, 162
  market, 72–*73*
  for money, 266–67, *267*

demand curves
  aggregate, 254
  definition of, 70–71
  effects of advertising on, *190*
  elastic/inelastic, 88–91
  examples of, *70, 72–73, 89–90, 185*
  for an oligopolist, 184–87, *185–87*
  in perfect competition, 170–72, *171*
demand pull inflation, 286–87
democratic capitalism, 218, 299
democratic socialism, 299
DIDMCA (Depository Institutions Deregulation and Monetary Control Act), 274
differing resources, in trade, 56–58, *57*
diffused benefits, in trade, 60
diminishing marginal utility, 117–21
discount rate, 270
discrimination:
  definition of, 143
  effects of, 144
  solutions to, 144–45. *See also* blacks, Hispanics, minorities, women
drugs, illegal
  supply and demand curves for, *95*
  U.S. policy toward, 95–96

E
earnings. *See* income; wages
economic concentration, 173–74, *174*. *See also* aggregate concentration; industry concentration
economic development
  comparative international statistics for, *282*
  definition of, 281–82
  desirability of, 283–84
  effects of, 286
  as hampered by military spending, 298
  keys to, 284
  measurement of, 284, *284*
  sources of, 284–85
  vs. underdevelopment, 282–83
economic growth
  definition of, 280
  effects of, 281
  measurement of, 281
  sources of, 281, *285*
economic questions, four, 5–6, 150
economic resources, four. *See* factors of production
economics
  definition of, 4
  key ideas in, 310–11
  normative, 12–13, 34, 56
  positive (descriptive), 12–13, 34
  problems in doing good, 11–13
  vs. politics, 297–99
  resources in, 7–8
  as a science, 4
  variations in, 297–99

economic stabilization, 231
economic systems, 211–20
   characteristics of, 213
   definitions of, 212
   mixed, 219, 299
   past, present, and future of, 299–305
   vs. political systems, 212, 297–99
   types of, 213. *See also* capitalism, socialism
economies of scale, 167
economy
   changes in U.S., 36–45
   circular flow of, 248, *248*
   global, 293–305
   national, 247–59
   tribal, 299
economy, global, 293–305
efficiency
   allocative, 169
   dynamic, 169
   equity and, 13–14, 312
   productive, 169
   as underlying issue of economics, 52
elasticity
   assumptions about, 92
   complements and, 94
   concept of, 88
   of demand, 88–93, 127–28
   equation for, 91
   factors affecting, 91–92
   other types of, 93–94
   price, 88–93
   public policy and, 94–97
   revenue and, 92–93
   substitutes and, 94
   of supply, 93–94
   using, 97
elasticity of demand, 88–93, 127–28
elasticity of supply, 93–94
employment/unemployment
   by government, *44*
   industrial composition of, *37*
   of men *vs.* women, 8, *42*
   of minority groups, 8, 40, *40*
   in selected countries, *22*
   trends in, 36–40
entrepreneurship
   as factor of production, 7–8, *196*
   riskiness of, 205
equilibrium
   analysis of, 77–79
   drawbacks to upsetting, 79–83
   markets and, 77–83
equity
   efficiency and, 13–14, 312
   taxes and, 233
   as underlying economic issue, 52
European Economic Community (EEC), 302

exchange
   as basis of economics, 9–10
   international trade and, 56–63
   money as medium of, 264
   as way of creating wealth, 52
explicit costs, 9, 103, 205
exports. *See* imports and exports
externalities
   definition of, 226–27
   negative, 227
   positive, 227
   possible government responses to, 227–28
extrapolation, trends and, 35

F

factors of production (inputs/resources), 7–8, 150, 196–207, *196*. *See also* capital; entrepreneurship; labor; land
fallacy of composition, 12–13
false-cause (*post hoc*) fallacy, 13
Federal Reserve System
   activities of, 269–70
   role of, 268–69
   structure of, 269, *269*
Financial System, U.S., 267–74
firms, 150–58
   controlling, 150–52
   definition of, 150
   labor-managed, 155
   major types of, 153–55, *154*
   managers of, 151–52
   markets and, 157–58
   multinational, 302, *302*
   not-for-profit, 155–56
   other ways of organizing, 155–57
   publicly owned, 157
   sizes of, *154*
fiscal year, 21
foreign aid, 287
fractional reserve system, 270–*71*
free enterprise, 214–15, 217

G

GATT (General Agreement on Tariffs and Trade), 300
Geis, Irving, 18
goods
   consumer, 8
   free, 9
   productive, 8
   public, 228–29
government in capitalism, 224, 232
   causes for intervention of in capitalism, 226–32
   role of, 224, 255–56
   in socialism, 218, 224
   state, *242*
   taxes and, 223–44
   of United States (*see* Government, U.S.)
Government, U.S.
   budget deficit of, 44–45, *44–45,* 240–44, *241, 243*

(*Continued*)
  defense spending by, *225*
  employment by, *44*
  growth of, 44
  tax revenues of, *23,* 42–43, *43*
government employee unions, 132–33
government franchise, 168
government license, 168
government ownership, 176–77
graphs, charts, and data tables, 17–30
  axes on (graphs), 22, 25–29
  bar, circle (pie), 21–22, *23*
  lying with, 24–29
  pictorial, 21–22, *22–23*
  reading of, 21–23
  relational (functional), 22–23
  variables on, 22
gross domestic product (GDP) of foreign countries, *24, 46*
  vs. gross national product (GNP), 251
  1929–1994 (in United States), *46*
  percentage distribution of, 6
  tax revenues as percentage of, *217*
gross national product (GNP)
  vs. gross domestic product (GDP), 251
  international living comparisons based on, 313
  for underdeveloped countries, *283*
growth rate, calculating, 216

H

health care supply and demand curves for, *97*
  U.S. policy toward, 96–97
higher education, exporting, 305
Hispanics
  discrimination against, 143
  employment/unemployment of, 8, 40, *40*
  relative income of, 41, *41–42*. *See also* minority groups
homogeneous product, 163–64
horizontal merger, 175
How to Lie with Statistics (Geis and Huff), 18
Huff, Darrell, 18
human capital
  as affecting labor supply and demand, 131–32
  creation of, 131
  definition of, 131

I

imperfect competition, 181–93
  definition of, 182
  models of, 182–84. *See also* monopolistic competition, oligopolies
implicit costs, 9, 103
imports and exports
  of automobiles, *27–28*
  of commodities (1994), *294–96*
  of higher education, 304
  of services, *304*
  by states, *58*
  by the United States, *45, 60*

income
  components of, 140–41
  disparities (by race and sex) in, 41, *41–42*
  distribution of, *10,* 139–43, *143,* 219
  of full-time workers, *41*
  hourly, *142*
  as increasing in America, 142
  per capita, *141*
  redistribution of, 230–31
income elasticity of demand, 94
industrial unions, 132
industry concentration, 173–74, *174*
infant industry argument, for trade barriers, 62–63
inflation
  anticipated/unanticipated, 288–89
  effects of, 288–89
  rate of, 204, 286, *288*
  types of, 286–88
information
  free, 165
  imperfect, 168
  perfect, 165
  types of, 34
infrastructure, 285–86
inputs. *See* factors of production
interdependency, of sellers, 184
interest/interest rates
  cost of, 204
  definition of, 274–75
  effects of, 275
  factors affecting, 201–202, 274
  nominal, 203–204
  overall, 202–203
  real, 203–204
  as return to factors of production, *196*
intermediate macroeconomic policy, 258
intermediate range, of aggregate supply curve, 255–56
international trade: exchange and, 56–63
  as a perspective on global economy, 294–97
  restrictions to, 62–63
  U.S. role in, 45

K

Keynesian macroeconomic policy, 258
Keynesian range, of aggregate supply curve, 255

L

labor
  costs, *25, 58*
  as factor of production, 7–8, *196*
  force, 37–40, *37*
  supply and demand for, 126–38, *129–30, 135–37*
labor/management relationships, 133–34
labor unions
  definition of, 132
  effect on wages of, 134–38
  history of, 132, 140
  management's relationship with, 133–34

membership in, 37–38, *38, 138,* 140
laissez faire policy, 177, 215, 257
land, as factor of production, 7, *196*
law of demand, 5, 69–71, 162
law of supply, 74
liability, limited/unlimited, 153, 155
lockout, worker, 134

M
macroeconomic policy
   current debates in, 259
   history of, 256–57
   vs. microeconomic policy, 11
   production possibilities curve and, 56
   purpose of adjustments to, 257–59
   types of, 258–59
managers, firm, 151–52
marginal analysis, 108
marginal benefit, 53, 108
marginal cost, 53, 108
marginal revenue, 108
marginal utility, 117–21
market(s)
   common, 300–302
   competitive, 215
   definition of, 10, 77, 157, 162
   equilibrium and, 77–83
   failure, 225–26
   firms and, 157–58
   for money, 267
   money and, 9–10
   open, 269
   types of, 158
market failure, 225–26
mark-up pricing, 189
Megatrends (Naisbitt), 35–37, *36,* 44. See also *Megatrends 2000*
Megatrends 2000 (Aburdene and Naisbitt), 36, *36,* 44. See also *Megatrends*
men
   discrimination and, 143
   employment of, 8
   in labor force, 8, 37, *37*
   relative income of, 41, *41–42*
mercantilism, 299
mergers
   concerns about, 175
   definition of, 174
   number of, 176
   types of, 175
microeconomic policy
   vs. macroeconomic policy, 11
   production possibilities curve and, 56
minority groups
   discrimination against, 143
   employment/underemployment of, 8, 40
   relative income of, 41–*42*

models, economic, 5
M1, 265
monetarist economic policy, 258–59
money
   in circulation, *11*
   creation of, 270–73
   definition of, 264
   demand for, 266–67, *267*
   functions of, 264
   market for, 267
   markets and, 9–11
   as medium of exchange, 264
   as store of value, 264–65
   supply components of, 265–66, *266*
   supply and demand for, *203, 268,* 275
money multiplier, 271, *271*
monopolistic competition, 183
monopoly
   benefits and costs of, 169
   competition and, 162–73
   conditions required for, 166
   definition of, 166
   as an economic model, 162–63
   frequency of, 169
   natural, 157
   nightmare of, 166
   prohibition of, 176
   regulation of, 226
   solutions to, 176–77
   supply and demand in, 170–72, *171*
moral suasion, of Federal Reserve, 270
most favored nation status, 300
M3, 265
M2, 265
multinational firm, 302, *302*
multiplier effect, 227

N
NAFTA (North American Free Trade Agreement), 302
Naisbitt, John, 35–37
national accounts/accounting
   definition of, 249
   differences in using, 251–52
   expenditure *vs.* income approach to, 249–50
   uses for, 250
national defense argument, for trade barriers, 62
Native Americans, relative income of, *41. See also* minority groups
natural barriers, to trade, 167–68
nonprice competition, 188
nontariff barriers, to trade, 61
normative approach, to economics/science, 12–13, 34, 56
North American Free Trade Agreement (NAFTA), 302

O
occupations, fastest-growing/declining, *311*
oligopolies
   advertising by, 190–91

(*Continued*)
   background for, 183
   competition between, 188–89
   conditions required for, 183–84
   demand curves for, 184–87, *185–87*
   raising prices in, 189
   supply and demand curve for, *188*
   understanding, 184–88, *185*
open market operations, 269
open shop, 133

P

partnerships, 154–55
patents, 168
perfect competition
   benefits and costs of, 169
   conditions required for, 163–65
   as economic model, 162–63
   frequency of, 165–66
   supply and demand in, 170–72, *171*
personal savings rate, *7*
political systems
   combinations of, 299
   vs. economic systems, 212, 297–99
   variations in, 297–99
positive approach, to economics/science, 12–13, 34
postal increases, *26*
poverty, vicious cycle of, 282–83, *283*
price, firms and, 150–51
price ceiling, 82–83, *82*
price elasticity of demand, 88–93
price floor, 80–81, *81*
price leader, 189
price regulation, 176
price taker, 164
prime rate, 201
production, 52–63, 201. *See also* factors of production
production possibilities curve, 53–*57, 54–55*
productive efficiency, *169*
productive process, *175*
profits
   accounting, 105–106, *106,* 205
   corporate, *206*
   economic, 105–106, 205
   measurement of, 105–106
   normal, 165
   rates of, 206, *206*
   as a residual, 205
   as return to factors of production, *196*
prohibition, of monopolies, 176
projections techniques
   Delphi, 46–47
   straight-line, 46–47
property
   private, 214
   in socialism, 217

R

rational expectations macroeconomic policy, 259
rational self-interest, 9
rent
   controls, 82–83
   definition of, 196
   inframarginal, 197–98, *198*
   monopoly, 200
   pure economic, 198–99
   quasi, 199
   as return to factors of production, *196*
reserve ratio, 270–71
reserve requirement, 270
residual claimant, 151–52
resources (factors of production), 7–8, 150, 196–207, *196*
   differing, 56–58, *57*
   unemployed, 55. *See also* capital; entrepreneurship; labor; land
revenue
   elasticity and, 92–93
   government (from taxes), *23,* 42–43, *43*
   marginal, 108. *See also* taxes
right-to-work laws, 133
risk, 8, 202, 205
round-about production, 201

S

savings and loan institutions, 273
Say's law, 258
scarcity (scarce goods)
   contrived, 169
   costs and, 9, 102
   as foundation of economy, 212
S corporation, 155
service sector, 304, *304*
shortage, 79
socialism
   competition in, 217–18
   conditions required for, 217
   definition of, 216–17
   democratic, 299
   as economic system, 6, 297–99
   effects of, 218–19
   enterprise in, 217
   history of, 300
   property under, 217
   role of government in, 218, 224
   totalitarian, 218, 299
sole proprietorships, 153–54
specialization, 213
static inefficiency, 169
sticky prices, 187
stock, 155, 201
stock market, 156
strikes, 134, *139*

substitutes, elasticity and, 94
supply
   aggregate, 255–56, *255, 257*
   definition of, 73–74
   factors affecting, 75–77, *76*
   law of, 74
   market, 77
   schedules, 74, *75–77, 129* (for labor)
supply curves
   aggregate, 255–56, *257*
   backward bending, 129–31, *130*
   examples of, *75–76, 78, 198–99*
   for labor, 129–32, *130,* 134–37, *135–36*
supply and demand, 67–84
   aggregate, *257*
   in automobile industry, 80
   equilibrium and, 77–83
   for money, *203, 268,* 275
   in perfect competition, 170–72, *171*
   schedules, *78*
supply and demand curves, examples of, *79, 81, 82, 95, 97, 135, 171, 188, 203, 257, 268*
surplus, 78–79, *243*

T

tables, data. *See* graphs, charts, and data tables
tariffs, 296–97, 300
taxes, 223–44
   capital gains, 234
   corporate, *23, 43*
   customs duties, 234
   definition of, 232–33
   effects of, 234–35, *234*
   estate and gift, 234
   excise, *23,* 233
   gasoline, *234,* 236
   incidence of, 235–37
   income, *23, 43,* 233, 239
   issues about, 233
   as percentage of gross domestic product, *217*
   progressive, 237, *237–38*
   property, 234–35
   proportional, 237, *238*
   regressive, 237–39, *238*
   sales, *43,* 233, *238*
   shifting of, 235–37
   social insurance, *23*
   types of, 233–34
total demand (Dm), for money, 267
totalitarian capitalism, 299
totalitarian socialism, 218, 299
trade
   barriers/restrictions to, 59–63, 164–65, 167–68, 296–97
   benefits from, 58–59
   comparative advantage in, 56, 58
   differing resources in, 56–58, *57*
   international, 45, 56–63, 294–97
   language of, 302
   personal, 59
   reasons for, 56, 58
transactional costs, 59–60
transactions demand (Dt), for money, 266
transfers, by government, 230–31
transportation costs, 59–60
trends
   economic, 36–47
   employment, 36–40
   extrapolation and, 35
   importance of, 34–35
   mega-, 35–37, *36,* 44
   projecting, 46–47
   social, 35–36
tribal economies, 299

U

unemployed resources, 55
unemployment. *See* employment/unemployment
unions. *See* labor unions
union shop, 133
U.S. Financial System, 267–74
utility
   costs and, 118–21
   definition of, 117
   diminishing marginal, 117–21
   marginal, 117–21, *119*
   total, 117, *118*

V

value
   creation of, 52
   idea of, 52
   money as store of, 264–65
vertical merger, 175

W

wages
   as return to factors of production, *196*
   unions and, 134–38. *See also* income
wealth, producing, 52–63
wheat production, *28–29*
whites
   discrimination and, 143
   employment of, 8, 40, *40*
   relative income of, 41, *41–42*
women
   discrimination against, 143
   employment of, 8, *42*
   relative income of, *19,* 41, *41–42*
work-to-rule, 134

X

x-efficiency, 169